Women and Politics:
The Pursuit of Equality

The *New Directions in Political Behavior* Series

GENERAL EDITOR
ALLAN J. CIGLER
University of Kansas

WOMEN AND POLITICS: THE PURSUIT OF EQUALITY

Lynne E. Ford

College of Charleston

Houghton Mifflin Company   Boston   New York

Editor-in-Chief: *Jean L. Woy*
Sponsoring Editor: *Mary Dougherty*
Associate Editor: *Jennifer DiDomenico*
Associate Project Editor: *Jane Lee*
Editorial Assistant: *Martha Rogers*
Production/Design Coordinator: *Lisa Jelly Smith*
Senior Manufacturing Coordinator: *Priscilla Bailey*
Marketing Associate: *Caroline Guy*

Cover image: Paul Hosefros/*The New York Times*

Printed in the U.S.A.

Library of Congress Catalogue Number: 2001091455

ISBN: 0-618-06338-2

123456789-CRS-05 04 03 02 01

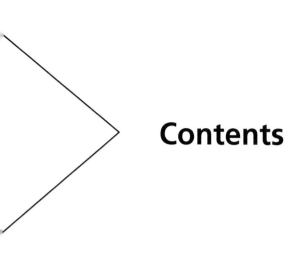

Contents

Preface

Women and Politics: The Pursuit of Equality is intended to serve as a core text for courses on women and politics. When I first developed the course in my own department nearly ten years ago, a colleague joked, "What will you cover in the second week?" On the contrary, I have found that the biggest challenges in teaching a course on women and politics are to introduce students to the vast history of women's movements, to acquaint them with the scholarship on women as political leaders and political participants, and to still leave time to address contemporary policy concerns. Never satisfied with a single book, I usually end up using parts of five or six books at a significant cost to my students. In *Women and Politics: The Pursuit of Equality*, I integrate the major topics related to women's political involvement in a single text.

To do so, I have created a strong central organizing theme that links topics across chapters but remains flexible enough to permit individual instructors to organize their courses in a variety of ways. The book is organized around what I've termed the *paradox of gender equality*: the need to reconcile demands for equality with biological differences between women and men. I argue that, in trying to resolve the paradox, women have primarily followed two paths. One path advocates a *legal equality doctrine* based on the belief that women and men must be treated the same in order to achieve equality. Therefore, differences must be erased in laws and public policies before equality can be achieved. Another just as viable path focuses on women's differences from men. Advocates of this approach believe that treating men and women the same when they are in fact different is unfair. The *fairness doctrine* requires that law and policy account for the consequences of biological difference by treating men and women differently, but fairly.

Resolving the paradox is complicated by the persistent and pervasive influence of the *separate spheres ideology*. Although this ideology impacts all women, it has affected different groups of women in different ways. Separate spheres ideology specifically excluded upper-class white women from employment and limited the type of employment opportunities and pay for low-income women and women of color in the workforce. Defining a contemporary role for women in the public sphere has been difficult because women's biological role in bearing children makes their traditional assignment to the home still seem "natural" to many people. Just as women's opportunities were once limited by the sharp demarcation between the private and public spheres, women today face conflicts created by a blurred line. Men and women alike are trying to sort out new gender roles. Presenting the paradox of gender equality within the context of separate spheres ideology enables students to examine their own preconceived notions of the "proper" roles for men and women and to connect events in their own lives with the theories and scholarship presented in the book. This approach also helps students understand why issues of gender equality seem to reappear for successive generations of political activists. In each chapter, a special effort is made to focus on the diversity of experiences among women of different races, economic classes, and political persuasions. The most compelling controversies of gender equality are often played out exclusively among women. Understanding how women differ from each other is as important as understanding how women are different from men. I've attempted to include as much scholarship as possible on the experiences of women of color, poor women, and women in other traditionally marginalized groups, including women who are opposed to equality altogether. Where such information is not available, I've challenged students to think carefully about why the gap in the literature exists.

The two dominant paths women have taken in resolving the paradox—the pursuit of legal equality and the pursuit of fairness—offer a way to organize women's politics historically as well as to present students with the live controversies of gender equality. Chapter 1 lays out the origins of the separate spheres ideology, distinguishes between sex as a biological designation and gender as a social construction, and details the roots of the legal equality and fairness doctrines. Both paths are presented as reasonable ways to resolve the paradox of gender equality on many issues. This chapter also acknowledges that women disagree as to which approach is the better way to proceed, and presents an overview of the major strands of feminism and their critiques. Chapter 2 evaluates two major women's movements in the United States: suffrage and the Equal Rights Amendment. The contrast between the success of the suffrage movement and the failure to ratify the ERA illuminates the differences between a legal approach to equality and women's interest in fair accommodations for biological differences. The histories of both movements present students with examples of women's political activism and highlight the contributions of young women and women of color in both movements.

Chapter 3 examines women as voters and political participants. Although initially slow to enter electoral politics, women are now registered at higher rates than men and have the power to dramatically shape elections. Chapter 3 addresses a variety of questions: How do women evaluate candidates? Which issues mobilize women's participation? How do women in their twenties approach politics? Under what circumstances will women vote for other women? Chapter 4 covers women as candidates for political office, evaluating the differences between male and female candidates, as well as differences among women in approaches to running for elective office. Research demonstrates that when women run for office they are as likely as men to win, but they are substantially less likely to run in the first place—why? Chapter 4 also examines the ways in which the United States electoral system has both a glass ceiling and a sticky floor for women. Chapter 5 provides an overview of women as agents of change and actors inside and outside formal politics. Women have a long tradition of acting as political outsiders because they were excluded from mainstream politics. Now that there are more women on the inside, how do they govern? Chapter 5 also looks at women's contemporary activism outside the formal channels of elective office. Women's participation in grassroots and nongovernmental organizations is examined in both United States and comparative contexts.

Chapters 6 through 8 focus on women and public policy. Chapter 6 examines education. Although Title IX is best known for opening athletic opportunities for women, it also opened doors to professional programs and eliminated quotas for women in "non-traditional" subjects such as math, science, and engineering. This chapter examines the link between education and income for women and men and explores the changing demographics of college admissions. Chapter 7 is focused on work, wages, and women's broad participation in the economy. This chapter addresses the pay gap—is it fact or fiction? In what ways does a segregated workforce impact pay rates, pensions, and poverty rates for women? Chapter 7 also evaluates the impact that recent changes in the welfare system and proposed changes in the social security system have had on women. Chapter 8 is dedicated to family and fertility issues. The definition of "family" has changed significantly in practice, but in many ways public policy regarding the family has not kept pace. This chapter examines the ways in which biology and gender intersect in very complex ways in shaping the roles men and women play in families. Should government be doing more to support families through paid leave and other social benefits? Who is responsible for guaranteeing high quality child care? What impact will emerging reproductive technologies have on women, men and gender roles? Why does abortion remain such an intractable issue in American politics? Finally, chapter 9 evaluates women's progress in achieving equality and challenges students to think about issues relating to women and politics that they will face in their own lives.

Women and Politics: The Pursuit of Equality provides a number of features designed to encourage critical thinking. In each chapter, at least one box titled

"Encountering the Controversies of Equality" presents students with a controversy or conflict generated by the paradox of gender equality, and prompts them to consider how it could be resolved. These boxes are intended to clarify the concept of the paradox and to encourage students to appreciate the complexity of women's demands for gender equality. By having students grapple with contemporary issues related to the core themes of the text, the parallels between central issues facing women centuries ago and issues facing students today become quite clear. Each chapter also relies on contemporary scholarship from a number of disciplines including political science, history, sociology, psychology, anthropology, philosophy and the natural sciences. The interdisciplinary approach enriches the analysis and makes the text appropriate for women's studies courses as well as courses in political science. Although politics changes daily, I have presented the most current data available, including figures for women's participation in the 2000 election. Internet resources in the text citations and the Suggested Readings and Web Resources section at the end of this text direct students to web sites where they can access the most current data, find additional information, and conduct independent research.

A unique web site, accessible via *college.hmco.com*, enhances and extends the theme and pedagogy of *Women and Politics: The Pursuit of Equality*. The site provides chapter outlines, web links, essay questions, and journal prompts for each chapter. A "Paths to Action" feature connects students to valuable resources for getting involved with issues relating to women and politics.

Finally, I could not have completed this book without tremendous support from a variety of sources. I remember reading somewhere that writing a book is similar to giving birth. It isn't. Although I didn't set out to test the proposition, in the process of writing this, my first book, my husband and I had our first child. There is no doubt in my mind that Grace's birth changed many aspects of the book, but it may take years for me to be able to articulate exactly how. I cannot imagine the multitude of opportunities that await her and the challenges that she will face as she makes her way through the world. I owe my husband, Frank Dirks, an enormous debt of gratitude for supporting me during the year I spent at home learning to be both a mother and an author. In choosing to take on more responsibility for Grace's care and devote less attention to his own career, he has experienced firsthand many of the issues I describe in the book. In his own way, he constantly confronts the paradox of gender equality and reminds me that men as well as women experience changes in gender role expectations. We both thank Melissa Jordan, Grace's loving companion and caregiver, for the peace of mind she affords us. My parents, now retired, also spent many hours with Grace so that Frank and I could both work. A semester-long sabbatical made it possible for me to begin this book, and understanding colleagues made it possible for me to finish the book in my first year as department chair. I owe many thanks to two undergraduate students, Angela Kouters and Amanda Deaton, who worked as my research assistants while I was on leave. Both women have since graduated and are working in Washington, D.C. I am grateful to all of the students in my Women and Politics courses over the years for their interest in the subject and the passion about gender equality they display as they become aware of women's history.

I would also like to extend special thanks to those scholars who provided useful suggestions for the development of this text: Rachel Anderson-Paul, University of Illinois at Urbana-Champaign; Susan C. Bourque, Smith College; Sally Friedman, State University of New York at Albany; Wendy Gunther-Canada, University of Alabama at Birmingham; Kathy Holland, L.A. Pierce College; Lauren Holland, University of Utah; Leonie Huddy, State University of New York at Stony Brook; Lynn H. Leverty, University of Florida; Kay L. Schlozman, Boston College; and Elizabeth G. Williams, James Madison University.

L. E. F.

This book is dedicated to women throughout the centuries, including those in my own family, whose bravery in the face of adversity will make it possible for Grace to live in a more equal world.

Two Paths to Equality

THIS IS a book about women's use of politics and the political system in pursuit of gender equality. At its core, this book explores the complexity, tension, and controversy created by an overarching paradox in the unique nature of women's claims to equality. A paradox occurs when two apparently contradictory positions coexist. In this case, the paradox is this: How can demands for gender equality be reconciled with sex differences? Because "equal" often means "the same," how can men and women be the same if they are different?

The story of women's relationship to politics is therefore complex because the most direct path to gender equality is not clearly marked. In fact, this book argues that there are two well-worn paths women have traveled in pursuit of equality. On the one hand, women have argued that equality is only possible when the differences between men and women are erased by laws that require men and women to be treated equally. We will refer to this path as the *legal equality doctrine*. The other path to equality consciously recognizes the differences between men and women and argues that women will always be disadvantaged if they are not somehow compensated for the social, economic, and political consequences of those differences. What matters most to advocates of this second approach is that women are treated fairly. Fairness may require laws, policies, and practices that treat women differently from men. We will refer to this path as the *fairness doctrine*.

The tension is evident in the disagreement among women themselves over which is the right path to take to improve women's status. Just because women share sex-linked biological characteristics with one another does not mean that they embrace a single understanding of gender equality nor does it mean that they possess a group identity or group consciousness as *women* in a way that easily translates into political action. In this regard, *feminism* only adds to the tension.

Encountering the Controversies of Equality

Memorializing Women's History

In January, 2000, after seven years of planning and fundraising, the Sojourner Truth Memorial Statue Committee announced its five design finalists. As soon as the names were released, local artists reacted with outrage and collected over 100 signatures in protest. It turns out that the five finalists, selected from a gender-balanced pool of 49 men and women designers, were all male. Known best among feminists for her "Ain't I a Woman" speech delivered at the Akron Convention in 1851, Sojourner Truth symbolizes the fight for equal rights on the dual fronts of race and gender. The Statue Committee announced in February that the list of design finalists had been increased to ten and that five women have been added to the original list. "The process that chose the first five men had integrity and was fair, but we had to have a gender-balanced diverse pool," said one committee member.[1]

SHOULD WOMEN designers have been equally represented in the final pool? If the original process was "fair," why were five women added later? Not surprisingly, the committee's solution did not satisfy anyone, nor should we have expected it to bring the dispute to a close. At the heart of this controversy lies the paradox of gender equality: a desire for equal-

As an ideology, feminism has been ineffective as an organizing philosophy for women's movements because feminism itself incorporates the equality paradox. Feminism promotes unity among women while recognizing diversity, and it pursues equality even while recognizing differences.

Controversy is inevitable anytime one group makes demands that require another group to relinquish power, resources, control, or the privileges they currently enjoy. *Patriarchy* literally means "rule of" (*arch*) "fathers" (*patri*). More generally, patriarchy characterizes the pervasive control men exercise over social, economic, and political power and resources; this is true not only in the United States, but also throughout the world. Feminism and women's movements directly challenge the privileged position of men and demand that women be viewed as individuals rather than simply derivatives of their relationships to men. The longstanding and persistent belief that men and women naturally occupy *separate spheres* strengthens the power of patriarchy. The separate spheres ideology promotes the belief that due to women's role in reproduction, they are best suited to occupy the private sphere of home and family. Alternatively, men are designed to occupy the public sphere of work and politics. Until the mid-1800s, common law, known as *coverture*, contributed to women's lack of power in the public sphere by defining married couples as one entity represented in civil society by the husband. Therefore, women could not vote, control property, or work for wages since they were indivisible from their husbands. Throughout the book, controversies about gender equality are

ity in the face of differences. Adding five female designers to the list of five male designers was a clear nod to *quantitative* equality of representation within the pool of finalists. Yet the action also reflected the persistent belief that women are somehow different from men in important ways and that the designs they submitted would therefore be *qualitatively* different from those submitted by the men. These two perspectives on gender equality appear inconsistent and yet have acted in tandem throughout history, rendering the story of women's integration into public life complex and unfinished even as we begin a new century.

What do you think?

In which instance did the Statue Committee treat men and women equally: when they selected the designs from among a gender-balanced pool of designers or when they made sure that the list of finalists included an equal number of men and women?

Who would be in the best position to memorialize women's history? Are both men and women equally capable of celebrating the contributions of a woman like Sojourner Truth? In what ways might men and women differ in their approach to the task? In what ways might a difference in how men and women approach the task matter?

1. "Women Added to Finalists for Abolitionist's Statue," *New York Times,* Sunday, 20 February 2000, p. A-24.

most evident when women demand autonomy and work toward acquiring the rights and privileges that flow from eliminating the distinction between the public and private spheres.

This text employs the equality-difference paradox to examine women's historic and contemporary participation in politics. In doing so, it is important to state two caveats: First, accepting the equality-difference paradox as a framework for examining women's political integration does not mean that these are the only two positions one might adopt. Dichotomies can sometimes be limiting in that they accentuate, or exaggerate, the positions at either end of a spectrum, while giving little attention to the space in between. History suggests that neither polar position provides an entirely satisfactory approach to the pursuit of gender equality. Similarly, neither position will provide a full explanation of women's successes and failures in working toward gender equality. Rather it is the tension produced by the coexistence of the legal equality doctrine and the fairness doctrine that provides the most fertile ground on which to examine gendered society, women and politics, and the continuing controversies of equality.

Second, equality is not the only goal of women's movements nor is the equality-difference framework the only way to understand women's pursuit of gender equality. This framework, however, does provide a very effective way to explore the multitude of controversies associated with the pursuit of gender equality and to examine the diverse perspectives among women, as well as differences between women and men. Many of the most interesting debates explored in this text, however, find women working in opposition to other women in defining and pursuing social, economic, and political goals.

POLITICS AND WOMEN'S PURSUIT OF EQUALITY

Why has it taken women so long to be recognized as important political actors? Why, in 2000, do women earn, on average, seventy-four cents to a man's dollar, despite passage of the 1963 Equal Pay Act? Why do many women, young and old alike, shy away from using *feminism* as a label yet express support for feminist positions? Why was allowing women to vote seen as the most radical demand expressed in the *Declaration of Sentiments* adopted in 1848 at the first organized women's rights convention, in Seneca Falls, New York? Is the gender gap in contemporary electoral politics real, and if so, what does it mean? Why are women still petitioning government to address problems like child-care, work, and family-leave issues; pay equity; funding for women's health concerns; and rape and domestic violence when these very same issues were also on the agenda at the Seneca Falls Convention? Answers to these questions lie in the controversies of gender equality created by the equality-difference paradox. Although women have been citizens of the United States since its founding, they have never shared equally with men in the rights or obligations of democratic citizenship.[1] Instead, women have struggled for admission to full and equal citizenship even while many argued that their particular brand of citizenship would be distinctively different from that of men.

The paradox of women's equality suggests that two paths toward the same end can coexist. Advocates of both legal equality and fairness have seen politics and the political system as a means to their preferred ends. The result has been a long history of disagreement among women about the surest path to full integration into public life and even about whether full public participation itself is desirable. Because women themselves hold different attitudes and opinions about their appropriate roles, their ability to effectively practice interest-group politics has been greatly diminished. If women could present a united front, their numbers alone would demand considerable respect and attention within the economy and from politicians at all levels of government. However, unable first to agree on unique sex and gender interests as women, and second, to disentangle gender interests from the powerful cross-pressures of race, ethnicity, class, marital status, motherhood, and sexuality women often find their interests allied with multiple groups. As a result, women's ability to speak with a single voice or act as a unified force on a single agenda is reduced. Thus women's relationship to politics and, more broadly, the development of women's movements have largely proceeded down two paths toward equality: one group advocating the legal equality doctrine and the other the fairness doctrine.

Feminists and nonfeminists alike find this division frustrating when a unified women's bloc would suit their needs. In 1920, both political parties worked feverishly to attract the female vote, and activists in the suffrage and women's rights movements worked diligently to turn out the women's vote in an effort to place their issues on the national policy agenda. When a coherent women's voice and vote failed to materialize, the parties eventually turned elsewhere, and activists were forced once again into an "outsider" strategy. More recently the media, trying to discover pivotal voting groups in the national electorate, have variously labeled female voters as "soccer moms" in the 1996 elections and "waitress moms" in the 1998 midterm elections. Obviously, these characterizations do not describe even the barest majority of women in the electorate, but the desire to understand women's political behavior and contribution to the nation by reducing their entire identity to a variation on motherhood is nothing new. Motherhood and women's unique role in nurturing future generations of citizens have exercised a powerful defining (and limiting) influence on women's relationship to politics.[2] In 1914, Congress passed a unanimous resolution establishing Mother's Day. The resolution's language emphasized mothers' contribution to the nation:

> Whereas the service rendered the United States by the American mother is the greatest source of the country's strength and inspiration . . . Whereas the American mother is doing so much for the home, for moral spirits and religion, hence so much for good government and humanity . . . Therefore, be it resolved that the second Sunday in May will be celebrated as Mother's Day.[3]

Women's role in good government in 1914, expressed by Congress in this resolution, was not one of direct action or participation but rather was limited to their functions in the private sphere of the home and in their socially defined role as mother and nurturer. While the constitutional right to vote in 1920 gave women a powerful form of direct participation, they were not newcomers to politics even then.

DEFINING WOMEN'S POLITICS

Defining *politics* beyond the traditional scope of electoral, party, or institutional behavior allows a more complete examination of women's political behavior. Until at least 1920, women had been legally excluded from many conventional forms of participation. As a result, an *insider's* definition of politics, focusing exclusively on political party activity, voting, campaigning, seeking office, or making direct contact with public officials, does not prove very useful in examining women's activism prior to suffrage or in understanding the complexity of women's politics today. Defining "politics" is in itself a political exercise since any definition necessarily expresses some judgment about which participants, actions, and issues are legitimate. The pervasiveness of the sepa-

Defining Politics

Politics involves the authoritative allocation of values for a society. (Easton, 1953)

Politics: who gets what, when, and how. (Lasswell, 1936)

The art and science of governance; the means by which the will of the community is arrived at and implemented; the activities of government, politician, or political party. (Shafritz, 1988)

WHEN GENDER is used as an analytic framework in the study of politics, politics itself needs to be redefined. Consider the following:

- Traditional definitions of politics make conflicts and terrain public, whereas many of the most significant issues and problems facing women are considered private. During the second wave, feminists adopted the slogan, "The personal is political" to call attention to the public-private boundary that often excluded certain issues like rape, domestic abuse, and contraception from public policy discussions. The public-private dichotomy may also shape the way we understand and evaluate men's and women's political participation.

- Traditional definitions of politics focus on elite behaviors and attitudes and dominant institutions. Feminists charge that this focus marginalizes the contributions, attitudes, and actions of multiple communities (of people of color, women, the poor, lesbians, and gays). When marginalized groups are included in politics or political analysis, it is often in a way that ignores the challenges created by the many intersections of identity.

- Traditional definitions of politics ignore the power and ubiquitous nature of patriarchy.

Given these concerns, crafting a single definition of politics is challenging, but give it a try. Write down your definition of politics now, and then come back to it as you read more of this text. Is your definition comprehensive enough to include the many and varied forms of women's participation and the issues that most directly have an impact on women's daily lives?

rate spheres ideology and the power of patriarchy limited women's opportunities to engage in politics as it has been traditionally defined. Even though women were seen as *outsiders* prior to suffrage, the range of activities they undertook, the tactics they employed, and the issues they cared about were indeed political.

In pre-Revolutionary America, women organized public demonstrations to protest the high cost of food and household goods and boycotted English tea to protest high taxes. To promote these activities, they formed organizations such as the Daughters of Liberty and the Anti-Tea Leagues. During the Revolutionary and Civil Wars, women participated both on the battlefield and in more traditional tasks consistent with their gender role such as nursing, cooking, and sewing clothes for soldiers. Although not yet seated in power, women nonetheless lobbied those closest to them for early political recognition. Abigail Adams issued the now famous plea to her husband John Adams, to " . . . remember the ladies and be more generous and favorable to them than your ancestors. . . . If particular care and attention is not paid to the ladies, we are determined to foment a rebellion, and will not hold ourselves bound by any laws in which we have no voice or representation."[4] Rejected (or at best ignored) in the constitutional framework, women organized through voluntary associations and social movements. Progressive women's organizations founded in the early twentieth century provided a model for the development of the welfare state in the 1930s, and women were integral in the abolition, temperance, and Progressive movements. When modern political campaigns began, women participated by performing duties "consistent with their temperament" (gender roles), by providing food, acting as hostesses and social organizers, and cleaning up afterward. In doing so, observers commented that women exhibited a partisan fervor equal to that of men.[5] Alexis de Tocqueville, noting in his essays that Americans were particularly preoccupied with politics, wrote that "even the women often go to public meetings and forget household cares while they listen to political speeches."[6] Although women were often relegated to support roles, they nonetheless participated in politics and acted politically long before they were awarded the franchise.

DISTINGUISHING SEX FROM GENDER

It is important at this juncture to distinguish between *sex* and *gender*. Sex identity as a male or female is a physically defined biological function of chemical hormones. Males and females differ most obviously in their unique contribution to human reproduction. Females alone can give birth and breastfeed. However, assigning women the job of raising children after birth is a socially defined gender role. Gender incorporates society's interpretation of sex-based characteristics and attaches a culturally constructed value to the differences and unique contributions of each sex. In a patriarchal culture, male characteristics are valued more highly than female qualities, and femininity is marginalized. This has significant implications for the ordering of society, the distribution of rights and power, and in the creation of public policy. Although most contemporary scholars, scientists, politicians, and jurists no longer view biology as the *sole* determinant of human potential, our culture is not entirely free of the view that sex carries an immutable quality linked to social, political, and economic competence. We now prefer to think of human behavior as a combination of nature (biology) and nurture (environment). The relative weight of biology and environment in producing an outcome is complex and subject to robust debate and research in a variety of disciplines. For our purposes, however, it is sufficient to state that simple sex differences do not create the greatest barriers to women's equality. Rather, it is how society interprets differences and values one quality over another that has the greatest impact on women's lives. *Gender* rather than *sex* differences will therefore be the focus of our inquiry in this book.

THE FIRST PATH: THE LEGAL EQUALITY DOCTRINE

For as long as women and men have inhabited organized society, three assumptions have governed their relations: men and women have fundamentally different psychological and sexual natures; men are inherently the dominant or superior sex; and male-female difference and male dominance are both natural.[7] Whether understood as a deity's grand plan or as biology's destiny, the presumption that men and women naturally occupy different spheres has dominated political, economic, and cultural thinking for centuries. Aristotle, writing in *The Politics*, ascribed society's rule and command function to men since "women are naturally subordinate to men" and "the male is naturally fitter to command than the female, except when there is some departure from nature."[8] Late nineteenth and early twentieth century psychiatrists and philosophers argued that education might actually be dangerous to a woman's reproductive system. Social Darwinists argued against women's suffrage, warning that because women are by nature the "nurturant and protective class," female voters might interfere with nature's progression by aiding the state in giving help to those who might otherwise not survive on their own (e.g., the poor, the sick, and the disabled).[9] While these theories may sound ludicrous, at their core lies a belief in a natural inevitability of sex and gender differences that enjoys support even today. This belief in the essential differences between women and men, more than any other perspective, separates women from one another and distinguishes between the two paths to equality. Gender equality accomplished through legal doctrine cannot coexist with gender differences if these differences are grounded in essential human nature. Yet equality of rights for women is exactly what many feminists argue is the most basic human right of all.

Although the concept of equality lies at the very heart of a liberal democracy, even politics and constitutions cannot make men and women equal when people believe they are essentially and immutably different. How else could the US founders so eloquently write: "We hold these truths to be self-evident: That all men are created equal; that they are endowed by their Creator with certain unalienable rights . . ." in the Declaration of Independence while they ignored the interests of women and slaves? The answer lies in the presumption that a patriarchal society is natural and therefore unalterable through social, economic, or political means. Thus a gendered system—one in which gender is inextricably linked to power, prestige, and fundamental rights—has been a force in American politics since the nation's founding. It is embedded in the very documents that define our institutions and governing practices, if not in the precise language then in the founder's assumptions about human nature. The path toward gender equality pursued by advocates of the legal equality doctrine proposes to alter the assumption of natural differences between men and women by changing the laws that govern human behavior. The presumption is that once behavior is altered, a change in attitude is sure to follow.

Roots of Women's Claims to Legal Equality

Those who argued for women's political equality in the late eighteenth century most often based their claims on the liberal challenge to aristocratic rule and the Enlightenment's legacy of reason and human improvement. Liberalism (or individualism) stresses the importance of rational thought, autonomous action, and choice on the part of each individual. An individual's status is therefore determined by that person's actions rather than by his or her station at birth. Gradually, individualism gained influence to the point that restrictions on the voting rights of free males imposed by property requirements fell by the wayside with the election of Andrew Jackson in 1828. As individuals, free from the barriers to political agency imposed by the requirements of inherited wealth or title, native-born, middle-class white men were able to exercise greater economic and political power. With this emphasis on individualism, education gained a prominent focus. Human beings were not purely subject to the whims of nature, liberals presumed, but open to developing their character through education and training. Individuals on equal footing would enter a social contract with one another to form a society of citizens. Unfortunately for women, early liberal theorists (such as Thomas Hobbes, John Locke, and Jean Jacques Rousseau) excluded women from full citizenship. Hobbes and Locke were willing to grant women a somewhat ambiguous state of equality in nature, but not in politics. Rousseau assumed from the start that women lacked the natural capacities for full citizenship. All three liberal theorists believed that natural and biological differences between men and women precluded women's full participation in a social contract.[10] In this sense, contemporary political theorist Carole Pateman argues that a *sexual contract* predated a *social contract*.[11] A sexual contract required women to transfer their natural rights to men in exchange for protection, thereby leaving women without any independent rights to exchange with others in forming a social contract. Within this patriarchal arrangement, women could never be men's political equals.

Mary Wollstonecraft, philosopher and author of *A Vindication of the Rights of Men* and *A Vindication of the Rights of Woman*, denied any fundamental difference in character or nature between men and women. She argued that any weaknesses exhibited by women resulted from their faulty education and isolated social position. Wollstonecraft argued that women would gladly trade their lofty, yet isolated, social position in return for their rights. Decades later, another liberal theorist, John Stuart Mill, published *The Subjection of Women* (1869). He too argued that women's "disability" in public life did not stem from her sex alone, but rather from her subjugation in marriage:

> [T]he principle which regulates the existing social relations between the two sexes—the legal subordination of one sex to the other—is wrong in itself, and now one of the chief hindrances to human improvement; and that it ought to be replaced by a principle of perfect equality, admitting no power or privilege on the one side, nor disability on the other.[12]

Mill unfavorably compared women's fate in marriage to the institution of slavery (universally discredited among liberals). While slaves were coerced into service, Mill wrote that every aspect of society leads women to willingly enter a state of subjugation and that men's dominion over all and the intimacy men and women share make it impossible for women to cast off their bonds. Suggesting that at one time both slavery and monarchy seemed natural in America, Mill wrote: "So true it is that unnatural generally means only uncustomary, and that everything which is usual appears natural. The subjection of women to men being a universal custom, any departure from it quite naturally appears unnatural."[13] Mill did not propose any solutions to the problem of women's subjection in marriage, but like Wollstonecraft, he believed that the vote could emancipate women's minds and admit them to the public dialogue. As a member of the British parliament, he introduced and supported women's suffrage.

Patriarchy and Limits to Legal Equality

Patriarchal systems are ancient in origin and ubiquitous. Mill captured the pervasiveness of patriarchy's reach in this passage from *The Subjection of Women*:

> Whatever gratification or pride there is in the possession of power, and whatever personal interest in its exercise, is in this case not confined to a limited class, but common to the whole male sex. Instead of being, to most of its supporters, a thing desirable chiefly in the abstract, or, like the political ends usually contended for by factions, of little private importance to any but the leaders; it comes home to the person and hearth of every male head of a family, and every one who looks forward to being so. The clodhopper exercises, or is to exercise, his share of the power equally with the highest nobleman.[14]

Mill rightly recognized that all men were empowered by patriarchy, regardless of their individual ability to exercise their power and privilege wisely. Likewise, all women were disempowered by patriarchy, regardless of their innate abilities for leadership and for the wise exercise of power. Patriarchy assumed that all women, by nature, were incapable of equality and therefore limited women's claims to the natural and political rights flowing from individualism as described by liberal theorists.

Contemporary feminist scholar Adrienne Rich describes the patriarchal tradition's limits on women's opportunities this way:

> Patriarchy . . . does not necessarily imply that no woman has power, or that all women in a given culture may not have certain powers. . . . Under patriarchy, I may live in *purdah* or drive a truck; . . . I may become a hereditary or elected head of state or wash the underwear of a millionaire's wife; I may serve my husband his early-morning coffee within the clay walls of a Berber village or march in an academic procession; whatever my status or situation, my derived economic class, or my sexual preference, I live under the power of the fathers, and I have access only to so much of privilege or influence as the patriarchy is willing to accede to me, and only for so long as I will pay the price for male approval.[15]

Patriarchy, as Rich describes it, leaves room for women to exercise considerable discretion and choice but only within the patriarchal framework in which men control power, resources, and access to both. In other words, even when women believe they are making independent choices and aspiring to and achieving great professional success, they do so within the realm of choices that males allow. So what sort of choices really exist for women within a patriarchal world? Patriarchy in this context poses serious problems for those who believe gender equality can best be accomplished by the legal equality doctrine. Can truly gender-neutral laws and policies exist when patriarchy is so pervasive?

Posing a slightly different but equally serious challenge for advocates of the legal equality doctrine, sociologist Sandra Bem contrasts patriarchy with the concept of *androcentrism*. Androcentrism is the practice of overvaluing the male experience and undervaluing the female experience. In an androcentric world, "males and the male experience are treated as a neutral standard or norm for the culture or the species as a whole, and females and female experience are treated as a sex-specific deviation from that allegedly universal standard."[16] Thus, feminists who aspire to equality as defined by the legal equality doctrine are faced with the fundamental dilemma: equality measured by whose standard? Can a standard be established apart from the dominance of the male experience? In a patriarchal system, the standard would appear to be whatever constitutes the male norm. Is the male norm an appropriate aspiration for women? Is it the appropriate standard for equality? Do we recognize the gendered character of standards of equality? More specifically, can laws based on the "male experience" adequately cover circumstances in the female experience? For many, particularly those who advocate the fairness doctrine, the answer is a resounding "No." The male standard can improve women's situation only when women and men are "similarly situated." In cases where men and women are differently situated, either because of biology or social norms, the male standard may actually mean additional burdens for women. Thus, while the legal equality doctrine as a path to gender equality has a solid basis in liberal democratic theory, making it an appropriate solution to the problems women face in gaining access to the public sphere, it is not without its theoretical or practical problems. The fairness doctrine addresses some of the problems inherent in the legal equality path but presents a different set of unique challenges for men and women seeking gender equality.

The Case of Pregnant Working Women

PREGNANCY AND motherhood, when combined with work outside the home, present feminists with a quandary: Is pregnancy a temporary disability comparable to physical disabilities men and nonpregnant women might experience, or is pregnancy a distinctive experience requiring special treatment by employers?

The tradition of protection

The issue of maternal health first arose late in the nineteenth century amid the debate over protective legislation. Most protective legislation that was aimed at all workers was struck down by the Supreme Court as unconstitutional interference with the free marketplace. Legislation aimed at protecting women only was, however, allowed in the case of *Muller* v. *Oregon*. The Court reasoned that men and women occupied separate spheres and women were naturally ordained to bear and raise children. Protections were further justified by the need to protect and sustain the race. The first major piece of social legislation, designed to provide health care to women and children, *regardless of employment status*, was passed in 1921. Known as the Sheppard-Towner Act, the law was a direct result of the potential power of newly enfranchised women voters. The law lapsed in 1929. The presumption that women were temporary participants in the work force, present only until they married or had their first child, dominated this period. Emphasis was on protecting the health of the mother—bearer of future citizens—rather than on employment rights for women.

Pregnancy as a disability

The next phase in maternity law came in the late 1950s when the women's bureau of the Department of Labor dropped its support for protective legislation and instead became an advocate for women's employment rights, including the right to equal pay. Since special treatment was incompatible with the new view of women as independent workers, the bureau adopted the concept of pregnancy as a temporary disability. Any policies or practices an employer might apply to cases of temporary disability must also be applied to a woman's incapacity from pregnancy or childbirth. While this approach assumed that women were in the paid work force to stay, it did not recognize the additional burdens a family added to women's dual roles and it did nothing to help workers balance family and job responsibilities. Two Supreme Court cases in the 1970s raised doubts about treating pregnancy as a disability. *Geduldig* v. *Aiello* (1974) and *General Electric* v. *Gilbert* (1976) involved whether an employer could remove pregnancy from a list of disabilities eligible for benefits. The Court ruled that an employer's failure to cover pregnancy as a disability was not a form of sex discrimination prohibited under Title VII because pregnancy was voluntary and because it only affected some, not all, women. Feminists reacted by lobbying Congress to amend Title VII. The Pregnancy Discrimination Act (PDA) was passed as an amendment to Title VII in 1978. The act requires pregnancy to be treated similarly to all other short-term disabilities for insurance purposes. The emphasis in the PDA is on the woman as a member of the labor force and not on her responsibilities as a mother.

Maternity leave becomes family and medical leave

In the 1980s, the battle among feminists as to the appropriate approach to pregnancy heated up once again. Some feminists argued that legal equality with regard to pregnancy as a temporary disability conformed to a male work standard and in fact, left women with two jobs and little support. Others argued that without gender-neutral laws, even with regard to pregnancy, women would be forced back to the days when special treatment was code language for job discrimination and wage inequities. Those favoring gender-neutral laws lobbied Congress to treat pregnancy as a medical condition and urged Congress to go even further and adopt a law requiring employers to offer unpaid family leave for any worker (male or female) with pressing family responsibilities that included job protections so that pay levels and seniority would be maintained. The Family and Medical Leave Act (FMLA) was first introduced in 1985, passing both houses of Congress in 1990. The Bush administration vetoed the legislation twice, arguing that the federal government should not mandate employment practices in an era of stiff economic competition. The FMLA was finally signed into law by Bill Clinton in February 1993, in his first act as president. FMLA applies to private employers with more than 50 workers and all public agencies. It provides for up to 12 weeks of unpaid leave for family-related illnesses, the birth or adoption of a child, or for a worker's own illness without sacrificing pay-level, position, or seniority after the leave has ended. In reality, the Women's Legal Defense Fund has estimated that the law covers only about 60 percent of U.S. workers, and fewer women than men since women are more likely than men to work in small businesses. The law still does not address the incompatibility of family and work responsibilities over the long term.

Provisions in other countries

The emphasis in the United States on individualism and the free market has resulted in relatively few national family policies. In fact, among major industrialized countries, only New Zealand and the United States do not mandate paid maternity leave. Alternatively, in many European countries, paid family leave is the norm for women and men. The form and duration of family leave differs by country, but generally ranges from one to six months and guarantees that the woman's job and health care benefits will be maintained as well as provides some portion of her salary while on leave. The salary is usually paid out of a government social security or health insurance program. In addition to paid maternity leave, some countries provide continuing support for families. In France the government pays every family a monthly sum for each child under the age of 18.

What do you think?

Can pregnancy be separated from child rearing in a way that returns a woman to her previous employment status after birth or does parenthood (for both women and men) conflict with work responsibilities and alter the relationship between employer and employee in a way that requires a totally new approach?

Arguably, it is in the nation's interest to both encourage a quality labor force and to encourage the regeneration of citizens through strong families. Can a national family policy be crafted to pursue both goals and at the same time be fair to both male and female workers, including those without children?

Would you describe current U.S. policy regarding pregnant women workers as gender neutral or as providing special treatment for women? Under which type of policy are women treated more *equally*? Explain.

THE SECOND PATH: THE FAIRNESS DOCTRINE

Colonial life in pre-Revolutionary America was largely agrarian and home-based. Women worked alongside men, and gender distinctions did not limit women's contribution or workday. However, as the means of production moved from the land to the factory and society was reorganized accordingly, specialization divided human laborers. At the time of the American Revolution, very few women were educated, and literacy rates among women were half those of men.[17] As society's child bearers, women's talents were quickly ascribed to the private sphere of home and hearth. Although women had been integral to the maintenance and survival of the agrarian economy, the duties of the home were now defined as distinct from the productive economy and paid labor force outside the home. Opportunities for women to earn money or to control property were severely limited by law and practice. Women constituted the reproductive unpaid labor force and men the productive paid labor force. In this sense, they complemented each other and were said to occupy *separate spheres*.[18]

Separate Spheres Ideology

Women's role in the private sphere was, by definition, incompatible with full participation in society. Separate sphere ideology, although not originally defined by law, clearly identified the activities available for women as consistent with their primary role as child bearers and nurturers. White women's role within the home was raised to new heights of glorification for middle- and upper-class women. The home was her exclusive domain, giving her a certain degree of autonomy. For working-class and lower-class women and for women of color, the separate sphere limited their access to the productive labor pool and depressed the wages paid for their work. Opportunities for work outside the home closely paralleled women's duties within the home. Immigrant women in the 1840s and 1850s, for example, worked in sex-segregated industries like textile, clothing, and shoe manufacturing. Teaching, sewing, and later nursing were also seen as consistent with women's domestic responsibilities, although the pay was almost negligible. Unpaid charitable and welfare activities, particularly those directed at women and children, were encouraged for all white women as appropriate extensions of the private sphere. Slave women in the South were at the bottom of the hierarchy in every respect. They were subject entirely to the white male patriarchal ruling class, and as such, African American women did not enjoy any of the privileges of autonomy that accompanied the separate station enjoyed by white women in the middle and upper classes.

Although separate spheres ideology was ultimately quite constraining for all women, it did provide limited opportunities for middle- and upper-class women to gain experience in forming welfare associations. It afforded them growing access to education and made it possible for women to interact with other women in quasi-public settings. These interactions enabled women to view their condition in a critical light and eventually to organize for a greater role as women and to advocate for more rights in the public sphere. In this sense, the separate sphere was empowering for white middle-class women. However, because power in a capitalist economy flows from those who control valued resources (namely money or goods), men continued to exercise decision-making power both within and outside the home. As separate spheres ideology found its way into court decisions and into the public's understanding of *normal* daily life, men used the ideology to solidify their control over women's lives and livelihoods.

Separate and Unequal Becomes the Law

Separate spheres ideology was reinforced and given the weight of law through the case of *Bradwell* v. *Illinois*, decided in 1873. Myra Bradwell, a feminist active in women's suffrage organizations, passed the Illinois bar exam in 1869, but the Supreme Court of Illinois refused to let her practice law. Under Illinois law, females were not permitted to practice law. Bradwell appealed to the U.S. Supreme Court, claiming that the state of Illinois had violated her rights under the Fourteenth Amendment in denying her one of the "privileges of citizenship" (the privilege of practicing law). The U.S. Supreme Court denied her claims and reaffirmed Illinois's power to determine the distinct privileges for men and women under state law. In a concurring opinion, Supreme Court Justice Joseph P. Bradley specifically noted the separate spheres ideology as justification for limiting women's role in the public sphere:

> Civil law, as well as nature herself, has always recognized a wide difference in the respective spheres and destinies of man and woman. Man is, or should be, woman's protector and defender. The natural and proper timidity and delicacy which belongs to the female sex evidently unfits it for many of the occupations of civil life. The constitution of the family organization, which is founded in the Devine ordinance, as well as in the nature of things, indicates the domestic sphere as that which properly belongs to the domain and functions of womanhood. The harmony, not to say identity, of interests and views which belong, or should belong, to the family institution is repugnant to the idea of a woman adopting a distinct and independent career from that of her husband. So firmly fixed was this sentiment in the founders of common law that it became a maxim of that system of jurisprudence that a woman had no legal existence apart from her husband, who was regarded as her head and representative in the social state. (83 U.S. 130, 21 L.Ed. 442)

Note that Justice Bradley relied on a series of assumptions in denying Bradwell's Fourteenth Amendment claim that she was entitled to practice law since she passed the Illinois bar. First, he clearly delineated separate spheres and destinies for men and women grounded not only in civil and common law, but in nature. Second, Justice Bradley said that the patriarchal family was not only natural but founded in "the Devine ordinance." Finally, he stated that the "law of the Creator" relegated women to the "offices of wife and mother." In other words, what was natural, ordained by the Creator, and made real through civil practice, the U.S. Supreme Court cannot change. Furthermore, all women were captives of nature, the Creator, and common law, since the Court refused to address the privileges and immunities of adult women apart from their marital status:

> It is true that many women are unmarried and not affected by any of the duties, complications, and incapacities arising out of the married state, but these are exceptions to the general rule. The paramount destiny and mission of woman are to fulfil the noble and benign offices of wife and mother. This is the law of the Creator. And the rules of civil society must be adapted to the general constitution of things, and cannot be based upon exceptional cases. (83 U.S. 130, 21 L.Ed. 442)

Like Aristotle in an earlier time, the U.S. Supreme Court treated all women as a group and ruled that even though there may be women whose exceptional abilities fit them for public life, society must be governed by the assumption that women's proper role is that of wife and mother. As such, women are dependent on men and cannot be treated as individuals in their own right. Although some women may have abilities that (but for their sex) would entitle them to practice law, society cannot be governed by such exceptions.

Later Court rulings would use the separate spheres ideology as a justification to protect women in the labor force and to accommodate her "special burden" by limiting her civic obligations (e.g., the vote, jury duty, military service). The Court rejected separate spheres ideology only during the last two decades of the twentieth century and then only piecemeal, not entirely. Although most would argue that both sex and race are immutable characteristics not subject to an individual's control, the Supreme Court still assumes that sex bears some relation to one's abilities; it does not, however, make similar assumptions about race. These distinctions and assumptions embedded in the philosophy of law in the United States will arise again in later chapters in examining education, work, and family issues.

The Basis of Restricted Citizenship for Married Women

Bradwell's status as a *femme covert* (which "covered" women entirely by their husbands' legal identity) also contributed to her being denied the ability to practice law. *Coverture,* imported to the colonies from the English legal tradition, defined the legal relationship between husband and wife and thus complicated women's claims to equality and their challenges to the constraints of separate spheres ideology. English jurist William Blackstone wrote:

> By marriage, the husband and wife are one person in law: that is, the very being or legal existence of the woman is suspended during the marriage, or at least is incorporated and consolidated into that of the husband; under whose wing, protection and *cover*, she performs every thing . . . [she] is said to be covert-baron, or under the

protection and influence of her husband, her baron, or lord; and her condition upon marriage is called her *coverture*.[19]

As a practical matter, coverture made the husband and wife one person—the husband. A married woman could not execute contracts independent of her husband, nor could she buy or sell property, dispose of personal assets like jewelry and household items, control the destiny of her children, or serve as their guardian apart from her husband's consent. Marital rape was inconceivable because husband and wife were one person. It was not until 1978, when New York included a spouse along with a stranger and an acquaintance in the list of perpetrators of rape that marital rape was outlawed anywhere in the United States.

In 1805, the U.S. Supreme Court articulated the nation's implicit understanding of married women's obligations to the state and her status as a citizen apart from her husband in the case of *Martin* v. *Massachusetts*. Anna Gordon Martin received approximately 844 acres of land from her father on his death. As was the custom, her husband, William Martin, controlled the land until his death. The "right of remainder" entitled the land to Anna's heir (her son James) on her husband's death. However, the Massachusetts Confiscation Act of 1779 allowed the state to confiscate properties of individuals who fled with the British during the war, which was considered an act of treason.[20] Anna fled the state with her husband William. James petitioned for the return of properties confiscated toward the close of the American Revolution, arguing that married women (his mother in this case) were inhabitants, not members, of the state, thereby making the property seizure illegal.

> Upon the strict principles of law, a *femme covert* is not a member; has no *political* relation to the *state* any more than an alien. . . . The legislature intended to exclude femmes-covert and infants from the operation of the act; otherwise the word inhabitant would have been used alone, and not coupled with the word member.[21]

As inhabitants of the state (citizens), all women were subject to its laws, and single women subject to taxation. The question before the Supreme Court was whether a married woman could have a relationship with the state distinct from that of her husband. There was no question that if William Martin held property, the statute would apply and the state of Massachusetts would have lawfully seized the property. But because Anna Martin owned the property and also met the conditions of the Massachusetts Confiscation Act of 1779, did the state have a right to the property? Attorneys for the Martins argued that Anna, as a femme covert, was incapable of defying her husband by remaining in Massachusetts while he fled. They further argued that the state did not expect married women to act independently and could expect no assistance from them in defending the country: "So far are women from being of service in the defence [sic] of a country against the attacks of an enemy that it is frequently thought expedient to send them out of the way, lest they impede the operations of their own party."[22]

Attorneys for the state crafted their argument based on the principles of natural law, reasoning that a precondition of citizenship was autonomous competence, and because women were considered citizens, they should also be responsible for their own actions even when their actions defied the theory of coverture marriage. They argued that "if patriarchy in politics is rejected, so too must patriarchy in marriage."[23] Despite this line of reasoning, the Court ruled unanimously in favor of the Martins, deciding in effect to abandon patriarchy in politics but maintain patriarchy in the family and in marital relationships. Although women might be citizens in a conceptual sense, marriage took away the privileges of citizenship in a real sense.

This line of reasoning was not merely a post-Revolutionary mindset clouded by a tradition of coverture. In 1907, Congress passed a law stating that women who married aliens lost their citizenship even if they remained in the United States. The Supreme Court upheld the law as late as 1915, ruling in *Mackenzie* v. *Hare* that if a woman voluntarily married an alien, she must give up her citizenship and adopt the nationality of her husband. This law remained in effect until passage of the Cable Act of 1922, which stated, "the right of a person to become a naturalized citizen shall not be denied to a person on account of sex or because she is a married woman." Even then, however, the law covered only marriages to men who were eligible to become naturalized citizens (excluding men from China or Japan, among others). American-born women who married aliens were treated as naturalized citizens, who could lose their citizenship if they lived abroad for two or more years.[24] Thus, well into the twentieth century, women's marital status governed her relationship to the state, in terms of both rights and obligations.

This gendered construction of citizenship for women differed from male citizenship in important ways. The same line of reasoning that denied married women property, guardianship of their children, and independent thought and action, found its way into debates over suffrage and subsequent Supreme Court rulings that rendered married women both sentimental and legal dependents of their husbands. The American Revolution challenged and abolished political patriarchy, yet even at the height of revolutionary spirit, familial patriarchy was continually reinforced through law, custom, and economic realities. Women remained in the same class as slaves and children when it came to extending the political rights of citizenship. Any attempt to challenge the natural order that kept women entirely in the private sphere was quashed.

Thus the separate spheres ideology, in which women occupy a natural position in the private sphere that is incompatible with public sphere responsibilities, presents the most serious challenge to those who advocate the fairness doctrine as the most appropriate path to gender equality. The logic that recognizes essential differences between men and women that suit them for different roles in society cannot be overcome by law alone. Advocates of the fairness doctrine argue that trying to make men and women alike when they are in fact different is an unproductive approach to improving women's lives. Instead, they urge that women be treated fairly. However, the pervasiveness of a separate spheres ideology makes it difficult to argue that women should participate fully in the public sphere, while believing that women need protection from and accommodation for the burdens of their sex that they bring to the public sphere. Like the legal equality doctrine discussed earlier, the fairness doctrine of gender equality is not without its theoretical and practical problems.

FEMINISM'S DIRECT CHALLENGE TO GENDER RELATIONS

Challenging long-entrenched gender roles and relationships is difficult even for the most committed individuals or groups. Gender exerts a powerful grip on each individual and on the social, political, and economic systems in which we live, study, and work. Without some sensitivity to the power of gendered life, it is easy to miss since gendered life seems so normal. Understanding the world in this way can consequently obscure the workings of an organizing system. The result is a system in which economic, political, social, and cultural forces interact with and reinforce one another in ways that continue to benefit one group and disadvantage the others. As participants in these interlocking systems, humans constantly reproduce the world we know through socialization, education, and role modeling as if we have no other choice. The effect is that the system continues as *normal*, becoming increasingly difficult to challenge as we each take our place within it. Those who suggest the system is corrupt or wrong threaten to upset centuries of tradition and custom that make life predictable and comfortable for the majority.

Feminism, then, provides a direct challenge to the gendered world, as well as to patriarchy, capitalism, and the sexist assumptions that women's difference from men renders them inherently inferior. Feminism is a complex and somewhat paradoxical ideology that defies a single approach or definition. In fact, feminists are rarely in agreement with one another over the ultimate aims of feminism or the means to achieve them. Although many feminists exhibit a commitment to absolute legal and practical equality, some feminists have argued for separate spheres of influence and an emphasis on difference and complementarity rather than equality.[25] In an oft-quoted passage, Rebecca West wrote in 1913, "I myself have never been able to find out precisely what feminism is. I only know that people call me a feminist whenever I express sentiments that differentiate me from a doormat or a prostitute."[26] Feminists of all descriptions wrestle with the question: How can demands for equality and fairness be reconciled with sex differences?

Feminism, as a word and concept, is a relatively recent addition to the lexicon, emerging only in the 1910s to express a broader set of goals than the suffrage movement embraced.[27] According to historian Nancy Cott, people in the nineteenth century talked about the "advancement of woman," the cause of woman, or woman's rights and woman suffrage. To our modern ears, the use of the singular "woman" sounds awkward—both grammatically and conceptually. "Nineteenth-century women's consistent usage of the singular *woman* symbolized, in a word, the unity of the female sex. It proposed that all women have one cause, one movement."[28] Now in the twenty-first century, individualism is valued so highly that it would be rare to encounter anyone who believed that all women share a single cause. Modern feminism reflects these sentiments and in doing so, embraces the paradox of gender equality that provides the foundation for the two paths to equality:

> Feminism asks for sexual equality that includes sexual difference. It posits that women recognize their unity while it stands for diversity among women. It requires gender consciousness for its basis yet calls for the elimination of prescribed gender roles. These are paradoxes rooted in the actual situation of women, who are the same as men in a species sense, but different from men in reproductive biology and the construction of gender. Men and women are alike as human beings, and yet categorically different from each other; their sameness and differences derive from nature *and* culture, how inextricably entwined we can hardly know.[29]

So, given this set of paradoxes, how might feminism be defined? Cott offers a very good three-part working definition of feminism:

- a belief in equality, defined not as "sameness" but rather as opposition to ranking one sex superior or inferior to the other, or opposition to one sex's categorical control of the rights and opportunities of the other
- a belief that women's condition is socially constructed, historically shaped rather than preordained by God or nature
- a belief that women's socially constructed position situates them on shared ground enabling a group identity or gender consciousness sufficient to mobilize women for change[30]

Approaches to Feminism

As an ideology, feminism has spawned a number of different "brands," among them liberal feminism, radical feminism, Marxist-socialist feminism, global feminism, black feminism, ecofeminism, and gender feminism. Scholars differ on how to label and divide the complex terrain of feminist theory, but the preceding list is fairly representative of the major strands of feminist thought today. Philosopher Rosemarie Tong distinguishes among these theories based on the locus of women's oppression in each. For example, liberal, radical, Marxist-socialist, and global feminists (as well as ecofeminists to some extent) attribute women's subordination to macro-level institutions, such as patriarchy, capitalism, or colonialism. Gender feminists, sometimes also called cultural feminists or maternal feminists, focus on the microcosm of the individual, claiming the roots of women's oppression are embedded deep within a woman's psyche.[31] A brief review and critique of each approach to feminism follows.[32]

Liberal Feminism

Liberal feminism is perhaps the oldest strand of feminism, rooted in the same ferment that promoted individual autonomy over aristocratic privilege in the French Revolution and the U.S. Revolutionary War. Liberalism stresses the importance of rational thought, autonomous action, and choice on the part of each person. Reason is what most clearly distinguishes humans from other forms of animal life. Individual autonomy empowers an individual to make choices in her or his own best interests, thereby elevating individual rights above the common good. Liberal theorists believe that the political and legal systems can be used to promote a liberal agenda for all people. Applied to feminism, early liberal feminists like Mary Wollstonecraft, J.S. Mill, and Harriet Taylor Mill stressed the importance of educating women, enfranchising women, and providing women equal access to both opportunities and resources in society. Liberal feminists tend to work within the existing political system and structures. Contemporary liberal feminists believe that by reforming the legal and political system to allow women equal access to opportunities and resources, men and women can achieve a state of equality. Liberal feminists target laws that distinguish between men and women based on sex. The *Declaration of Sentiments,* issued by women at the Seneca Falls Convention in 1848, was a liberal feminist document. It called for the reform of laws restricting women's right to hold property, to control resources, and to vote. The U.S. suffrage movement and suffrage organizations, such as the National American Women's Suffrage Association (NAWSA), extended women's liberal feminist claims that suffrage was an integral step in achieving political and social equality across three generations. The Equal Rights Amendment (ERA) in the United States and the United Nations Convention to End All Forms of Discrimination Against Women (CEDAW) are examples of contemporary legal reforms in this tradition.

During the early 1960s, President John F. Kennedy responded to feminists' concerns about equality for women by forming the Commission on the Status of Women. The commission studied various forms of discrimination against women, collected and made public new data on the condition of women, and spawned a number of state-based commissions that had similar missions. As a result of the data presented, the Equal Pay Act was passed in 1963; it promised equal pay for equal work, regardless of sex. Political action groups—the National Organization for Women (NOW), the National Women's Political Caucus (NWPC), and the Women's Equity Action League (WEAL), for example—were formed in the late 1960s to pursue the liberal feminist agenda. This agenda was based largely on a plan to demand enforcement of civil rights laws protecting women from discrimination. All but WEAL are still in existence today.

A variety of criticisms have been leveled against liberal feminism. Early and contemporary liberal feminists alike concentrate almost exclusively on the

Revolution or Reform?

WHETHER YOU describe yourself as a radical feminist dedicated to revolutionary change or a liberal feminist dedicated to legal reforms in pursuit of equality most likely depends on whether you see sexism as a form of *oppression* or *discrimination*. Viewing sexism as a form of oppression emphasizes change affecting women collectively—a level of change only possible through a radical reordering of patriarchal society. Women's oppression refers to patriarchy's grip on all women, regardless of class, race, or sexual orientation. Ending oppression requires ending patriarchy, capitalism, and Western dominance. Viewing sexism as a form of discrimination emphasizes the individual. Discrimination refers to "the act of singling out a person for special treatment, not on the basis of individual merit, but on the basis of prejudices about the group to which the person belongs."[1] Ending discrimination against women in employment or education, for example, requires that laws and practices be changed so that women have the same opportunities as men within these institutions.

Feminist scholar bell hooks illustrates the distinction:

> While the contemporary feminist movement has successfully stimulated an awareness of the impact of sexual discrimination on the social status of women in the U.S., it has done little to eliminate sexist oppression. Teaching women how to defend themselves against male rapists is not the same as working to change society so that men will not rape. Establishing houses for battered women does not change the psyches of the men who batter them, nor does it change the culture than promotes and condones their brutality. . . . Demanding an end to institutionalized sexism does not insure an end to sexist oppression.[2]

1. Virginia Sapiro, *Women in American Society,* 4th ed. (Mountain View, Calif.: Mayfield Publishing, 1999), p. 109.
2. bell hooks, *Ain't I A Woman: Black Women and Feminism* (Boston: South End Press, 1981).

public sphere. Women's unpaid labor in the home, domestic abuse, marital rape, and traditional practices that discriminate against women in many cultures are not addressed within the liberal approach because they occur in the private sphere. These issues are labeled *personal* and therefore are not subject to public scrutiny or redress in the public policy arena. Radical feminists charge that liberal feminism has been co-opted by the male establishment since its goals are to reform the existing system rather than to replace it, as radical feminists demand. Global feminists equate liberal feminists' embrace of individualism with Western values that do not fit well in other cultures where community values are favored over the individual. Additionally, individualism makes sex solidarity and the development of a movement difficult as liberal feminists have discovered repeatedly throughout history.

Conservative critics charge that liberal feminists, with their concentration on ending legal sex discrimination in society, are out of touch with mainstream women who still value marriage, motherhood, and family—all traditionally private sphere concerns. Finally, liberal feminism has been labeled racist, classist, and heterosexist. This last charge suggests that liberal feminism speaks only to concerns of white, middle- and upper-class, heterosexual women. The history of the women's movement to date has offered ample evidence that the concerns of women of color, the working poor, and lesbians have been on the periphery of the agenda.

Radical Feminism

Radical feminism is difficult to define because of the many subgroups within the larger approach. However, there are some common distinguishing features. Unlike liberal feminists who believe that it is possible to produce systemic reforms that would yield women more rights (ultimately leading to equality of rights), radical feminists believe it is the "sex-gender system" itself that is the source of women's oppression.[33] Radical feminists are interested in women's liberation from the bounds of this system and therefore have advocated a total revolution. For this reason, scholars often classify women's organizations as either "reform-minded" or "revolutionary" and link them to liberal or radical feminist theory accordingly.[34] Radical feminist theory spawned a variety of activist groups in the 1960s. Many, although not all, were associated with the political left. Such radical organizations as the Redstockings, Women's International Terrorist Conspiracy from Hell (WITCH), the Feminists, and the New York Radical Feminists were among some of the largest groups formed.

Sexism, as the first form of human oppression, must take precedence over other forms of oppression and must be eradicated first. Beyond agreement on this basic issue, radical feminists differ on the best way to eliminate sexism. Radical-libertarian feminists believe that femininity, women's sex and reproductive roles limit women's development. They often promote androgyny (eliminating masculine-feminine distinctions) as a way to overcome the limits of femininity and to break the socially constructed link between sex and gender. Radical-cultural feminists, on the other hand, believe that female-feminine qualities are vastly superior to male-masculine characteristics. Women should not try to be like men, but rather they should try to be like women. By this they mean a return to women's essential nature. Therefore, culturally associated feminine traits—interdependence, community, sharing, emotion, nature, peace, and life—should be celebrated over hierarchy, power, war, domination, and death. Androgyny simply clouds the female nature with undesirable male qualities. For these reasons, radical-cultural feminists are often associated with lesbian separatism.

Critics of radical feminism often target the stark choices women have been asked to make. Issues of separatism, lesbianism, and the promotion of reproductive technology over traditional means of conception and biological motherhood draw fire from conservative critics who charge that radical feminists are out to eradicate the family. Others criticize radical cultural feminists' belief in the essential nature of women, charging that it unnecessarily polarizes men and women.

Marxist-Socialist Feminism

In contrast to liberal theory's emphasis on the individual, Marxist-socialist theory stresses the collective aspect of human development. Men and women, through production and reproduction, have collectively created society that in turn shapes them. Capitalism and patriarchy work hand in hand, although Marxist-socialists believe that capitalism, more than sexism, is at the root of women's oppression. Women's economic dependence on men gives them little leverage in other aspects of society. However, rather than singling out women as *the* oppressed class, Marxist-socialist theories focus on the worker. Women's situation then can only be understood in terms of her productive work and its relationship to her life. In a capitalist system, women are exploited both in the marketplace (lowest-paying and most menial jobs) and at home (no wages for her domestic labor). Marxist-socialist feminists advocate public policy that aims to redistribute wealth and opportunity. For example, some have argued that women be paid a wage for their housework; others have concentrated their actions on issues of the workplace outside the home and the disparities in pay and position between men and women. The concept of "equal pay for equal work" does not cover women working in traditional occupations that are undervalued. Advocates of equal pay for jobs of comparable worth argue that wage inequities will persist as long as jobs are segregated on the basis of gender.

Critics of Marxist-socialist feminism most often point to the sizable gap between the ideal and the reality in contemporary Marxist-socialist regimes (those remaining and those recently dissolved). Women have filled the majority of low-status and low-paying occupations and, contrary to theory, are still taking primary responsibility for home and child care.

Global Feminism

The forces of colonialism and nationalism have conspired to divide the world into *the haves*, known as the First World, and the *have nots*, known as the Third World. Global feminists seek to expand feminist thought to include issues vital to women in the Third World. They argue that economic and political oppression are every bit as severe as sexual oppression. "For global feminists, the personal and political are one."[35] The way in which various forms of oppression interconnect and affect women has been the focus of many global feminists. Some charge that First World women are blinded by sexual oppression. As a result, they overlook their own complicity in the oppression of women that multinational corporations and exploitative labor practices cause. Others suggest that color, class, and nationality cannot be separated from sex when addressing the forms of oppression people face. Western feminists, they argue, have been too narrow in their agendas, particularly liberal feminists who were guided by legal reforms in the public sphere. Political participation is a hollow victory for those who cannot feed their families, earn a living wage, control their reproduction, and live free of violence.

Cultural practices that Western feminists and others deem exploitative or damaging to women have presented the most vexing problems for global feminists. Dowry, bride price, female circumcision, and many religious customs are examples of practices that, when taken out of a cultural context, are indefensible in any feminist theory. However, the importance and power of culture, tradition, and religion make passing judgment on these and other issues problematic. Differences among women of various cultures present many challenges to global feminists who attempt to create a feminist theory and set of practices that unite rather than divide women.

Black Feminism

Most feminist anthologies use the term "multicultural feminism" to encompass the diversity of feminist thought among diverse populations. African American feminists in the United States, however, have been among the most vocal critics of the mainstream liberal feminist tradition, and so black feminism is included here as a unique category of feminist thought.

One of the thorniest questions arising in black feminist thought, according to Patricia Hill Collins, is who can be a black feminist?[36] Does authentic voice flow from one's race, one's experiences with the dual oppressions of race and gender, or one's ideas and ideologies regardless of race and gender? The core of the black feminist tradition encompasses several themes: the legacy of struggle, the experience born of multiple oppressions, and the interdependence of thought and action. Black feminists often express frustration that white women seem incapable of understanding the "multiple jeopardy" that black women face on a daily basis. Sexism cannot be separated from racism or classism or any of the other "isms" women must deal with. To pursue a single-minded gender equality strategy is to ignore profound forms of oppression and to exclude women of color from the women's movement. Black women have experienced discrimination in the women's movement (discussed in greater detail in the next chapter) and continue to press feminists to expand the definition of feminism.

Alice Walker has offered the term *womanist* as an alternative to feminist, saying "womanist is to feminist as purple is to lavender."[37] A womanist is at heart a *humanist* pursuing political action as a means to human empowerment—including both men and women of all races, ethnicities, and abilities.

Critics of black feminism are most often African American women themselves. Some critics argue that black feminists have failed to confront sexism strongly enough as it occurs within the black community. Believing that black males are under siege by the dominant white community, some black women have been reticent to press for stronger laws protecting women's interests, believing that black males would be disproportionately harmed in the process. In 1991, when lawyer Anita Hill charged Clarence Thomas, her former boss at the Equal Employment Opportunity Commission (EEOC), with sexual harassment, the nation was introduced to the divisions within the African American community and among black feminists. Hill's charges became public during Clarence Thomas's Supreme Court confirmation hearings before the Senate Judiciary Committee. Criticism of Hill and her decision to make her charges public came from a variety of quarters, but it was especially strong among blacks. They considered her "disloyal" and criticized her for potentially derailing a black man's chances for a seat on the Supreme Court. Public opinion polls revealed support for Hill among feminists, although 49 percent of American women (black and white) either sided with Thomas or declared the dispute a "draw."[38] Further probing by pollsters found that Hill's Yale law degree and successful law career made her identity as a "black woman" problematic because it did not fit the stereotype many held. This revelation again raised questions about who represents or speaks for black feminists.

Ecofeminism

Ecofeminism is an emerging branch of feminism that most resembles global feminism in its emphasis on "connectedness." In this case, however, feminists are interested in the connections between all living things—human and nature. Ecofeminists charge that patriarchy's hierarchical framework not only damages women but harms nature as well. "Because women have been 'naturalized' and nature has been 'feminized' it is difficult to know where the oppression of one ends and the other begins."[39] Ecofeminists disagree over how closely women should be associated with nature, but all agree that ending women's and nature's oppression should be a joint endeavor.

Critics of ecofeminism warn that equating women with nature harkens back to essentialist arguments of other feminists. Others charge that feminists should invest their energy in understanding other women and in bridging the divide between nations and cultures before addressing nature.

Gender Feminism

Gender feminists, unlike any of the theories previously described, believe that the root of women's oppression lies somewhere at the intersection of biology, psychology, and culture. They believe that the traits culture associates with women and femininity are superior in many respects to masculine traits, and therefore both men and women should strive to develop relational webs. The issues most closely associated with gender feminism include the superiority of women's moral development, women's ways of knowing and thinking, and women's mothering abilities. Because gender feminists argue that men and women are developmentally different, they are sometimes also known as *difference feminists*. However, difference in this case works in favor of women. Among the best-known gender feminists is Carol Gilligan who challenged Lawrence Kohlberg's theory of moral development in her book, *In a Different Voice*.[40] She argued that Kohlberg's widely accepted model of moral development did not account for differences between male and female moral development. While males resolve moral dilemmas using an *ethic of justice*, females use an *ethic of care*. While Gilligan did not at first argue that one was superior to the other, her work has been widely used to promote gender feminism's claim to women's moral superiority.

Maternalism, a subset of gender feminism, celebrates the power of women's reproductive capacity. Mothers in many Latin American nations, for example, have politicized motherhood in opposing dictatorships, raising sensitive political questions, and serving as visible reminders of the repression of immoral regimes. In the United States, mothers' movements are enjoying a contemporary resurgence. On Mother's Day 2000, tens of thousands of mothers marched on Washington, D.C., in the Million Moms' March to protest gun violence against children and to petition the government to take action in the form of tougher gun control legislation.

Critics of gender feminism argue that associating women with caring reinforces the traditional view of women as nurturers, rather than women as autonomous and strong. Particularly in relation to electoral politics, a nurturant posture of care has proven to be a somewhat limited virtue depending on the domestic political climate in any one election. Others charge that labeling women as the only sex responsible for caring releases men from important social and familial obligations and unnecessarily polarizes men's and women's gender roles. Some also object to the nomenclature of maternal feminism, arguing that not all women are or aspire to be mothers.

USING POLITICS TO BRING ABOUT CHANGE

How will we know if and when women realize equality? Most likely the answer to this question depends in part on which path to gender equality you favor. If you favor the legal equality doctrine, you most likely believe that women's equality will resemble a gender-neutral state in which men and women exist as equals. If you favor the fairness doctrine, you probably believe that women are different from men and should remain so, but should not be disadvantaged by those differences. The central question of gender equality is this: Do differences between men and women *require* a sensitivity to sexual difference resulting in special provisions that compensate women for their biological role in childbearing or does gender neutrality *require* that no distinctions of any kind be made on the basis of sex? In effect, an affirmative answer to one question or the other delineates the two paths traveled by activists in women's movements—both of which have been traveled in the name of improving women's status. While the two approaches may not be entirely mutually exclusive, their dual existence and favor among women have confounded the ability of women to exhibit sex solidarity around the issues of discrimination and gender inequality. Those who believe men and women are the same, except for their sex-linked contributions to human reproduction, are confident that gender-neutral laws can remedy the discrimination women face by eliminating sex-based barriers to opportunities in the public sphere. However, those who believe that men and women are essentially different are convinced that special legislation is the remedy for the social, economic, and political disadvantages women endure as a result of motherhood and traditional gender roles. Thus women are often most at odds with other women over their common interests.

The Plan for this Book

This book examines how women participate in and use politics to pursue gender equality. Regardless of their chosen path and strategy, women have worked for nearly two centuries to gain access to the public sphere and to improve the quality of their lives. To effect this change, women have used such conventional forms of political participation as lobbying for constitutional changes, fighting for the right to vote, and pursuing elective office, as well as less conventional methods, including working in organizations outside government and protesting public and private sector inequities. In addition, women have lobbied for policy changes before state legislatures and the U.S. Congress. At various times, the courts have facilitated or hampered their efforts. To quote the National Women's Equality Act (1998), women have "lobbied, litigated, picketed, marched, petitioned, engaged in civil disobedience, and boycotted to win women's rights."[41] However, women have still not gained full political, legal, social, economic, and educational equality. This book examines and analyzes women's political experiences, attitudes, and behaviors and looks at their successes as well as their failures, to understand more clearly where women stand today in their pursuit of gender equality.

The next chapter evaluates two major women's movements in American history: suffrage and the Equal Rights Amendment (ERA). In both cases, the mechanism for change was a constitutional amendment. With the vote, women gained a potentially powerful political tool but did not gain legal equality. Those who favored the legal equality doctrine immediately pressed for the ERA as a way to finish the work that suffrage had begun. The ERA was first introduced in 1923, but it did not become a movement until the second wave of feminism arrived in the early 1970s. By 1981 it was clear that the ERA would not be ratified. A comparison of the successful arguments for suffrage and the unsuccessful push for the ERA illuminates the limits of using the legal equality doctrine to pursue gender equality.

Chapter 3 evaluates how women have used the vote to effect political change and examine patterns of participation, issues of representation, and policy preferences among women in the electorate. We will be sensitive to the ways in which women differ from one another as well as how women differ from men. The analysis also pays special attention to the political attitudes and behavior of young women and, in the process, attempts to answer a number of questions: How do women evaluate candidates? Which issues mobilize women to participate in politics? Under what circumstances will women vote for other women? Are women adequately represented if only 13 percent of Congress is female?

Chapter 4 examines women's pursuit of elective office. We will look at how female candidates differ both from male candidates and from one another. Under what circumstances are women most likely to run for office and under what conditions are they most likely to win? What role does gender play in elections today? In what ways does the U.S. electoral system have both a *glass ceiling* and a *sticky floor*? How do the media act to define female candidates? What types of systemic reforms might get more women elected to office? In what ways do the gendered patterns of political representation reflect positively or negatively on American democracy?

Women have two established political traditions: as emerging insiders and as accomplished outsiders. Chapter 5 examines women as agents of change inside and outside political institutions. First we will examine how women govern once elected or appointed to office. One argument for electing women is that they bring a distinctive style to politics. What role does gender play in women's ambition, leadership, agendas, and conduct in office? How does the United States compare to other developed nations in promoting women's political leadership? How successful are women in office in effecting change and promoting equality? The chapter also focuses on women working *outside* the system and evaluates the roles that nongovernmental organizations, international treaties, and activism play in advancing women's agendas.

Chapters 6, 7, and 8 examine how women have used the public policy process to effect change and evaluate how women fare under current policies. Education, one of women's first equality battlegrounds, is the focus of chapter six. Although Title IX is most often associated with high school and collegiate athletics today, it was designed to provide women with equal access to all kinds of educational opportunities. How effective has it been in advancing educational equity? Are the ultimate payoffs from education the same for men and women? Why are more women than men going to college today? What impact will the college gender gap have on the workplace of the future?

Chapter 7 examines issues relating to work, wages, and women's participation in the economy. The workplace has undergone a number of changes as a result of globalization, competition, and advances in technology. How will these changes affect men and women in the workplace? Why, nearly forty years after the Equal Pay Act was passed, do women still earn less than men? Is the separate spheres ideology still prevalent in our view of work for men and women? Given the facts about gender and wages, can you expect to make more or less than your classmates of the opposite sex? What impact do the gendered patterns of employment in the United States have on the pay gap? Why are poverty rates among elderly women so high even in prosperous times? How might the proposed changes in social security affect you? Is the move toward privatization of social security supported by the Bush administration of 2001 a positive change for women?

Chapter 8 is dedicated to family, fertility, and reproductive-health issues. Separate spheres ideology excluded women from public life, but now that women are active in the public sphere, who is taking care of the family and home? Is the second shift a reality for all women with children? Why do some conservatives argue that "women" should stay home with their children while also arguing that welfare mothers should work? What role will technology play in the future of fertility and reproduction? How might emerging reproductive technology transform our understanding of sex and gender? Does government have a legitimate role to play in family policy and reproductive decisions? How have the changes in reproduction, family life, and women's participation in the work force altered our understanding of the public and private spheres? How have men fared as a result of the changes in work and family expectations?

Finally, chapter 9 challenges you to design an agenda for the future. Many feminist activists of the 1960s and 1970s long for the days of radical political activism that centered on women's issues and despair that young women no longer appear interested in the cause. Young feminists, on the other hand, often say that the old radicals "need to get on with things." What are the current controversies of gender equality? How have they been shaped by the history of women's pursuit of gender equality and the paradox of gender equality? How might you get those issues on the political agenda in the future? How can you apply what you've learned in this book and in your class to planning for your own future? Is feminism a concept that has meaning for you? What will gender relations look like in the future? Will men and women develop more similar interests and behaviors or will gender roles become more distinctive in this century? How will political, social, or economic forces affect gender relations in the future? Which path to gender equality do you favor?

Throughout the book you will find a number of features to help you think through the issues raised here. A boxed feature might reference the Web site associated with this book. That site has links to other resources and data sets, text of articles or court cases referenced in this book, and other useful information. In addition, throughout the book you will find a feature called "Encountering the Controversies of Equality." This feature presents you with a situation involving questions and issues of gender equality that you might encounter in your own life and that challenges you to think through conflicting positions. There is not one correct way to resolve these dilemmas, but thinking about them now and talking with your professor and your classmates may help you develop and clarify your own position and become a more careful and critical thinker in the process.

Notes

1. Linda Kerber, "The Paradox of Women's Citizenship in the Early Republic: The Case of *Martin* v. *Massachusetts*, 1805," *American Historical Review* (April 1992).

2. Maxine Margolis, *Mothers and Such: Views of American Women and Why They Changed* (Berkeley: University of California Press, 1984).

3. Ibid., p. 47.

4. Abigail Adams to John Adams, March 31, 1776.

5. Virginia Sapiro, *The Political Integration of Women: Roles, Socialization, and Politics* (Chicago: University of Chicago Press, 1983), p. 19.

6. Alexis de Tocqueville, *Democracy in America* (1835; reprint, New York: Doubleday, 1969), p. 243.

7. Sandra Lipsitz Bem, *The Lenses of Gender: Transforming the Debate on Sexual Inequality* (New Haven: Yale University Press, 1993), p. 1.

8. Aristotle, *The Politics of Aristotle*, trans. Ernest Barker (London: Oxford University Press, 1947), pp. 43–45.

9. Bem, *The Lenses of Gender,* p. 11.

10. Suzanne M. Marilley, *Woman Suffrage and the Origins of Liberal Feminism in the United States, 1820–1920* (Cambridge: Harvard University Press, 1996).

11. Carole Pateman, *The Sexual Contract* (Stanford, Calif.: Stanford University Press, 1988).

12. J. S. Mill, "The Subjection of Women," in *The Feminist Papers*, ed. Alice S. Rossi (Boston: Northeastern University Press, 1972).

13. Ibid., p. 201.

14. Ibid., p. 199.

15. Adrienne Rich, *Of Woman Born: Motherhood as Experience and Institution* (New York: Norton, 1976), pp. 40–41.

16. Bem, *The Lenses of Gender,* p. 41.

17. It has been estimated that 70 percent of the men in northern cities could read and only 35 percent of women. See Linda K. Kerber and Jane Sherron De Hart, *Women's America: Refocusing the Past,* 4th ed. (New York: Oxford University Press, 1995).

18. Nadine Taub and Elizabeth M. Schneider, "Perspectives on Women's Subordination and the Law," in *The Politics of Law*, ed. D. Kairys (New York: Pantheon, 1982), pp. 125–126.

19. William Blackstone, Chapter 15, in *Commentaries on the Laws of England,* 4 vol. book 1 (1765–1769).

20. Massachusetts Confiscation Act of April 20, 1779.

21. Linda Kerber, "The Paradox of Women's Citizenship in the Early Republic," *American Historical Review* (1992): 369.

22. Ibid.

23. Ibid., p. 375.

24. Ibid.

25. Imelda Whelan, *Modern Feminist Thought: From the Second Wave to "Post Feminism"* (New York: New York University Press, 1995).

26. Nancy Gibbs, "The War against Feminism," *Time* (March 9, 1992): 51.

27. Nancy F. Cott, *The Grounding of Modern Feminism* (New Haven, Conn.: Yale University Press, 1987).

28. Ibid., p. 3.

29. Ibid., p. 5.

30. Ibid., pp. 4–5.

31. Rosemarie Putnam Tong, *Feminist Thought: a More Comprehensive Introduction* (Boulder, Colo.: Westview Press, 1998), p. 5.

32. For a more complete description and historical account of each approach to feminism, see Tong, *Feminist Thought*; Whelan, *Modern Feminist Thought*; Allison M. Jagger, *Feminist Politics and Human Nature* (Totowa, N.J.: Roman and Allanheld, 1983); Susan Moller Okin, *Women in Western Political Thought* (Princeton, N.J.: Princeton University Press, 1979); Shulamith Firestone, *The Dialectic of Sex* (New York: Bantam Books, 1970); Mary Daly, *Gyn/Ecology: The Metaethics of Radical Feminism* (Boston: Beacon Press, 1978); Nancy Chodorow, *The Reproduction of Mothering: Psychoanalysis and the Sociology of Gender* (Berkeley: University of California Press, 1978); Carol Gilligan, *In a Different Voice* (Cambridge: Harvard University Press, 1982); Patricia Hill Collins, *Black Feminist Thought: Knowledge, Consciousness, and the Politics of Empowerment* (Boston: Unwin Hyman, 1990); Robin Morgan, *Sisterhood is Global* (Garden City, N.Y.: Anchor, 1984).

33. Tong, *Feminist Thought,* p. 46.

34. There are, however, notable exceptions. Jo Freeman, for example, believed that it was a mistake to label some women's organizations as merely reformist since all groups were breaking away from established gender norms, an act "revolutionary"

in itself. She'd prefer to divide branches of the movement into a "younger branch" and an "older branch." Barbara Ryan grouped organizations within the movement into "mass movement" and "small groups."

35. Tong, *Feminist Thought*, p. 227.

36. Patricia Hill Collins, *Black Feminist Thought: Knowledge, Consciousness, and the Politics of Empowerment* (Boston: Unwin Hyman, 1990), p. 19.

37. Ibid., p. 37.

38. Tong, *Feminist Thought*, p. 222.

39. Ibid., p. 247.

40. Carol Gilligan, *In a Different Voice* (Cambridge: Harvard University Press, 1982).

41. National Council of Women's Organizations, "National Women's Equality Act for the 21st Century," 1998, p. 3, accessed at *http://www.womensorganizations.org*.

All Rights are Not Equal: Suffrage Versus the Equal Rights Amendment

THERE HAVE been two major points in American history when women have undertaken concerted action in the form of a *movement* in an attempt to effect a significant change in their public status. The first was the campaign for suffrage, especially between 1910 and 1920, the final phase of women's efforts. The second was during the 1970s, when women mobilized around the Equal Rights Amendment (ERA). In both cases, women eventually organized to achieve a single goal and were willing to make compromises on other important issues to realize that goal. In both cases, women constituted the majority of the proponents for and opponents to the change in their status. In both cases, women's support for or opposition to the vote and to the ERA was grounded in their understanding of *equality,* their perspective on women's roles in the private and public spheres, and their concept of *fairness.* Women are not a homogenous political force, and there is no sex solidarity among women regarding gender equality. In the case of suffrage, the campaign was successful, albeit after more than seventy-two years of advocacy. When the Nineteenth Amendment reached the states for ratification, public attitudes had already changed. By then, women were viewed as independent from their husbands and fathers when it came to owning property and earning wages. Additionally, women already had full voting rights in fifteen states and presidential suffrage in another twelve. In effect, the constitutional change that gave women the vote followed a change that had already taken place in social attitudes. This was not so with the Equal Rights Amendment. The Constitution still has no equal rights amendment, even after nearly eighty years of episodic campaigning and an unprecedented thirty-nine month extension to the ratification deadline granted by Congress in 1978. Why? What can we learn about women's relationship to politics and the controversies of equality in the contrast? This chapter sets out to answer these questions, first by briefly examining the history of both movements and then by analyzing the arguments for and against each change in light of the paradox of gender equality.

FROM SENECA FALLS TO SUFFRAGE: THREE GENERATIONS OF WOMEN WORK FOR THE VOTE

Although the vote is now considered the most basic act of citizenship, it took women more than seventy-two years of political activism to win the elective franchise. Three generations of women joined the cause, each believing that theirs would be the final effort required to convince enough state and federal legislators that women deserved and required political representation. Initially suffragists argued that admitting women to the political system would result in positive change. Within a generation, they discovered that it was more effective to argue that suffrage for women would not result in any change—positive or negative—but rather was required out of a sense of basic fairness. By the third generation, women were again divided over how to approach the civic gatekeepers. A younger group, led by Alice Paul, trained in militant tactics of political resistance, argued that women should not be begging the establishment for the vote; they should be demanding the right to vote. The more established suffragists, led by long-time activist Carrie Chapman Catt, believed that women would win the vote in time, but threatening politicians would only delay their victory. In the end, winning the vote required both approaches and a fundamental shift in public attitudes of legislators and average citizens alike. Women were admitted to the political franchise only after public opinion supported the view that women were capable of rational thought and action independent of their husbands.

Female Social Activists Discover the Suffrage Cause: 1840–1869

Many early advocates of equality and rights for women came to the cause via their dedication to the abolition of slavery or their experiences with other charitable societies.[1] In their drive to help others, women were able to transcend the line between private and public life and, in the process, began to share informally the "problems of their sex" with one another. As they labored for racial equality and political rights for African Americans, they became conscious of their own inequality. Historian Carol Ellen Dubois argues that women working in the abolition movement gained something even more significant than a discovery of their own second-class status: "What American women learned from abolition was less that they were oppressed than what to do with that perception, how to

Declaration of Sentiments

WHEN IN the course of human events, it becomes necessary for one portion of the family of man to assume among the people of the earth a position different from that which they have hitherto occupied, but one to which the laws of nature and of nature's God entitle them, a decent respect to the opinions of mankind requires that they should declare the causes that impel them to such a course.

We hold these truths to be self-evident: that all men and women are created equal; that they are endowed by their Creator with certain inalienable rights; that among these are life, liberty, and the pursuit of happiness; that to secure these rights governments are instituted, deriving their just powers from the consent of the governed. Whenever any form of government becomes destructive of these ends, it is the right of those who suffer from it to refuse allegiance to it, and to insist upon the institution of a new government, laying its foundation on such principles, and organizing its powers in such form, as to them shall seem most likely to effect their safety and happiness. Prudence indeed, will dictate that governments long established should not be changed for light and transient causes; and accordingly all experience hath shown that mankind are more disposed to suffer, while evils are sufferable, than to right themselves by abolishing the forms to which they were accustomed. But when a long train of abuses and usurpations, pursuing invariably the same object evinces a design to reduce them under absolute despotism, it is their duty to throw off such government, and to provide new guards for their future security. Such has been the patient sufferance of the women under this government, and such is now the necessity which constrains them to demand the equal station to which they are entitled.

The history of mankind is a history of repeated injuries and usurpations on the part of man toward woman, having in direct object the establishment of an absolute tyranny over her. To prove this, let facts be submitted to a candid world.

He has never permitted her to exercise her inalienable right to the elective franchise.

He has compelled her to submit to laws, in the formation of which she had no voice.

He has withheld from her rights which are given to the most ignorant and degraded men—both natives and foreigners.

Having deprived her of this first right of a citizen, the elective franchise, thereby leaving her without representation in the halls of legislation, he has oppressed her on all sides.

He has made her, if married, in the eye of the law, civilly dead.

He has taken from her all right in property, even to the wages she earns.

He has made her, morally, an irresponsible being, as she can commit many crimes with impunity, provided they be done in the presence of her husband. In the covenant of marriage, she is compelled to promise obedience to her husband, he becoming, to all intents and purposes, her master—the law giving him power to deprive her of her liberty, and to administer chastisement.

He has so framed the laws of divorce, as to what shall be the proper causes, and in case of separation, to whom the guardianship of the children shall be given, as to wholly regardless of the happiness of women—the law in all cases, going upon a false supposition of the supremacy of man, and giving all power into his hands.

After depriving her of all rights as a married woman, if single, and the owner of property, he has taxed her to support a government which recognizes her only when her property can be made profitable to it.

He has monopolized nearly all of the profitable employments, and from those she is permitted to follow, she receives but a scanty remuneration. He closes against her all the avenues to wealth and distinction which he considers most honorable to himself. As a teacher of theology, medicine, or law, she is not known.

He has denied her the facilities for obtaining a thorough education, all colleges being closed against her.

He allows her in Church, as well as State, but a subordinate position, claiming Apostolic authority for her exclusion from the ministry, and, with some exceptions, from any public participation in the affairs of the Church.

He has created a false public sentiment by giving to the world a different code of morals for men and women, but which moral delinquencies which exclude women from society, are not only tolerated, but deemed of little account in man.

He has usurped the prerogative of Jehovah himself, claiming it as his right to assign for her a sphere of action, when that belongs to her conscience and to her God.

He has endeavored, in every way that he could, to destroy her confidence in her own powers, to lessen her self-respect, and to make her willing to lead a dependent and abject life.

Now, in view of this entire disfranchisement of one-half the people of this country, their social and religious degradation—in view of the unjust laws above mentioned, and because women do feel themselves aggrieved, oppressed, and fraudulently deprived of their most sacred rights, we insist that they have immediate admission to all the rights and privileges which belong to them as citizens of the United States.

In entering upon the great work before us, we anticipate no small amount of misconception, misrepresentation, and ridicule; but we shall use every instrumentality within our power to effect our object. We shall employ agents, circulate tracts, petition the State and National legislatures, and endeavor to enlist the pulpit and the press in our behalf. We hope this Convention will be followed by a series of Conventions embracing every part of the country.

Elizabeth Cady Stanton, Susan B. Anthony, and Matilda Joslyn Gage, Eds., *History of Women's Suffrage*, vol. 1 (Rochester, N.Y.: Charles Mann, 1881), pp. 67–74.

turn it into a political movement."[2] The seed for that political movement germinated with a sex-discrimination incident at the World Anti-Slavery Convention held in London in 1840. Although women were part of the official U.S. delegation, they were not allowed to participate in the proceedings and were relegated to seats in the balcony. Here Elizabeth Cady Stanton and Lucretia Mott began to discuss holding a meeting for the express purpose of discussing women's rights.

In 1848, Stanton and Mott issued a call for participating in a meeting organized to talk about the "social, civil, and religious rights of women."[3] More than 300 people participated in the two-day Seneca Falls Convention and ratified the *Declaration of Sentiments and Resolutions,* as drafted by Stanton. The meeting was odd by contemporary standards. Called to consider the question of women's equality, none of the conveners felt qualified to chair the meeting, and so the task fell to Lucretia Mott's husband, James. The taboo against "public women" fell away slowly, and subsequent conventions often relied on noted male abolitionists as speakers. Education activist Emma Willard, for example, always asked a man to speak on her behalf, or if forced to speak for herself, she did so while seated. Others delivered their remarks from behind a curtain. Historian Glenna Matthews refers to this phenomenon as the social geography of gender.[4] Elizabeth Cady Stanton, after speaking in public for the first time at Seneca Falls, added "access to the public lectern" to the other demands in the Declaration of Sentiments. Not until 1850, at a meeting in Salem, Ohio, was the social geography of gender transformed entirely. At that meeting, only women were allowed to speak, whether from the platform or the audience.

The Declaration of Sentiments mirrored the Declaration of Independence in form, word, and tone. These similarities suggest that the early advocates for women's rights based their equality claims in the liberal tradition of individualism. The Declaration of Sentiments began, "We hold these truths to be self-evident: that all men and women are created equal" and then lists 18 injuries "on the part of man toward woman," including exclusion from the franchise, coverture in marriage, denial of property rights, blocking access to higher education, and undermining "confidence in her own powers . . . and willing to lead a dependent and abject life." The list was a curious mix of political and personal grievances against men. All of the resolutions passed unanimously at the convention with the exception of suffrage, which passed by a narrow margin. Of all of the demands, the franchise was the most radical and controversial among the conference participants, as well as among women throughout the country. Even Lucretia Mott counseled Stanton against including suffrage in the Declaration's resolutions saying, "Thou will make us ridiculous. We must go slowly."[5] Frederick Douglass, former slave and noted abolitionist leader, reassured Stanton and promised to speak in favor of the suffrage resolution. The reticence among Seneca conventioneers to embrace woman suffrage immediately was a bellwether of the long struggle ahead. Of all those in attendance at Seneca Falls, only one nineteen-year-old woman, Charlotte Woodward, lived long enough to exercise her right to vote.[6]

Soujourner Truth (1797–1883), abolitionist and women's rights activist. *Hulton Getty Picture Archive.*

Within months of the Seneca Falls meeting, women's rights conventions were held in other cities, beginning in Rochester, New York. Susan B. Anthony, a tireless crusader for suffrage later in the movement, was at first slow to join. She heard about the Rochester meeting from her mother and sister, but she was already immersed in the abolition and temperance movements and felt those causes more consistent with her Quaker beliefs. In 1851, when men in Akron, Ohio, directly challenged women's ability even to hold such conventions, let alone demand civil and political rights, a former slave named Sojourner Truth responded forthrightly from the floor. Truth's indignant oratory reflects her dual oppression as a black former slave and as a woman:

> Well, children, where there is so much racket there must be something out of kilter. I think that 'twixt the Negroes of the South and the women at the North, all talking about rights, the white men will be in a fix pretty soon. But what's all this here talking about?

That man over there says women need to be helped into carriages, and lifted over ditches, and to have the best place everywhere. Nobody ever helps me into carriages, or over mud-puddles, or gives me any best place! And ain't I a woman? Look at me! Look at my arm! I have ploughed, and planted, and gathered into barns, and no man could head me! And ain't I a woman? I could work as much and eat as much as a man—when I could get it—and bear the lash as well! And ain't I a woman? I have borne thirteen children, and seen them most all sold off to slavery, and when I cried out with my mother's grief, none but Jesus heard me! And ain't I a woman?

Then they talk about this thing in the head; what's this they call it? ["Intellect," whispered someone near.] That's it, honey. What's that got to do with women's rights or Negroes rights? If my cup won't hold but a pint, and yours holds a quart, wouldn't you be mean not to let me have my little half-measure full?

Then that little man in black there, he says women can't have as much rights as men, because Christ wasn't a woman! Where did your Christ come from? Where did your Christ come from? From God and a woman! Man had nothing to do with Him. . . .

If the first woman God ever made was strong enough to turn the world upside down all alone, these women together ought to be able to turn it back, and get it right side up again! And now they are asking to do it, the men better let them.[7]

Woman's rights and abolition shared a common philosophical claim to equal rights, and the movements were closely linked until divisions surfaced over the Civil War amendments. The start of the war all but suspended the campaign for women's rights. Women in the North and South dedicated themselves to their respective causes, but most suffragists at the time supported the Union effort. In 1863, Stanton and Anthony organized the Women's Loyal National League in the North to promote the emancipation of all slaves through constitutional amendment.[8] The amendment proposed universal suffrage and was intended to include freed slaves *and* women. Many abolitionists objected to women's inclusion in the suffrage clause, fearing that it would cause the amendment to fail. The Republican Party argued that an attempt to enfranchise women would jeopardize efforts to enfranchise black men in the South.[9] The Thirteenth Amendment (1865) was ratified without any mention of the franchise. Then attention turned to the Fourteenth Amendment, which granted citizenship rights to freed slaves.

The American Equal Rights Association (AERA) was formed in 1866 to advance the cause of universal suffrage, and many active in the organization believed that suffrage was already implied in the language of citizenship. Several prominent African American reformers held leadership positions in the AERA including Harriet Purvis, Sarah Redmond, and Sojourner Truth.[10] Black men and women active in the movement clearly linked women's rights with the vote and focused their efforts on universal suffrage and universal reforms. However, the AERA was embroiled in a battle between those whose first priority was black male suffrage and those who were dedicated first to woman suffrage. The tension found a target in the Fourteenth Amendment. If the Fourteenth

Amendment was ratified as proposed, the word "male" would appear in the Constitution for the first time, thereby establishing two categories of citizens: male and female. Suffragists disagreed among themselves as to how they ought to react to the language of the proposed amendment. Anthony and Stanton believed that the amendment should be defeated unless it included women, while others like Lucy Stone argued that it was "the Negroes hour, and that the women must wait for their rights."[11]

Those who believed in the precedence of women's suffrage could not get past the willingness of others to accept the word "male" in the text of the Fourteenth Amendment and the exclusion of women from the Fifteenth Amendment, which removed race as a disqualifier for the franchise. Having been told to wait their turn during the ratification of the Thirteenth and Fourteenth Amendments, woman suffragists saw the Fifteenth Amendment as their last opportunity to be included in the post-war reconstruction of the nation via Constitutional amendment. White female suffragists left the AERA, blaming male abolitionists for sacrificing women in the name of expediency. Black women "remained quiet or divided among the prevailing forces."[12] The disunity resulted in the dissolution of the AERA and the formation of two rival organizations for women's rights in 1869: first, the National Woman Suffrage Association (NWSA), led by Stanton and Anthony, and later the American Woman Suffrage Association (AWSA), led by Lucy Stone and Henry Ward Beecher. The NWSA turned its immediate attention to the fight over women's inclusion in the Fifteenth Amendment, whereas the AWSA continued to support the Fifteenth Amendment as written, vowing to support a Sixteenth Amendment dedicated to woman suffrage.[13]

Historian Rosalyn Terborg-Penn, writing about African American women's participation in the early suffrage movement, argues that the schism within the movement and black women's reaction to the divide reveals how "they were often torn between identifying with racial priorities or gender priorities."[14] In the process, black women are often left out of accounts of the divisions, and black males are often blamed. The racist overtones of Stanton's and Anthony's woman-first claims have been ignored in many contemporary accounts, according to Terborg-Penn, and worse still, feminists writing historical accounts in the 1970s and 1980s justify white suffragists' racism as expedient, "but often [do] not justify the pro-'Negro suffrage' male behavior as expedient."[15]

The disagreement with abolitionists and the divide among suffragists is significant because it signals an end to women's quest for universal suffrage and a start to the often ugly nativist and racist rhetoric and action that characterized some claims to the woman's vote. Women dove into social activism, dedicated to the universality of natural rights and to full citizenship rights and privileges for all adults grounded in the liberal tradition. However, their negative experiences with allied groups in the formative years of the rights movement pushed women toward exclusivity and self-interest, transforming the women's rights movement into a women's suffrage movement. In a broader sense, it also forced them to give up the philosophical and moral high ground, and to sacrifice forever the most radical notion of all: transforming the social and political structure itself.

Suffragists Disagree over Amending the U.S. Constitution: 1870–1910

Having been divided primarily over strategic disagreements rather than deeper ideological differences, the NWSA and AWSA advanced along similar paths, courted many of the same potential constituents, and advocated many of the same arguments in favor of women's suffrage. There were some differences, however. The NWSA worked for both a federal amendment and state referendums. Of the two organizations, the NWSA was more revolutionary because it at first refused to admit men,[16] attacked the institution of marriage, and published essays on "free love" in its journal, *The Revolution*. Elizabeth Cady Stanton, in particular, targeted the church as a primary source of sexism in society, which led her to reject the Bible.[17] In the 1870s, NWSA used such confrontational tactics as attempting to vote, sponsoring female candidates, and mounting protests at public events.[18] The AWSA maintained their working relationship with abolitionists of both sexes, and its membership reflected a more conservative, middle- and upper-class slice of society. AWSA's publication, the *Woman's Journal*, supported the institutions of family, church, and marriage. For the most part, women's efforts in both organizations to educate the public and legislators involved petitioning legislatures, testifying before legislative committees, giving public speeches, and conducting public referendum campaigns.

Divisions between the two organizations and the NWSA's embrace of "free love" tarnished the woman suffrage organization's claim to moral superiority. In the void, the Women's Christian Temperance Union (WCTU) took up the cause of suffrage. Frances Willard, WCTU president from 1879 to 1897, linked suffrage to temperance by arguing that only women could be counted on to cast the votes necessary to prohibit the sale and consumption of alcohol. Alcohol abuse was a leading cause of domestic violence, abandonment, and poverty for women and children. The WCTU was larger than any women's suffrage organization and contributed vast resources to the cause during Willard's presidency.[19] The combination of efforts yielded success. Two western territories, Wyoming and Utah, granted women the vote, and state legislatures in other regions (except for the south) considered woman suffrage legislation. Political scientist Lee Ann Banaszak calculated that on average, "in every year between 1870 and 1890, 4.4 states considered legislation giving women the vote."[20]

From 1869 to 1874, NWSA members urged female activists to adopt a more revolutionary strategy. Missouri suffragists Virginia Minor and her husband Francis took the lead in developing a reinterpretation of the Fourteenth Amendment and applying its definition of citizenship to enfranchise women.[21]

Victoria Woodhull took the same argument to the 1871 NWSA convention in the District of Columbia. Calling the strategy the "new departure," she urged delegates to adopt the tactic in their own communities.[22] African American suffragist Mary Ann Shad Cary, having studied law at Howard University, constructed a legal argument applying the Fourteenth and Fifteenth Amendments to black women as well as black men. In testimony before the House Judiciary Committee, Cary argued that if women were denied the vote, the emancipation amendments would leave women free in name only. She called for an amendment to strike the word "male" from the Constitution.[23]

In the November election of 1872, several women attempted to vote. Susan B. Anthony and a small group of women voted in Rochester, New York. Anthony was arrested several weeks later and charged with "illegal voting." Rather than pay her fine and win her release, Anthony instead applied for a *writ of habeas corpus*, in an effort to get her case before the Supreme Court. When the judge asked if Anthony had anything to say, she used her trial and conviction to plead the case of women's suffrage before the court of public opinion:

> Yes, your honor, I have many things to say; for in your ordered verdict of guilty, you have trampled underfoot every vital principle of our government. My natural rights, my civil rights, my political rights, are all alike ignored. Robbed of the fundamental privilege of citizenship, I am degraded from the status of citizen to that of a subject; and not only myself individually, but all of my sex, are, by your honor's verdict, doomed to political subjection under this so-called Republican government.[24]

Although the judge at Albany refused to issue the writ and raised her bail to $1,000, Anthony remained steadfast. Unfortunately, her attorney did not. Writing a personal check for her bail, attorney Henry Seldon scuttled any chances for Anthony to present her case to the Supreme Court. When Anthony asked Seldon if he realized what he had done by paying her bail, he replied, "Yes, but I could not see a lady I respected put in jail."[25] Misplaced chauvinism denied Anthony the opportunity to make her case to the Court.

In the same election, Virginia Minor cast her illegal vote in Missouri and was arrested. But unlike Anthony, Minor's case was eventually heard before the U.S. Supreme Court. She argued that in denying her the vote, the state of Missouri had denied her rights under the Fourteenth Amendment guarantee to the privileges and immunities of citizenship. The right to vote, she claimed, is a privilege of citizenship. The Court rejected her claim in *Minor* v. *Happersett* 1875. While admitting that women may be citizens, the Court said that not all citizens are voters. The Court based its opinion on the fact that the federal Constitution does not explicitly grant women the right to vote (" . . . if it had been intended to make all citizens of the United States voters, the framers of the Constitution would not have left it to implication") and the fact that no new state added to the Union after ratification had granted suffrage to women.[26] Without constitutional instruction, the states could decide for themselves who had the privilege of voting. In closing the Court said,

We have given this case the careful consideration its importance demands. If the law is wrong, it ought to be changed; but the power for that is not with us. The arguments addressed to us bearing upon such a view of the subject may perhaps be sufficient to induce those having the power, to make the alteration, but they ought not to be permitted to influence our judgement in determining the present rights of the parties now litigating before us. No argument as to woman's need of suffrage can be considered.[27]

The ruling in *Minor* led suffragists to the inevitable conclusion that a legal strategy would not advance their cause, and therefore they were left with only two choices: a federal amendment or constitutional amendments in each state. In 1877, the NWSA was once again dedicated to a federal constitutional amendment. This time, however, the goal was not universal suffrage, but rather woman suffrage.

By 1890, old animosities between the NWSA and AWSA had faded sufficiently for a merger to take place. The new organization, the National American Woman Suffrage Association (NAWSA), elected Elizabeth Cady Stanton president. Stanton served only two years before she was forced out after publishing the *Woman's Bible*, a feminist reinterpretation of the Bible. Anthony replaced her, but found herself at the helm of a younger, more moderate membership. The merger did not immediately inject new enthusiasm or success into the movement. In fact, suffrage leaders referred to this period as "the doldrums."[28] After Utah and Idaho enfranchised women in 1896, no other state gave women the vote until 1910 when the state of Washington acted. NAWSA's membership had fallen to fewer than 100,000.[29] Women's rights organizations had been formed in most states by then and were spawning new leaders for the movement. Women formed literary and social organizations as well, eventually leading to the Women's Club Movement.[30] During the same period, African American women organized into clubs, initiating the Black Women's Club Movement. Most of the early black women's clubs (1880s–1895) were not affiliated with national organizations and formed to deal with local issues facing women of color. In 1896, the largest national black women's clubs merged to form the National Association of Colored Women (NACW), a federation of women's clubs with Mary Church Terrell at the helm as president. The rise of the NACW coincided with the disenfranchisement of black males in the South, and so issues on its agenda included "Jim Crow" laws and lynchings, as well as women's suffrage.[31] An organization of southern white women came last, was slow to get started, and required the NAWSA to adopt a questionable "states' rights" policy on organizational structure, allowing segregated organizations to flourish in the South. Once again, suffragist leaders sacrificed a basic organizing principle in favor of expediency. This time, women's suffrage gave way to "white women's suffrage" in an effort to bring in southern states.

Toward the end of the century, the founding leaders of the movement—Stanton, Stone, and Anthony—were aging and dying. Carrie Chapman Catt briefly replaced Stanton as president of the NAWSA in 1900, before Dr. Anna Howard Shaw assumed the role in 1904. Shaw represented the "intergenerational" leaders of the suffrage movement and provided a bridge between the pioneers and the new younger leadership, including Alice Paul and Lucy Burns. Shaw concentrated the NAWSA's efforts on state referendums and on lobbying state legislatures, forgoing a federal amendment for a time.

The Final Push: 1910–1920

With the new century came new challenges for women's rights organizations. A multitude of clubs and organizations were mobilizing in favor of and in opposition to women's suffrage. Coordinating efforts and strategies was nearly impossible, and in the end, it was two openly divergent strategies that together delivered women's suffrage.

The NAWSA continued to organize, petition, and lobby in the states. Emmeline Pankhurst had been pioneering direct protest tactics in the English suffrage movement. Harriet Stanton Blatch (Elizabeth Cady Stanton's daughter), Alice Paul, and Lucy Burns traveled to England to participate in this new method of campaigning for women's suffrage. On their return, Paul and Burns lobbied the NAWSA to return to a federal amendment strategy. Although the NAWSA formed a congressional committee in 1912, support for a federal strategy was so meager that the committee was given an annual budget of ten dollars.[32] Paul and her followers, referred to as the "new suffragists" by some scholars,[33] were different from the "old suffragists." Although the suffrage cause connected both groups, the new suffragists viewed the fight for suffrage as a means to "challenge a social system that attempted to refute their feminist ideology and deny them their identities."[34] Rather than begging for their rights, they intended to demand them. The NAWSA grudgingly agreed to support the congressional committee's proposal (in name only, since they refused to give Paul any funds) to hold a massive parade in Washington, D.C., designed to coincide with Woodrow Wilson's presidential inauguration. Paul was convinced, contrary to the NAWSA leadership, that if suffrage was to become reality, the focus must be on a federal amendment. To Paul that meant that Congress must be convinced to pass legislation and send it on to the states. However, Congress was unlikely to act without some prodding, a task Paul assigned to the president of the United States. The March 3 parade was intended to put both Congress and President Wilson on notice that women would not wait any longer for action on the suffrage question.

Paul and the NAWSA's congressional committee devised a strategy by which local suffrage organizations would sponsor (and pay for) their own parade participants. When Howard University women volunteered to march in the college section of the parade, some white marchers threatened to pull out. To Paul's credit, she did not back down. Instead she found sympathetic white male marchers to provide a protective buffer for the Howard women. On the day of the parade, some 8,000 marchers, including twenty-six floats, ten bands, and

Encountering the Controversies of Equality

Two Means to the Same End: A Contrast in the Styles of Alice Paul and Carrie Chapman Catt

THE LEADERS of the women's suffrage movement are enjoying renewed public attention in the wake of women's recent electoral gains. The PBS documentary, *Not for Ourselves Alone*, written and produced by Geoffrey Ward and Ken Burns, introduced thousands of viewers to Susan B. Anthony and Elizabeth Cady Stanton for the first time. What many people do not realize is that both of these pioneering women were dead long before the Nineteenth Amendment was ratified. Carrie Chapman Catt (1859–1947) and Alice Paul (1885–1977) led the final battle for women's suffrage, but in dramatically different styles.

Catt worked her way through Iowa State University, serving as a school principal and later as one of the nation's first female superintendents. She began her suffrage work with the Iowa Suffrage Association upon the death of her first husband. The prenuptial agreement, signed before her second marriage to George Catt in 1890, guaranteed her four months each year to work on suffrage activities. Known for her strong organizational skills, Catt took the helm of the National American Women's Suffrage Association (NAWSA) in 1917 and implemented the "Winning Plan," which combined a careful congressional lobbying strategy for a federal amendment with continued efforts to win suffrage in individual states. Catt believed that Congress would act only when women in enough states had the votes to make them listen. She further believed that rational appeals and careful persuasion would lead Congress and President Wilson to support suffrage in ways that punishing Democrats at the polls would not. She urged NAWSA members to remain nonpartisan in their calls on lawmakers. After the Nineteenth Amendment was ratified, Catt founded the League of Women Voters, a nonpartisan organization dedicated to educating women for full civic participation.

Alice Paul, born to affluent Quaker parents, graduated from Swarthmore College in 1905, earned a master's degree from the University of Pennsylvania in 1907, and a Ph.D. in 1912. Her studies combined her overlapping interests in economics, political

five squadrons of cavalry with six chariots, participated.[35] More than half a million people watched as the parade headed down Pennsylvania Avenue toward the White House. Although the congressional committee had sought additional police protection for the marchers, the superintendent of police refused, saying it was a job for the War Department, not the police department. Trouble started when spectators began insulting participants and pushing the crowd into the parade line. As police stood idle, the situation deteriorated into a near riot. In all, 175 calls for ambulances were sent out, and more than 200 people were treated at local hospitals.[36] A subsequent Senate investigation

science, social work, and women's equality. Later in her life she would also earn three law degrees. While pursuing a graduate fellowship in England, Paul met the Pankhurst sisters and was introduced to the militant tactics of the British suffrage movement. When she returned to the United States in 1910, she brought with her an appreciation for the direct and aggressive methods of the English suffragettes. Paul was convinced that suffrage rights needed to be taken and demanded, not begged for. Initially working within the NAWSA as chair of the Congressional Committee, Paul organized a massive suffrage demonstration in Washington, D.C., held the day prior to Woodrow Wilson's inauguration. She believed that the party in power and incumbent politicians should be held accountable for their lack of support for suffrage and eventually (after being ousted from the NAWSA) organized the National Woman's Party to facilitate women's direct political action. She organized and coordinated the actions of hundreds of women who demonstrated in front of the White House and engaged in hunger strikes while imprisoned. She too had a gift for organizing. As her friend Lucy Burns said of her, "Her great assets, I should say, are her power to make plans on a national scale; and a supplementary power to see that it is done down to the last postage stamp."[1] Paul's methods were viewed as controversial and radical. In an editorial condemning the picketing as such a female thing to do, the *New York Times* wrote, "That the female mind is inferior to the male mind need not be assumed. That there is something about it essentially different, and that this difference is of a kind and degree that with votes for women would constitute a political danger is or ought to be plain to everybody."[2]

What do you think?

Under what circumstances is direct action warranted in pursuit of women's equality? Evaluate Catt's and Paul's respective strategies in light of what you've learned about the history of the suffrage movement and the political climate between 1917 and 1920. Which was more effective in moving the Nineteenth Amendment toward ratification? Would one strategy have been as effective without the other?

[1]Lunardini, Christine, *From Equal Suffrage to Equal Rights: Alice Paul and the National Woman's Party, 1910–1928* (New York: New York University Press, 1986), p. 10.

[2]Ibid., p. 108.

turned up numerous examples of police ineptitude and complicity with the rioters. The publicity the parade generated and the claims Paul made that the police and top civilian officials had conspired to break up the parade, brought unparalleled attention to the suffrage cause. Not all of it was positive. Newspaper editorials chided the female participants for their unruly behavior, and such criticism made the NAWSA's leadership nervous. In the leaders' minds, the congressional committee, and not the NAWSA, was pursuing a federal strategy. The NAWSA was still committed to a state-by-state campaign. Conflict between the congressional committee and the NAWSA escalated.

March 3, 1913. Suffrage Parade down Pennsylvania Avenue, Washington, D.C. The procession included 26 floats, ten bands, four mounted brigades, three heralds, and more than 8,000 marchers. Women from countries that had enfranchised women marched first in the procession, followed by the pioneers in the U.S. struggle. They were followed by sections celebrating working women by occupation, state delegations and finally, a separate section for male supporters of woman suffrage. *Copyright 1997 State Historical Society of Wisconsin.*

Allegations and conspiracy theories (none of which were ever proven) began surfacing that Paul and her supporters were working to undermine the state campaign by focusing exclusively on the federal amendment and on financial improprieties.

Frustrated, Paul broke with the NAWSA and established the Congressional Union (CU) as an independent organization in 1914. The CU's first action was to hold Democratic party elected officials responsible for the failure of federal suffrage legislation. The CU targeted Democratic congressmen in close races and actively campaigned against candidates who did not support enfranchising women. Following the same logic, Paul turned her attention to Woodrow Wilson. She organized pickets in front of the White House and called on Wilson to pressure Congress to consider and pass the federal amendment (known by then as the Susan B. Anthony Amendment). On January 10, 1917, the first "Silent Sentinels" appeared.[37] These were women who stood motionless holding banners that read, "Mr. President, What Will You Do for Woman Suffrage?" and "How Long Must Women Wait for Liberty?" These suffragist picketers were the first pickets ever to appear before the White House.

The NAWSA, although not specifically endorsing the pickets, took a wait-and-see attitude under the new leadership of Carrie Chapman Catt. Catt, who had replaced Shaw as president in 1915, made reforming the organization her first priority. Although Shaw led with great intelligence and moral authority, she did not have Catt's political savvy or her skills in managing the unwieldy NAWSA bureaucracy. Catt's first action was to obtain the allegiance of the national and state association leaders. Her goal was to "enable campaigners in the field and lobbyists in Washington to feel a united organization behind them."[38] Catt did not believe that the NAWSA or the suffrage question should be tied too closely to either of the two major political parties and instead pursued a nonpartisan strategy through ratification and beyond.

At first, the pickets attracted sympathy from the public, and donations poured in from women nationwide. However, in 1917, while other suffragists debated how to respond to the country's war on Germany, Alice Paul transformed the Congressional Union into the National Woman's Party (NWP) and stepped up efforts to call attention to women's disenfranchisement. Ignoring the war, NWP picketers carried signs reading: "Kaiser Wilson, have you forgotten your sympathy with the poor Germans because they were not self-governed? Twenty million American women are not self-governed. Take the beam out of your eye."[39] As the rhetoric heated up, police began arresting picketers, some of whom were physically attacked by daily crowds of onlookers. Each time police arrested a group of marchers or a woman was felled by attack, another woman was there to take her place. States sent delegations to the picket lines, and those who couldn't picket, sent donations to support those marching in their place. When jailed, women refused to pay their fines and remained in jail. In an attempt to scare off new picketers, prison terms of up to 60 days were imposed. The women engaged in several hunger strikes to protest their unjust incarceration. Prison officials responded by force-feeding them through the nose, a dangerous and terribly painful practice. Public reaction was swift and overwhelmingly sympathetic to the suffragists, prompting early releases. Women released from prison capitalized on the public's sympathy by campaigning for suffrage in their prison garb.

The NWP's militant tactics offended many within and outside of the movement, including many NAWSA members. Under Catt's leadership, the NAWSA was pursuing a state strategy for a federal amendment labeled the "Winning Plan." Under Catt's plan, each state would be accorded the resources and attention in proportion to its chances of passing a state constitutional amendment. Members also lobbied Congress to pass the Anthony Amendment. Catt believed that President Wilson could be persuaded to support the federal amendment in time.[40] She feared that the NWP's tactics would only antagonize him and drive him farther from the cause. The "Winning Plan" was carefully orchestrated so that the NAWSA was perceived as "playing by the rules" contrary to the NWP. Catt and others in the NAWSA believed that Paul's tactics were hurting suffrage as a whole. Most scholars, however, attribute the amendment's final passage to a combination of efforts. "Between 1910 and 1920 an average of 15 states considered suffrage legislation each year, and there were more state referenda on women's voting rights than in the previous forty years combined."[41] As women won suffrage rights in increasing numbers of states, pressure mounted on Congress to pass the Nineteenth Amendment and to send it to the states for ratification. In 1918, the federal amendment failed in the Senate by two votes after passing the House of Representatives. In 1919, the NAWSA demonstrated the significance of the women's vote by targeting and defeating two antisuffrage incumbents in the Senate. As a result, the Nineteenth Amendment was sent to the states in 1919. The battle for ratification was waged in the states for fifteen months. The NAWSA state network, built as a part of the "Winning Plan," proved invaluable in mobilizing men and women to pressure state legislatures for timely ratification. On August 26, 1920, by a one-vote margin in Tennessee, the final state to ratify the amendment, the Anthony Amendment was added to the Constitution.

Never Underestimate the Value of One Vote

Tennessee tested women's ability to directly confront opponents and their tactics. It took pressure from President Wilson to convince Tennessee's governor to call the legislature into special session to consider the amendment. Court challenges to the amendment had been dismissed, clearing the way for the summer session called for August 9. Opponents poured into Nashville, and the state suffrage association issued a call for help from the national associations. The NAWSA and NWP worked together polling for support across the state. At first it looked promising, but support eroded in the face of well-funded and well-organized opposition. "Legislators who had expressed favorable sentiments toward woman suffrage were threatened with the ruin of their business and political careers, some were all but kidnaped, and they were all systematically plied with liquor."[42] The Senate quickly passed the amendment and sent it to the House where it stayed for ten days. During those ten days, members of the opposition were alleged to have bought votes, tried to break the quorum, appealed to "Negro phobia" and states'-rights claims, and threatened legislators, saying that a favorable vote would lead to their political death. Suffrage forces relentlessly counted votes in the House, and when the bill finally reached the floor on August 18, it was two votes short of passage. An attempt to table the bill resulted in a tie and failed when an opponent, Representative Banks Turner, turned proponent. When the final vote was called, it was the youngest member of the chamber, twenty-four-year-old Harry Burns, who cast the surprise "yea." In his pocket was a letter from his mother, an active suffragist,

> Hurrah! And vote for suffrage and don't keep them in doubt. I notice some of the speeches against. They were very bitter. I have been watching to see how you stood, but have noticed nothing yet. Don't forget to be a good boy and help Mrs. Catt put "Rat" in Ratification.[43]

The amendment passed, forty-nine to forty-seven, just in time for twenty-six million women of voting age to participate in the 1920 elections.

TABLE 2.1 Women's Voting Rights

1893	New Zealand	1931	Chile		Vietnam	1957	Colombia
1902	Australia		Spain	1947	Argentina		Honduras
1906	Finland		Sri Lanka		Mexico		Zimbabwe
1913	Norway	1932	Brazil		Pakistan	1958	Chad
1915	Denmark		Thailand		Singapore		Guinea
1918	Austria	1934	Cuba	1948	Belgium	1959	Madagascar
	Canada	1935	Puerto Rico		Israel		Morocco
	Georgia	1937	Philippines		Korea, South	1960	Zaire
	Poland	1939	El Salvador		Niger	1961	Rwanda
	Russia	1942	Dominican Republic	1949	China		Sierra Leone
1919	Belarus	1943	Yugoslavia		Costa Rica	1962	Paraguay
	Germany	1944	Bulgaria		Greece		Uganda
	Netherlands		France	1950	Haiti		Zambia
	Sweden		Jamaica		India	1963	Congo
	Ukraine	1945	Croatia	1951	Nepal		Iran
1920	Albania		Hungary	1952	Bolivia	1963	Kenya
	Czech Republic		Indonesia	1953	Syria	1964	Afghanistan
	Slovakia		Italy	1954	Ghana		Libya
	United States		Japan	1955	Cambodia	1965	Sudan
1921	Armenia	1946	Guatemala		Ethiopia	1971	Switzerland
	Lithuania		Korea, North		Nicaragua	1974	Jordan
1924	Kazakhstan		Macedonia		Peru	1975	Mozambique
1928	Ecuador		Panama	1956	Egypt	1976	Portugal
	Ireland		Romania		Mali	1978	Nigeria
	United Kingdom		Taiwan		Somalia	1980	Iraq
1930	Turkey		Venezuela		Tunisia	1994	South Africa

Source: Naomi Neft and Ann Levine. *Where Women Stand.* (New York: Random House, 1997).

OPPOSITION TO WOMEN'S SUFFRAGE

Traditionally opponents to suffrage were the liquor industry, big business, and the church. The liquor industry, represented by the U.S. Brewers' Association, the Wholesale Distillers' Association, and the Retail Dealers' Association, held significant power in U.S. politics, particularly in state legislatures. Its direct interest, however, was preventing prohibition rather than preventing women's suffrage. Since many women suffragists were also temperance advocates, the liquor industry believed keeping women away from the voting booth would be in its best long-term economic interests. Businesses, primarily textiles and agriculture, that would be directly affected by women's voting on progressive reform agendas, provided a welcome ally for antisuffragists. A relative latecomer to the antisuffrage coalition was the Catholic Church. Suffrage opponents initially shied away from the church because of fears of foreigners and papists. The

Catholic Church opposed suffrage primarily on ideological grounds, arguing that the church desired "to prevent a moral deterioration which suffrage could bring and feared the development of a political structure and social climate deleterious to Catholicism."[44] Like other hierarchically organized religions opposed to women's suffrage, the Catholic Church believed that a traditionally constituted society was ordained by God, and any move by either sex on the terrain of the other was viewed as unnatural and a threat to the universal order. The association of the birth control movement with women's rights and suffrage after 1885 only solidified Catholics' official opposition to a more public role for women.

Beginning in about 1880, female suffragists encountered their most vexing opponents to the cause: other women. At first suffragists dismissed the "remonstrants" (as they were called) as inconsequential and misguided. Later these opponents were attacked as fronts for male corporate interests, particularly the interests of their wealthy husbands. To suffragists Carrie Chapman Catt and Nettie Rogers Shuler, the "antis" served to "confuse public thinking by standing conspicuously in the limelight while the potent enemy worked in the darkness."[45] They further dismissed antisuffragists as throwbacks to outdated gender norms. Associating the antis with traditional gender relations spawned a destructive and false dichotomy between "true women" and "new women" that would surface again in the 1970s in relation to the Equal Rights Amendment.

Historian Susan Marshall expresses regret about the simplicity with which antisuffragists have been treated, arguing instead that their very existence is an important element in understanding women as political actors.[46] To suggest that the antis were merely fronts for more powerful males is to rob them of their autonomy and political agency, as well as to undermine the suffragists' own arguments about women's equality. The dichotomy between "modernists" and "traditionalists" or "careerists" and "traditionalists/homemakers" ignores the complex, changing social conditions most women faced at the turn of the century. Opportunities for new roles as well as the increasing economic pressure on families created by periodic recessions meant that women of all classes bridged the divide between private and public life by combining work and family obligations. According to Marshall, antisuffragists had their own gendered class interests that motivated them to undertake political action to "protect their own positions of privilege as elite volunteers, political appointees, and custodians of prosperity." The ideology of separate spheres, so evident in antisuffrage rhetoric, "enhanced their social influence as cultural arbiters, maintaining the exclusivity of elite social networks while simultaneously promoting new standards of domesticity that enhanced class control . . . From their perspective, the franchise was an inferior form of power to that which they already enjoyed."[47] Antisuffragists' access to money, leisure, and extensive social networks enabled their political action, while "the confines of class mandated a circumspect public image."[48]

Numerous organizations dedicated themselves to preventing women's suffrage. Many of these were organized at the state level in response to statewide women's suffrage referendum campaigns. These organizations included the Maine Association Opposed to Suffrage for Women and the Massachusetts Association Opposed to Further Extension of Suffrage to Women. The southern states were the last to grant women the vote, and for most, it came only with the federal amendment. Groups like the Southern Woman's League for the Rejection of the Susan B. Anthony Amendment linked the preservation of the southern "way of life" to protecting women's honor from degradation at the polling place. There were also more nationally focused groups like the National Association Opposed to Woman Suffrage and, by extension, *The Woman Patriot*, the organization's national publication that extended the antis' fight beyond ratification in 1920. The Daughters of the American Revolution supported post-ratification agitation by linking supporters of women's rights with the abolition of family relations.

The majority of those in support of suffrage and those opposed shared important characteristics, first among them being their sex. Like most of the suffragists of this era, women opposed to women's equality tended to be wealthy, well-educated, and well-connected to the political power elite. Historian Susan Marshall argues that it was only after suffragists turned to direct electoral strategies aimed at defeating state legislators and members of Congress opposed to suffrage and stepped up the populist state referendum campaigns, that the antis' lost their edge. As long as the decision remained in the hands of a few insulated elite male politicians, the antisuffragists were well positioned to exert their brand of influence exercised through kinship and shared class interests even while maintaining an image of self-sacrificing womanhood.[49] Suffragists, however, were forced to adopt an expedient political strategy that moved them closer to antisuffragists' conservatism. This conservatism is evident in posters proclaiming "Votes for Mothers" and their claim that women's unique gender-linked perspective would "clean house" in the political system. Gone were the demands for women's natural rights, and the suffrage movement succumbed to the "cult of domesticity" in the final years before ratification in an effort to expand their base of support—a calculated reaction to the success of the antisuffrage movement.[50]

POST-SUFFRAGE DIVISIONS: THE EQUAL RIGHTS AMENDMENT OR SPECIAL PROTECTIONS FOR WOMEN?

For the NAWSA and the NWP, the aftermath of suffrage was a time to savor the victory and re-evaluate their missions. Much of the scholarly literature chronicles the demise of the organized women's movement in the period immediately following suffrage. Although membership in these two major women's organizations did decline somewhat, that was to be expected since their organizational focal point had been accomplished. Historian Nancy Cott writes that the 1920s, rather than the end of feminism, signaled the end of the suffrage movement and the emergence of the early struggle of modern feminism. "That struggle was, and is, to find language, organization, and goals adequate to the paradoxical situation of modern women, diverse individuals and subgroups who 'can't avoid being women whatever they do,' who inhabit the same world as men, not in the same way."[51] The two paths to gender equality clearly emerged during the period immediately following the ratification of the Anthony Amendment.

Women associated with the NAWSA under Catt's leadership had been persuaded to act as nonpartisans in the battle for suffrage and many remained active in the organization in its new nonpartisan incarnation: the League of Women Voters. Rather than directly entering electoral politics, the League dedicated its efforts to educating newly enfranchised women, studying national legislation and social policy, and participating in local civic matters. Catt's earlier admonition against allegiance to any one party held, and the League separated itself from partisan politics entirely, even refusing to endorse specific candidates or to promote women from within its own ranks as candidates. Ironically, the period immediately following ratification may have yielded the largest "eligibility pool" of potential female candidates with prior political experience, education, and political interest in history, and yet that pool went untapped. The transition from nonpartisan reformers to partisan "insider pols" never took place. Some suffrage activists were offered positions in the administration but turned them down suspecting tokenism. Other strong leaders who might have been viable candidates for national office turned their attention to suffrage battles in Europe and divorced themselves from American politics almost entirely.

Even Alice Paul, who pushed hardest for the introduction of an Equal Rights Amendment, spent the better part of the 1920s abroad. Like the NAWSA, the National Women's Party underwent substantial reorganization between 1920 and 1923. It too eschewed a partisan electoral agenda and instead focused on achieving complete legal equality between men and women. For the remainder of the decade, members pursued three avenues toward that objective: the Equal Rights Amendment; its international equivalent, the Equal Rights Treaty; and the Equal Nationality Treaty dealing in a more limited way with citizenship rights.[52]

The history of the Equal Rights Amendment (ERA) is similar to the battle for suffrage, with one major exception: The ERA was not ratified. Once women had the vote, disagreements surfaced over how the vote could best be translated into political power so that women could exert influence over issues and legislation. Initially political parties courted women voters by offering reform proposals and including progressive planks designed to appeal to female voters in their party platforms. In 1921, for example, Congress passed the Sheppard-Towner bill for maternity and infant care. However, the *gender gap* that many predicted in 1920 did not actually materialize for another six decades. It wasn't until the election of Ronald Reagan in 1980 when women were significantly more likely than men to support Democratic candidates. When a women's voting bloc failed to materialize after two election cycles, the parties left women to themselves to set a political action agenda for the future.

The Fight for an Equal Rights Amendment: The First Generation

Not all women believed that the vote alone would bring about significant change. After all, the Thirteenth Amendment, which abolished slavery, was not enough to guarantee full citizenship rights to former slaves, thereby requiring the ratification of the Fourteenth and Fifteenth Amendments. Similarly, some suffragists argued that another constitutional amendment was required to guarantee women equal rights under the law. At a 1923 National Woman's Party convention called to identify state laws that discriminated against women, Alice Paul proposed the Equal Rights Amendment. Daniel Anthony, a Kansas representative and nephew of Susan B. Anthony, introduced it into Congress that same year.[53] The language read,

> Men and women shall have equal rights throughout the United States and every place subject to its jurisdiction. Congress shall have the power to enforce this article by appropriate legislation.

The rift between liberal feminists (advocates of the legal equality doctrine) and social reform feminists (advocates of the fairness doctrine) was always present in the movement, but the single-minded pursuit of suffrage obscured its importance. Historian Nancy Cott argues that the *unity* attributed to the women's rights movement during the decades preceding ratification was overblown and quite unrealistic to expect.[54] As noted previously, each generation of women's rights activists has had divisions over strategy as well as divisions born of race, class, ethnic, and religious differences among women. It is no more realistic to expect women to agree with one another than it would be to expect all men to agree with one another on every issue and political strategy. In fact, some scholars argue that the Nineteenth Amendment actually freed women to disagree among themselves and to pursue a wide range of political interests as full citizens and active political participants.[55] The two paths to gender equality were once again clearly at issue.

Introduction of the ERA brought to the surface the deep divide within the women's movement and society as a whole between those who believed that equality meant special treatment and enactment of protective legislation that considered the burdens women bore (consistent with the fairness doctrine) and those who believed that only gender-neutral law and policies could achieve equality (consistent with the legal equality doctrine). Those favoring the legal equality path argued that protective legislation, although superficially designed to discriminate *in favor* of women, in reality kept women from the best paying jobs and denied them the ability to competitively negotiate the terms of their labor as individuals. Women who had worked tirelessly to see fair protective legislation enacted now accused NWP members of elitism, charging that they had never worked a twelve-hour factory shift, so they did not, and could not, understand the issues of working-class women. Labor unions quickly mobilized their membership in opposition to the ERA and remained opposed to the amendment until 1973.

The rift over the ERA was exacerbated by the ambiguity of feminism as an organizing ideology. NWP members, themselves arguably the strongest proponents of a legalistic, rights-based form of equality for women, held mixed views about women's maternal function in society. The NWP primarily focused on the similarities between men and women, but it also believed that the biological fact of motherhood led men and women to possess different values. On the one hand, motherhood was a force for justice in the world and a check on social and sexual debasement. Yet, they also believed "motherhood has been the rod held over the backs of women to drive them into submission; it has been the chain to hold them in dependence and to close-rivet them to a condition of slavery."[56] Women's moral superiority, which flowed directly from maternalism (actual or anticipatory) in the eyes of some NWP members, required that women be admitted to all quarters of society on an equal basis. Protective legislation proponents also used this same maternal role to argue for special compensatory measures for women only—laws that the NWP found inherently discriminatory and economically restrictive. When the NWP approached Alfred E. Smith, governor of New York, to speak in opposition to protective legislation, he replied, "I believe in equality, but I cannot nurse a baby."[57] For many, this summed up the dilemma of equal rights. Women wanted equal opportunities, particularly in the economic marketplace, but also in education, access to health care, and in marriage and family law. Yet the biological differences that left women with a unique role in perpetuating the species could not be denied. The crux of the debate over equal rights, both then and now, lies in how best to render the two compatible. The NWP and other liberal feminists argued that a blanket constitutional amendment was the only way to guarantee women equal opportunities across the board. Social reform feminists maintained that the only way to "make women equal" was to recognize and compensate women for the burdens they bore relative to childbirth and family responsibilities. To them, gender-neutral laws were inherently unfair to women because such laws would always be blind to women's maternity issues. The ERA provided a foil for all sides to wrangle with the competing visions of women's role in society. In the end, opposition to the ERA from Progressive organizations, such as the National Consumer's League, labor unions, and prominent female reformers like Eleanor Roosevelt, scuttled any chance the legislation had of a formal hearing before Congress in the 1920s.

Over the next three decades support grew slowly but steadily for the amendment. During the 1930s, the National Association of Women Lawyers and the

National Federation of Business and Professional Women's Clubs became sponsors of the ERA. In 1940, the Republican Party supported the ERA in its party platform, and the Democrats followed suit in 1944. In 1950 and 1953, the Senate passed the ERA but attached the "Hayden rider," which provided that the amendment "shall not be construed to impair any rights, benefits or exemptions now or hereinafter conferred by law upon persons of the female sex."[58] Women's organizations immediately declared the Hayden rider an unacceptable attempt to have it both ways by allowing states to retain laws providing special benefits for women in employment.

The Second Generation

In the 1960s with the rise of the civil rights movement, the context in which the ERA was debated changed dramatically. When Congress passed the 1964 Civil Rights Act, it effectively removed protective legislation from the controversy over the ERA and paved the way for its eventual consideration. The 1964 act sought, among other things, to alleviate racial discrimination in employment, education, and public accommodations. Title VII of the act dealt with banning discrimination in employment. As the bill moved closer to passage, southern conservatives offered an amendment they thought would surely kill the entire bill. Judge Howard Smith, a Democratic congressman from Virginia, proposed to amend Title VII to include sex in the employment discrimination section. He offered his amendment, he said, "in a spirit of satire and cajolery," and the House promptly designated the day "Ladies Day." Supporters of the Civil Rights Bill feared that adding women to the employment-discrimination section would defeat the entire bill. However, a group of Republican and Democratic women joined Smith's coalition of conservative southern Democrats having planned to offer a similar amendment themselves. No committee hearings were ever held on the potential impact of the Smith amendment, nor did anyone pay much attention since it was offered "in jest." The amendment passed the House (and was not touched by the Senate). When the Civil Rights Bill was finally passed and signed into law later that summer, liberal feminists gained their most powerful tool yet to combat sex discrimination in the workplace. Since protective employment law designed for women only is inherently discriminatory, such laws quickly fell by the wayside and with them organized labor's opposition to the ERA.

In 1970, two forces brought the ERA to the forefront of Congress's attention. First, the Pittsburgh chapter of the National Organization for Women (NOW) disrupted Senator Birch Bayh's hearings on giving eighteen-year-olds the vote (ultimately the Twenty-sixth Amendment), prompting Bayh to promise to hold hearings on the ERA in the following spring.[59] Second, congresswomen Martha Griffiths and Edith Green freed the ERA from twenty-two years of captivity in committee without a hearing.[60] Green capitalized on a concurrent campaign to expand the scope of Title VII to include discrimination in education by holding hearings on the topic that eventually became hearings on discrimination against women in all facets of life. The official record from the education subcommittee hearings created a compelling case for equal rights. Representative Griffiths mounted a discharge petition drive to free the ERA from the House Judiciary Committee, chaired by the very powerful octogenarian, Emanuel Celler. A discharge petition is a procedural mechanism for circumventing committee inaction and bringing a resolution directly to the floor of the House of Representatives. It is a bold move and rarely successful. Of the 829 petitions filed prior to Griffith's, only twenty-four bills were ever successfully discharged, and of those, only twenty passed the House. Of those twenty, only two were enacted into law.[61] Griffiths not only managed to convince 218 House members to sign the discharge petition, but she also got 332 of the 435 members to vote for the discharge resolution on the floor, effectively removing the ERA from the Judiciary Committee's grasp. On the Senate side, however, the resolution was amended exempting women from the draft, effectively killing the chances for congressional passage in 1970. It was not until 1972, after more than a year of successive hearings, failed amendment attempts, and wording changes, that both houses of Congress successfully passed the bill by the constitutionally required two-thirds margin, enabling the resolution to be sent to the states.[62] Ironically, Emanuel Celler's congressional career, which began in 1923, the same year the ERA was introduced for the first time, ended in 1972, the year Congress finally passed the ERA. The opponent who defeated him in the Brooklyn district primary was herself an ardent supporter of the amendment.[63]

Unlike the precarious support for suffrage, the ERA enjoyed overwhelming bipartisan congressional favor. Supporters therefore predicted ratification by the states in record time. The experience in the first few months seemed to confirm their optimism. State legislatures competed with one another for the honor of being the first to ratify the ERA. Hawaii ratified the amendment on March 22, 1972—the same day the resolution passed the U.S. Senate. Five additional states ratified the amendment over the next two days, and by early 1973, twenty-four more states were added to the list. By 1977, however, only thirty-five states of the thirty-eight required to add the amendment to the Constitution had ratified. A rare extension to the ratification deadline was granted in 1978, giving proponents until 1982 to gather the remaining three affirmative state votes. When the deadline again passed in 1982, not a single state had been added, and several states were actively working to rescind their prior ratification as the amendment died. The language of the defeated ERA read:

1. Equality of rights under the law shall not be denied or abridged by the United States or any State on account of sex.
2. The Congress shall have the power to enforce, by appropriate legislation, the provisions of this article.
3. This amendment shall take effect two years after the date of ratification.

THE FAILURE OF THE ERA

The debate that prevented the ERA from receiving congressional attention in the 1920s largely centered on economic and workplace issues, particularly special protective legislation that compensated women in the workplace for the additional burdens of caring for children and a family. Equal pay, equal access to educational opportunities, and the right to advance in employment were all tied intimately to the economic debate. Proponents argued that freeing women to act as individuals in the marketplace would empower them to be more effective advocates of their self-interest at home and in politics. They also believed that the ERA would strike down oppressive marriage and divorce laws, provide access to birth-control information, and would allow women the right to make contracts distinct from their husbands, to control their children, to maintain their names in marriage, to exercise independent citizenship, to equalize moral standards and treatment of sexually transmitted diseases, and to even out penalties for sexual offenses.[64] Opponents, however, successfully convinced a majority of men and women that the ERA would radically change the way society was organized along gender lines. Moreover, this reorganization would not only have an impact on the workplace but, more important, would also affect the home and potentially the marital bed. This was more change than most citizens at the time were willing to accept. Opponents did not have to invest much in organized opposition because there was never a consensus in favor of the ERA in the 1920s, even among feminists active in major women's organizations. Most women favored fair treatment within the family and society at large. They did not view absolute legal equality as promised by the amendment as fair to women since the law might require that women be treated the same as men were. Any compensatory advantage women gained through progressive employment would be lost, and for many women, this was not the sort of equality they favored.

The climate was quite different in 1972. This time, issues of women's vulnerability in the workplace had largely been settled in the courts. Additionally, protective legislation aimed solely at women had been struck down as incompatible with Title VII of the 1964 Civil Rights Act. The issue of equal pay was broached by the Equal Pay Act of 1963. The debate now, framed largely by the opposition after 1973, centered on home protection and the preservation of traditional family values, including women's *right* to the role of primary caregiver and homemaker. By 1972, a considerable number of women had entered the paid workforce (43.9 percent, comprising 38.5 percent of the total paid workforce[65]), yet women in opposition to the ERA voiced fears that full-time homemakers would be *forced* into the paid labor force. They argued that a change in the rules of gender relations would be inherently unfair to women and would lead to a rise in divorce rates, family and child abandonment, and poverty among women and children. They were, in effect, arguing that the separate spheres ideology protected women from the unfair burdens of the paid labor force. By 1982, the year the ERA effectively died, more than 50 percent of married women were in the paid work force. For African Americans, the percentage topped 60 percent.[66] For these women, the glorification of the separate spheres ideology by ERA opponents created a reality gap. They were not free to advocate for the *right* to be a full-time homemaker. Additionally, the Supreme Court acted in 1973 on the issue of abortion. Arguably, abortion was not directly related to the substantive content of the ERA, but opponents nonetheless used the *Roe* v. *Wade* decision to argue that ratification would inevitably lead to on-demand, government-funded abortions. Conservative groups effectively linked people's unease with the federal government's involvement in the abortion issue, cautioning that the ERA would give the federal government the power to enter private and family life. The conservative movement, organized largely by the fundamentalist Christian Right, gained strength and new members by linking abortion and states'-rights issues to the ERA.

Surprisingly few scholarly studies have been published on the failure of the Equal Rights Amendment. Jane Mansbridge's *Why We Lost the ERA* (1986) is probably the best-known book on the subject. She argues that the ERA's failure can be attributed to a variety of causes, among them a backlash against Supreme Court decisions in the 1960s and 1970s (particularly *Roe* v. *Wade*, 1973), the political mobilization of fundamentalist Christians, the gender imbalance in the state legislatures of nonratifying states, the emergence of new ultraconservative, anti-ERA leadership in the Republican Party (Ronald Reagan, first among them), and a general deceleration in progressive reforms of all types during the 1970s.[67] Mary Frances Berry, in *Why ERA Failed* (1986), compares the ERA to other successful and unsuccessful campaigns to ratify amendments that attempt to make major changes in American life. Berry argues that in order for the ERA to have succeeded, a majority of voters would have had to recognize that a problem existed that had not been remedied by the courts, state legislatures, or the Congress, and which could only be solved by changing the Constitution.[68] She claims that supporters did too little, too late to effect the magnitude of change that was promised (or threatened, depending on one's perspective) by the ERA. Political scientist Janet Boles's book, *The Politics of the Equal Rights Amendment* (1978), examines political decision making under conditions of intense conflict. Her book is unique in that it was published prior to the ERA's final defeat. She argues that state legislators in unratifying states actually voted against the conflict the ERA created rather than the amendment itself. In *Constitutional Inequality* (1985), Gilbert Steiner claims that between 1971 and 1973 there was a brief window of opportunity during which the ERA could have been ratified. That window was closed forever by three factors: legalization of abortion, the increasing saliency of the draft in the wake of the Soviet-Afghanistan invasion, and the increased prominence of Senator Sam Ervin (a long-time ERA opponent) after Watergate. Finally, *Sex, Gender, and the ERA* (1990) is the most recent book on the demise of the ERA. Authors Donald G. Mathews and Jane Sherron De Hart examine the politicization of women as a result of the ERA fight, and offer a unique state-level perspective.[69] Despite the ERA's defeat, women who became politicized during the ratification fight, regardless of which side they were on, remained active in politics, ushering in the second wave of feminist (and antifeminist) political activity.

Women Opposed to the Equal Rights Amendment

There is no question that opposition forces to the ERA were well organized and more effectively mobilized within individual states than pro-ERA organizations were immediately after congressional passage. Pro-ERA groups were located primarily in Washington, D.C., enabling them to lobby effectively for congressional passage. Once the resolution went to the states, however, these organizations lacked a network of state-based chapters that could effectively work for ratification. Alternatively, opposition groups were founded primarily in the states and worked almost exclusively at the state level to oppose ratification. Two national organizations were formed to oppose the ERA and have remained active even today: the Eagle Forum, founded in 1972 by Phyllis Schlafly, and Concerned Women for America (CWA), founded in 1979 by Beverly LaHaye. CWA developed a national network of anti-ERA prayer chains that sought God's direct intervention weekly. Stop-ERA, a Schlafly spinoff from the Eagle Forum, was dedicated specifically to the anti-ratification campaign in the states and has long been suspected of having direct ties to the John Birch Society. Other John Birch Society ad-hoc groups, such as HOTDOG (Humanitarians Opposed to Degrading Our Girls) in Utah and POW (Protect Our Women) in Wisconsin, formed in the unratified states. Even Stop-ERA spawned ad-hoc groups like AWARE (American Women Already Richly Endowed), Scratch Women's Lib, and the League for the Protection of Women and Children.[70] Most of these spinoff opposition groups were organized on the principle of protecting what was perceived as traditional family values. Operating from their self-appointed positions of true defenders of women's interests, Eagle Forum and CWA leaders charged that the feminist agenda "deliberately degrades the homemaker."[71] They warned women that ratification of the ERA would radically alter the balance of power within families and would free men from their traditional economic obligations to their families.

Similar to the gap in the antisuffrage leadership's rhetoric and conduct, Schlafly and LaHaye are both relatively privileged, well-educated women who head organizations with multimillion dollar budgets. Yet these women denounce careers for other married women. Both movements claimed the separate spheres ideology as the source of women's fulfillment as well as God's plan for human survival. Married women who worked outside the home did so for selfish, narcissistic reasons and threatened the health and safety of their children and the very stability of the family by doing so. The anti-ERA forces ignored the new economic realities that often drove women into the paid workforce. Schlafly skillfully harkened back to the rhetoric of the antisuffrage campaign by labeling the ERA the "extra responsibilities amendment," a claim reminiscent of the charge that voting constituted an "unfair burden" on women already laden with home and child-care responsibilities. Similar to the 1910s, anti-ERA leaders, although elites themselves, successfully portrayed the ERA as harmful to nonprofessional women and the poor. Both the CWA and the Eagle Forum have attracted a base of members from the middle and lower-middle classes and convinced them that ideal womanhood is characterized by the virtue of occupying a distinct and separate private sphere. Influence over men and the power to control men, they argued, flows from this privileged position, not government protection. "True women" are characterized by an attractive femininity that empowers them to speak for women, unlike the "amazons," "feminoids," or feminist "freaks" of the "third sex." By legitimizing an expanded political role for women, historian Susan Marshall concludes, "the feminist movement has bequeathed a much larger legacy to contemporary political culture: the mobilization of conservative women. . . . They serve as ironic testimony to feminist assertions of female equality."[72]

THREE POLITICAL LESSONS ABOUT GENDER EQUALITY

1. A change in social norms and attitudes about women must precede a legal change, particularly in the case of a constitutional amendment.

The biggest obstacle to enfranchising women was the prevailing social attitude that women were not autonomous beings.[73] For women to be seen as competent in the public sphere, the power of the separate spheres ideology and coverture had to be overcome in the minds of those with the power to change existing law. It is no surprise then that it took so long for women to gain the vote. Centuries of socialization and custom and generations of attitudes had to be significantly altered so that adult women could be viewed as independent actors capable of making informed decisions apart from their fathers, brothers, and husbands. By the time the Nineteenth Amendment was ratified, women already had full voting rights in fifteen states, presidential voting rights in another twelve, and the right to participate in local and school elections in several others.[74] The full effect of the coverture doctrine was diminished when several states passed *Married Women's Property Acts* in the 1840s, giving free married women the right to control property for the first time. This single change—a woman's right to control her own property—was perhaps more democratizing than suffrage itself. Property gave women access to wealth, power, and additional rights that flowed from property ownership, such as the right to enter into and enforce contracts.

Coverture's grip on women's citizenship was, however, more difficult to sever and serves as an example of the principle that rights granted can be taken away. In the 1880s, Congress acted to link women's citizenship automatically to that of her husband. If a foreign-born woman married an American, she automatically gained American citizenship. But if an American-born woman married a foreign man, her American citizenship was stripped and she became an alien in her own country. Congress did not equalize citizenship rights until 1934.[75] So, while the ratification of the Nineteenth Amendment was law following a change that had already taken place in attitude and practice, it also offered women constitutional protection for their voting rights and by extension, the protection of other granted rights since they now had a tool by which to hold legislators accountable.

By the time the Equal Rights Amendment passed both houses of Congress by the required two-thirds majorities in 1972, supporters believed that women's equality had achieved the same "bygone conclusion" status as suffrage did. They were wrong. Unlike the vote, which was a well-defined, single political act, *equality* was a much more ambiguous concept. While suffragists began their fight by arguing that admitting women to the voting population would radically change America for the better, they quickly learned to argue instead that votes for women would actually produce little noticeable change and could point to experience in suffrage states as evidence. Arguing that granting suffrage was really an issue of *fairness* was more palatable and successful than arguing that it would be an agent of change. Advocates of the ERA also tried to argue that fairness required an extension of equal rights to women. Because these rights did not take on a concrete form, it was difficult to persuade people that the radical changes to daily life predicted by Phyllis Schlafly and others opposed to the ERA would not come to pass. The ambiguity of *equal rights* allowed the opposition to suggest that ERA ratification would bring about unisex toilets, wives and daughters in military combat, and homosexual marriages. Despite the lack of evidence that any of their predictions would come true, *proving* otherwise was impossible. Additionally, people who supported women's equality but who were not ERA activists could point to more than a decade of change for the better through legislative action and favorable decisions by the courts. Why clutter the Constitution with rights already granted? Supporters were unable to convey the complexities and vagaries of relying on the court and legislatures, which were historically unreliable. As long as other federal venues could be pursued, a constitutional change was unlikely.[76] In short, ERA supporters were unsuccessful in convincing the American public that the ERA would simply affirm the country's commitment to women's rights in ways that were consistent with current values. Furthermore, anti-ERA forces were very successful in raising fears about radical social change, the federal government's active intrusion into personal lives, and a loss of the traditional family. The ERA was dead.

2. The role that states play in the pursuit of gender equality should not be underestimated.

Another lesson from the contrast has to do with the role that states play in determining women's rights. The United States is organized as a federal system with power shared between the national and fifty state governments. As a result, each state plays a significant role in defining the rights and privileges of its citizens. Although the supremacy clause of the Constitution constrains states to act within the bounds set by the national government, in the absence of national action, the states may act alone. Therefore, the laws regarding women's rights differ by state. Two states (Utah and Wyoming) not only gave women the right to vote but also extended equal legal rights when those states first joined the union. Nine other states adopted their own ERAs in the 1970s, while another eight have included language resembling the Fourteenth Amendment's Equal Protection clause in their state constitutions. This leaves a patchwork of rights for women wholly dependent on their residence. (In chapters six, seven, and eight, the policy implications of federalism are explored further.) Those working for suffrage were able to convince the public and three-fourths of the state legislatures that the right to vote was so fundamental to a functioning democracy that it could not be left to each state to decide. The wisdom of this strategy came only after decades of working in the states on suffrage referendums and state constitutional amendments. Proponents of the ERA were not successful in making a similar case. ERA supporters were also slow to realize the power each state held in determining the fate of the federal amendment and so delayed in organizing a state-based ratification strategy. Missing from the ERA ratification strategy was a 1970s version of Carrie Chapman Catt's "Winning Plan" that recognized the value of cultivating early allies in the states and state legislatures.

3. All women are not alike. There is no sex solidarity in pursuit of gender equality.

Women do not constitute a homogeneous population. Women proved to be some of the most vociferous opponents of both suffrage and the Equal Rights Amendment, much to the surprise of many female supporters. The same fault lines that divide the social, economic, and political interests of men, divide women from one another. Empirical evidence from the 1970s and 1980s suggests that women do not act politically on the basis of shared interests with other women. "On most issues and candidacies that are seemingly relevant to gender, women do not differ materially from men, and both genders show considerable disunity."[77] In other words, gender does not bind women as a group any more than it binds men to one another in constructing and enacting a political agenda. While developing sex solidarity on a limited set of issues may be possible, the pursuit of gender equality is clearly not one of them. Women have developed alliances with African Americans and others similarly disadvantaged by the status quo only to break away when they felt their interests were being subsumed by those of other groups. Because women of different social, racial, or economic groups rarely interact as equals, they have difficulty making gender and common experiences as wives, mothers, and daughters a basis for political solidarity.[78]

The political equality promised women by the Nineteenth Amendment is only now slowly emerging as we enter the twenty-first century. Suffragists argued that the vote could also be used as a tool to extend women's rights and equality in the social and economic spheres, however, that has proven a slow, incremental process. The broad-brush equality in all spheres promised by the ERA threatened too much unpredictable change too quickly for many women. Equality and fairness are sometimes two different, albeit related, concepts. Suffragists started their campaign in 1848 by claiming in the Declaration of Sentiments that men and women are created equal and therefore eligible for the same rights and privileges of citizenship. This line of reasoning did not get very far since it said that men and women are the same and therefore should be accorded the same rights. ERA opponents convinced Americans that changing the "rules" (otherwise known as social norms) midway through the game was "unfair" to women who had remained at home to raise their children and support their husbands' careers. To now suggest that men and women be treated equally (the same) meant that women would be responsible for earning a living, paying child support, planning for retirement, and maintaining a mortgage. To many, this was incomprehensible.

The relationship between political, social, and economic equality is complex and illuminates the fault lines in how women's equality is understood and accepted. In order for political equality to be extended, women had to make significant progress in crossing the divide between the public and private spheres and to demonstrate their social and economic competence. However, once granted the vote, some women saw an opening to extend equality of rights even further while others viewed the vote as an end in itself. With the death of the ERA in 1982, women in America are once again faced with the prospect of fighting over equality issue by issue. The paradox that characterizes women's equality—the desire to eliminate sex-specific laws and classifications on the one hand, and the desire to recognize women's differences on the other—ensures that the debate will continue for some time. Suffrage for women guarantees that women will be active on all sides of the debates, from inside the political system and as outside activists. Suffrage does not ensure that all women will act on a single agenda or set of interests.

CONCLUSION

It is with some sense of irony that scholars marked women's entrance into the electorate at precisely the moment the power of the vote declined.[79] Women's experience with politics prior to the Nineteenth Amendment (and even after they won the vote) was primarily a nonpartisan model based in voluntary associations. Whether political parties themselves declined in importance, or whether women viewed partisan activity as a "male model" and therefore chose a different strategy, women and partisan politics have been slow to mix. After suffrage was ratified, activists pursued a divided agenda consistent with the two paths to equality: One branch proposed the ERA and pushed for gender-neutral legal reforms; the other remained dedicated to nonpartisan civic participation in pursuit of fairness and inclusion in the existing social, political, and economic system. Although the language of equality has remained important to both groups, there was little agreement on the meaning of full equality for women or on a strategy in pursuit of gender equality. Feminism as an ideology provided little guidance or cohesion in this regard.

Women and men are divided over the role women *should* play in politics and in society. In the fight for suffrage and legal equality, the National Women's Party adopted the view that women would achieve equality only when they were so fully integrated into politics, society, and the economy that sex no longer served as a useful way to classify citizens. This is consistent with the legal equality doctrine. Other women, some active in the League of Women Voters, viewed eradicating sex classifications as dangerous for women. They viewed women's role in public life as every bit as important as men's but distinctively female in its character. This perspective (which is consistent with the fairness doctrine) sees women as society's caretakers, government's watchdog, and politics' conscience. Some women supported neither path because they viewed any move by women to participate in public affairs as a violation of God's plan and dangerous to the well-being of the traditional family. That these themes dominated the debates over the failed ERA some fifty years after the Nineteenth Amendment was ratified suggests that the controversies of equality have not yet been settled. The next chapter continues the examination of the two paths in pursuit of women's equality by looking at women as voters and participants in the political process.

Notes

1. Glenna Matthews, *The Rise of Public Woman* (New York: Oxford University Press, 1992).

2. Carol Ellen Dubois, *Feminism and Suffrage: The Emergence of an Independent Women's Movement in America 1848–1869* (Ithaca, N.Y.: Cornell University Press, 1978), p. 32.

3. Jeffrey D. Schultz and Laura van Assendelft, eds., *Encyclopedia of Women in American Politics* (Phoenix, Ariz: Oryx Press, 1999), p. 205.

4. Matthews, *Rise of Public Woman,* p. 117.

5. Eleanor Flexnor and Ellen Fitzpatrick, *Century of Struggle: The Woman's Rights Movement in the United States*, enlarged ed. (Cambridge, Mass.: Harvard University Press, 1996), p. 70.

6. Ibid.

7. Elizabeth Cady Stanton, Susan B. Anthony, and Matilda Joslyn Gage, eds., *History of Woman Suffrage*, vol. 1 (Rochester, N.Y.: Charles Mann, 1881), p. 116. Sojourner Truth could neither read nor write, so Mrs. Frances D. Gage wrote down part of the speech. Mrs. Gage tried to capture Truth's unique dialect and speaking style in

her record, but that has been dropped here. Some feminists today have accused white suffragists of recording Truth's words in ways that best served their cause and in the process robbed her of her "authentic voice." See Rosalyn Terborg-Penn, 1998, for more on this debate. The most complete biography of Sojourner Truth is by Nell Irvin Painter, *Sojourner Truth: A Life, A Symbol* (New York: Norton, 1996). Painter has argued that Gage embellished Truth's oratory to create a feminist symbol. In fact, we will never know for sure what Sojourner Truth actually said at the Akron meeting (or at any other time in her life) since she could not write down her own thoughts and words.

8. Barbara Ryan, *Feminism and the Women's Movement: Dynamics of Change in Social Movement, Ideology, and Activism* (New York: Routledge, 1992).

9. Aileen S. Kraditor, *The Ideas of the Woman Suffrage Movement: 1890–1920* (New York: Norton, 1981).

10. Rosalyn Terborg-Penn, *African American Women in the Struggle for the Vote, 1850–1920* (Bloomington: Indiana University Press, 1998), p. 24.

11. Kraditor, *Ideas of the Woman Suffrage Movement*, p. 3.

12. Terborg-Penn, *African American Women in the Struggle for the Vote*, p. 26.

13. Lee Ann Banaszak, *Why Movements Succeed or Fail: Opportunity, Culture, and the Struggle for Woman Suffrage* (Princeton, N.J.: Princeton University Press, 1996). See also Ryan, *Feminism and the Women's Movement*, p. 20.

14. Terborg-Penn, *African American Women in the Struggle for the Vote*, p. 27.

15. Ibid.

16. Terborg-Penn wrote (in *African American Women in the Struggle for the Vote*, p. 34) that Stanton and Anthony eventually relented in the face of strong opposition to the anti-male stance taken by potential women members. She reported that although males were grudgingly admitted, no male was permitted to hold office in the organization.

17. Banaszak, *Why Movements Succeed or Fail*, p. 7.

18. Ibid., p. 8.

19. Barbara Sinclair Deckard, *The Women's Movement: Political, Socioeconomic, and Psychological Issues* (New York: HarperRow, 1983).

20. Banaszak, *Why Movements Succeed or Fail*, p. 8.

21. Terborg-Penn, *African American Women in the Struggle for the Vote*, p. 37.

22. Ibid., p. 38.

23. Terborg-Penn, *African American Women in the Struggle for the Vote*, p. 39.

24. Stanton, Anthony, and Gage, eds., *History of Woman Suffrage*, vol. 2.

25. Geoffrey C. Ward and Ken Burns, *Not For Ourselves Alone: The Story of Elizabeth Cady Stanton and Susan B. Anthony* (New York: Knopf, 1999), p. 144.

26. *Minor v. Happersett*, 88 US 162 (1875).

27. Ibid.

28. Eleanor Flexnor and Ellen Fitzpatrick, *Century of Struggle: The Women's Rights Movement in the United States* (Cambridge, Mass.: The President and Fellows of Harvard College, 1975), p. 256.

29. Ryan, *Feminism and the Women's Movement*, p. 28.

30. Ibid., p. 26.

31. Terborg-Penn, *African American Women in the Struggle for the Vote,* p. 91.

32. Ryan, *Feminism and the Women's Movement.*

33. Christine A. Lunardini, *From Equal Suffrage to Equal Rights: Alice Paul and the National Woman's Party, 1910–1928* (New York: New York University Press, 1986).

34. Ibid., p. 17.

35. Ibid., p. 29.

36. Ibid., p. 31.

37. Flexnor and Fitzpatrick, *Century of Struggle,* p. 275.

38. Ibid., p. 273.

39. Flexnor, 1975.

40. Flexnor and Fitzpatrick, *Century of Struggle,* p. 271.

41. Banaszak, *Why Movements Succeed or Fail,* p. 11.

42. Flexnor and Fitzpatrick, *Century of Struggle,* p. 315.

43. Ibid., p. 316.

44. Jane Jerome Camhi, *Women Against Women: American Anti-Suffragism, 1880–1920* (Brooklyn, N.Y.: Carlson Publishing, 1994), p. 111.

45. Susan B. Anthony and Ida Husted Harper, eds., *The History of Woman Suffrage,* vol. 4 (Rochester, N.Y.: Charles Mann, 1902), p. xxix.

46. Susan E. Marshall, *Splintered Sisterhood: Gender and Class in the Campaign against Woman Suffrage* (Madison: University of Wisconsin Press, 1997).

47. Ibid., p. 224.

48. Ibid., pp. 12–13.

49. Ibid., pp. 226–227.

50. Ibid., p. 229.

51. Nancy F. Cott, *The Grounding of Modern Feminism* (New Haven, Conn.: Yale University Press, 1987), p. 10.

52. Susan D. Becker, *The Origins of the Equal Rights Amendment: American Feminism Between the Wars* (Westport, Conn.: Greenwood Press, 1981).

53. Doris Stevens, *Jailed for Freedom: American Women Win the Vote,* ed. Carol O'Hare (1920; reprint, Troutdale, Ore.: New Sage Press, 1995).

54. Nancy Cott, "Across the Great Divide: Women in Politics Before and After 1920," in *Women Politics and Change,* eds. Louise A. Tilly and Patricia Gurin (New York: Russell Sage Foundation, 1990), pp. 153–176.

55. Marjorie Spruill Wheeler, ed., *One Woman, One Vote: Rediscovering the Woman Suffrage Movement* (Troutdale, Ore.: New Sage Press, 1995), p. 355.

56. Becker, *Origins of the Equal Rights Amendment,* p. 51.

57. Ibid.

58. Jane J. Mansbridge, *Why We Lost the ERA* (Chicago: University of Chicago Press, 1986), p. 9.

59. Ibid., p. 10.

60. Gilbert Y. Steiner, *Constitutional Inequality: The Political Fortunes of the Equal Rights Amendment* (Washington, D.C.: Brookings Institution, 1985), p. 13.

61. Ibid., p. 15.

62. For a more detailed account of the congressional debates over the ERA, see Mansbridge, *Why We Lost the ERA*, pp. 8–19; Steiner, *Constitutional Inequality*, pp. 1–25.

63. Steiner, *Constitutional Inequality*, p. 22.

64. Becker, *Origins of the Equal Rights Amendment*, p. 53.

65. Bureau of Labor Statistics, *Handbook of Labor Statistics*, 1989, Table 2; *Employment and Earnings*, January 1997, Table 2.

66. Cynthia B. Costello, Shari Miles, and Anne J. Stone, eds., *The American Woman: 1999–2000* (New York: Norton, 1998), p. 294.

67. Mansbridge, *Why We Lost the ERA*. See also, Mansbridge, "Organizing for the ERA: Cracks in the Façade of Unity," in *Women, Politics, and Change*, eds. Tilly and Gurin, pp. 323–338.

68. Mary Frances Berry, *Why ERA Failed: Politics, Women's Rights and the Amending Process of the Constitution* (Bloomington: Indiana University Press, 1986), pp. 2-3.

69. Donald G. Mathews and Jane Sherron DeHart, *Sex, Gender, and the Politics of the ERA: A State and the Nation* (New York: Oxford University Press, 1990).

70. Janet K. Boles, *The Politics of the Equal Rights Amendment: Conflict and the Decision Process* (New York: Longman, 1979).

71. Marshall, *Splintered Sisterhood*, p. 232.

72. Ibid., p. 235.

73. Ryan, *Feminism and the Women's Movement*, p. 33.

74. Kristi Anderson, *After Suffrage: Women in Partisan and Electoral Politics before the New Deal* (Chicago: University of Chicago Press, 1996), p. 50.

75. Virginia Sapiro, *Women in American Society*, 4th ed. (Mountain View, Calif.: Mayfield Publishing, 1999).

76. Mansbridge, *Why We Lost the ERA*, p. 35. See also, Mary Frances Berry, *Why ERA Failed: Politics, Women's Rights, and the Amending Process of the Constitution*.

77. David O. Sears and Leonie Huddy, "On the Origins of Political Disunity Among Women," in *Women Politics and Change*, eds. Tilly and Gurin, pp. 252–253.

78. Louise A. Tilly and Patricia Gurin, "Women, Politics, and Change," in *Women, Politics, and Change*, eds. Tilly and Gurin, pp. 24–26.

79. See Suzanne Lebsock, "Women and American Politics, 1880–1920," in *Women, Politics, and Change*, eds. Tilly and Gurin, pp. 35–62.

Suffrage Accomplished: Women as Political Participants

O NCE THE legal barrier to the ballot was removed, women entered the electorate slowly. By and large, they voted similarly to men, but initially in smaller numbers. This slow start led one commentator to declare that women's suffrage was a colossal failure. Women's suffrage was not a failure but rather a casualty of unrealistic expectations—both positive and negative. "Men said that woman suffrage had promised almost everything and accomplished almost nothing when neither of these were true."[1] The vote opened the door to the public sphere and a corresponding host of politically relevant activities. Now, nearly eighty years after gaining the vote, women are more likely than men to register to vote and to actually vote; they are as likely as men to engage in a whole range of extra-electoral activities. Women are, however, less likely than men to donate large sums of money to campaigns, to express interest in running for elective office, and to be recruited for office by political party elites. Also, the forces that attract women to politics are different from those that attract men. The vote did not, however, make women think alike, act alike, or view issues of gender equality similarly. As we saw in the previous chapter, women differ from one another along roughly the same social, economic, and political lines that divide men. These differences influence women's levels and types of political engagement. This chapter examines women's political participation in the electorate as voters, partisans, and members of political organizations. In the process we will analyze how women's participation differs from men's and how women differ from one another as they pursue gender equality through political participation.

When Did Your State Permit Women to Vote?

INFORMATION ON when women were included in the franchise by state is available at *http://www.gendergap.com*. This Web site, created and maintained by Marilyn Brown, offers a rich history of women's participation at the state level. For each of the fifty states, the site provides the year in which women were first able to vote and the circumstances of their admission to the franchise if the date came after ratification of the Nineteenth Amendment. The site also includes historical information about women from each state in public office, the state's support or opposition to the Equal Rights Amendment, and population demographics for each state. Other areas of the site cover electoral politics, women in the military, and issues dealing with the glass ceiling. This Web site is an excellent example of one woman's commitment to providing information on issues of gender equality.

WOMEN ENTER THE ELECTORATE AS VOTERS

After ratification of the Nineteenth Amendment, procedures had to be clarified before women could actually cast their ballots. For instance, states had to change their laws and practices to allow women to register, and the pace of change varied by region. Women in Mississippi and Georgia, for example, did not vote in the November 1920 election because the state registrars upheld the existing four-month residency requirement.[2] Because counties and states did not always keep records of voting registration rates and hardly ever noted the sex of the voter in their records, little data are available to evaluate women's suffrage during the first decade following ratification. As with other new groups of voters, it took time for women to develop voting habits, including accepting the idea that voting was appropriate behavior for women. Interviews with nonvoting women in Chicago conducted in 1923 found that more than 10 percent still believed it was *wrong* for a woman to vote.[3]

Although many attribute decreases in overall voter turnout rates during the 1920s to women entering the eligible electorate but not actually casting a ballot, some evidence contradicts that notion. It now seems just as likely that political parties experienced a de-aligning period during which partisans of both genders moved away from the existing political parties and were therefore not attracted to vote for a party's candidate.[4] Sophinisba Breckinridge conducted the first empirical study of women's political participation in 1933.[5] In *Women in the Twentieth Century*, Breckinridge examined registration rates of men and women in Illinois, the only state to keep records separated by sex. Between 1914[6] and 1931, women's registration rates in Chicago increased by 10 percent whereas men's decreased by the same percentage. The resulting "male advantage" in registration in 1931 was just 16 percent.[7]

Women Voters Outnumber Men at the Polls

By 1980 the gap in registration rates had narrowed considerably, with 80 percent of men and 77 percent of women registered to vote. Women's registration rates surpassed those of men in the 1984 election and have remained higher in every subsequent national election (see Table 3.1). Since 1980, the proportion of female voters has surpassed the proportion of male voters in every presidential election. In 1992, for example, 62.3 percent of voting-age women cast ballots compared to 60.2 percent of voting-age men. The absolute number of women voting has also been higher than that of men in every presidential election since 1964. In nonpresidential years, women have outvoted men since 1986. In the midterm election of 1994, labeled the "Year of the Angry White Male," 44.9 percent of women and 44.4 percent of men turned out. In the 1996 presidential election, 55.5 percent of voting-age women cast their vote, compared to 52.8 percent of men. In real numbers, more than 7 million more women cast votes than men did in the 1996 presidential contest.[8]

Estimates of men's and women's voting habits are generally based on post-election surveys. This methodology relies on individuals' correctly recalling whether they actually voted on election day. While remembering such information seems like a simple task, the considerable social pressure to fulfill one's civic duty to vote causes many people to misreport having voted thereby slightly inflating the turnout statistics. Evidence from vote validation studies has shown that men are slightly more likely to misreport voting than are women, making the gap between male and female turnout rates potentially even larger than reported.[9]

TABLE 3.1 Voter Registration: Number Reported They Are Registered Voters

	Women	Men
1996	67.9 million	59.6 million
1994	62.7 million	55.3 million
1992	67.3 million	59.3 million
1990	60.2 million	53.0 million
1988	63.4 million	55.1 million
1986	59.5 million	52.5 million
1984	62.1 million	54.0 million

Source: Center for American Women and Politics (CAWP), Eagleton Institute of Politics, Rutgers University

The gap between men and women at the polls varies depending on a number of socio-demographic characteristics, such as age, race, region of the country, and education. In recent years, women under forty-five years old voted at significantly higher rates than did men in the same age group. However, after fifty-five years of age, the percentage of women voting declined while the percentage of male voters held steady, thus reversing the gender advantage seen in younger age cohorts. For example, among citizens between the ages of sixty-five and seventy-four, 67 percent of the men reported voting compared to only 61.3 percent of women in the 1994 election.[10] Researchers are not sure why women's participation tends to decline after age fifty-five when arguably they would have more, not less, resources and time to dedicate to politics. Among African American voters, the gender gap in voter turnout has been consistently larger than in the population at large. In 1994, for example, 38.2 percent of black women voted compared to 35.5 percent of black men. This gap is 2.1 points larger than that of the entire population. In the South, where states were slow to admit women to the voting population even after the federal amendment was ratified, the gender gap was largest prior to the election of 1970. In 1964, the gender gap in the South was nearly double that of the rest of the nation. More recently regional disparities have largely disappeared. Among those with an elementary-school education, males vote at higher rates than women do. However, a high-school diploma reverses the gap with women voting at higher rates than similarly educated men. Among those who have some college or a college degree, men and women report voting at roughly the same rates.[11]

Other factors beyond gender influence a person's decision to vote or to abstain. Since voter turnout in the United States is consistently lower than in most other developed nations, researchers have studied the motives and behaviors of voters for several decades to answer: Why *don't* people vote? To cast a ballot, citizens must register to vote, which often means navigating a complex bureaucratic process. The 1993 National Voter Registration Act (NVRA), also known as "Motor Voter," made registering somewhat easier. The NVRA requires states to allow citizens to register to vote at the same time they do other business with the state, such as register a car, renew a driver's license, or apply for some forms of government benefits. Although this program registered more people and created a slightly more diverse voter pool in terms of education, age, and race, the effects of the NVRA on actual voter turnout are not as great as had once been predicted.

Political scientists have also investigated why people *do* vote. After years of investigation and countless theories, the answer remains a mystery. Some political scientists posit that citizens undertake a rational calculation of the costs and benefits of voting. If the benefits outweigh the costs, the people appear at the polls. However, the benefits one person derives are difficult to determine since, according to some calculations, a voter is more likely to be struck by lightning on the way to the polls than it is for that person's vote to change an election's outcome.[12] So the benefits of voting are more often such intangibles as altruism or a sense of duty fulfilled. The costs vary, depending on an individual's circumstances. For women, the costs may be higher than for men since women are still considered the primary caregivers to children and elderly parents and are more likely to have jobs with less flexible schedules or that pay on an hourly basis, all of which affect the time that women have to go to the polls. And yet, women vote at higher rates than men, so other factors must be at work. Most likely, voting is a standing decision or a habit that individuals develop as they join communities and become integrated into the social and political life of their communities. Voting, in this context, is an act of social participation or civic involvement. In general, voters are connected to the larger society and to their communities in ways that nonvoters are not.[13] Women have a history of community-based involvement, and this tradition may help explain why women are more likely to vote than men.

Twenty-Something Citizens

Among young men and women between the ages of 20 and 29, the female advantage holds in voter-turnout statistics (see Table 3.2). Yet when first-year college students were asked about the importance of influencing the political structure, only 18.5 percent of men and 13.9 percent of women felt that voting was essential or very important (see Table 3.3). Similarly, 30 percent of college-age males and only 19 percent of college-age females said that they visited a campaign's Web site. The electronic gap also extends to contacting public officials. Forty-three percent of men and 31 percent of women of the same demographic said they used e-mail to contact Congress in the last year.[14]

TABLE 3.2 Percentages of Young Women and Men Voting 1978–1996

	Ages 20–24		Ages 25–29		All Ages	
	Women	Men	Women	Men	Women	Men
1996	36.1	30.7	43.7	36.5	55.5	52.8
1994	23.8	20.3	28.7	27.4	63.2	60.8
1992	47.2	42.1	52.8	46.8	62.3	60.2
1990	22.2	21.1	31.1	27.0	45.4	44.6
1988	39.7	35.8	46.0	41.2	58.3	56.4
1986	24.7	22.6	31.7	29.8	46.1	45.8
1984	44.6	41.0	53.3	48.2	60.8	59.0
1982	26.7	27.8	37.2	35.1	48.4	48.7
1980	43.9	40.4	52.4	50.0	59.4	59.1
1978	26.1	25.3	34.0	33.3	45.3	46.6

Source: Center for American Women and Politics (CAWP), Eagleton Institute of Politics, Rutgers University

TABLE 3.3 Percentages of First-Year College Students Who Consider It Essential or Very Important that They Influence the Political Structure

	(%) Women	(%) Men	Male Advantage
1998	13.9	18.5	4.6
1996	15.4	20.6	5.2
1994	17.5	20.0	2.5
1992	18.5	21.9	3.4
1990	18.6	22.9	4.3
1988	14.2	19.8	5.6
1986	12.3	17.1	4.8
1984	12.4	17.9	5.5
1982	11.7	18.1	6.4
1980	12.6	20.1	7.5
1978	11.4	17.9	6.5
1976	11.7	18.5	6.8
1974	9.6	15.3	5.7

Source: Center for American Women and Politics (CAWP), Eagleton Institute of Politics, Rutgers University

A spring 2000 study of young people between the ages of 18 and 24 conducted by the White House Project Education Fund supported the connection between community involvement and voting, particularly among women. Forty-one percent of men and 55 percent of women reported being very or somewhat involved in their communities and with issues important to those communities. Women, however, volunteered at significantly higher rates than men did. Twenty-eight percent of the young women and only 19 percent of men reported volunteering at least a couple of times a month. Of the women who frequently volunteered, 43 percent had parents who voted in every election, 34 percent reported that they themselves would probably vote, and 30 percent were registered to vote. For those least involved in their communities, 15 percent of the young women said they were not likely to vote, 21 percent were not registered voters, and 21 percent had parents who did not vote.[15]

THE GENDER GAP

Pick up a daily newspaper during the months preceding an election, and you'll find evidence that journalists and politicians alike perceive the *gender gap* to be a powerful political phenomenon.[16] The gender gap is said to exist when women as a group vote significantly different from men. The term originated during the 1980 presidential election when the victor, Republican Ronald Reagan, ran a campaign dominated by his opposition to the Equal Rights Amendment and to abortion and his support of "traditional family values," which many interpreted as a return to traditional roles for women. The Republican Party's continuing affinity for these themes is presumed to have alienated many women voters throughout the 1990s.[17]

The gender gap should be calculated by subtracting the percentage of men who voted for a particular candidate from the percentage of women who voted for the same candidate (or vice versa), not by looking at how one candidate did among either women or men alone. Although after 1980, the gender gap referred to the greater likelihood of women's voting for a Democratic Party candidate, a candidate cannot be said to have lost an election because she or he lost the "women's vote." Conceptually, when a single candidate fares well against her opponent among female voters, for example, her opponent fares equally well among male voters. "By definition, the Republicans' 'problem with women' is exactly the same size as the Democrats' 'problem with men'."[18] Since the size of the gender gap in the last two presidential contests and in a number of high-profile congressional races was larger than the margin of victory, women have become the target of appeals by both parties designed to attract female voters. The Center for American Women and Politics (CAWP) estimates that the gender gap affected thirteen of the races in the 1998 midterm elections. Five Democratic victors benefited from women's votes, and eight Republican winners owed their victories to men.[19] Similarly, the Feminist Majority Foundation estimates that Al Gore received 54 percent of the female vote, but only 42 percent of the male vote, creating a twelve-point gender gap in the 2000 presidential contest. The Foundation also estimates that women voters delivered all five of the U.S. Senate races in which Democrats picked up seats

TABLE 3.4 Voter Choice for Recent Presidential Elections

1996	Women	Men
Bill Clinton	54%	43%
Bob Dole	38%	44%
Ross Perot	7%	10%
1992		
Bill Clinton	45%	41%
George Bush	37%	38%
Ross Perot	17%	21%

Source: Center for American Women and Politics (CAWP), Eagleton Institute of Politics, Rutgers University

in 2000. For example, Debbie Stabenow of Michigan won a close race with an eleven-point gender gap. Similarly, Bill Nelson of Florida enjoyed an eleven-point advantage among women voters; Thomas Carper of Delaware won with a twelve-point gender gap; Mark Dayton won the Minnesota Senate seat with a nine-point gap; and Mel Carnahan posthumously won the Missouri Senate seat with a six-point gender gap. In each of these races, the surplus of women's votes made up for less than a majority of men's votes.[20]

The contemporary gender gap generally ranges from 7 to 12 percentage points in congressional elections and hovers at about 6 percentage points on average in presidential contests. President Clinton enjoyed a significantly larger gender gap in both 1992 and 1996. The impact of the gender gap, therefore, depends wholly on the proportion of men and women voting in any single election. As noted earlier, women have been turning out in both higher proportions and larger numbers than men have in recent elections, making a gender gap favoring women a determining force in the outcome of these elections. The 1996 presidential contest attracted attention in this regard since the gender gap was estimated at 14 percentage points—the largest since World War II—and increased by 40 percent compared to the male-female difference in the 1992 vote. It is important to remember though, that gender differences do not make up the largest gap within the electorate. The gap created by race (consistently 50 points between whites and blacks) and economic differences (19 points between the rich and poor in 1994) in voting behavior far surpasses gender in size, if not in significance. The gender gap attracts media attention because a political "war of the sexes" is more socially acceptable than competition between the races or economic classes.

The Source of the Gender Gap

The definitive source of the gender gap continues to elude scholars, but evidence supports a number of theories. Some attribute the gap to the changing employment circumstances and attitudes of women,[21] while others attribute the male-female difference to the changing politics of men.[22] More broadly, scholars explain the different candidate preferences of men and women as differences in policy preferences, most especially those regarding government social welfare spending and the importance of a government "safety net." Additionally, "women's issues," such as abortion and women's rights, along with "men's issues," such as the use of force and military expansion, have been investigated as root causes of the gender gap. Perceptions of the economy, either in general (most important to women) or in regard to an individual's personal finances (most salient to men) have been shown to differ by gender.[23] In the 2000 election, the Feminist Majority Foundation estimates that the gender gap was fueled by issues like abortion rights, gun control, military spending, women's rights, and human services.[24] However, even when men and women hold the same policy positions, the levels of salience may differ to the extent that a single issue may determine the vote for one sex, while being relatively unimportant to the other sex's final decision. This is most evident in the issue of abortion. While men and women do not differ significantly in their relative positions on abortion policy, the salience of the issue acts as a political mobilizing force for women, but not for men.[25] Most likely, it is some combination of these various theories that account for the gender gap.

In analyzing presidential elections between 1980 and 1992, political scientists Carole Kennedy Chaney, R. Michael Alvarez, and Jonathan Nagler developed a model based on multiple differences in the political preferences of men and women. Men and women constitute distinctive and separate voting blocs on issues of compassion, feminism, and use of force. Additionally, women are more supportive of an expanded role for government in providing a safety net, presumably because they are more apt to find themselves and their dependents financially vulnerable. These researchers attribute policy gender differences to socio-psychological forces that have a different impact on men than they have on women. Women's comparative aversion to using force and their greater likelihood to base economic evaluations on the health of the national economy rather than on the state of their own wallets can be attributed to gender socialization and women's concern for the welfare of others over their own self-interest.[26] Interestingly, partisanship does not independently contribute to the gap between men and women. This research suggests that the Republican leadership's efforts to attract women by making women politicians more visible (e.g., by appointing or electing women to party leadership positions or by nominating a woman to be the vice presidential candidate) are not likely to close the gender gap—that is, not without making significant changes in the Republican party's issue positions.

GENDER DIFFERENCES IN POLITICAL PARTICIPATION BEYOND THE BALLOT

One unique feature of the U.S. political system is the sheer number of opportunities to engage in political activity apart from elections. For our purposes, we can define *political participation* as "activity that has the intent or effect of influencing government action—either directly by affecting the making or implementation of public policy or indirectly by influencing the selection of people who make those policies."[27] For example, an individual might work on a campaign, contribute funds to candidates or an important cause, serve on a local board or commission, contact public officials, join political or interest-based organizations, or volunteer for a community-based organization. Some forms of participation require resources, whereas others ask for nothing more than interest. Passionate interest sometimes results in protests or other unconventional forms of participation. Women who petitioned for suffrage rights engaged in protests to attract attention in the absence of power and access to other important political resources. Political participation is not equally distributed throughout the population. Ironically, those who stand to benefit the most from working on a cause or for a candidate (e.g., the poor, minorities, women), often participate less frequently than others. Conventional wisdom holds that women participate beyond the ballot box at lower rates than men do. However, a closer examination reveals that if demographic characteristics are held constant, men and women participate at roughly equal levels across many, but not all, forms of political activity.

Do Men and Women Specialize in Forms of Political Participation?

In the largest study of its kind, political scientists Sidney Verba, Kay Schlozman, and Henry Brady surveyed more than 15,000 Americans by telephone and then interviewed more than 2,500 citizens in person to understand voluntary civic participation.[28] The researchers used the data to compare men's and women's behavior in traditional political activity and other forms of volunteerism to test the hypothesis that men and women specialize in different types of political engagement. In examining political participation,[29] they found that women engaged in an average of 2.0 political acts, while men undertook 2.3, a minor but statistically significant difference.[30] In other words, generally men are slightly more actively involved in traditional forms of political engagement than are women. More substantively important differences appear in specific acts. The largest differences appear in making a campaign contribution, contacting a government official, and affiliating with a political organization. In each case, men are more likely than women to have engaged in these political activities.[31]

The picture is slightly different for nonpolitical voluntary activities, but perhaps not as different as we might have expected. For nearly two centuries, women have participated at the periphery of politics through community and religious organizations. However, the data here shows that men and women engage in about the same number of nonpolitical activities with a few notable exceptions. Women are more likely than men to attend church and donate their time and money to the church. However, once men and women get involved, the amount of time and money given is significantly different. Men give more hours to the church than women do, whereas women give more hours to politics than men do. When it comes to money though, compared to women, men contribute more frequently and are likely to contribute larger sums of money to both the church and to political causes and candidates. This raises the resource question.

Access to Monetary and Political Resources

Do men have access to more monetary resources and do they use those resources to greater political effect than women? Political scientists do not have
a complete answer to this question. Research has shown that the propensity to
give and the amount contributed depend on both the total family income and
the portion of family income derived from the respondent's income. Women's
mean family income is lower than men's, and women's personal share of the
family income is lower even in cases where both spouses work outside the
home. Most often clustered in lower-paying jobs, women have less money to
give to the candidates and causes they support. Democratic consultant Nikki
Heidepriem observes:

> Women tend to give in smaller amounts, and they give ideologically. They give for
> abortion rights or because they want to see someone fighting for Anita Hill. Men
> tend to give for economic reasons, with an eye on the bottom line. The big money
> comes from entrepreneurs and corporate types who do business in Washington, and
> they tend not to be women.[32]

Money is only one type of resource though; others include time and civic skills.
Men and women in the Verba, Schlozman, and Brady civic-participation study
had roughly the same number of free hours per week, although among full-
time workers and full-time workers with preschool children, men had an average of 24 more free minutes per week than women did. Essentially, this
suggests that life and family circumstances, not gender, determine the time
available for civic activity. With respect to skills, the researchers included civic
skills acquired on the job, through organizational affiliation, and through
church membership. Among those working outside the home and those affiliated with an organization or church, altogether, men have significantly more
opportunity to practice civic skills on the job than women do. In other settings,
there are no differences between men and women. " . . . [M]en's advantage
with respect to civic skills exercised on the job results from a process by which
men have differential access to jobs that require education and training and not
from differential access to skill opportunities in these jobs."[33]

In translating the role that resources play in laying a path to political participation, the researchers found that by and large men and women do not significantly differ in how they engage in politics. Voluntary organizational
involvement is an important avenue for women, particularly for women who
do not work outside the home. This finding confirms the historical role voluntary associations have played for women in politics. The most striking finding,
however, has to do with monetary resources. Women have less money than
men, and less control over the money in their households, disadvantaging them
in an increasingly important form of political activity: making political contributions. The wage gap between men and women is well known; but less well

TABLE 3.5 Men's and Women's Civic Participation

	Women	Men
Political Participation		
Worked on a campaign	8%	9%
Attended a protest	6%	6%
Made a campaign contribution	20%	27%*
Contacted a government official	30%	38%*
Affiliated with a political organization	44%	53%*
Nonpolitical Participation		
Affiliated with a nonpolitical organization	68%	68%
Gave time to charity	39%	36%
Attended church services once/month or more	62%	50%*
Gave time to religious activity	31%	24%*
Made a contribution to church	69%	55%*

*Statistically significant difference between men and women at .01 level.
Source: Kay Lehman Schlozman, Nancy Burns, and Sidney Verba, "Gender and the Pathways to Participation: The Role of Resources," *The Journal of Politics* 56, no. 4 (1994): 969–971.

known is the way in which the household economic gap exacerbates inequalities in political activity.[34]

Do Men And Women Speak in Different Political Voices?

From the same citizen participation data set described above, the same researchers investigated whether men and women speak "in a different voice" when it comes to politics.[35] Do men and women follow their respective *voices* by undertaking particularized political action? Verba, Schlozman, and Brady also investigated the type of rewards men and women received from their political participation. This research is significant because it connects attitudes with action. Previous studies have only examined this connection among political elites, such as officeholders or political-party officials. We know, for example, that female legislators' distinctive attitudes are reflected in their choice of legislative priorities and roll-call voting behavior, most notably in sponsoring and promoting legislation dealing with women, children, and the family.[36]

Among the citizenry at large, however, the researchers found that men and women are more similar than dissimilar. Again, conventional generalizations can be misleading in this regard. Gender exercised little direct pressure on defining political voice, rewards gained through participation, or issues that mobilized participation. Rather, race and ethnicity, level of education, and family circumstances—like the presence of school-aged children—were most powerful for both men and women. The differences that exist between men and women are not always predictable. For example, women have historically engaged most directly in grassroots, organizational, and local activities, but researchers were surprised to learn that at least in 1990 (the year in which this survey was conducted), women were often less locally and organizationally focused than men. Men and women gained similar gratifications from political participation. While voting was motivated by civic gratifications, activities involving campaigns were more likely driven by social motivations. In short, researchers found that across genders, the nature of the act rather than the sex of the actor determined the type of gratification experienced. Finally, researchers hypothesized that men and women would be moved by different issues. From a list of eleven issues mentioned by respondents as important in motivating their participation, men and women differed substantially on only two: education and abortion. For women, concern about education motivated 20 percent of their issue-based activity, compared to 13 percent for men. The issue of abortion motivated 14 percent of women's activity, compared to 8 percent of men's activity. Gaps between the advantaged and disadvantaged and among racial and ethnic groups surpassed gender gaps in almost every case. With regard to children and family issues, previous findings led researchers to hypothesize that women would be moved more directly than men by issues related to children. However, for both men and women, action was prompted by having school-aged children in the home rather than by the respondent's gender. In short, this research cautions that expectations about citizen participation based on gender can best be understood by looking at the complex relational webs that define people's lives. Race, ethnicity, socioeconomic status, and family circumstances are greater predictors of motivation, gratification, and issue interests than gender alone.

Levels of Political Interest Among Men and Women

Researchers have long believed that interest motivates political activity.[37] Women in previous generations were conditioned to believe that politics was a "man's world" and therefore beyond the scope of their interest. Perhaps this legacy continues even today. Significant gaps in interest and attentiveness to politics remain between men and women. In analysis based on the 1989 American National Election Study, for example, 61 percent of men, as opposed to only 45 percent of women, reported that they followed politics some or most of the time. In 1996, 74 percent of women, compared to 59 percent of men, said they sometimes did not feel competent to understand public affairs. Interestingly, statistically controlling for differences in level of education between men and women does not eliminate this gap in perceived political competence. Actually, the gap is greatest among college-educated people! Sixty-one percent of college-educated women but only 36 percent of similarly educated men find politics too complicated to understand, according to a March 2000 study conducted by researchers at the University of Pennsylvania's Annenberg Public Policy Center.[38]

At the root of this gender difference may lie a political knowledge gap. Researchers remain puzzled as to why women answer fewer questions on political knowledge correctly than men. This gap continues as recently as the 2000 primary elections. Using a national sample of adults, researchers at the Annenberg Center asked thirteen questions about the major presidential candidates' backgrounds and their positions on issues to test political knowledge during the 2000 primary campaign. In addition to analyzing the number of correct answers, researchers also paid attention to how often respondents answered incorrectly or stated that they did not know an answer. Previous research on political knowledge found that women were more likely than men to answer that they did not know an answer, while men more often answered questions correctly. In the Annenberg survey, men were more likely to answer correctly, whereas women were more likely to answer incorrectly *and* to state that they did not know an answer. The knowledge deficit for women persisted even when several sociodemographic variables, such as level of education, age, race, income, marital status, party identification, and media exposure, were statistically controlled. Simply being male added one correct answer out of the thirteen knowledge items in the scale.[39]

EXPLAINING THE PATTERNS OF PARTICIPATION

The patterns of political participation present us with a puzzle: Women vote at higher rates than men do, but men exhibit more interest in and attentiveness to national politics and demonstrate more knowledge about politics than women. Among other forms of political participation, gender does not appear to exert a more significant influence than other factors related to a person's life circumstances. There are a variety of plausible explanations for the lingering gender differences in politics, including the power of socialization, real and perceived structural barriers to participation, and cultural counterpressures.

Socialization

The role of socialization is best characterized by Simone de Beauvoir's claim that "Women are made and not born."[40] Socialization is the process by which we, first as children and later as adults, learn and internalize the values, norms, and expectations of the culture and society around us. Gender socialization is the process by which girls and boys learn to differentiate between the sexes and act according to the norms and expectations appropriate to their sex. As early as five years old, most children understand gender differentiation. Along with understanding that boys/men differ from girls/women biologically, children internalize the images of power and the sense of importance that separate the genders. Very quickly they describe the sexual hierarchy they see around them as *natural* or *normal*.[41] Thus when boys show a stronger preference for "boys'" toys and same-sex playmates, researchers link their preference to the effects of this gender stratification.[42] Further, girls are more likely to wish that they were boys than the reverse. Researcher Ann Beuf asked sixty-three children, ages three to six, what they would do if they grew up as the opposite sex. More girls had answers, meaning that they had already thought about the possibility. The boys didn't even want to answer the question. "That's a weird question, you know," one replied. When another boy was pressed, he said, "If I were a girl, I'd have to grow up to be nothing."[43] In similar research conducted by Myra Sadker and David Sadker, 42 percent of girls saw positive outcomes in becoming a boy, whereas 95 percent of the boys saw no advantage whatsoever in becoming a girl. In fact, for 16 percent of the boys interviewed, becoming a girl was so unacceptable that they fantasized about committing suicide. In the words of one boy, "I would stab myself in the heart fifty times with a dull butter knife."[44] At a very young age, children have already learned about the gendered world including which gender is more valued by society. How do they learn the rules of gender hierarchy so quickly?

Gendered norms and expectations are communicated in a variety of ways. According to socialization research, *agents of socialization,* such as the family, school, peers, religion, and the media, play a role in shaping children's attitudes toward, knowledge of, and behavior in both gender and political roles. Early research on children and political learning found that the family transmitted the earliest messages about authority. In two-parent households, more prevalent in the 1950s and early 1960s when this research was conducted, the father was labeled the authority figure, and he was assumed to transmit political information to his children. It was further assumed that if a father was absent, children's political sophistication would suffer. A study of college students in the 1980s, however, examined the impact of family structure and found that it exerted little independent influence on students' political attitudes and voting predilections.[45] Experiences in school reinforce the norms of democratic society. By high school, civics classes transmit specific political information to adolescents. Studies of textbooks have consistently found males depicted as the primary figures in political life, while females are rarely mentioned. When Ann Richards, former governor of Texas, was asked about the historical significance of her governorship, she replied that beyond any policy change she might facilitate, her picture would appear in textbooks and offer a role model for girls to emulate.[46]

Gendered behavior is further encouraged through play with "appropriate" toys. Toy stores are shockingly clear in color-coding "boy" and "girl" aisles (in pink and blue, of course) and choosing displays ("hands-on" versus "look, don't touch"). Social psychologists confirm that children are equally serious about maintaining the separation, "One fourth-grade male reported that if he saw a boy playing with a doll, 'I'd yell at him first, but if he didn't stop, I'd punch him in the nose and call the police'."[47]

Governments are interested in learning about political socialization because of its power to maintain stable political systems. Socialization processes may also reinforce and maintain patriarchal gender relations. Research done in the 1960s is now criticized for the way in which it interpreted differences between boys and girls on measures of political interest, knowledge, and political awareness. Researchers, presumably viewing the data through their own gendered expectations, overestimated the size and significance of differences between primary-school boys and girls.[48] Additionally, the main body of political socialization research suggested that adult political behavior was a direct result of early childhood experiences, overlooking the possibility of change later in life. Only recently have researchers lengthened the time of observation to in-

A role model? The White House Project, Girls, Inc., and Mattel launched the Barbie for President doll in April 2000. The doll is accompanied by a Girl's Bill of Rights, created by Girls Inc., inspiring girls to be "strong, smart, and bold." *T. Levette Bagwell/Atlanta Journal-Constitution.*

clude adult experiences, such as those in the workplace, as well as the power of social, political, and economic events to reshape attitudes and behaviors.

Since politics in its traditional forms is limited to adults, how might gender socialization translate to political activity? Children learn through imitation, modeling, and apprenticeship opportunities. The study by the White House Project Education Fund, cited earlier, found that the young men and women who are most engaged in politics are also involved and invested in their communities. They come from families in which their parents model civic behavior by voting. These young people are more likely to be registered to vote than those who are least involved in their communities. The men and women in this study who indicate an interest in someday seeking political office themselves are those who have gained leadership experience through school or other apprentice organizations, have been encouraged to run by adults or peers, and are the most likely to believe that they can make a positive difference and the least likely to find politics too complicated.[49] The research suggests that providing girls with role models, mentors, and opportunities to practice politics before they reach adulthood makes a positive difference in women's interest and political ambition. One initiative in this regard that draws ridicule from some quarters and praise from others is the "Barbie for President" doll, released in April 2000 by Mattel in conjunction with the White House Project and Girls, Inc. Each doll comes with a copy of the White House Project's Girls' Action Agenda, which encourages girls to pursue leadership in their schools, communities, and homes.[50]

Structural Barriers to Women's Participation

Political scientists have long confirmed that certain characteristics make some citizens more likely to participate in politics than others. Education, for example, followed by income, and certain occupations are good relative predictors of the frequency and types of citizen participation. Since women lag behind men on several economic indicators and have only recently matched men on years of formal education, lingering barriers to women's full participation remain, reinforcing the gaps found between male and female participation. One additional factor distinguishes women from one another: gender consciousness, or a feminist identity.

A group consciousness that ties an individual woman's interests to those of other women and provides an outlet for her discontent over gender inequities has been found to facilitate women's participation and to set those women apart from others.[51] Feminist consciousness may be shaped by generational forces. Those who come of age during eras of active public feminism—for example, those who turned 18 during the early 1970s (the start of the second wave of feminism) or during the Clinton administration in the 1990s—are not only more likely to develop feminist consciousness, but also to act on it by supporting collective action advocating feminist policies. Those who come of age in more conservative periods (e.g., the Reagan administration) may also support feminist policies, but are less likely to develop a feminist consciousness leading to support for and engagement in collective action.[52]

Additional research examining the relationship of feminist identity and group consciousness to political attitudes and policy positions finds that feminists differ significantly from nonfeminists. Analysis based on the 1992 National Election Study revealed that women categorized as feminists were more likely than other women to support increased federal spending for child care, unemployment benefits, environmental and welfare programs, and programs to address homelessness, public schools, and urban problems.[53] Nonfeminists were significantly more likely to support additional spending on the military to maintain the United States as a military power. Differences also exist with respect to women's positions on abortion and sexual harassment, with the majority of feminists supporting choice positions and nonfeminists opposing abortion. The 1992 study also found that significantly more feminists than nonfeminists believed that sexual harassment in the workplace is a serious problem for women. A majority of all the women believed that too little was being done to protect women from harassment. Fifty-three percent of nonfeminists and 68 percent of feminists reported that they would be more likely to believe the woman in a case of conflicting stories about sexual harassment.

Feminist consciousness also appears to motivate some types of political participation. For example, feminists are more likely to vote than nonfeminists. During the 1992 presidential election, 41 percent of feminists and only 33 percent of nonfeminists reported that they were very interested in the campaign. Interest led feminists to participate in campaigns at higher rates than nonfeminists and to exhibit a higher level of interest in politics overall.[54]

Cultural Messages: Counterpressures to Political Activity

Among the many potential barriers to women's participation are the daily messages present in popular culture and directed at shaping women's identity, expectations, ambitions, and habits. As we learned above, women remain less interested in politics and less knowledgeable about politics than men even in 2000, nearly 80 years after wining the vote. Powerful socialization forces in the nineteenth and early twentieth centuries led women to believe that politics was better left to men.[55] However, contemporary media images of women in politics may be sending the message that women are "damned if they do, and damned if they don't." In October 1992, Deborah Tannen, best known for her work on gender differences in communication styles, wrote an article for the op-ed page of the *New York Times*. In it, she addressed the "Hillary Factor." The term was originally coined to refer to the question of whether Hillary Rodham Clinton would help or hurt her husband Bill Clinton's chances to win the presidency. Tannen, however, took the term one step further, saying it represented the double bind that affects accomplished women who do not fit the stereotype of femininity and the expectations of motherhood. When, for example, the Clintons acted to protect their daughter's privacy by shielding her from the press, they were surprised to learn that a majority of Americans thought they were childless and held Hillary Clinton responsible for that misconception. The "Motherhood Bind" has an impact on all women. As Tannen describes it, "If you're not a Mother, you're a Failed Woman. If you are a Mother, you can't have enough attention to pay to serious work. If you are paying attention to serious work, you must be a Bad Mother."[56] She goes on: "By what logic could it be scary rather than comforting for a president's wife, who everyone knows will have his ear, to be unusually intelligent, knowledgeable and accomplished? And to answer: by no logic at all. The hope was to incite emotions—fear and anger—that confront women who do not conform to the old molds."

Women face a variety of cultural expectations that may vary depending on a woman's physical appearance, race, or ethnicity. In each case, men do not have the same expectations placed on them, and in each case there are significant political implications for women as a result. Ambrose Bierce once wrote, "To men a man is but a mind. Who cares what face he carries or what he wears? But woman's body is the woman."[57] Although Bierce wrote this passage in 1958, consumer-spending statistics suggest his words still ring true. In 1990 alone, women spent well over $1.2 billion on elective cosmetic surgery, and more than $20 billion on cosmetics. The standards of beauty differ across cultures and vary over time, but women are universally expected to aspire to the current standards of beauty in ways that men are not. Men are referred to as *handsome*, connoting achievement and strength. Such terms do not accompany *beautiful*, which is applied only to females, scenes, or objects. This common terminology leads one set of researchers to conclude, "Men are instrumental; women are ornamental."[58] These observations and statistics would be trivial if not for their consequences on how individuals are judged. In a classic 1972 study entitled, "What is Beautiful is Good," psychologists asked college students to rate photographs of strangers on a variety of personal qualities. Those who were judged attractive were also more likely to be characterized as intelligent, flexible, interesting, confident, assertive, strong, outgoing, friendly, poised, and successful than those considered unattractive. Women are judged more harshly than men.[59] The same attributions are made when considering candidates seeking public office.

The media facilitate the public's attention to appearance by focusing on female candidates' hairstyles and the color or design of their clothes rather than on the content of their message. Bush campaign operative Mary Matalin described it this way, "Women in politics who look chic are perceived as frivolous. If you're pulled together that means you've been shopping . . . instead of laboring over papers . . . fifteen hours a day. . . . Besides, every woman who looks good gets hit on, and after a while they just don't want to be hassled."[60] Josie Heath, a 1990 and 1992 Democratic senatorial candidate from Colorado, claimed that she could describe her wardrobe during that period by reading her press clippings.[61] Following the 2000 presidential election, Katherine Harris, Florida's secretary of state who was responsible for several significant decisions affecting the state's presidential ballot count, became the object of public ridicule based on her appearance. The *Washington Post* noted that Harris's lipstick was of "the creamy sort that smears all over a coffee cup and leaves smudges on shirt collars," that she "applied her makeup with a trowel," and compared the texture of her skin to that of a plastered wall.[62]

Similar to attractiveness, race and ethnicity modify expectations as well. Scholar Patricia Hill Collins writes that, "[P]ortraying African American women as stereotypical mammies, matriarchs, welfare recipients, and hot mommas has been essential to the political economy of domination fostering Black women's oppression. Challenging these controlling images has long been a core theme in Black feminist thought."[63] Leaders in the women's movement were relatively silent during the congressional debate over welfare reform even when the tone and content became a thinly veiled racist attack on poor, single mothers. African American women lag behind white women in winning legislative seats at both the state and the federal level.[64] Part of the reason is the lingering belief that black women are not serious and credible candidates.[65] To overcome this hurdle, more women of color need to seek and hold office, but the obstacles to public office are substantial. Money constitutes a barrier for many women, but particularly for women of color. Beyond money, many minority women have little public exposure beyond their immediate communities, yet they face resistance even within their own communities. As Shirley Chisholm said, "Black males feel that the political seats are owed to them because of historical circumstances; therefore, opportunities should redound to them first of all."[66] The Center for American Women and Politics at Rutgers recently partnered with the National Organization of Black Elected Legislative Women (NOBEL) to develop a leadership and training program for African American women interested in pursuing elected and appointive office.[67]

Asian American women, Latina women, and Native American women have also been slow to ascend to public life. Besides having to overcome the previously described barriers, women in these groups (especially Asian and Latina women) face cultural expectations that limit their role to the home and family. Native American women, although historically active in tribal politics and fully integrated in many tribal systems of governance, have only recently explored public life beyond their community of origin. Without role models to give voice to their concerns, women of color are also less likely to be involved in electoral politics as voters.

MOBILIZING WOMEN'S POLITICAL PARTICIPATION

As this chapter has shown, men and women approach politics similarly and from different perspectives depending on the activity and on the individual's life circumstances. While women vote at higher rates than men do, women remain less likely to donate money to a candidate, participate in political organizations, or seek elective office themselves. This chapter concludes by examining three factors that may increase women's political participation: events and issues, organizations that target women, and the role of political parties.

Political Events and Issues Stimulate Interest and Raise Gender Consciousness

Although many factors combined to make 1992 an especially good year for women in politics, two distinctly mobilizing events stand out: the Clarence Thomas Supreme Court confirmation hearings and the Tailhook scandal.

On July 1, 1991, President Bush nominated Clarence Thomas to fill a vacancy on the U.S. Supreme Court. By October 6, 1991, the Senate Judiciary Committee had already voted to forward Thomas's nomination to the full Senate for a vote. On that date, however, Nina Totenberg, of National Public Radio, alleged that the committee had suppressed allegations of sexual harassment against Thomas brought by a University of Oklahoma law professor, Anita Hill. Hill had worked for Thomas at the Equal Employment Opportunity Commission (EEOC), the federal agency that enforces antidiscrimination policy. On October 8, Democratic congresswomen marched from the House to the Senate to demand an investigation. The Senate relented, and new hearings were called with Anita Hill as the primary witness. Her testimony before the Senate Judiciary Committee was televised giving many voters, particularly female voters, their first glimpse at the all-male, all-white committee. Interest in the hearings was incredibly intense. Senator Paul Simon reported receiving nearly 20,000 letters on the subject, compared to fewer than 16,000 on the Gulf War. Millions watched the televised hearings, which had a larger audience than the NFL games that were on at the same time.[68] Women were outraged at what they saw and what many perceived as the unfair and condescending treatment of Hill. Tee shirts proclaiming "I Believe Anita Hill," "He did it," and "She Lied" sprang up across the country. A full episode of a prime-time sitcom, *Designing Women,* was dedicated to the controversy. After the show's airing, CBS received more than fifteen hundred, mostly positive, phone calls—the largest number in the network's history in response to a single show.[69]

Sexual harassment as an issue separated men from women in many ways. Women, regardless of race or class, shared experiences similar in nature, if not in severity, to those described by Anita Hill. It appeared clear to even the most uneducated in fair-trial norms, that the deck was stacked against Hill. Senator Arlen Specter stated that Professor Hill's testimony "was flat-out perjury,"[70] and Senators speculated openly on national television about various psychological disorders Hill might be suffering from. The phrase, "men just don't get it" was born.

One of the first political victims of the Hill-Thomas hearings was Senator

Alan Dixon who lost his seat in the Illinois primary to political newcomer Carol Mosely Braun. Ms. Braun went on to win Dixon's Senate seat and ultimately a seat on the Judiciary Committee. Braun was one of several women moved by the Hill-Thomas debacle to seek public office themselves. An unusually large number of seats opened up in Congress as a result of retirements and reapportionment, which further encouraged women to announce their candidacies. In all, twenty-two women sought Senate seats in 1992, compared to just eight in the previous election. A record four new women entered the Senate, raising the total to six in 1992,[71] including Braun, who was the first African American woman to be elected to the Senate. In the House of Representatives, forty-eight women were elected, nearly doubling the number of female members. Facilitating this increase were a number of grassroots women's organizations whose membership also rose after the Hill-Thomas event. Membership in EMILY'S (Early Money Is Like Yeast) List, an organization supporting prochoice, Democratic female candidates, went from 3,000 to 23,000 in just one year. EMILY'S List contributed more than $6 million to candidates in the 1992 elections, a fourfold increase over the elections of 1990.[72] The National Organization for Women (NOW) reported that anger over the Senate's handling of Hill's charges "has translated into 13,000 new members in the final months of 1991," and the Feminist Majority reported receiving an unsolicited contribution of $10,000 after the hearings and a 30 percent rise in contributions overall.[73] Clearly a single event can have powerful organizational implications in mobilizing women to attend to and participate in politics.

In September 1991, naval aviators belonging to the Tailhook Association, held their annual convention in Las Vegas. The revelry became assaultive, alleged Lt. Paula Coughlin, as male aviators "formed a gauntlet down a narrow hallway and tore at her clothes, grabbed at her breasts, and seized her buttocks with such force she was hoisted airborne."[74] Other women reported that they were thrown to the ground, had their clothes torn off, and were molested by drunken airmen. In all, 119 Navy and 21 Marine Corps officers were referred by Pentagon investigators for possible disciplinary actions. None of these 140 cases ever went to trial, however, and nearly half were dropped for lack of evidence. Twenty-eight junior officers were eventually disciplined for "indecent exposure" and "conduct unbecoming an officer." None of the aviators were charged with sexual assault, and Coughlin's charges against a specific Marine captain for sexual molestation were dropped for lack of evidence. The investigation and disciplinary hearings stretched on for more than three years, culminating in the resignation of Secretary of the Navy Lawrence Garrett III and the early retirement of Admiral Frank Kelso, the navy's top officer, who was found to have witnessed several incidents, but failed to intervene. Women following the progress of the investigation were introduced to the dark side of military culture. Outraged that sexual assault charges were dismissed as "high jinks" and dismayed to learn that the "gauntlet" had been a fixture at every Tailhook Convention since 1986 without any intervention by navy officials, civilian women's groups rallied to Coughlin's cause. The fallout resulted in new sexual

Encountering the Controversies of Equality

When Should a Woman "Blow the Whistle"?

ANITA HILL began her career in Washington as an associate at the law firm of Wald, Harkrader and Ross in September 1980. Eleven months later, she left the firm to join Clarence Thomas as his only special assistant at the Department of Education. Hill was described by colleagues and friends as bright, ambitious, and interested in pursuing civil rights work. Nine months later, Thomas was nominated for chairman of the Equal Employment Opportunity Commission (EEOC). Hill later testified that harassment from Thomas had started at the Department of Education, where Thomas had been pressuring her for a date and engaging in an "unwelcome discussion of sexual matters." Despite such incidences, Hill followed Thomas to the EEOC. In later testimony, she said that she feared she would lose her job at Education once Thomas had gone. She also testified that she knew Thomas was going places and that she liked her work in civil rights law.

Within three to five months of her move to the EEOC, Hill testified that Thomas's bizarre behavior had returned. This time he allegedly moved from pressuring her to date him socially to commenting on her physical appearance, describing whether the dress she was wearing made her more or less physically appealing, and discussing pornographic movies. At no time while employed at the EEOC did Hill lodge a formal complaint against her boss. On July 1, 1991, Thomas was nominated to a seat on the U.S. Supreme Court. Hill was by then a law professor at the University of Oklahoma and had to decide whether to come forward. She later testified about her regret at not filing charges earlier against Thomas, "I can only say that when I made the decision to just withdraw from the situation and not press a claim or charge against him that I may have shirked a duty, a responsibility that I had. And to that extent I confess that I am very sorry that I did not do something or say something, but at the time that was my best judgment. Maybe it was poor judgment, but it wasn't dishonest and it wasn't a completely unreasonable choice that I made given the circumstances."[1] She later said, "I was aware that telling at any point in my career could adversely affect my future career." Eventually Hill did testify before the Senate Judiciary Committee in a hastily arranged, nationally televised hearing. By all accounts, the committee's treatment of Hill was despicable, and several senators later apologized for their behavior. Thomas was nevertheless confirmed by a 52–48 Senate vote, the largest number of negative votes ever cast for a successful Supreme Court nominee. He is now the youngest U.S. Supreme Court justice on the bench.

Lieutenant Paula Coughlin was a 30-year-old helicopter pilot and an aide to Rear Admiral Jack Snyder at Maryland's Patuxent River Naval Air Test Center in 1991 when she attended the annual Tailhook Convention in Las Vegas, Nevada. She was a victim of "the gauntlet," a tradition since 1986. In a narrow hallway, several drunken aviators engulfed her, mauled her, and tried to rip off her clothes. As she yelled for help, the men laughed and chanted "admiral's aide, admiral's aide," leaving only to grab more women coming down the hall. When she reported her story to her supervisors, she was told, "That is what you get when you go to a hotel party with a bunch of drunken aviators." In the weeks that followed, she was told to get counseling, warned that if she aired her complaint, she would be blackballed, ridiculed, and ignored by the aviation community. The report she filed languished with her supervisor, and although the Navy conducted its own internal investigation of the charges, little was done. In fact, the civilian hired by the Naval Investigative Service to interview Coughlin had himself pressured her to see him socially, calling her "sweet cakes" (his punishment when Coughlin reported his behavior was a three-day suspension without pay). Coughlin decided to take her story to the national evening news and to the *Washington Post*. Once she went public, more than a dozen other female officers came forward to tell similar stories. The subsequent external investigation took months, and the final report was more than 2,200 pages long, detailing incidents of assault, drunken violence, and lewd behavior. Several top Navy officials either resigned, chose early retirement, or were demoted. Although there were several Navy trials, none of the junior officers were convicted of assault and none of those charged lost their jobs. In the end, Paula Coughlin left the Navy on February 11, 1994, the day after the final three assault charges were dismissed for lack of evidence.[2]

What do you think?

The sexual-harassment cases described in connection with Anita Hill and Lt. Paula Coughlin are different in a number of ways, however, taken together, they raise an important question. If you encounter sexual harassment, are you obligated to other women to blow the whistle immediately, even if there's a possibility of negative repercussions to your own job or career? Or have we reached a level of awareness about sexual harassment that each woman should decide what is best for herself and her own career?

Discuss the short- and long-term implications of the answer you've given.

Locate and evaluate the procedures at your own college or university to report sexual harassment. When were they developed? (Before or after Hill-Thomas?) Are they adequate to protect both the person making the allegation and the accused until an investigation takes place? Would you feel comfortable reporting an incident of sexual harassment using these procedures? What kinds of changes would you make to the procedures if you had the chance to do so?

[1]Jane Mayer and Jill Abramson, *Strange Justice: The Selling of Clarence Thomas* (Boston: Houghton Mifflin, 1994), p. 223.

[2]Frances Pohl, "Ritual and Sacrifice at Tailhook '91" in *Women Transforming Politics*, eds. Cathy J. Cohen, Kathleen B. Jones, and Joan C. Tronto (New York: New York University Press, 1997), pp. 238–255. See also Katherine Boo, "Universal Soldier: What Paula Coughlin Can Teach American Women," *Washington Monthly* (September 1992).

harassment policies and training for personnel along with the slogan, "Not in Our Navy."[75] Women in and outside the military service are more aware of policies and procedures designed to ensure a safe and productive workplace as a result of this incident.

Organizations

In both the Hill-Thomas hearings and the Tailhook incident, women's organizations rallied to the cause. Groups such as NOW and the National Women's Political Caucus (NWPC), as well as such conservative organizations at the other end of the ideological spectrum as the Independent Women's Forum enjoy membership surges when highly publicized events remind women that the controversies of equality are not yet settled. A "women's organization" should not be construed to mean a "feminist organization, " although many explicitly political organizations dedicated to women share some feminist aims. NOW, for example, is an organization in the liberal feminist tradition. It was founded in 1966 in response to concern that the discrimination provisions of the 1964 Civil Rights Act and Title VII were not being properly enforced. NOW focuses on eliminating sexism in American society through legislation and court action. The NWPC, founded in 1971, is a bipartisan organization with the explicit goal of bringing more women, Republicans and Democrats alike, into office. Both organizations' activities are most consistent with the goals of the legal equality doctrine.

There is tremendous variety in organizations for women, and groups have been organized around every point along the ideological spectrum. Organizational involvement is intimately tied to participation in larger political arenas.[76] Organizations do this in a number of ways. First, a member's contact with the organization extends her social network to include political activists and introduces political newcomers to the efficacy of political action to solve public problems. Further, in local chapters, members gain valuable political and leadership skills that allow them to access politics at all levels. In this way, associations may act as a feeder network to political-party activity. Organizations may also facilitate citizen contact with public officials by encouraging letter-writing campaigns, visits to elected officials, or participation in organized demonstrations.[77]

Apart from mobilizing participation, women's organizations provide a wide range of services to members and nonmembers alike. The Internet provides women's groups even greater visibility and allows women around the world to access political information and resources twenty-four hours a day. Candidates and women who are thinking of seeking office can use the Internet to access training seminars, consultants, and networks of volunteers. A majority of women serving in state legislatures today list a women's organization as an important source of support. Women's organizations can mobilize women to vote and to participate in politics by drawing attention to important issues at stake in an election or to a contest between two evenly matched candidates. Women's organizations have, at times, joined forces to propose policy agendas and to lobby for congressional action on women's issues. The National Council of Women's Organizations is a bipartisan network of leaders from more than 100 organizations representing more than six million women in the United States. The council proposes a "National Women's Agenda" every two years, which corresponds to a new session of Congress. The agenda adopted in November 1998 includes issues like protecting social security and ending disadvantages to women in the social security system, making quality, affordable child care a national priority, improving access to health care, strengthening Violence Against Women legislation, supporting ratification of the ERA and CEDAW, and urging the Senate to take action to oppose gender apartheid in Afghanistan, among others.[78] The NCWO's agenda combines the two paths to equality—legal equality and fairness.

The Role of Political Parties

Although political parties made early overtures to female voters in anticipation of the immediate post-suffrage elections, they largely abandoned the "women's vote" when no such voting bloc materialized. Many women continued their activities with political parties, but, as political scientist Jo Freeman said, they entered mainstream parties "one room at a time":

> Party women had their own style of action. Whereas feminists had assaulted the citadel, and reformers had banged on the door, party women had infiltrated the basement of politics. But while their actions were incremental and only occasionally attracted notice, their numbers expanded and they helped bring about significant changes to the parties. They also built a base of well-informed women with years of party service who were quick to take advantage of the opportunities created by the new feminist movement that arose in the late 1960s.[79]

Both national political parties, as well as many state party organizations, created special women's auxiliaries designed to educate and mobilize female voters. Women's divisions proved both a facilitator and a ghetto for women interested in ascending to political power. At the same time that parties recruited women to organize other women, they denounced "sex solidarity" and encouraged their female organizers to do the same. Party loyalty was the first priority for parties. For party women, inclusion was the first priority. Party women, according to Freeman, were not interested in promoting a "women first" agenda, but rather in receiving "equal rewards for equal service."[80] The odd waltz between parties and feminists continued with women and parties alike trying to argue both sides: Parties tried to appeal to women by identifying women's issues in their platforms but appealing to their partisan loyalty first. Women worked tirelessly for the party, but always held out the possibility of a women's bloc vote to motivate the party to listen to women.

Political scientists have given contemporary parties mixed reviews on their ability to promote women as candidates and to motivate women to participate in politics. Although women have continued to labor in the basement, as Freeman said, they have also slowly ascended to the ranks of party leadership. By 1972, 40 percent of the delegates at the Democratic presidential nominating convention were female, and 32 percent of the delegates at the Republican convention were female. A woman has never been head of the Democratic Party, and only one woman, Mary L. Smith, has headed the Republican Party (1974–1977). Within the parties, women work as strategists, fundraisers, and administrators. However, when it comes to nominating women from among the ranks to run for political office, lingering forms of discrimination are evident. Often women serve as "sacrificial lamb" candidates by running against strong incumbents from the other party or are chosen to run for a "woman's seat"—one vacated by a female incumbent.[81]

In recent elections, both political parties have reached out to female voters and made an effort to showcase female candidates. In 1992, labeled the "Year of the Woman," the major party convention stages were filled with female candidates and speakers, and network cameras lingered on the faces of female delegates. A commitment to a political party is a strong vote motivator. Studies have shown, however, that women are no more committed to political parties than men are.[82] Attachment to political parties in general is on the decline, making it essential that new groups of voters be recruited into the ranks of the faithful. For example, in 1998, both parties targeted "waitress moms." Their profile (older than 50, white, working multiple hourly wage jobs to support children) fit the Democratic Party best, and yet their votes were in play largely because of the Clinton-Lewinsky scandal. "They're values oriented," said pollster Celinda Lake who coined the term. "They've been swung back and forth by events, so they're a question mark."[83] Republicans appealed to women fitting the waitress-mom profile because of the party's promise to lower taxes. At a fundraising dinner, former Vice President Quayle said, "Think of the waitress that works extra hours at night so she can buy a book for her child. She might want to be at her son or daughter's soccer game, but she has to work because of high taxes."[84] In the end, women remained divided between the parties along demographic lines and by the issues that directly affect them. As in the 1920s though, both parties are busily courting what would be for any party a political holy grail—a women's voting bloc.

CONCLUSION

Women constitute a substantial political force in the abstract. However, a variety of historical and contemporary forces work to minimize the chances that women will act in concert *as women* in politics. Despite the gender gap, a "women's bloc" did not materialize immediately following ratification of the Nineteenth Amendment nor has it since materialized in American politics. Most likely even the possibility of a women's voting bloc was the stuff of political myth-making or propaganda depending on one's perspective. The evidence suggests that men and women, for the most part, participate in politics at about the same rates and in about the same ways. Women are divided by race, class, marital status, and education in the same ways that men are politically stratified. Where men and women differ in their rates or modes of participation, resources are most likely at issue rather than gender. Women still lag behind men in their wages and therefore in the amount each can contribute to family earnings. As a result, women lag behind men in their ability to spend precious capital on politics. It remains to be seen whether political organizations, parties, or episodic events and issues can help women overcome the remaining barriers to full political participation and mobilize women's involvement. Achieving gender equality, even if merely political equality, depends not only on a woman's ability to vote but also on her ability to express her will and her interests effectively through other forms of participation. So far, women have been unable to coordinate their goals in a way that easily translates into a unified women's agenda. Gender equality does not easily translate into policy platforms or campaign promises, particularly considering the complexities introduced by the paradox and the two different paths to the realization of gender equality.

The fact remains that women make up 53 percent of the U.S. population in 2000, and women constitute the majority of registered voters. In this sense, women's votes are key to winning elections for both male and female candidates. Empirical studies caution that women candidates and Democratic candidates should not take women's votes for granted any more than males or Republican candidates should write them off. The next chapter examines another form of political participation that could translate into the power to more directly set the political agenda: women as candidates for public office.

Notes

1. Jo Freeman, *A Room at a Time: How Women Entered Party Politics* (Lanham, Md.: Rowman & Littlefield, 2000), p. 3.

2. Kristi Anderson, *After Suffrage: Women in Partisan and Electoral Politics before the New Deal* (Chicago: University of Chicago Press, 1996), p. 50.

3. Charles Merriam and Harold Gosnell, *Non-Voting: Causes and Methods of Control* (Chicago: University of Chicago Press, 1924), pp. 36–37.

4. Anderson, *After Suffrage*.

5. Sophinisba Breckinridge, *Women in the Twentieth Century: A Study of their Political, Social, and Economic Activities* (New York: McGraw Hill, 1933).

6. Illinois granted women presidential suffrage in 1914.

7. Virginia Sapiro, *The Political Integration of Women* (Urbana: University of Illinois Press, 1983), p. 22.

8. Turnout and registration statistics from "Sex Differences in Voter Turnout," fact sheet compiled by the Center for American Women and Politics, Eagleton Institute of Politics (New Brunswick, N.J.: Rutgers University, December 1997).

9. Sidney Verba, Kay Lehman Schlozman, and Henry E. Brady, *Voice and Equality: Civic Voluntarism in American Politics* (Cambridge: Harvard University Press, 1995), p. 254n.

10. Richard A. Seltzer, Jody Newman, and Melissa Vorhees Leighton, *Sex as a Political Variable: Women as Candidates and Voters in U.S. Elections* (Boulder, Colo.: Lynne Rienner Publishers, 1997), p. 68.

11. Ibid., pp. 68–69.

12. Nelson W. Polsby and Aaron Wildavsky, *Presidential Elections: Strategies and Structures of American Politics* (New York: Chatham House, 2000), p. 8.

13. Ibid., p. 9

14. Statistics on Internet use came from a study by Bruce Bimber, *The Government and Politics on the Net Study,* quoted in "Young Women and Politics," fact sheet compiled by the Center for American Women and Politics, Eagleton Institute of Politics (New Brunswick, N.J.: Rutgers University, July 1999).

15. Kathleen Hall Jamieson, Richard Johnston, and Michael Hagen, "The Primary Campaign: What did the Candidates Say, What did the Public Learn, and What did it Matter?" (Philadelphia: Annenberg Public Policy Center, University of Pennsylvania, March 27, 2000), accessed at *http://www.appcpenn.org.*

16. Kathleen A. Frankovic, "Why the Gender Gap Became News in 1996," *PS: Political Science and Politics* 32, no. 1 (March 1999): 20–23.

17. Jeff Manza and Clem Brooks, "The Gender Gap in U.S. Presidential Elections: When? Why? Implications?," *American Journal of Sociology* 103, no. 5 (March 1998): 1235–1266.

18. Seltzer, Newman, and Leighton, *Sex as a Political Variable,* p. 4.

19. "Gender Gap Evident in Numerous 1998 Races," fact sheet compiled by the Center for American Women and Politics, Eagleton Institute of Politics (New Brunswick, N.J.: Rutgers University, 1999).

20. Feminist Majority Foundation, "Gender Gap Decisive in Election 2000," accessed at *http://www.feminist.org,* November 8, 2000.

21. Manza and Brooks, "The Gender Gap in U.S. Presidential Elections."

22. Karen M. Kaufmann and John R. Petrocik, "The Changing Politics of American Men: Understanding the Sources of the Gender Gap," *American Journal of Political Science* 43, no. 3 (July 1999): 864–887.

23. Susan Welch and John Hibbing, "Financial Conditions, Gender and Voting in American National Elections," *Journal of Politics* 54 (1992): 343–359.

24. Feminist Majority Foundation, "Gender Gap Decisive in Election 2000."

25. Kay Lehman Schlozman, Nancy Burns, Sidney Verba, and Jesse Donahue, "Gender and Citizen Participation: Is there a Different Voice?" *American Journal of Political Science* 39 (1995): 267–293.

26. Carole Kennedy Chaney, R. Michael Alvarez, and Jonathan Nagler, "Explaining the Gender Gap in U.S. Presidential Elections, 1980-1992," *Political Research Quarterly* 51, no. 2 (June 1998): 311–339.

27. Verba, Schlozman, and Brady, *Voice and Equality,* p. 38.

28. For information on the sample and methodology, see Verba, Schlozman, and Brady, *Voice and Equality,* Appendix A.

29. Defined in this study as whether the respondent voted, worked on a campaign, made a campaign contribution, worked informally or in the community, served on a local governing board, contacted a government official, attended a protest, or was affiliated with a political organization.

30. Kay Schlozman, Nancy Burns, and Sidney Verba, "Gender and the Pathways to Participation: the Role of Resources," *The Journal of Politics* 56, no. 4 (November 1994): 969.

31. Ibid., pp. 968–969. In each case, the gender differences were statistically significant.

32. Wendy Kaminer, "Crashing the Locker Room," *The Atlantic* 270, no.1 (July 1992): 58–70.

33. Scholzman, Burns, and Verba, "Gender and the Pathways to Participation," p. 977.

34. Ibid., p. 987.

35. Schlozman, Burns, Verba, and Donahue, "Gender and Citizen Participation." The phrase "in a different voice" is from Carol Gilligan's 1982 book of the same title.

36. See, for example, Susan Welch and Sue Thomas, "Do Women in Public Office Make a Difference?," in *Gender and Policymaking,* eds. Susan J. Carroll, Debra Dodson, and Ruth B. Mandel (New Brunswick, N.J.: Center for American Women and Politics, Eagleton Institute of Politics, Rutgers University, 1991).

37. Sidney Verba and Norman Nie, *Participation in America: Political Democracy and Social Equality* (New York: Harper & Row, 1972).

38. Jamieson, Johnston, and Hagen, "The Primary Campaign: What did the Candidates Say, What did the Public Learn, and What did it Matter?"

39. Ibid.

40. Simone de Beauvoir, *The Second Sex* (New York: Knopf, 1952).

41. Sapiro, *Political Integration of Women,* p. 40.

42. Paul H. Mussen, "Early Sex Role Development," in *Handbook of Socialization Theory and Research,* ed. David Goslin (New York: Rand McNally, 1969).

43. Katherine Blick Hoyenga and Kermit T. Hoyenga, *Gender-Related Differences: Origins and Outcomes* (Boston: Allyn and Bacon, 1993), p. 265.

44. David Sadker and Myra Sadker, *Failing at Fairness: How America's Schools Cheat Girls* (New York: Scribner, 1994), pp. 84–85.

45. Kathleen Dolan, "Political Development and the Family: An Examination of Alternative Family Structures" (dissertation, University of Maryland, 1991).

46. Sue Thomas, *How Women Legislate* (New York: Oxford University Press, 1994), p. 56.

47. Hoyenga and Hoyenga, *Gender-Related Differences,* p. 266.

48. See Roberta S. Sigel, *Ambition and Accommodation: How Women View Gender Relations* (Chicago: University of Chicago Press, 1996), 9-17; Sue Tolleson Rinehart, *Gender Consciousness and Politics* (New York: Routledge, 1992), pp. 21–27.

49. "Pipeline to the Future: Young Women and Political Leadership," (findings on mobilizing young women, from a survey and focus groups conducted by Lake Snell Perry and Associates for the White House Project Education Fund, April 12, 2000), p. 22.

50. The White House Project Education Fund, "Barbie is Running for President!" accessed at *http://www.whitehouseproject.org,* April 19, 2000, press release.

51. M. Margaret Conway, Gertrude A. Steuernagel, and David Ahern, *Women and Political Participation: Cultural Change in the Political Arena* (Washington, D.C.: Congressional Quarterly Press, 1997).

52. Elizabeth Adell Cook, "The Generations of Feminism," in *Women in Politics: Insiders or Outsiders,* ed. Lois Duke Whitaker, 3d ed. (Upper Saddle River, N.J.: Prentice Hall, 1999), pp. 45–55.

53. Conway, Steuernagel, and Ahern, *Women and Political Participation,* pp. 66–68.

54. Ibid., pp. 87–91.

55. Gerhard Falk, *Sex, Gender and Social Change: The Great Revolution* (Lanham, Md.: University Press of America, 1998), p. 175.

56. Deborah Tannen, "The Real Hillary Factor," *New York Times,* 12 October 1992, op-ed section.

57. Estelle Disch, *Reconstructing Gender: A Multicultural Anthology,* 2d ed. (Mountain View, Calif.: Mayfield Publishing, 2000), p. 308.

58. Ibid., p. 306.

59. Kenneth Dion, Ellen Berscheid, and Elain Walster, "What is Beautiful is Good," *Journal of Personality and Social Psychology* 24 (1972): 285–290.

60. Linda Witt, Karen M. Paget, and Glenna Mathews, *Running as a Woman: Gender and Power in American Politics* (New York: Free Press, 1993), pp. 59–60.

61. Kaminer, "Crashing the Locker Room," pp. 58–70.

62. For more on this story, see Caryl Rivers, "Commentary: Mockery of Katherine Harris Shows Double Standard," -accessed at *http://www.womensenews.org,* 2000.

63. Patricia Hill Collins, *Black Feminist Thought* (London: Routledge Press, 1991), p. 67.

64. R. Darcy, Charles D. Hadley, and Jason F. Kirksey, "Electoral Systems and the Representation of Black Women in American State Legislatures," *Women and Politics,* vol.13, pp. 73–76.

65. Irene Natividad, "Women of Color on the Campaign Trail," *The American Woman: 1992–1993,* eds. Paula Ries and Anne J. Stone (New York: Norton, 1992).

66. Ibid., p. 136.

67. Center for American Women and Politics, "CAWP in Partnership with NOBEL Women," *CAWP News* (Fall 2000): 4.

68. Charles J. Olgetree Jr., "The People vs. Anita Hill: A Case for Client Centered Advocacy," in *Race, Gender, and Power in America,* eds. Anita Faye Hill and Emma Coleman Jordan (New York: Oxford University Press, 1995), pp. 142–176.

69. Anna Deavere Smith, "Anita Hill and the Year of the Woman" in *Race, Gender, and Power in America,* eds. Anita Faye Hill and Emma Coleman Jordan (New York: Oxford University Press, 1995), pp. 248–270.

70. Ibid., p. 250.

71. A seventh female senator, Kay Bailey Huchison, Republican from Texas, was seated after winning a special election to replace Senator Lloyd Bentsen.

72. Cynthia B. Costello, Shari Miles, and Anne J. Stone, eds., *The American Woman: 1999–2000* (New York: Norton, 1998), p. 97.

73. Toni Cabrillo, et al., *The Feminist Chronicles* (Los Angeles: Women's Graphics, 1994), p. 143.

74. Susan Faludi, "Going Wild: Debating Tailhook," *Frontline,* accessed at *http:// www.pbs.org/wgbh/frontline/shows/navy/tailhook/debate.html,* 1994.

75. Katherine Boo, "Universal Soldier: What Paula Coughlin Can Teach American Women," *Washington Monthly* (September 1992).

76. David Knoke, "The Mobilization of Members of Women's Associations," in *Women, Politics, and Change,* eds. Louise A. Tilly and Patricia Gurin (New York: Russell Sage Foundation, 1990), pp. 383–409.

77. Ibid.

78. National Council of Women's Organizations, accessed at *www.womensorganizations. org.*

79. Freeman, *A Room at a Time,* p. 6.

80. Ibid.

81. Amy H. Handlin, *Whatever Happened to the Year of the Woman: Why Women Still Aren't Making it to the Top in Politics* (Denver, Colo.: Arden Press, 1998), p. 116.

82. Conway, Steuernagel, and Ahern, *Women and Political Participation,* p. 87.

83. Melinda Henneberger, "Want Votes with That? Get the 'Waitress Moms,'" *New York Times,* 25 October 1998, p. 3.

84. Ibid.

Women Seeking Office: The Next Phase of Political Integration

As of 1995, 197 women have served in the U.S. Congress since Jeanette Rankin was first elected in 1916. In 1968, frustrated with women's slow progress over the years, Congresswoman Martha Griffiths asked congressional researchers to calculate how long it would take for women to become the majority if the incremental pace continued. The answer? Four hundred thirty-two years.[1]

Eighty years after suffrage, what is the status of women in office? The 2000 elections resulted in women occupying 72 (13 percent) of the 535 seats available in the U.S. Congress. A record 59 women were elected to serve in the House of Representatives, with an additional two women serving as nonvoting delegates. In the Senate, women have won 13 of the 100 available seats. For the first time in history, three states (California, Maine, and Washington) are represented by two female senators. By winning the New York Senate seat, Hillary Rodham Clinton became the first, first lady to hold elective office. Her victory also marks the first time a woman has represented New York in the Senate and the first time a New York woman has been elected to a statewide office in her own right.

In addition, women were elected to fill 22.4 percent of the available seats in state legislatures, and 27.6 percent of the 323 statewide elective offices available. Five women were elected governor of their state, sixteen women serve as lieutenant governor, eight as attorney general, thirteen as secretary of state, and eleven as state treasurer. Five women governors serving in 2001 has surpassed the previous record of four women serving at one time and brings to 18 the total number of women to have ever served as governor of their state.

Local offices have been much harder to track, but as of January 1997, twelve of the nation's largest cities had female mayors and 20.7 percent (202 of 975) of U.S. cities with populations greater than 30,000 had female may-

TABLE 4.1 Women's Representation in Elective Office Over Time, 1977–2001

Year	U.S. Congress	Statewide Elective	State Legislature
1977	4%	10 %	9 %
1979	3%	11 %	10 %
1981	4%	11 %	12 %
1983	4%	11 %	13 %
1985	5%	14 %	15 %
1987	5%	14 %	16 %
1989	5%	14 %	17 %
1991	6%	18 %	18 %
1993	10%	22 %	21 %
1995	10%	26 %	21 %
1997	11%	26 %	22 %
1999	12%	28 %	22.5%
2001	13%	27.5%	22.4%

Source: Center for American Women and Politics (CAWP), National Information Bank on Women in Public Office, Eagleton Institute of Politics, Rutgers University.

ors.[2] In 1992 the Center for American Women and Politics estimated that about 20.2 percent of elected officials at the local level were women. At the highest levels of government, no woman has ever been nominated to run at the top of a major party ticket, and only one woman, Geraldine Ferraro in 1984, has run in the second spot on a major party ticket. Only two women have actually sought the presidential nomination of a major party, while a third got as far as an exploratory committee before bowing out. A total of twenty-one women have been appointed to presidential cabinets since Frances Perkins first assumed her post as Secretary of Labor, representing about 4.3 percent of the total appointments. Eight of the twenty-one (just over one-third) were appointed by the Clinton administration alone. President George W. Bush's cabinet includes four women and a fifth as national security adviser.

When the United States is compared to other developed nations in terms of the number of women in political office, the United States clearly lags behind. The reason for the deficit is not clear. Conventional wisdom used to explain women's political underrepresentation by saying that the country was not ready for women in high office; voters, particularly women voters, would not support a woman candidate; women could not raise sufficient funds to mount successful campaigns; or political-party elites conspired to keep women from being nominated to winnable seats.[3] The reality today is that women candidates are as likely to win elections as men. "The reason there aren't more women in public office is not that women don't win, but that not enough women have been candidates in general elections."[4] So why aren't there more women candidates? The answer is multifaceted and constitutes a major portion of this chapter. Also included is a detailed examination of women's experiences as candidates for elective office and an analysis of how their experiences differ from their male counterparts. Finally, this chapter looks at potential reforms and current initiatives designed to increase the number of women running for public office.

WOMEN CANDIDATES ARE AS LIKELY TO WIN ELECTIONS AS MEN

The long-held conventional wisdom that a woman has a poor chance of electoral victory is empirically unsubstantiated. That does not mean, however, that the myth does not continue to scare women away from running for office. A study conducted by Richard A. Seltzer, Jody Newman, and Melissa Vorhees Leighton comparing the actual success rates of male and female candidates for general elections for state legislature, U.S. House and Senate, and governor during comparable time periods found that "a candidate's sex does not affect his or her chances of winning an election."[5] Researchers in this study were careful to compare like candidates in like situations. In other words, they compare challengers with challengers and incumbents with incumbents in both open-seat races and those with incumbents running for re-election. This is a crucial point of distinction. Previous studies looked only at the electoral landscape as a whole and simply compared winners to losers on the basis of sex. Since more men have run for office overall and more men have been incumbents, men seemed to have won more often than women. These findings were in fact inaccurate, the result of an error in the methodology used in the earlier studies. Incumbency, not sex, is the main determinant of victory in general elections in the United States.

Seltzer, Newman, and Leighton found that in state house races, female incumbents won 93.6 percent of their elections, compared to 93.8 percent for male incumbents. Women vying for open seats won 52.2 percent of their contests, compared to men, who won 53 percent of the time. What's more, women challengers won 10.9 percent of their elections, compared to 9.7 percent for men. In state senate races, incumbent women won 90.1 percent of their elections, compared with 92.2 percent for men; women running for open seats won 55.8 percent of their races compared with 54.9 percent for men; and women challengers won 15.2 percent of their elections compared with 11.6 percent for men.[6] Interestingly, men's and women's chances of victory are similar across the country except for New England and East North Central regions where female incumbents and challengers did slightly better than males. Southern women, who have been the most politically disadvantaged by their sex, suffered no disability.

Because state legislative seats have historically been most accessible to women, a better test of the influence of a candidate's sex might be found at the national level. Here, too, researchers found that women fare as well as men in general elections. Incumbent women in U.S. House races won 93.6 percent of their elections, compared to 94.8 percent for incumbent men. Women running for open seats won 47.9 percent of the time, compared to 51.2 percent for men, and women challengers won 4 percent of their contests, compared to 6.2 percent for men. Analysis by party found that in the Republican Party, women did better than men, whereas in the Democratic Party, men were more successful. Researchers were unable to calculate similar statistics for gubernatorial and U.S. Senate races because of the small number of women running for these offices.[7]

Success rates for women compared to men do not vary significantly, even in 1992. The media attention surrounding the "Year of the Woman" in politics should really be a celebration of the number of women who *sought* office rather than the number of women who *won* their races. A number of factors expanded women's opportunities to run including a record number of open seats in the U.S. House resulting from retirements, resignations, and reapportionment. Women fare much better in open-seat contests than as challengers to incumbents as evidenced in the statistics above. Recall that incumbent women in U.S. House races won 93.6 percent of their races, female candidates for open seats won 47.9 percent of the time, and challengers to incumbents won only 4 percent of their elections. As Jody Newman of the National Women's Political Caucus (NWPC) notes:

> Consider what would happen if women made up half of all open seat candidates and challengers in the general elections for the U.S. House starting in 1994. Assuming 50 open seats per election cycle and the same success rates as those found in this study, then women would hold a third of the seats in the U.S. House by the year 2000.[8]

Whether spurred by the Anita Hill-Clarence Thomas spectacle or by a rational assessment of their chances for victory, by April 30, 1992, more than 213 women had announced they would seek their party's nomination for the U.S. House or Senate. The most striking increase was in the number of women who announced their bids for the Senate, which historically has been the hardest office for women to win. By early spring 1992, 22 women had announced candidacies, compared to only 8 in 1990.[9] Ultimately 29 women filed, and 11 won their primaries in 1992.[10] From 1972 to 1994, only 7.9 percent of the candidates for the Senate were women. Likewise, only 7.8 percent of the candidates for the House, and 6.6 percent of gubernatorial candidates were women. From 1986 to 1994, just 21.3 percent of state house and 17.3 percent of state senate candidates were women.[11] But in open-seat races for higher office in 1994, only one candidate in ten was a woman. Despite the big surge in 1992, fewer than one candidate in four was a woman in open-seat contests for state legislatures in 1994. By contrast, 20 women ran in thirty-five open House races in the 2000 election. In all, 122 women won their 2000 primary elections while only 46 women lost in the primaries, resulting in a record twelve woman-to-woman races

Democratic House candidates greet the 2000 Democratic Convention delegates, Los Angeles, CA. *AP Photo/Ron Edmonds.*

for the U.S. House.[12] Women are as likely as men to win political office when they run, but they are still less likely than men to seek office in the first place.

WOMEN ARE NOT AS LIKELY TO BE CANDIDATES

The decision to seek political office is not one that can be empirically tested or objectively quantified. The decision is intensely personal, and studies show that family, friends, and confidants have usually had more of an impact on potential candidates than national parties or other organizational appeals.[13] There are, however, some factors that all candidates take into consideration when deciding whether to seek public office. Many of these factors play differently for men and women. The first and foremost calculation has to be the chance of winning the election.

Perception of Electability

A 1994 study conducted by pollster Celinda Lake for the National Women's Political Caucus found that two-thirds of voters believed that women have a tougher time winning elections than men do.[14] This belief was based on assumptions that women face discrimination from the gatekeepers in elections—the party elites responsible for recruitment of new candidates. Those surveyed also felt that voters would not support a woman and that women would have a tougher time raising money. Although these perceptions may or may not be true in any single contest, their power lies in the fact that women may not see themselves as viable candidates and party leaders may not see women as viable candidates purely as a result of the perception. Studies find that women are more likely than men to carefully consider their qualifications for office and often to undervalue their credentials. On the other hand, similarly situated men tend to overestimate their qualifications. These factors combine to produce the *pipeline* thesis, which argues that there are fewer women candidates and officeholders because not enough women possess the qualifications or have met the requirements to hold elective office. The pipeline refers to the group of vetted potential candidates that have met the formal and informal requirements and have been deemed electable. Although age, citizenship, and residence are the only formal qualifications for most offices, the informal requirements might include experience and name recognition, which may be more difficult for women to meet. Education, previous experience holding political office, occupational prestige, and even marital status combine to create the *eligibility pool* from which viable candidates are drawn. In many cases, previous experience in political office is a crucial characteristic of those in the eligibility pool. Political scientist Sue Carroll notes the importance of experience in constructing the pipeline for women candidates:

> The importance of this women's political base—of the development of a sizable pool of potential candidates with experience at state and local levels—is evident from an examination of the 24 women elected to the U.S. House of Representatives for the first time in 1992. Of these 24 women, 11 had served in state legislatures. Of the 13 who had not been state legislators, two had been county commissioners, four had served on city councils, one had been municipal court judge, one had been a state party chair, and one had held a cabinet position in state government.[15]

The characteristics of electable candidates depend in part on the level office in question (national, state, or local). The higher the office, the more experience, education, and professional prestige are required. Candidates for the U.S. Senate are drawn from a select pool of individuals, many of whom come from corporate boardrooms, the ranks of senior management, prestigious law firms, or the U.S. House. Women have only recently broken into this select group, and their numbers are still very small. In 2000, there were no women CEOs of *Fortune* 500 companies, women held roughly 5 percent of senior management positions in the nation's largest companies, constituted only 11 percent of the partners of large law firms, held 12.8 percent of the seats in the U.S. House, and made up only 15 percent of full professors nationwide. For many, this suggests that the reason for women's lack of representation in politics rests with their small numbers in the pipeline to office. In other words, there are simply not enough qualified female candidates. Advocates for more women in office are advised to be patient. As more women enter the public sphere overall, there will be more female candidates and therefore more women elected officials. Chapter seven explores the validity of the pipeline thesis as it relates to occupational choices and wages.

There is no doubt that levels of preparation for the eligibility pool are already changing among young men and women. In 1997, the educational attainment levels of women between the ages of 25 and 29 exceeded those of men in the same age group for the first time. More women than men are enrolled in four-year colleges and universities, and more women are completing bachelor's degrees than men.[16] Women are approaching parity in law schools, but there is a considerable drop-off in the number of women who are actually practicing law. Women still lag behind men in completing advanced degrees. Beyond education, the progress into other avenues of power has proceeded more slowly. One path to higher office has traditionally been to work in local or state politics to gain experience as well as visibility within a political party. Women's numbers at this level are increasing, but at a very slow rate.

Women face additional obstacles in filling the pipeline for higher office. While women's numbers have been growing at the local and state legislative levels, the average age when first elected to office remains significantly higher for women than for men. Women often wait to seek office until their children are grown,[17] which limits their ability to climb the ladder to progressively higher positions. In a study released in 1991, only 15 percent of women officeholders were forty years old or younger, compared to 28 percent of the men. Men in office were twice as likely as women to have preteenage children at home.[18] While fatherhood is seen as compatible with a professional career and political office, motherhood is seen as a full-time job.[19] Women with small children face tough questioning as candidates about how they expect to handle both jobs. Men, however, are rarely asked whether their political responsibilities will take them away from their children. Congresswoman Connie Morella of Maryland recalls a party slating meeting in 1976, the year in which she first sought office: "One of the men who hoped he would get the nomination . . . asked, 'Well, Ms. Morella, in light of your extended family do you think you'll really have time to run for Congress, much less serve?'"[20] In 1972, Patricia Schroeder, former Democratic congresswoman from Colorado, had a two-year-old daughter when she was first elected to the House. She spent the first few days in office answering queries from constituents, as well as from her new congressional colleagues, about how she was going to "do it."[21] Unmarried women face questions about their sexuality. "A single woman politician, without family to provide the paternalistic equivalent of coverture, will be gay-baited, or lusted after, or pestered with questions about why she can't get a man."[22]

Men and women may also seek political office for different reasons. Historically, women have sought local office to solve a particular problem rather than to start a career in politics. Once the community problem is solved, many women choose to leave public service rather than seek higher office, limiting their numbers in the pipeline. Women are less likely than men to see themselves as politicians, let alone career politicians. For a long time, women's primary path to elective office was in the wake of a male relative, usually a father or a husband. The *widow tradition* has a long history in the United States and accounts for many of the "first" women in Congress, state legislatures, and governors' offices. Women who ran for national office in their own right as recently as the early 1970s were likely to have come from a political family and carry the legacy of a political name. Now retired Senator Nancy Kassebaum, for example, is the daughter of one-time presidential contender Alf Landon. As Marion Saunders, a defeated 1954 congressional candidate said, "Those who take to politics like ducks to water have generally grown up in the pond."[23] Women today are not limited by family legacy or the widow's tradition. Instead they can aspire to public service based on their own motivations and undertake the preparation necessary to be successfully elected.

In a study conducted in the spring of 2000 for the White House Project Education Fund, researchers interviewed young women and men to learn more about the pipeline of the future. The study found that young people, particularly women, are extraordinarily dedicated to their communities and to solving problems within their communities. Although they hold negative attitudes about politics and politicians in general, more than four in ten young adults would consider running for office themselves. Young women are more inclined to get involved in politics if they believe they will be able to accomplish their goals and address issues they care about through political involvement. Young women who have held leadership positions in their school or community and who have been encouraged to seek office are far more likely than other women to express a desire to seek political office. Encouragement has twice the power of any other factor in predicting whether a young woman will consider running for office. Therefore, young women can be cultivated to seek elective office.[24]

Political Parties: A Help or a Hindrance?

Political parties serve a unique role in recruiting potential candidates to run in primary elections where voters select one candidate to represent their party in the general election. Scholars have long suspected that party leaders are biased against women, but conclusive research to back up those suspicions has been mixed. Research using party financial contributions to candidates as a proxy measure of party support for women candidates has found no evidence of bias.[25] Bias, however, was detected in a 1998 study conducted by David Niven in which both county-level party chairs and potential women candidates were interviewed about their experiences and preferences.[26] Niven hypothesized that because as many as 97 percent of county-level party chairs are male in some states, male attitudes toward potential women candidates may take on the form of assumptions about women as a group. This phenomenon is known as the *outgroup effect*. A prior study of male and female state legislators found some evidence of the outgroup effect. Younger, less-experienced males were encouraged by the party to run for office, while only those women who had extensive party experience and a strong background were considered acceptable candidates. In other words, party elites judged males on their potential whereas females were not. In interviewing potential women candidates, Niven discovered that 64 percent of those who ran for state legislative or congressional seats had experienced some form of discrimination at the hands of party leaders. Niven found support that this perception of bias was real and attributed its cause to the outgroup effect. Party elites consistently recruited and preferred potential candidates they judged most similar to themselves. This is significant because 85 percent of the same women reported that they would not seek higher office if their party was unsupportive.

Other studies have found that in recruiting candidates for office, party elites tend to look for candidates similar to themselves in order to ensure shared values.[27] Since women are seen as a part of the other group, they do not pass the similarity test during the initial screening. Another phenomenon explored in this research is the *distribution effect*. In this case, men's and women's distribution in productive roles (jobs and occupations) results in abstractions of the sexes in general. As a result, men are judged more likely to succeed based on the prevalence of men in occupations viewed as feeders for political office.

Women experience this bias in a number of different contexts, such as being chosen only for unwinnable contests while being overlooked for races in which the party has a good chance of winning the seat.

> In 1974, when Barbara Mikulski first ran, unsuccessfully, for the U.S. Senate, she told a television audience that Maryland's Democratic Party appeared "very happy to support a woman against someone who they thought couldn't be beat . . . [It was] Okay, good old Barb. . . . Let her take the nosedive for the party. When the race was winnable, like most women candidates, I was not considered a good investment."[28]

Harriett Woods, former lieutenant governor of Missouri and former president of the National Women's Political Caucus, experienced a similar slight when she first ran for the Missouri state senate in 1974:

> I had been in the city council eight years, a television producer for ten years, two years on the state highway commission . . . Well, it was the shock of my life when the party said, "We have to have a man for the job." [29]

Woods ran anyway and won the race. Candidates for the U.S. Senate in 1990 reported similar experiences, particularly within the Democratic Party. Political parties are not completely oblivious to the potential voter draw of women candidates. There is some evidence that the political parties have undertaken initiatives specifically designed to identify and support female candidates. In 1984, for example, the Republican Senate Campaign Committee offered $17,500 (the maximum allowable amount under Federal Election Campaign

Act [FECA] guidelines) in start-up funds to any willing woman candidate.[30] National parties are somewhat constrained in offering financial aid to political newcomers like women since the congressional campaign committees have finite resources, and their first and foremost responsibilities are to incumbent members.[31] Political parties have also sponsored training workshops for female candidates covering such topics as campaign advertising, fundraising, and get-out-the-vote techniques. Political parties have not shown a willingness to practice *negative recruitment* in favor of women. Negative recruitment is used to discourage challengers to the party's anointed candidate during primary elections.

Prior to the 1996 election cycle, consultant Celinda Lake advised the Democrats to recruit women who had successfully "started their own businesses, become prominent in community-based organizations, or served in local offices, especially school boards and other appointive or elective boards such as those dealing with health care, safety issues and environmental regulation."[32] Because women remain outsiders, in many cases, successful party recruitment strategies require that party elites look beyond the traditional occupations (law and business) and sources for candidates and be willing to put aside their strong preference for candidates that are similar to themselves.

The Pressure to Raise Money

When asked what would prevent them from seeking political office, young men and women interviewed for the White House Project Education Fund study listed as the number-one barrier raising large sums of money for the campaign.[33] Conventional wisdom suggests that women have had a harder time than men in raising and spending money to get themselves elected to public office. Women are not equally represented in prestigious companies that have access to large single donations, nor have they traditionally attracted equal amounts of political action committee (PAC) money. In the 1990s, however, this situation seems to have turned around. Political scientist Barbara Burrell studied major party nominees for the U.S. House over a number of years and found that as early as 1972, female candidates for the House began raising and spending nearly as much money as male candidates. In House races between 1974 and 1980, a period that saw the number of women candidates increase dramatically, women raised and spent about 75 percent of what men raised and spent. In 1988, women raised 119 percent of what men raised, and in 1992, they raised 111 percent and spent 108 percent of what men raised and spent.[34]

Some of this money comes from women's PACs, a relatively new breed of Political Action Committee dedicated to electing women to office. The Women's Campaign Fund, founded in 1974, and the PAC associated with the NWPC were among the first to dedicate money specifically to electing women. EMILY'S LIST (Early Money Is Like Yeast—it makes the dough rise), founded by Eleanor Malcom, was one of the first partisan PACs. EMILY'S List supports Democratic, pro-choice women who have been carefully screened and judged to be strong candidates. Women have traditionally had the hardest time raising early money that in turn allows them to purchase television airtime for advertisements and increase their name recognition as well as ultimately their donor base. The List pioneered the practice of *bundling*, an effective and creative way to circumvent the FECA's $5,000 limit on PAC contributions to a single candidate. Members of EMILY'S List join the organization with a membership fee and then agree to write three checks in the amount of at least $100 to each of three candidates selected from the List. These candidates have been interviewed and their contests thoroughly analyzed by Malcom and her staff. Through bundling, candidates receive an envelop full of checks written directly to them, rather than to the organization, that total far more than the $5,000 limit.

The first high-profile test for a women's PAC came in 1986 when Congresswoman Barbara Mikulski of Maryland decided to seek a vacant Senate seat by challenging a popular congressman and an incumbent governor in the Democratic primary. Donations from EMILY'S List have been credited with allowing her to purchase an early poll that provided solid evidence of her support throughout the state. This evidence made it possible to raise additional funds and eventually win the primary and the Senate seat. Since that race, EMILY'S List has become one of the largest and most powerful PACs in the nation. In 1994 EMILY'S List distributed $8.7 million to pro-choice Democratic women candidates, which made it the third-highest PAC money raiser in the 1994 election cycle.[35] Republican women quickly formed WISH (Women in the House and Senate) supporting pro-choice Republican candidates. WISH was then countered by an establishment group (formed by wives whose husbands were serving in the Bush administration), called the Republican Women's Leadership Network (WLN). The WLN's philosophy is more in keeping with the Republican Party's stand on abortion.[36] Another recent pro-life addition is the Susan B. Anthony List, which reportedly distributed $34,000 to pro-life female candidates in 1994. These national PACs have now spawned local and statewide affiliates dedicated to raising money for women who seek all levels of office. Listed in the appendix of Handlin's *Whatever Happened to the Year of the Woman* are fifty-seven PACs and donor networks that either give money predominantly to women candidates or have a predominantly female donor base, including twelve national and forty-five state-based organizations. In addition to raising and contributing money, many of these groups also engage in recruitment, training, and providing other forms of aid to female candidates. In 1978, the National Organization for Women formed NOW-PAC, which is the only PAC that contributes to both men and women based on their "feminist credentials."[37]

Gender Stereotypes and the Campaign Experience

Gender stereotypes affect campaigns in a number of ways. Although such stereotyping is difficult to isolate as *the* cause of women's reticence to run for office, researchers have demonstrated how gender stereotypes have caused voters and the media to view men differently from women and therefore to judge them differently within a political context. Political scientists Leonie Huddy and Nayda Terkildsen found that voters' gender stereotypes have had potentially negative implications for women candidates, particularly when running for higher national office. Voters prefer male characteristics in candidates seeking higher office. Policy areas in which males are typically judged more competent, including the military and economics, are given greater importance the higher the level of office. Competence in female policy areas, such as poverty, education, children and health-care policy, are viewed less favorably the higher the level of office. This may explain, in part, why voters are less willing to back women for president or vice president but overwhelmingly likely to vote for women at the state and local levels.[38] These findings also suggest that women interested in seeking top national elective office must convince voters of their atypicality by emphasizing their "male traits." This is not easy to do, nor are candidates in total control of the images and message presented to voters.

The media plays a significant role in defining both the candidate and the campaign to voters. Research on U.S. Senate races in the 1980s found that female candidates consistently receive less coverage than their male opponents.[39] A more recent study of 1998 gubernatorial campaigns found that newspaper reporters treat male and female candidates equitably in terms of the quantity of coverage, but the qualitative differences in coverage create contrasting images consistent with gender stereotypes. For example, journalists were more likely to focus on personal characteristics (age, marital status, whether the woman had children, personality, and appearance) of female executive candidates (16.9 percent of all paragraphs) than those of male candidates (12.3 percent of all paragraphs). By contrast, male candidates were more likely to be identified by their occupation, experience, or accomplishments.[40] Reporters are more likely to highlight the male candidates' issue positions or records on the issues (31.2 percent of all paragraphs) than those of female candidates (27.4 percent). Male candidates were also more likely to be quoted backing their campaign claims with evidence or reasoning than were female candidates (62.2 percent of the time for men, 56.2 percent of the time for women).[41] Another study found that women were more likely to be subject to *negative gender distinctions*, a reference to one's gender that is described as a hindrance or barrier to office, while men were more likely described in gender-neutral terms.[42]

Press coverage of candidates is a crucial component of elections. "Because a small proportion of the electorate has the opportunity to meet candidates in person, voters rely on news coverage—and other forms of mass media, such as paid advertising—in forming their opinions of those running for office."[43] The

Encountering the Controversies of Equality

Elizabeth Dole's Campaign and the Press

Six months after Elizabeth Dole entered the race for the Republican nomination for the presidency, she announced that she was withdrawing. Her candidacy represented the longest and most serious attempt by a woman to secure a major party's nomination for the U.S. presidency. Throughout the early primary season, public opinion polls consistently showed Dole running a strong second to George W. Bush while others showed her beating the leading Democratic contender, Vice President Al Gore, in hypothetical head-to-head contests. With such a promising position in the race, we would expect to find that Elizabeth Dole received extensive media coverage and significantly more coverage than other Republican hopefuls farther down in the polls. However, a recent study comparing the print media coverage of Elizabeth Dole with the other five contenders for the Republican nomination found significant inequities in the press coverage of Dole's campaign.[1]

Consistent with other research on gender bias in the media's coverage of women candidates discussed in this chapter, political scientists Heldman, Carroll, and Olson found gender differences in the way the print media covered the Republican's primary campaigns. Elizabeth Dole received less media coverage overall than either Bush or Senator John McCain. The amount of press coverage Dole received was consistent with candidates Steve Forbes and Gary Bauer. The press paid consistently more attention to her dress, personality traits, and personal story than they did to the other candidates' appearance and personal life. About one in six stories examined in the study mentioned Dole's appearance and more than three-fifths of the stories made reference to at least one personality trait, often in a negative context. For example, a columnist for the *De-*

use of stereotyping to render a decision increases within three contexts. Stereotyping will be more common when a voter must make a decision but lacks information and has neither the time nor the motivation to get that information. Because many women are newcomers to politics and more likely to be challengers, voters are more likely to have information about male candidates and to rely on sex as a relevant cue. Second, stereotyping is more likely to occur when individual characteristics, such as sex, are especially salient. If, for example, a pool of candidates includes only one woman, gender stereotypes will be more prevalent and will exert more influence on a voter's ultimate decision. Finally, the act of stereotyping itself encourages the confirmation of preexisting stereotypes. When voters are exposed to stereotyping in media accounts of a campaign, they are more likely to pay attention to gender characteristics and to interpret new information about the candidate in ways that are consistent with their preexisting gender stereotypes.[44]

troit News wrote that Dole's "public speaking style looks and sounds like Tammy Faye Baker meets the Home Shopping Network."[2] Nearly 62 percent of the print stories on Dole made multiple references to her husband, Bob. The press covered Dole's issue positions in ways comparable to her opponent's coverage, but more stories were written about the viability of her campaign than were written for any other single candidate. Journalists often framed Dole's candidacy in gendered terms as the "first woman" to be a serious presidential candidate. Previous research has shown that when female candidates are framed in gendered terms, the public is more likely to see them as anomalies rather than serious contenders for the office at stake.[3]

What do you think?

The research discussed here suggests that Dole's candidacy was covered very differently from the campaigns of other candidates. Might Dole have been able to remain in the race longer if her press coverage had been more equitable and presented in less gendered terms?

What role should gender play in political campaigns? Did Dole enjoy some advantages as a woman candidate? How might the press treat the next woman candidate more equitably?

When do you predict the United States will inaugurate its first woman president? In your lifetime? Who might the viable candidates be for the next presidential contest? What characteristics make them viable candidates in your judgment?

1. Caroline Heldman, Susan J. Carroll, and Stephanie Olson, "Gender Differences in Print Media Coverage of Presidential Candidates: Elizabeth Dole's Bid for the Republican Nomination," delivered at the 2000 Annual Meeting of the American Political Science Association, Washington, D.C., accessed at *http://www.cawp. rutgers.edu.*
2. Ibid., p. 7.
3. Maria Braden, *Women Politicians and the Media* (Lexington: University of Kentucky Press, 1996).

In a similar study, Monika McDermott used a quasi-experimental design to examine voters' stereotypes of women and African Americans.[45] She found that race and gender signal voters in two ways: on ideology and on issues. Women and black candidates are stereotyped as more liberal than the average white male. While African American candidates are more closely associated with minority rights than whites, women are viewed as more dedicated to honest government. McDermott found that voters decide on which candidates to support by considering how much the candidate agrees or disagrees with the ideologies and issues attributed to the stereotype of that candidate, rather than on a candidate's actual ideology and position on an issue. This leaves women candidates in a quandary about how to craft a campaign message and establish credibility as a viable candidate.

Women who decide to seek public office know that they will face tough opposition in a primary or a general election or maybe both. And yet women who announce as candidates are often unprepared for the level of combat a campaign entails. Nancy Pelosi, congresswoman from California, warns women, "Don't think of this as some League of Women Voters type of thing to do. It's brutal. It's tough. You are going for power. It's never been just given away. It's highly competitive trying to take power, and as long as you understand that and are ready to take a punch square in the face, then you'll love it."[46]

Women candidates face a number of dilemmas associated with their gender when they try to craft a campaign message. They want to appear tough, but not so tough or aggressive that voters will be scared away. Harriett Woods learned this lesson from her "crying farmer" ad when she ran for the Senate in 1986 on the Democratic ticket against Republican Kit Bond. Woods thought that she had found *the* issue to counter the effects of President Reagan's high approval ratings when she came out in strong support of farmers who were facing the worst agricultural crisis since the 1930s. Bob Squier, a noted Democratic consultant who was working on her campaign, came up with an ad that showed Woods firmly denouncing farm foreclosures. In the ad, Woods talked to a farmer who was crying about the foreclosure of his farm by an insurance company on whose board Kit Bond served as director. Woods later said, "When Squier previewed it, I told him he might win an award, but I would lose the election."[47] When the commercial finally aired it backfired terribly when Bond's campaign learned that Squier had not informed the farmer that the footage would be used as part of a "political attack." The farmer's wife was quoted as saying, "I kinda felt like we had been used." Although Woods fired Squier, the damage was never repaired in the minds of Missouri voters. Bond's ratings fell, but Woods's fell too. "All the years of building a reputation as the high-minded campaigner for truth and good government, of asserting my identity as not just another politician, were going down the drain," Woods said. In her recent book, *Women Stepping up to Power*, she reflects:

> Voters often see women candidates as different, more honest and not playing the usual political games. We're seen as outsiders who are less likely to be corrupted or get caught in any shenanigans. This generalized image is part of the advantage that balances the automatic no votes against us as too weak and unassertive. If anything happens to puncture that image, it can mean a disproportionate loss in support.[48]

Here again, the paradox of gender equality is evident. Woods eloquently captures the delicate balancing act a female candidate must master in seeking public office. If she decides to use the argument that women are different from men and says (or implies) that women are also *better* than men, she runs the risk of being held to a higher standard—perhaps one that is too high for any mortal to meet. Alternatively, if she decides to pursue political office by arguing that she is the same as a man, voters might rebel against what they view as a challenge to appropriate gender roles.

CAN WOMEN CANDIDATES EXPECT SUPPORT FROM WOMEN VOTERS?

When women step forward as candidates, can they count on the support of women voters? While all candidates can count on some women's support, is there any evidence that women actually prefer a woman candidate? We've already learned that women are more likely to support a Democratic candidate—the gender-gap phenomenon. We also know that the majority of women candidates are Democrats. However, to accurately test whether women voters prefer women candidates, apart from their running on the Democratic ticket, we need to look at the size of the gender gap in races where one or the other candidate is a woman. Researchers Seltzer, Newman, and Leighton analyzed 167 statewide races: 90 for U.S. Senate and 77 for governor in 1990, 1992, and 1994. One fourth (42) of those races were contests between a man and a woman. The researchers found a gender gap in almost all of the 167 races, with the percentage of women who voted for the Democratic candidate sometimes being as much as 15 points higher than the percentage of men who voted for the Democrat. The gender gap grew by several points on average when the Democratic candidate was a woman, and it shrank by several points when the Republican candidate was a woman:

> In ninety U.S. Senate races, the gender gap averaged 5.4 points in races between two men, 8.6 points in races between a Democratic woman and a Republican man, and 1.2 points in races between a Republican woman and a Democratic man. In the seventy-seven gubernatorial races, the gender gap averaged 4.8 points in races between two men, 8.2 points in races between a Democratic woman and a Republican man, and 1.4 points in races between a Republican woman and a Democratic man.[49]

In several cases, a reverse gender gap occurred when the Republican candidate was a woman and more women voted Republican than men did. This reveals that the sex of the candidate affects the gender gap and confirms that women have given an edge to women candidates in the races studied. However, we cannot say that women make the difference for women candidates in all cases. In 130 of the 167 elections studied, the outcome of the race would have been the same if only one sex had voted. On average, though, women supported women candidates slightly more often than men did.[50] As we learned in chapter 3, women do not constitute a monolithic voting bloc. They do, however, constitute over half the voting population and as such should be carefully analyzed and courted in the same way that serious candidates have treated male voters. Women candidates should not assume that the female electorate is a natural ally.

Some women candidates have learned this lesson the hard way. Author Amy Handlin includes a story about Carol, a founder and director of a women's shelter, in her book *Whatever Happened to the Year of the Woman.*[51] After running the shelter for five years, Carol decided to seek election to the all-male city council. She had been active in party politics for years, networking and organizing fundraisers for other candidates, so she felt she had valuable personal connections to politicians in "high places." She was confident that she could count on a base of support from women in her party and from women in the community she had met in the process of developing the shelter.

> I learned that there's this invisible line you cross when you decide to run for office . . . all of a sudden you're competing for this position that's very desirable, and some people look at you differently . . . Before you were like them; now you seem very threatening. . . . What really bothered me, though, was when I learned that several key women officials in my party were working against me. They said that I didn't deserve a council seat because I hadn't worked hard enough for the party—in other words, I hadn't done the same things they did. Some told me that I had to "wait my turn," because I was younger than the men who also wanted the seat.[52]

The NWPC commissioned a study in 1987 to learn more about voters' attitudes toward women candidates. Voters who said they would be most supportive of a woman candidate were "younger voters, minorities, voters [who] never married, Catholics, urban residents, and higher educated, white-collar workers—and especially women in these groups." Voters who said they were least likely to support a woman candidate tended to be "over 60, live in small towns or rural areas, . . . [have] lower levels of formal education, . . . [work] in lower-white-collar and blue-collar jobs, [be] homemakers [or] . . . retired, and . . . [from] the South. . . ."[53] Consistent with other studies, the female voters who were least supportive of women candidates were older women and homemakers. In 1990, a survey of 7,000 women commissioned by *McCalls* magazine found that 35 percent of the respondents preferred voting for a woman, though 25 percent still said they preferred voting for a man.[54]

Research among college undergraduates suggests that women are more supportive of female candidates than are men. In a study conducted in 1989, political scientist Kathleen Dolan found that while men and women were about equally likely to support female candidates at the local level, as the level of office increased, the gap between men and women also increased. When asked if they would support a woman candidate for local office, 92 percent of the men and 96 percent of the women responded affirmatively. When similar questions were asked about a woman running for office at the state level, 87 percent of males and 96 percent of females were supportive. The gap widened to 14 points when the students were asked about candidates for national office in general (82 percent of the men were supportive versus 96 percent of the women) and increased to a full 26 points when asked if they would support a woman for president (54 percent of the men and 80 percent of the women).[55] Note the sizable dropoff for both men and women when they were asked about supporting a woman for president of the United States.

More evidence comes from focus groups in Sherrye Henry's *The Deep Divide*. About seven out of ten women (69 percent) said that the country would be different if more women held powerful positions. Forty-four percent believe this is so because they think women in power will improve the quality of life,

14 percent believe women will formulate a better economic policy, and 31 percent think women will do a better job with social policy. Seventy-four percent of women said that they think more women in powerful positions will lead to greater equality, including 67 percent of the nonfeminists in the groups. However, when asked if they plan to vote for a woman "because another woman understands the problems women face, or does sex not make a difference," 74 percent said that sex does not make any difference! While the majority of these women believed that women in power would make some positive difference, they were unwilling to give women the advantage at the polls.[56] These findings reflect the power of the paradox of gender equality. Although voters in a variety of studies discussed in this section clearly feel that female officeholders can offer something different from males, they are hesitant to act on that belief at the polls. Women candidates are caught within the paradox. Voters say that they believe women in office might result in substantively different policies, which suggests that candidates might effectively appeal to this belief during the campaign. However, women voters also say that gender does not make any difference in their decision at the polls, so female candidates might be encouraged to campaign on the basis of no difference from male candidates.

SYSTEMIC SOURCES OF ELECTORAL BIAS AGAINST WOMEN CANDIDATES

Aside from voter perceptions of women candidates, some sources of bias remain within the electoral system itself. Incumbency is a powerful force in American politics that limits access to political office for both male and female challengers, but it appears to be a more powerful deterrent for women candidates. Likewise, research suggests that women fared better as candidates in multimember districts than in the single-seat districts that characterize most state legislatures as well as the U.S. Congress. Popular initiatives to limit politicians' terms in office have been approved in a number of states to remedy the power of incumbency, but it is not clear whether these changes will result in more women being elected to office.

Incumbency and the Potential of Term Limits

We have already discussed the negative effects that incumbency exerts on women challengers. Term limits, if enacted, may remedy this problem. Term limits enforced at the state level (term limits enacted by states and intended to apply to congressional seats were ruled unconstitutional) would require an officeholder to give up his or her seat after that person had served a preset number of terms in office. While term limits are a relatively recent reform, the effects are already being felt in some state legislatures as long-time incumbents are forced to leave office. As of February 1996, twenty-one states had passed ballot initiatives limiting terms of office. Obviously, term-limit induced retirements increase the number of open-seat contests, thereby potentially improving the climate for female candidates.[57] Additionally, one study found that 93 percent of state legislators initially affected by term limits were male.[58] Speculative research and research based on simulations and forecasting suggest that term limits would benefit groups that serve for a limited time anyway (male incumbents have served for an average of 13.8 years, compared to female incumbents' 11.9 years of service) and would have the greatest impact in opening leadership positions to women. Assemblywoman Carol Migden of California, chair of the Appropriations Committee, states it this way: "Most people don't get Appropriations in six years . . . but I got it in six months. Who says term limits aren't working?"[59] Similar successes in Maine have been reported in the *Wall Street Journal*, "As part of the increased turnover—40 percent of the legislators are freshmen—Maine has its first female House speaker and half of the legislature's leaders are women, the most ever."[60]

Research beyond speculation and modeling has only recently become available as the first states (California, Colorado, and Oklahoma) have implemented term limits. With the 1996 election, California became the first state to "retire" an entire assembly of incumbent members. In evaluating the impact of term limits on women's progress in the California assembly, Stanley Caress cautions that term limits in themselves will not be sufficient to increase the number of women in office. More than term limits, it is the political climate—reflected in improved prospects for women candidates nationwide between 1990 and 1992—combined with reapportionment's opening up a number of open-seat races, that account for more women being elected to office. Caress concludes that "initially, term limits may provide an advantage for women if there is not already a large number of women incumbents. But as the 1994 and 1996 elections suggest, term limits do not provide women candidates with an advantage if they already are well represented in a legislature's membership."[61]

Preliminary analyses of state legislatures affected by term limits in the 1998 elections, conducted by CAWP, shows mixed results. The number of women serving in seats vacated by term-limited incumbents increased in the state senates, but decreased in the state houses. The number of minority women serving in term-limited state house seats decreased slightly following the 1998 elections.[62] CAWP also found that a large proportion of women were replaced by men when term limits forced them to vacate their seats. In many cases, no women even sought to replace them. Women were most successful in term-limited states in 1998 when there were organized efforts to recruit, support, and fund women candidates for state legislative seats.[63]

Single Districts Versus Multimember Districts

The electoral system itself is another source of potential bias or discouragement for women candidates. Most people take it for granted that elections are neutral contests, at least as far as the formal rules are concerned. However, political arrangements are not neutral.[64] African Americans and other minority groups have challenged electoral systems, though women have not. Research comparing electoral contests in which representation was chosen through single-member districts versus multimember districts has found that more women ran and more women were elected through multimember systems. Researchers have identified four main reasons why women have done better in multimember districts. First, party and community leaders who are under some pressure to respond to interests in a district are more sensitive to including and supporting women candidates. Second, voters may be more comfortable voting for a woman if she is among a slate of candidates than if she is their only representative. Third, running as a woman among a group of candidates may produce some novelty value and attract more publicity and ultimately more votes. Finally, women are more willing to run for office in multimember districts since there is no specific opponent and women would therefore be running on their own qualifications and program ideas.[65]

Political scientists R. Darcy, Susan Welch, and Janet Clark examined state legislatures in the United States in an effort to empirically test the theory that women fare better under some electoral systems over others. Since states are constitutionally free to adopt any election method, there are a variety of experiences to examine. The findings are clear. In states that use both single- and multi-member district systems, women ran in greater proportions in multi-member districts and in seventeen out of twenty-one cases, the proportion of women running and winning in multimember districts was about double the proportion of those running and winning in the single-member districts. Further, in states with all single-member districts, the proportion of women elected was less than in states with multimember or mixed systems.[66]

INITIATIVES DESIGNED TO INCREASE THE NUMBER OF WOMEN CANDIDATES

In addition to the structural reforms we've discussed, a number of organizations have undertaken special initiatives to identify, recruit, and support women candidates. Here are a sample of these initiatives:

- *The White House Project* is a nonprofit, nonpartisan public-awareness campaign to change the political climate so that women can launch successful campaigns for the U.S. presidency and other key positions. The project is

Encountering the Controversies of Equality

Is this a Sign of Progress?

A S A RESULT of the 2000 elections, thirteen women represent ten states in the U.S. Senate. Nearly half of the women in the Senate represent three states. California, Maine, and Washington State are each represented by two female senators. A fourth state, Kansas, followed California briefly in 1996 as the second state to seat two women, but it is now represented by two men. Only thirty-one women have held seats in the history of the U.S. Senate, including seventeen who first entered the Senate to complete unexpired terms of their husbands or others. There is no doubt that most observers would say that increasing the number of women in the Senate from nine to thirteen in a single election is a sign of progress, but what about the concentration of six of the thirteen women representing just three states? Is that a sign of progress too?

committed to raising awareness of women's leadership in U.S. politics and mobilizing Americans of all ages to participate in civic life.[67]

- *Pipeline to the Presidency* is an initiative undertaken by the White House Project Education Fund, a project of the Women's Leadership Fund. The Women's Leadership Fund is dedicated to enhancing public perceptions of women's capacity to lead, changing biases against women's leadership ability, and fostering the entry of women into positions of leadership. Using surveys and focus groups, researchers have developed a plan to mobilize young women to engage in politics. Young women are best motivated to seek office by having mentors, receiving practical training on what to do and how to do it, and knowing that they will be able to accomplish their goals through political involvement.[68]

- *NRCC Buddy System* was established in 1994. Twelve incumbent Republican House women campaigned in districts where women GOP candidates were running. They offered advice and eased the entry of new women into politics. As a result, new Republican women were elected and the incumbent "buddies" were rewarded with leadership positions in the House.[69]

- *EMILY'S List WOMEN VOTE!* was originally designed to recapture the more than 16 million women who sat out the 1994 midterm election and to convince them to vote for women candidates. The majority of these nonvoters fall into the non-college educated category and are among the least likely to support female candidates. Proponents of the program boasted that a pilot version of WOMEN VOTE! turned out 415,000 women in the 1994 California Senate race in which Dianne Feinstein defeated multimillionaire Michael Huffington. Before the elections in 2000, EMILY'S List planned to spend $10 million to mobilize nonvoting women in fifteen states.[70]

What do you think?

Brainstorm some of the possible explanations for three states electing women to fill both of their U.S. Senate seats:

- Could it be the political culture of the state? If so, how are the four states that have seated two women similar and different from one another?
- Might it be that once one woman is elected to the Senate from a state, a second woman has an easier time winning a seat? You can research this proposition by analyzing the campaigns of the following senators: Susan Collins, Republican from Maine, who followed Olympia Snowe, Republican from Maine, or Barbara Boxer, who followed Dianne Feinstein, both of whom are Democrats from California.

In your judgment, is it a sign of progress that six of the thirteen women serve three states? Alternatively, might it mean that women can only be elected from certain states or under certain conditions and therefore be an indication of structural limits on women's election to political office at the highest levels? What do you think?

- *American Association of University Women—The Power of One Vote* (AAUW) has undertaken an Internet campaign to mobilize progressive women voters. AAUW launched the Voter Education Project in 1995 in the wake of the conservative tide that swept through Congress in 1994. "AAUW believes that to prevent the erosion of hard-won gains on issues important to women—educational equity, health care, civil rights, workplace equity, reproductive choice, social security, welfare reform—women need to know how legislation being considered in Congress affects their lives and their families."[71] Through a national e-mail and fax network, women are updated regularly on congressional action. Additionally, AAUW members have conducted get-out-the-vote campaigns in local communities. AAUW has the support of more than forty other organization in this effort through the Women's Network for Change.
- *The Women's Campaign School at Yale University* is cosponsored by Yale Law School and Gender Studies Program. Each year the school offers a four-day training session designed to teach a wide range of campaign skills and introduce participants to professionals in the campaign and political arena. The school also offers a series of regular one-day workshops that cover such topics as "Secrets of Successful Fundraising," "Campaign Message and Strategy," and "Politics: The Uncommon Career Choice," among others.[72]
- *Women Under Forty Political Action Committee* is a multipartisan political action committee that supports women under the age of forty who run for state and federal office. Discouraged by the low number of young women in political office, a group of interested women gathered in Washington, D.C., in January 1999 and organized WUFPAC. During the 2000 election cycle, WUFPAC focused on raising money and making contributions to women

under 40 running for Congress. In the future, there are plans to support statewide candidates under 40, develop a youth outreach program designed to encourage civic and political participation by high-school-aged women across the country.[73]

- *Young Women Vote '98* was first organized in anticipation of the 1998 elections and in reaction to the conservative actions of the 105th Congress. The Third Wave Foundation and the Young Women's Leadership Institute have co-sponsored the coalition of young women. The Third Wave, a national organization for women between the ages of 15 and 30, has also sponsored a lecture series "Why Vote?" designed to mobilize young women voters. NEW Leadership, sponsored by the Center for the American Woman and Politics (CAWP), is a year-long program aimed at college women and includes a summer institute connecting young women with women currently in office and policy-making roles.[74]

- *Elect Women for a Change*, sponsored by the National Organization for Women (NOW), provides feminist candidates with experienced organizers, resources, and connections to other women's campaign experiences.[75]

- *Ready to Run* is a bipartisan initiative aimed at encouraging women in New Jersey to run for public office and to position themselves for political appointments. Cosponsored by the Institute for Women's Leadership and the Center for American Women and Politics, the initiative offers workshops and training sessions for potential candidates. New Jersey Governor Christine Todd Whitman cochairs the initiative. At least three women who attended the first conference in 1998 were later successful in their bids for elective office in New Jersey. The initiative also identifies qualified women to serve on gubernatorially appointed boards, commissions, and other public bodies.[76]

POLITICAL APPOINTMENTS: AN ALTERNATIVE PATH TO POLITICAL OFFICE

In addition to elective office, women also gain political power through appointments to governmental positions. Frances Perkins, appointed by President Franklin D. Roosevelt in 1933 as secretary of labor, was the first woman to serve in a presidential cabinet. Since the cabinet was established in 1789, twenty-five female cabinet members (4.8 percent) out of the 498 individuals, have served. In December 1996, President Bill Clinton named Madeleine K. Albright secretary of state, making her the highest ranking woman ever to serve in the U.S. government.[77]

When Clinton was elected in 1992, he pledged to appoint a first-term cabinet that "looked like America." In keeping that promise, he appointed four women to cabinet positions, including Janet Reno, the first woman ever appointed attorney general. Women, when they have held executive appoint-

TABLE 4.2 Women Appointed to Presidential Cabinets

Madeleine K. Albright	Secretary of State	1997–2001
	U.N. Ambassador	1993–1997
Charlene Barshefsky	U.S. Trade Representative	1997–2001
Carol M. Browner	Administrator, Environmental Protection Agency	1993–2001
Elaine Chao	Secretary of Labor	2001–
Elizabeth Hanford Dole	Secretary of Labor	1989–1991
	Secretary of Transportation	1983–1987
Barbara H. Franklin	Secretary of Commerce	1992–1993
Patricia R. Harris	Secretary of Health and Human Services	1979–1981
	Secretary of Housing and Urban Development	1977–1979
Magaret M. Heckler	Secretary of Health and Human Services	1983–1985
Alexis Herman	Secretary of Labor	1997–2001
Carla Anderson Hills	Special Trade Representative	1989–1993
	Secretary of Housing and Urban Development	1975–1977
Oveta Culp Hobby	Secretary of Health, Education, and Welfare	1953–1955
Shirley M. Hufstedler	Secretary of Education	1979–1981
Jeane J. Kirkpatrick	U.N. Ambassador	1981–1985
Juanita M. Kreps	Secretary of Commerce	1977–1979
Lynn Morely Martin	Secretary of Labor	1991–1993
Ann Dore McLaughlin	Secretary of Labor	1987–1989
Gale Norton	Secretary of Interior	2001–
Hazel R. O'Leary	Secretary of Energy	1993–1997
Frances Perkins	Secretary of Labor	1933–1945
Janet Reno	Attorney General	1993–2001
Alice M. Rivlin	Director, Office of Management and Budget	1994–1996
Donna E. Shalala	Secretary of Health and Human Services	1993–2001
Laura D'Andrea Tyson	Chair, National Economic Council	1995–2001
Ann Veneman	Secretary of Agriculture	2001–
Christine Todd Whitman	Administrator, Environmental Protection Agency	2001–

Source: Gender Gap Web Site, accessed at *www.gendergap.com*

ments, have traditionally served as secretary of labor; health and human services; housing and urban development or education—offices consistent with women's traditional points of intersection between the private and public spheres. In order to expand women's sphere of influence by diversifying women's appointments, the NWPC established the Coalition for Women's Appointments, made up of about sixty women's professional and issue groups. The Coalition identified qualified women candidates for appointed positions and provided the new administration with "seven hundred resumes of highly qualified, individually vetted women, including many who filled break-through positions in the military, economic, and scientific areas, such as chief scientist at the National Aeronautics and Space Administration."[78] Similarly, The National Political Congress of Black Women (NPCBW), through its Commission for the Presidential Appointment of African American Women, has created a talent bank of highly qualified African American women for top political appointments.[79] Ultimately, more than 40 percent of Clinton's appointments were women, including six women in cabinet-level positions and a record 32 percent of all Senate-confirmed positions. More African American women have been appointed to high level positions in the Clinton administration than in any other administration. The previous administration under President George Bush had appointed women to 22 percent of Senate-confirmed positions.

President Ronald Reagan appointed Sandra Day O'Connor, the first woman to the U.S. Supreme Court, early in his first term. While his record of appointing women and minorities to his administration had been poor, O'Connor's appointment was met with overwhelming enthusiasm.[80] The Senate unanimously confirmed her appointment. President Clinton added the second woman, Ruth Bader Ginsberg, to the Court in 1993.

In addition to providing role models for other women, some evidence also suggests that women in appointed positions govern differently from men. President Jimmy Carter's female appointees were more feminist than his male appointees, while the women in the Clinton administration selected more women to serve under them than men did.[81] Alternatively, analysis of women in the executive branch over several administrations since the 1960s suggests that women had difficulty overcoming the status of token or "other" in providing substantive governance on the basis of their gender.[82] In a contrary example, Secretary of State Madeleine Albright was an active participant and leader in international conferences dedicated to improving women's rights and exhibited a greater sensitivity to women's concerns in shaping U.S. policy toward refugees.

CONCLUSION

The assumption underlying this chapter has been, of course, that it is desirable to increase the number of women in office and that the goal could best be accomplished by increasing the number of women candidates who seek office. This may be challenged by those who are happy with the status quo and so should be addressed. Women should participate fully as citizens and rulers within government for a variety of important reasons. The quality of representation suffers when women are excluded from elective office. Men and women hold different views on issues and exhibit different policy preferences for dealing with public problems. When women are absent from legislative bodies or executive administrations, their perspective is also absent, robbing the country of valuable insight. As long as society is gendered, women will live a different life from men. Compared to men, women are more likely to earn less money, to work in hourly wage jobs and in part-time rather than in full-time positions, and to rely on government assistance to feed, house, and educate their children. They are less likely than men to carry health insurance for themselves or their children. Priorities born of these experiences play an important part in establishing the priorities for a nation. The next chapter discusses in greater detail how women govern once they are elected or appointed to office and how women have continued to work for change outside the bounds of formal power. Women now have two traditions in affecting government: the first as part of a long tradition as *outsiders*, and the second as relatively new *insiders* as more women are successfully elected and appointed to political office.

Notes

1. Irwin L. Gertzog, *Congressional Women: Their Recruitment, Integration and Behavior,* 2d ed. (Westport, Conn.: Praeger, 1995), p. 3.

2. "2000 Fact Sheet," compiled by the Center for American Women and Politics, Eagleton Institute of Politics (New Brunswick, N.J.: Rutgers University, 2000).

3. Richard A. Seltzer, Jody Newman, and Melissa Vorhees Leighton, *Sex as a Political Variable: Women as Candidates and Voters in U.S. Elections* (Boulder, Colo.: Lynne Rienner Publishers, 1997), p. 76.

4. Jody Newman, *Perception and Reality: A Study Comparing the Success of Men and Women Candidates* (Washington, D.C.: National Women's Political Caucus, 1994).

5. Seltzer, Newman, and Leighton, *Sex as a Political Variable*, p. 79.

6. Ibid., p. 80.

7. Seltzer, Newman, and Leighton, *Sex as a Political Variable*, pp. 82–83.

8. Newman, *Perception and Reality*, p. 35.

9. Linda Witt, Karen M. Paget, and Glenna Mathews, *Running as a Woman: Gender and Power in American Politics* (New York: Free Press, 1993), p. 4.

10. "Women Candidates in 2000: An Early Glimpse," fact sheet compiled by the Center for American Women and Politics, Eagleton Institute of Politics (New Brunswick, N.J.: Rutgers University, February 28, 2000), accessed at *http://www.rci.rutgers.edu/~cawp/facts/CandLook2000.html.*

11. Seltzer, Newman, and Leighton, *Sex as a Political Variable*, p. 85.

12. "Women Candidates in 2000," accessed at *http://www.rci.rutgers.edu/~cawp/facts/CandLook2000.html.*

13. Paul Herrnson, *Party Campaigning in the 1980s* (Cambridge: Harvard University Press, 1988).

14. Georgia Duerst-Lahti, "The Bottleneck: Women Becoming Candidates," in *Women and Elective Office: Past, Present, and Future,* eds. Sue Thomas and Clyde Wilcox (New York: Oxford University Press, 1998), pp. 15–25.

15. Susan J. Carroll, *Women as Candidates in American Politics,* 2d ed. (Bloomington: Indiana University Press, 1994), p. 161.

16. U.S. Department of Commerce, Bureau of the Census, "Young Women Surpass Young Men in Educational Attainment" (Washington, D.C., 1998), accessed at *http://www.census.gov/population/www/socdemo/educ-attn.html.*

17. Susan Carroll and Wendy Strimling, *Women's Routes to Elective Office* (Brunswick N.J.: Center for American Women and Politics, Rutgers University, 1983).

18. Witt, et al., p. 95.

19. R. Darcy, Susan Welch, and Janet Clark, *Women, Elections and Representation,* 2d ed. (Lincoln: University of Nebraska Press, 1994), p. 106.

20. Witt, et al., p. 97.

21. Ibid.

22. Witt, et al., p. 62.

23. Ibid., p. 105.

24. "Pipeline to the Future: Young Women and Political Leadership," findings on mobilizing young women from a survey and focus groups conducted by Lake Snell Perry and Associates for the White House Project Education Fund, April 12, 2000, accessed at *http://www.womensleadershipfund.org/programs/research.html#content.*

25. See, for example, Barbara Burrell, *A Woman's Place is in the House: Campaigning for Congress in the Feminist Era* (Ann Arbor: University of Michigan Press, 1994).

26. David Niven, "Party Elites and Women Candidates: The Shape of Bias," *Women and Politics* 19, no. 2 (1998): 57–80.

27. Kenneth Prewitt, *The Recruitment of Political Leaders* (Indianapolis: Bobbs-Merrill, 1970).

28. Witt, et al., p. 217.

29. Ibid., p. 218.

30. Duerst-Lahti, "The Bottleneck," p. 19.

31. Robert Biersack and Paul Herrnson, "Political Parties and the Year of the Woman" in *The Year of the Woman: Myths and Realities,* eds. Elizabeth Adell Cook, Sue Thomas, and Clyde Wilcox (Boulder, Colo.: Westview, 1994), pp. 161–180.

32. Ibid., p. 21.

33. "Pipeline to the Future," p. 16.

34. Barbara Burrell, "Campaign Finance: Women's Experience in the Modern Era," in *Women and Elective Office: Past, Present, and Future,* eds. Sue Thomas and Clyde Wilcox (New York: Oxford University Press, 1998), pp. 26–37.

35. Ibid., p. 36.

36. Witt, et. al., p. 139.

37. Burrell, "Campaign Finance," p. 128.

38. Leonie Huddy and Nayda Terkildsen, "The Consequences of Gender Stereotypes for Women Candidates at Different Levels of Office," *Political Research Quarterly* 43, no. 3 (1993): 503–525.

39. Kim Fridkin Kahn, *The Political Consequences of Being a Woman* (New York: Columbia University Press, 1996).

40. L. B. Joliffe, "Comparing Gender Differentiation in the *New York Times*, 1885 to 1985," *Journalism Quarterly* 66 (1989): 683–691.

41. James Devitt, *Framing Gender on the Campaign Trail: Women's Executive Leadership and the Press* (Philadelphia: Annenberg Public Policy Center, University of Pennsylvania, 2000).

42. Kathleen Hall Jamieson, *The Double Bind: Women and Leadership* (New York: Oxford University Press, 1995).

43. Devitt, "Framing Gender on the Campaign Trail," p. 4.

44. Kahn, *Political Consequences of Being a Woman*, pp. 4–6.

45. Monika McDermott, "Race and Gender Cues in Low-Information Elections," *Political Research Quarterly* 51, no. 4 (1998): 895–918.

46. Witt, et al., p. 214.

47. Harriett Woods, *Stepping Up to Power: The Political Journey of American Women* (Boulder, Colo.: Westview Press, 2000), pp. 117–119.

48. Ibid., p. 118.

49. Seltzer, Newman, and Leighton, *Sex as a Political Variable*, p. 100.

50. Ibid., p. 102.

51. Amy Handlin, *Whatever Happened to the Year of the Woman: Why Women Still Aren't Making it to the Top in Politics* (Denver, Colo.: Arden Press, 1998).

52. Ibid., pp. 41–42.

53. "The New Political Woman Survey," in Witt, et al., p. 172.

54. Handlin, *Whatever Happened to the Year of the Woman*, p. 62.

55. Kathleen Dolan, "Gender Differences in Support for Women Candidates: Is there a Glass Ceiling in American Politics?," *Women and Politics* 17, no. 2 (1997): 27–41.

56. Sherrye Henry, *The Deep Divide: Why American Women Resist Equality* (New York: Macmillan, 1994), pp. 320–322.

57. See Joel A. Thompson and Gary F. Moncrief, "The Implications of Term Limits for Women and Minorities: Some Evidence from the States," *Social Science Quarterly* 74, no. 2 (1993): 300–309.

58. Darcy, Welch, and Clark, *Women, Elections and Representation*, p. 165.

59. Handlin, *Whatever Happened to the Year of the Woman*, p. 158.

60. Ibid.

61. Stanley M. Caress, "The Influence of Term Limits on the Electoral Success of Women," *Women and Politics* 20, no. 3 (1999): 45–63.

62. Susan Caroll and Krista Jenkins, *Term Limits and the Representation of Women, Minorities, and Minority Women: Evidence from the State Legislative Elections of 1998* (New Brunswick, N.J.: Center for American Women and Politics, Rutgers University, 1999), accessed at *http://www.rci.rutgers.edu/~cawp*.

63. Susan Carroll and Krista Jenkins, "The Effect of Term Limits on the Representation of Women: An Analysis of the 1998 Elections" (New Brunswick, N.J.: Center for American Women and Politics, Rutgers University, 1999), accessed at *http://Awww.rci.rutgers.edu/~cawp*.

64. Darcy, Welch, and Clark, *Women, Elections and Representation,* p. 140.

65. Ibid., p. 158.

66. Ibid., p. 163.

67. White House Project, accessed at *http://www.thewhitehouseproject.org.*

68. "Pipeline to the Future," p. 27.

69. Tanya Melich, *The Republican War Against Women: An Insider's Report from Behind the Lines* (New York: Bantam Books, 1996), p. 286.

70. Jean Reith Schroedel and Nicola Mazumdar, "Into the Twenty-First Century: Will Women Break the Political Glass Ceiling?," in *Women and Elective Office: Past, Present, and Future,* eds. Sue Thomas and Clyde Wilcox (New York: Oxford University Press, 1998), pp. 203–219.

71. American Association of University Women, accessed at *http://www.aauw.org/5000/vecbod.html.*

72. The Women's Campaign School, accessed at *http://www.yale.edu/wcsyale.*

73. Women Under Forty Political Action Committee, accessed at *http://www.wufpac.org.*

74. Young Women Vote '98, accessed at *http://www.feminist.com/ywvote98.html.*

75. National Organization for Women, accessed at *http://www.now.org/issues/election/elect.html.*

76. Center for American Women and Politics, Eagleton Institute of Politics, Rutgers University, New Brunswick, N.J., accessed at *http://www.rci.rutgers.edu/~cawp.*

77. "Gender Gap in Government," accessed at *http://www.gendergap.com.*

78. Woods, *Stepping Up to Power,* p. 2.

79. National Political Congress of Black Women, profile, accessed at *http://www.npcbw.org.profile.html.*

80. Melich, *Republican War Against Women,* pp. 155–157.

81. Center for American Women and Politics, n.d. "Women Appointed to the Carter Administration."

82. MaryAnne Borrelli and Janet M. Martin, eds., *The Other Elites: Women, Politics, and Power in the Executive Branch* (Boulder, Colo.: Lynne Rienner Publishers, 1997).

Women as Political Actors: Emerging Insiders and Seasoned Outsiders

DESPITE STEADY progress over the last twenty years and even more rapid gains in recent elections, the number of women in political office in the United States is still significantly smaller than the number of men in politics. Does it matter if more men than women are in politics? Are we concerned about this issue from a purely numerical standpoint, or is it that women in office govern differently from men and are therefore better able to represent women's interests? The paradox of gender equality again provides a useful way to evaluate our expectations about the number of women in office as well as how we think women will (or should) behave once in office. Those who believe that equality stems from the similarities between men and women view parity (equal numbers of men and women) as the standard for equality of representation in political office. Therefore, equal numbers of women serving is paramount for *descriptive representation*. Women in this regard provide role models, and a diverse, descriptively representative government lends legitimacy to its decisions and actions. A political institution like Congress or a presidential administration appears to be more representative of the people when its membership reflects the characteristics of the population it serves. Alternatively, for those who believe that equality requires a recognition of the differences between men and women, women's involvement in politics is important because of their unique perspective as women. Therefore, having women in public office is important for what they bring to the job and in the ways they *substantively represent* women and their interests. Of course, as we've seen repeatedly, these perspectives are not mutually exclusive and, in the case of political representation, are quite complimentary. Both paths in pursuit of equality embrace the goal of bringing more women into politics.

This chapter examines women as political actors, defined broadly to include women working within the formal channels of government as *insiders* as well as women working as *outsiders*, pressuring government from beyond the boundaries of formal office. The previous chapter reviewed a number of initiatives designed to increase the number of women candidates and, by extension, the number of women elected officials. Here we examine women's experience and behavior as legislators and appointed public officials working as political insiders. We also look at the ways in which men and women are similar and different in their actions as political insiders. We will also examine the ways women differ from one another as political actors. Women have had a long-standing tradition of working as political outsiders, initially because they were legally excluded from participating as insiders. Now, women have both strategies at their disposal. How do they differ in their means and ends? Outside activists work with nongovernmental organizations and within a variety of social movements to influence politics and promote policies favorable to the interests of gender equality. Often their goals include trying to change the system itself as well as its outputs. As participants in international conferences, feminists have broadened their pursuit of equality to address issues that not only affect women in the United States, but women around the world as well. We will look at how some of these initiatives impact women in this country as well as women abroad and evaluate whether the issues women address as insiders vary from those women address as outsiders. In both cases, women are engaged in political representation through their actions.

POLITICAL REPRESENTATION

On October 25, 1991, the National Women's Political Caucus ran a full-page ad in the New York Times. *Under a pen and ink drawing of a diverse hearing panel made up entirely of women, the heading read: "What If . . . " "What if fourteen women, instead of fourteen men had sat on the Senate Judiciary Committee during the confirmation hearings of Clarence Thomas? . . . Sound Unfair? Just as unfair as fourteen men and no women."*[1]

As this advertisement illustrates, feminists believe that more women in office will translate into a more woman-friendly political system which in turn will generate government actions responsive to women's unique concerns. The ad further implies that it is "unfair" when one group in society dominates political representation so completely and that women, if elected, will act differently than men once in office. This is a complicated set of expectations born of our conceptual understanding of *political representation*.

Contemporary political theorist Hannah Fenichel Pitkin describes four types of political representation: formal, descriptive, symbolic, and substantive.[2] *Formal* representation refers to mechanisms in a political system that ensure representation exists and allows citizens to hold representatives accountable for their actions. In the United States political system, elections are the mechanisms of

WHAT IF?

What if 14 women, instead of 14 men, had sat on the Senate Judiciary Committee during the confirmation hearings of Clarence Thomas?

Sound unfair? Just as unfair as fourteen men and no women.

What if even **half** the Senators had been women? Women are, after all, more than half the population. Maybe, just maybe, women's voices would have been heard. Maybe the experiences and concerns of women would not have been so quickly dismissed or ridiculed. And maybe all of America would have benefited.

The behavior and performance of the United States Senate during the Clarence Thomas confirmation hearings demonstrated a stark truth: women are tragically under-represented politically. As long as men make up 98% of the U.S. Senate and 93% of the U.S. House of Representatives, women's voices can be ignored, their experiences and concerns trivialized.

The need for women in public office has never been more obvious. Or essential.

Men control the White House, the Congress, the courthouse and the statehouse. Men have political power over women's lives. It's time that women help make the rules, create the policies, and pass the laws about sexual harassment, day care, affordable health care, and hundreds of decisions that affect American families every day.

The National Women's Political Caucus is determined to even the odds. To hear the voices of women echo in the halls of power.

If you're angry about what you've witnessed in the United States Senate, don't just raise your fist, raise your pen. Join us. The goal of the National Women's Political Caucus is to increase the number of women elected and appointed to public office. We're the only national bi-partisan grassroots organization working across this country to recruit, train and elect women into office at all levels of government.

Turn your anger into action. Join us.

Count me in. I want to help the National Women's Political Caucus increase the number of women elected and appointed to public office.

Enclosed is my check payable to NWPC Inc. for:

( )$250   ( )$100   ( )$50   ( )$35   OTHER $____

NWPC

Name _____

Address _____

City/State/Zip _____

Please bill my ( ) Mastercard   ( ) Visa   Amount $____

Account Number _____ Expiration Date _____

Signature _____ Date _____

Contributions to NWPC are not tax deductible.

National Women's Political Caucus
1275 K Street, N.W., Suite 750, Washington, D.C. 20005

Paid for by the National Women's Political Caucus

Compare the image presented in this advertisement with the photograph of the actual Senate Judiciary Committee on the next page. Might the outcome of the Clarence Thomas's confirmation hearing have been different if women sat on the Judiciary Committee as this ad implies? *National Women's Political Caucus.*

Feminists reacted strongly to the all-white, all-male Senate Judiciary Committee's treatment of witness Anita Hill. The reaction spawned an effort to elect more women to the U.S. Senate in the next election. *AP Photo/Greg Gibson.*

formal representation. This explains why women were so anxious to participate in elections as voters and ultimately as elected representatives.

The next three types of representation refer to *how* a person is represented. When demands for more women in office stem from claims of justice and equity, descriptive and symbolic representation are in play. When women represent other women simply by their presence in government, women are *descriptively* represented. We assume that if someone shares our descriptive characteristics like sex, race, or other defining features, they will also share and protect our interests. Our image and interests are mirrored by the representative who is "like us." *Symbolic* representation adds an emotional or affective component to representation in that it occurs when we *feel* represented by another. When women looked at the all-male, all-white Senate Judiciary Committee, it neither mirrored their image nor made them feel as if their interests were represented, and the palpable disconnect produced a strong, negative reaction in many. Thus, women's numeric representation in Congress, state legislatures, or other halls of power is important for symbolic reasons in the sense that women *stand for* other women. Women standing for women act as important role models in that they challenge the mental image of political leadership as male in its embodiment. "When we don't see women as leaders, we continue to think of leaders as men. . . . In a circular fashion, the absence of women as political leaders contributes to the continued absence of women as political leaders."[3] *Substan-*

June, 1992. Life Magazine asked 98 women and two men to assemble on the U.S. Capitol steps to show what the U.S. Senate would look like if its male-female proportions were reversed. At the time, only Nancy Kassebaum (R-Kansas) and Barbara Mikulski (D-Maryland) actually held Senate seats. In 2001, thirteen women serve in the U.S. Senate. *Henry Groskimsky/ Time Life.*

tive representation occurs when women *act for* other women by pursuing distinctive interests and policy preferences unique to women. This is perhaps the most important form of representation, although it is also the most problematic to implement. As we have seen repeatedly throughout this volume, women do not constitute a homogeneous group. As such, defining "women's interests" along a single dimension is nearly impossible. Therefore women acting for other women will reflect the diversity of ideological perspectives and issue positions among the women elected representatives. Rarely will all women adopt the same substantive position simply because they are women. In fact, many women in public office do not view themselves as acting for other women. Descriptive representation, therefore, may not have any predictable relation to support for women's substantive interests.[4]

Arguably substantive representation could exist without descriptive or symbolic representation. In other words, men could act for women, but do they? In 1970, a CBS news poll found that more than 78 percent of women favored federally established day-care centers. In 1970, women held less than 4 percent of the seats in Congress, and no action was taken. For that matter, no action has been taken in the more than thirty years since.[5] Is that because women are not present in large enough numbers or because female representatives share no solidarity on this issue? Alternatively, a lack of action could be because this particular issue does not have the popular support needed to pressure Congress to act regardless of how many of its members are women. As of the 2000 election, women held 13 percent of the seats in Congress, and as this chapter shows, that small percentage often makes it difficult to get particular issues on the official agenda. It is impossible to tell for certain whether gender parity in representation would alter the public agenda, but some evidence suggests that it would.

Are Women Unique as Representatives?

Descriptive, symbolic, and substantive representation, although conceptually distinct, are in reality interwoven in complex ways that form the assumptions we make and the expectations we hold for women in political office. For example, because of the power of sex role socialization, we believe women are different from men and possess different traits and characteristics that are stereotypically feminine (e.g., compassionate, conciliatory, compromising). Some feminists see this difference as empowering and therefore expect women to behave differently from men within political institutions, to pursue different policy solutions, to hold different attitudes, and to act to shape the political processes and institutions into being more responsive to women's particular concerns. In recent elections, female candidates have been able to capitalize on voters' desires for change by promising that if elected, women would be different—whatever that means. The meaning of "different" is left to the voters' (and the media's) imagination, but the invitation to rely on positive stereotypes in evaluating women candidates and their promises is clear. Implicit in the message is also the suggestion that women will not only be different, but they will also be *better* than men. Some of these expectations have been confirmed by research studies, while others have not. Simply electing more women to office will not directly translate into the adoption of feminist policies. There is considerable diversity among women as a whole, as well as among women officeholders—particularly by the late 1990s.[6] Assuming that all women share some essential quality that can be translated into a single political voice ignores the diversity among women and, in effect, silences the interests of some women in favor of more dominant women's interests.[7]

An alternative perspective among feminists considers women's claim of difference as somewhat dangerous in the sense that it recalls the theory of separate spheres which relegated women to second-class status and largely confined them to the private sphere purely on the basis of their perceived difference from men. If women encourage voters to rely on stereotypes and place an emphasis on difference, it may backfire when the electoral context or public mood changes. Supreme Court Justice Sandra Day O'Connor, for one, is skeptical of the wisdom of women's claims to virtue and difference:

> The gender differences cited currently are surprisingly similar to stereotypes from years past. They recall the old myths we have struggled to put behind us. For example, asking whether women attorneys speak in a 'different voice' than men do is a question that is both dangerous and unanswerable. . . . It threatens, indeed, to establish new categories of 'women's work' to which women are confined and from which men are excluded.[8]

Others worry that women will be held to a higher standard and be judged ineffective in short order if they cannot alter the political system after taking office. Madeline Kunin, former governor of Vermont, said, "We cannot expect the few women in political life to change the values and the rules of the game alone, although that is sometimes precisely the expectation."[9] Key in her warning is "the few." Even in 2001, women still constituted the minority in Congress and in all fifty state legislatures. Some research suggests that until women make up a critical mass, they cannot be expected to exert much influence over the institution in which they serve.[10] Whether women are in fact different from men may be unanswerable, as Justice O'Connor claims. Nonetheless, the perception of difference is a powerful force in American politics.

POLITICAL INSIDERS: HOW DO MEN AND WOMEN DIFFER?

The research on differences between male and female political actors offers some direction in analyzing women as insiders and evaluating the type of representation they provide. Later in this chapter we will evaluate whether men and women differ in their ideological outlooks on politics and whether women pursue policies that are distinctly different from the policy priorities of male legislators.[11] We will then examine the results of research on gender and policymaking and investigate whether women adopt a particularized style as political actors that differs from their male colleagues.[12]

Ideology and Attitudes

A number of studies have found that women officeholders, at both the state and the federal levels, are more liberal than their male counterparts, regardless of their political party. In an early study of women in Congress, political scientist Freda Gehlen found that female representatives were more likely than males to support such liberal initiatives as the 1964 Civil Rights Act and the Equal Rights Amendment.[13] Women during that period, which also corresponded to the early years of the second wave of the feminist movement, supported a tentative feminist coalition (or at least a coalition of female members) in the House of Representatives.[14] Longitudinal analysis of women in office from 1972 to 1980 found that the nature of the issue and the influence of a representative's constituency were as important or more important than gender in explaining male and female voting behavior. Although women voted more liberally than men in the early 1970s, the size of the difference in voting records decreased over time and did not exist in some regions of the country. Researchers thus concluded that legislative districts that supported liberal policies were more likely to elect women legislators during the 1970s and 1980s.[15] What initially appeared to be gender differences in voting behavior was actually a result of unique characteristics of the relatively few women elected to Congress at the time.

Political scientist Barbara Burrell replicated the early longitudinal analysis of House voting patterns in three sessions of Congress between 1987 and 1992 to see whether gender differences between male and female legislators' voting records remained even after accounting for the fact that women may disproportionately represent more liberal districts.[16] She found, similar to research from prior decades, that liberal ideology is strongest among Democratic women who represent northern urban districts. However, even when controlling for political party and constituent factors, sex remained a significant point of departure in predicting a legislator's liberal voting record across social, economic, and foreign-policy issues. Political party is a slightly greater determinant than sex. Democratic women make the Democratic Party more liberal, whereas Republican women moderate the Republican Party. "In terms of general political ideology, female representatives as a group continue to influence the policy preferences of Congress from what they would be if only men served."[17] Burrell concluded that after taking into account all of the external factors that might make women appear more liberal than men (e.g., district characteristics, political party), women in Congress, as a group, do indeed vote differently from men on issues.

In state legislatures, the trend is similar. A 1988 survey of state legislators from twelve states found that women tend to describe themselves as liberal and that women's voting records reflected greater support for issues related to women, to families, and to general social welfare concerns—particularly on issues like child care and the ERA.[18] A similar study sponsored by the Center for American Women and Politics (CAWP) found a gender gap on a variety of issues, from the death penalty to construction of nuclear power plants; however, the gap was largest on issues of abortion policy. For example, only 26 percent of women agreed that abortion should be prohibited in almost all circumstances, compared to 39 percent of men. Fifty-seven percent of women opposed mandatory parental consent for minors wanting abortions, whereas only 33 percent of men opposed the restriction.[19]

A 1995 study found that women were more ideologically liberal than men on almost all issues, although they were somewhat less so on fiscal matters. Women are far more likely to oppose the death penalty, mandatory prayer in schools, and tax cuts that also require a cut in government spending and to support abortion rights.[20] Relative to their constituents, women are consistently more liberal than men in either party. These ideological and attitudinal differences are also reflected in the interest groups that legislators associate with. For example, the Christian Coalition, as well as groups that support term limits and oppose abortion rights and gun control are all more likely to support Republican men than Republican women and Democratic men and women. As it turns out, groups that support Republican men were more active in the 2000 election than were labor unions, feminist groups, environmentalists, and abortion-rights and gun-control groups—all of which most often favor women and Democrats. The authors conclude that these data "suggest that the electoral tides of the early 1990s may be shifting to the disadvantage of women state legislative candidates."[21] Indeed, although women made substantial one-time gains at the state legislative level in 1992, subsequent gains have been minimal. Women's percentage of state legislative seats rose from 17 percent in 1989 to 21 percent in 1993, but increased only to 22.5 percent in 1999, and dropped slightly to 22.4 percent in 2001.[22]

Male and female state legislators also have different perceptions of their political roles and the impact their gender has on career and effectiveness in office.[23] Public opinion surveys suggest that voters view women legislators as "more nurturant than men, more compassionate, more accessible, more honest, and more moral, the flip side of the perception that women are less swayed by 'politics as usual.'"[24] Women state representatives view themselves differently as well. For example, they see themselves as more hardworking, more patient, more attentive to detail, better prepared in their daily tasks, and better equipped to deal with female constituents' concerns than their male colleagues. As for their work, they think of themselves as more interested in long-term implications of policy and are driven more by the common good than by personal gain. In short, most female legislators see themselves as distinct "outsiders" even within the confines of their respective legislatures. About a quarter of the women interviewed did not see any connection between their sex and their role as a legislator, believing that women are no different from men. The author of the study concludes that such stark differences among women in how they view the intersection of gender and their legislative role leave women officeholders with a need for more complete models of how best to combine gender and political roles.

"Styles" of Political Behavior

In carrying out their role as legislator, several studies have found that women spend considerably more time "keeping in touch" with constituents and helping constituents solve problems than men do. Within the legislature itself, women tend to be "team players" more often than men, spending more time building coalitions within and across political parties.[25] Women's interest in building bridges also extends to their leadership styles. Researchers developed a typology of leadership along two major dimensions: leadership styles (command, coordinating, and consensus) and leadership goals (power, policy, and process). Along each dimension qualities range from a narrow focus on the self to a broader focus on others and the system as a whole. Previous evidence suggests that women would be more likely to be found among the consensus and process oriented leaders. Interviews with ninety legislative leaders in twenty-two states found that women more often considered their leadership styles to be based on cooperation and consensus building qualities, while men usually described their styles as strong, directive, and oriented toward power and control.[26] Significantly, the trend toward professionalized legislatures (higher salaries, more days in session, larger staffs) is also producing a trend toward the feminization of leadership. As legislatures have become more professional, membership has become more resistant to autocratic leadership styles. Thus, women have benefited in two distinct ways: First, the number of women in leadership positions has increased almost in proportion to the number of women serving in state legislative institutions. Second, both male and female leaders are more prone to adopt a "female" style of leadership that emphasizes consensus building and broader concerns about the political system as a whole in response to underlying changes in the institutions themselves.[27] By contrast, a study of female committee chairs found that legislative professionalization produced a negative effect on the collaborative style favored by women.[28]

One of the most important leadership positions within legislative institutions is the committee chair. Legislatures divide the work of detailed policy development and scrutiny among committees that are charged with drafting legislation, holding hearings, reaching compromises on competing interests, and ultimately with presenting the draft legislation to the full body for consideration. This makes committees a central force of power and influence within the institution. Two important studies of chairwomen's performance were done in the 1990s. The first, conducted by political scientist Lyn Kathlene, examined the gendered dynamics of verbal exchanges within committee hearings that were chaired by a man or a woman.[29] When women chaired committees, they spoke less, took fewer turns at speaking, and interrupted less frequently than chairmen. Male chairs influenced committee hearings, by engaging in substantive comments more than females did and, in the process, interjected their opinions more often. In one out of six turns, men "interjected personal opinions or guided the committee members and witnesses to a topic of their interest."[30] Chairwomen used their position of power to facilitate discussion among participants and only rarely interjected personal opinions. Among committee members, the gendered patterns of participation persisted as well. Male members spoke up earlier in the hearing than women (half-way versus two-thirds of the way through) and spoke longer, took more turns, and encountered more interruptions than women did. As the proportion of women on a committee increased, men became significantly more vocal. When a sponsor of a bill before the committee was female, men both spoke earlier and began questioning her or female witnesses as soon as the bill was introduced. Men did not engage in this same type of eager scrutiny when a male sponsored a bill or was a supporting witness.[31] To increase women's effectiveness as chairs and members of committees, Kathlene observes, each woman should either be seated beside a woman or be within the line of sight of other women. This is consistent with the findings of a 1985 study of county supervisors in Santa Clara, California. Political scientist Janet Flamang found that the presence of supportive female colleagues allowed women to speak out and participate in the legislative process where they might otherwise exhibit reticence.[32]

In the second study of female committee chairs, conducted in 1994, political scientist Cindy Simon Rosenthal found important demographic differences between male and female chairs. Because leadership positions have most often been awarded to those with the greatest seniority, Rosenthal found that chairwomen were significantly older than chairmen and were less likely to hold advanced degrees. They were also less likely to have worked outside the home and more likely to have developed their leadership skills in community or volunteer settings rather than in political office.[33] In many ways, the profile of female chairs in this 1994 study more closely resembles the majority of women serving in the 1970s and early 1980s than the women elected after 1988.[34] Chairwomen in this study viewed themselves as task and team oriented, managerial, assertive, skilled at interpersonal dealings, and frank and direct. Males, on the other hand, viewed themselves as more competitive, willing to intimidate, and opportunistic.[35] Ironically, Rosenthal concludes that women's task-oriented style of leadership, rather than facilitating their rise to power, may actually act as a barrier. Women feel obligated to finish a task or to "get things done," even if it means passing up an opportunity to seek higher office or pursue progressively higher leadership positions.

Policy Priorities

The contemporary focus on women as "different" is in part fueled by psychologist Carol Gilligan's work on the moral reasoning of men and women. Her book, *In a Different Voice*, provides theoretical fuel for political scientists to empirically test whether men's and women's approaches to policymaking differ in substantive ways. Lyn Kathlene's research shows that men tend to be more instrumental in their attitudes and behavior as policymakers, while women approach the world from a more contextual viewpoint.[36] As instrumentalists, men view individuals situated within a hierarchical and competitive world, they value the protection of individual rights and are more likely to solve problems using an "ethic of justice." Alternatively, women view the world as a series of interdependent, connected relationships. Because Gilligan believes that women are more likely to see individuals in terms of their "symbiotic relationships" to others, she argues that women will approach problem-solving from an "ethic of care." Using this framework, Kathlene interviewed state legislators in Colorado, analyzed transcripts of committee hearings, and conducted content analyses of 360 proposed bills in an effort to understand how men and women conceptualize problems and formulate policy solutions.[37] She found that on average women consulted more sources and used more resources to define the problem and explore solutions. Men were more likely to rely on a few experts or to rely more heavily on information from lobbyists. These differences persisted regardless of party, age, or number of terms in the legislature.

Applying this research to a specific policy area, Kathlene interviewed forty-seven Colorado legislators about the problem of crime.[38] Again she found differences between the way men and women conceptualized the problem and the type of solutions they proposed as bills. Men tended to see criminals as individuals who had chosen a life of crime, whereas women most often viewed criminals within the broad context of social opportunities or, more accurately, the inequalities of social opportunities (e.g., disintegrating families, poverty, educational inequities). These differences persisted even across political party lines. In proposing policy solutions to stop crime, men focused on the crime itself and proposed bills with a short-term legal focus (increasing penalties, addressing criminal justice, prison administrative issues, and legal proceedings, or expanding existing laws to include new crimes). Women, however, adopted a long-term perspective and focused on crime prevention and proposed bills that focused on intervention or rehabilitation. Some woman-sponsored bills also had a legal focus, but these constituted only 37 percent of the total crime-related bills sponsored by women. Eighty-three percent of the bills proposed by men became law in the year of Kathlene's study, while only 37 percent of the women's bills were passed. More specifically, all of the prevention and intervention bills sponsored by women were indefinitely postponed. Kathlene concludes, "Women's policy approaches are not understood or appreciated, but seen at best as tangential to the problem at hand."[39] At least in this narrow case, women did not substantively change the nature of the legislative discourse or policy outcomes regarding crime.

Sociologist Rosabeth Moss Kanter found that when members of a minority group made up 15 percent or less of the total, the larger group perceived them as tokens. This token status changed their behavior, and these minority-group members tended to respond to their differential status in "unnatural" ways. As minorities in organizations reached "tilted" status (between 15 and 40 percent of the whole) or approached a "balanced" status (defined as a 60–40 split), they were able to respond in an unrestrained fashion. Building on a theoretical framework first proposed by Kanter, [40] political scientist Sue Thomas hypothesized that as the percentage of women in a legislative body increases, so too does the likelihood that women legislators will sponsor more bills relating to women, children, and the family. Likewise, in states with more women legislators, the passage rates for bills on women, children, and the family will be higher. [41] Thomas's study of women in twelve state legislatures found that in states with more than 20 percent women legislators, women gave priority to bills related to women, children, and the family more often than men did. In states that had the lowest percentages of women in their legislatures, no bills related to women, children, and the family were introduced by either men or women.[42] Although women's presence alone did not alter the ethic of the legislature, in states with higher percentages of women or in legislatures with organized women's caucuses, both women and men were more attentive to "women's issues."

HOW EFFECTIVELY DO WOMEN *STAND FOR* WOMEN'S INTERESTS?

Thomas's research, to some extent, tested the assumption that more women in office led to better representation of women's interests and shows that women officeholders render substantive representation, or stand for women and their interests. There is also some evidence that women officeholders provide an important form of symbolic representation in the form of political empowerment. Women represented by other women are more interested in politics, participate more, and have a greater sense of efficacy and political competence.[43] A study of men and women living in congressional districts served by female legislators found that women exhibited a sense of political empowerment, a sort of psychic benefit from being represented by a woman in Congress. Men, however, did not derive the same benefit. The statistical differences noted between men's empowerment when represented by a woman and alternatively by a man suggest that the effect on women is derived from a type of symbolic representation and not district-specific characteristics that could also explain the election of a woman. Interestingly, women do not appear to expect more in the way of tangible benefits when they are represented by a woman.[44] Whether women's satisfaction with mere symbolic representation will decline over time as female officeholders become a more integral part of governing remains to be seen. Presumably tangible benefits could combine with symbolic empowerment to produce an even stronger relationship between the gender of constituents and their representatives.

African American women in Congress constitute a rather small, but highly visible group that faces additional expectations about their behavior as legislators and feels pressure to represent the interests of both women and African Americans. Their dilemma again stems from difficulty in defining a constituency based on some essential characteristic that may or may not unite members of the minority group around a common agenda. "We're expected to be representatives on economic issues, health issues, housing issues, the issue of incarceration of black males and drugs," says Maxine Waters, a Democratic congresswoman from California. "But at the same time, because of the nature of this job and the nature of our work, it creates the need to be assertive. And sometimes [women lawmakers] are criticized for being too aggressive. Somehow, there is a desire for [women] to be tough, but not to show it, or to be aggressive, but to mask it in ways that men are not asked to do."[45] Eleanor Holmes Norton, the nonvoting delegate from the District of Columbia, says that her preparation to represent dual interests stems from a lifetime's experience with both racism and sexism:

> Much of my view of women comes out of the life I've lived and the commitments I've made long before even thinking about running for Congress. Growing up in a segregated city and going to segregated schools raised my consciousness very early about [racial] discrimination. . . . The transfer of that from blacks to women was almost automatic. . . . By the time I got to Congress, my view on women and my feeling of responsibility for pressing forward their demands was very well formed. . . . This was just another place, another forum, to act on them.[46]

Very few studies have been conducted on minority women's behavior as public officials, maybe because of the relatively small sample of minority officials to study. More research in this area would enrich our understanding of the diversity among women and of the way individual politicians deal with the dual identities of race and gender when representing their constituents.

Comparative research on women politicians shows that the context in which women serve is an important factor in whether women can effectively stand for other women. A 1998 study investigated whether the presence of female members of the Canadian House of Commons made a substantive difference in representing women's interests.[47] Manon Tremblay found that although women did make a difference, their impact was slight. Women, more than their male colleagues, tried to shape the legislative agenda and the legislative discourse to promote the interests of women, but their efforts were quite small. Their numbers, which reached a record high of fifty-three women in 1993, did not permit them to exert the level of influence necessary to make substantial changes in the parliament's culture or in the political parties' primary legislative agendas. Tremblay notes that simply having women represent women does not in itself result in substantive representation. Rather, "it is the election of feminists which constitutes the best guarantee that a correlation between *standing for* and *acting for* representation will be established. It is feminists who are more likely to speak and act in favour of women's interests."[48]

The Role of a Women's Caucus in Facilitating Legislation for Women

Several studies note that an organized caucus for women's interests facilitates favorable legislation for women. Sue Thomas found that without gender balance or a critical mass of women in state legislatures, women's caucuses were instrumental in bringing attention to issues related to women, children, and families.[49] "When a caucus bands together, the result is political clout—a weapon with the potential to overcome skewed groups."[50] The percentage of women in the U.S. Congress has increased more slowly than the number of women in state legislatures. In 1977, when only eighteen women (a little more than 3 percent) sat in Congress, fifteen of those eighteen women founded the Congresswomen's Caucus, later renamed the Congressional Caucus for Women's Issues (CCWI). Since its inception, the women's caucus has been a bipartisan organization co-chaired by a Democrat and a Republican. To extend the caucus's influence, the Women's Research and Education Institute (WREI) was also founded in 1977 and remained organizationally linked to the caucus until 1985.[51] The caucus had two early policy successes in the 95th Congress: a bill preventing employer discrimination against pregnant women and attention to gender disparities in federal employment and social security benefits.[52] Beyond these, women had little success convincing the overwhelmingly male Congress that women's issues were not only linked to one another, but they were also imbedded in programs that initially seemed unrelated to "women's issues." That changed in 1978 when the caucus mobilized colleagues to extend the life of the Equal Rights Amendment. Besides the extension, which few thought possible, its members put Congress on notice that they were capable of moving legislation and setting policy priorities favorable to women's interests.

The CCWI provided two functions: to advocate for women and families and to serve as an information clearing-house on women's issues in Congress. During the 1980s and early 1990s, CCWI introduced and sponsored several omnibus legislative packages including the Economic Equity Act (1981), the Family and Medical Leave Act (1985), the Women's Health Equity Act (1990), and the Violence Against Women Act (1993). Portions of each of these packages have now been adopted into law. In addition, the caucus brought new attention to the issue of breast cancer and won approval to earmark more than $500 million for breast cancer research. The caucus's most successful legislative session was the 103rd Congress (1993–1994), during which sixty-six measures of direct benefit to women and families were passed and signed into law. The caucus also endorsed reproductive rights, ending a fifteen-year self-imposed silence on the divisive issue. Patricia Schroeder remarked that the 103rd Congress "should finally put to rest the question, 'What difference does having more women in Congress make?'"[53] Although there were victories, how successful was the CCWI in establishing a legislative agenda that was compatible with women's interests?

The CCWI suffered organizational difficulties during the early 1980s as founding members either retired, were defeated, or passed away. Attracting new members proved difficult in the 1980s, particularly among newly elected Republican women. For a variety of reasons (unwillingness to pay membership dues, wariness of affiliation with "women's issues," or a fear of alienating the conservative Reagan administration), membership lagged, and the caucus's ability to influence the legislative agenda diminished substantially. In 1981, the CCWI took dramatic steps to extend its influence and opened its membership to men. Over time, the caucus grew from one of the smallest legislative service organizations to one of the largest. New bylaws restricted membership on its executive committee to women only but retained the bipartisan co-chair arrangement, as well as its tradition of focusing on issues that united women. During the 103rd Congress, the caucus's membership included forty-two of the forty-eight women in the House as well as the speaker of the house, the majority leader, the majority whip, and a number of powerful committee and subcommittee chairs.[54] This resurgence was short-lived. When the Republicans took over Congress after the 1994 elections, rule changes stripped legislative service organizations of their budgets, staff and office space. As a result, the CCWI reorganized as a congressional member organization, and three former staff members established a nonprofit organization called Women's Policy, Inc. (WPI) to carry on the caucus's weekly newsletter and information services.[55]

Research on the CCWI's effectiveness prior to its change in status showed that the organization was moderately successful in shaping the agenda of the 103rd Congress on issues of women's health, abortion rights, and health-care reform.[56] Women in the CCWI were able to transform the area of women's health from an invisible issue to one that is politically highly charged. As one Capitol Hill lobbyist explained, "If the women had not been there, there would be no women's health agenda. There never would have been. I think they are wholly and completely responsible. . . ."[57] The caucus began work on women's health in the 101st Congress by introducing the Women's Health Equity Act (WHEA), an eighteen-item omnibus bill designed to address inequities in the treatment of women's health issues. By using the WHEA as the cornerstone of future initiatives on women's health, legislators increased the number of bills on women's health to thirty-two by the 103rd Congress. What's more, women had sponsored twenty-three of those thirty-two bills. Women's health is a good example of an issue that brings women together regardless of party or political ideology. The bills on women's health came from women on both sides of the partisan aisle. Researcher Debra Dodson attributes three factors to women's success in getting Congress to focus on women's health: First, allocating more federal dollars for health research allowed women to avoid partisan or ideological divides that often derailed other initiatives. Second, the rise of a grassroots movement to fight breast cancer put pressure on members of Congress from their constituents to support women's health issues and to take women's health more seriously overall. Finally, there was no organized opposition to women's health. Of all the issues the CCWI pursued, it was most successful in shaping the overall congressional agenda and in seeing legislation enacted in the area of women's health.

Abortion rights was a more divisive issue than women's health, both within and outside the caucus. Although the caucus had voted to take a pro-choice stance on abortion rights, not every member agreed, and the internal divisions limited the organization's ability to promote bipartisan solidarity on the issue. Unlike women's health, abortion rights had a well-developed opposition to overcome. African American women were instrumental in setting the CCWI's priorities on reproductive rights. Until then, the focus on reproductive rights had been the Freedom of Choice Act (FOCA). FOCA attempted to protect a woman's access to abortion and to limit the restrictions states could impose on abortion services. Rather than support FOCA, African American members argued that the CCWI should push for funding and the removal of barriers to funding for poor women covered under Medicaid. The differences in priorities reflected the differences among the women members themselves and among the constituencies they were elected to represent. Ultimately the caucus agreed to push for funding as their top priority. In the same session, Congressman Don Edwards reintroduced FOCA without consulting either the senior congresswomen or the CCWI. The caucus's dedication to pursuing funding for poor women eventually robbed Edwards of the energy he needed to push FOCA, which died before reaching the floor for debate. Although women were ultimately unsuccessful in procuring funding guarantees, House members clearly understood that neither senior women nor the caucus could be ignored in setting the reproductive-rights agenda in the future. The caucus's success in the area of reproductive rights was limited to demonstrating their power to grant or to withhold its support for particular legislation consistent with its own priorities as an organization. To many, the caucus's decision to forgo support for FOCA in favor of pursuing Medicaid funding seemed shortsighted since in the end they lost both bills. In the long-term though, the caucus strengthened its position within the institution as an integral player in setting the congressional agenda.

Finally, in the area of health-care reform, women were able to insert into the Clinton health-care package a number of narrow provisions on services for women. Women were less successful in shaping health-care reform than in either of the previous two issue areas because of the breadth of the overall initiative and the level of organized opposition that quickly developed to the Clinton plan. Women were successful in highlighting women's health concerns within the larger debate. Members of the caucus met with Hillary Rodham Clinton, chair of the Health Care Task Force, early in the process to talk about women's health priorities. The caucus urged the Task Force to improve the coverage for mammograms, pap smears, and pelvic exams in the basic benefits package.

Researcher Debra Dodson concluded that although women and the CCWI were successful in bringing significant new attention to health, reproductive rights, and health care reform, successfully passing legislation still largely depends on women's positions within the traditional institutional power structure—serving on relevant committees, chairing committees and subcommittees, and earning seniority as legislative leaders. "Until women are chairs of powerful and key committees, hold half the leadership positions, and have the expertise that comes through years of experience, they will have to continue to build the strong ties to male colleagues that enable them to accomplish goals they could not otherwise accomplish."[58] This also implies that until more women are elected, rise to power, and become a more visible presence in the institution, their power to set and to enact legislation that is favorable to women's interests will be limited.

The Difficulty in Defining "Women's Interests"

Although the CCWI was a bipartisan organization, members often differed along partisan lines in defining "women's interests." Historically, if feminists have felt comfortable with either of the two parties, it has been with the Democrats. As women officeholders become more diverse in terms of their ideology, partisanship, and interests, it produces interesting controversies as to who is actually "standing for" women. Additionally, women officeholders must make decisions and take actions "inside" that appear to "outsiders" as if they are compromising their feminist principles and selling out women's interests. Two cases illustrate this point: the debates leading up the Persian Gulf War and the welfare reform vote in the 104th Congress.

In 1991, Congress spent three days debating resolutions authorizing the use of force in Iraq. The debate was prompted by the news that Saddam Hussein and his Iraqi military force had invaded Kuwait, removed the ruling family, and taken over the oil production facilities. The Persian Gulf War ensued in an attempt to drive Hussein from Kuwait, restore the previous government and ruling family to power, and maintain the stability of the Middle East. The terms of the debate were largely framed around world power, the importance of stability in the Middle East, and the United States' strategic interests in maintaining the flow of oil from the region. Only one woman, Barbara Boxer, raised issues related to women and war during the congressional debates. More than 32,000 women soldiers served in the Persian Gulf War, the highest number of women ever to serve in an armed conflict. Some in the media dubbed the operation a "mommy's war" because of the large number of women with children in the U.S. forces. The footage of women in fatigues kissing their children good-bye again raised questions among some about the appropriateness of women in the armed forces. However, others believed that women's presence in both the military force and the Congress should have influenced the decision to go to war in the first place. Arguing that power-over politics silenced congresswomen during the debates over the war, author Adrienne Elizabeth Christiansen suggests that women nevertheless should have spoken out in defense of women and war issues. Power-over politics is defined as the use of force to get one's way. In her essay, she argues that even though women were present in Congress for the debate, they were effectively silenced since they lacked the military experience that lends legitimacy to participants in such a debate. Without legitimacy, the issues they might have raised about women, children, and the environment went unaddressed. In short, "until women and men are able to directly challenge the underlying assumptions of power-over politics and this conceptual framework, wars will continue to be fought and the effect on women and the environment will continue to seem irrelevant."[59] This argument assumes that women's perspective on issues related to war differs substantively from men's and it again raises the question of "essential" characteristics related to gender. Are men by nature more aggressive and prone to violence than women?[60] Is a government run by men more likely to engage in wars than a government run by women? These remain hypothetical questions since we do not have any empirical observations on which to base an answer. However, these questions and others about the Persian Gulf War, as well as those about women in the military and women's role in Congress as it debates the use of force again raise the paradox of gender equality as it relates to women's ability to define and stand for women's interests. Are women's interests the same as men's or do women have a unique set of concerns that only women representatives in government can adequately address?

The same questions have been raised about women's interests and welfare reform. As the Republican leadership and the Clinton administration worked to "end welfare as we know it," women members were openly chastised in several quarters for failing to influence the content and character of the legislation. Republicans, in control of both houses of Congress by 1995, proposed to replace the welfare system known as Aid to Families with Dependent Children (AFDC) with a much smaller program administered largely by the states through block grants. The biggest change in the proposal was to eliminate entitlement to welfare benefits. Under AFDC, single women with children who met the income qualifications were entitled to receive support for their children. The new legislation proposed a five-year lifetime benefit cap with some leeway for states to enact their own restrictions. Welfare-rights advocates cited studies that predicted the new legislation would force 1.1 million more children into poverty. When the final vote came, only Senator Carol Mosely Braun joined ten male Democratic senators to vote against the bill. The sharp rhetoric surrounding the welfare debate and its particular focus on blaming poor women for the ills of the welfare system prompted few public objections from women in Congress. This silence led columnist and feminist critic Katha Pollitt to condemn the congresswomen's inaction as more "business as usual." "The truth is," Pollitt wrote, "except on a few high-profile issues—abortion rights, sexual harassment, violence against women—electoral feminism is a pretty pallid affair: a little money for breast cancer research here, a boost for women business owners there. The main job of the women is the same as that of the men: playing toward the center, amassing campaign funds, keeping business and big donors happy, and currying favor with the leadership in hopes of receiving plums."[61] One Washington-based activist summed up her disappointment, characterizing the conflict women officeholders face in trying to become effective insiders, "They [congresswomen] didn't want to be marginalized, they wanted to be at the table, and they wanted Bill Clinton to like them."[62]

The National Organization for Women, while it committed considerable resources to fighting the welfare changes, still felt compelled to write an op-ed piece defending the women who voted in favor of the bill that NOW labeled "anti-woman":

> When the Senate voted recently for the harsh Republican welfare repeal bill, Senator Carol Mosely-Braun stood alone among the women senators in opposing it. This did not go unnoticed by reporters. Despite their invitations, we resisted the temptation to lash out at the other women senators and renounce our strategy of electing more

THIS POLITICAL cartoon depicts Secretary of State Madeleine Albright and Attorney General Janet Reno sharing tea as they discuss the war in Kosovo and a Justice Department investigation into security breaches at the Los Alamos nuclear research facility. Secretary Albright and Attorney General Reno are the first women ever appointed to their respective cabinet positions. In what ways does this cartoon depict gender stereotypes? Are they positive or negative stereotypes? In what ways do gender stereotypes of women political actors enhance or detract from the public's perception of their competence and power?

feminist women. We are convinced that real, lasting change can only come from having women's rights supporters both outside and inside the system—in much larger numbers. While activists must hold insiders accountable, even when they are operating in an ugly, hostile climate, we must also recognize the valuable roles each of us plays. . . . It took more than 70 years to get women the vote in this country. We know it will take years longer before we build the critical mass to wield a fair share of power on Capitol Hill.[63]

What is women's role in defining and promoting women's interests? To argue that women alone are responsible for protecting women, children, and the vulnerable in society suggests again that women have some quality in their nature that men lack. Does this line of reasoning promote women's equality or relegate women to the sidelines of institutional politics? As we've seen repeatedly, not all women think alike or act alike. The conflicting expectations for women in public office, born of the paradox of gender equality, create a complex environment for women insiders.

As the number of women in Congress and in other powerful government institutions grows, women will increasingly face the contradictions inherent in the pursuit of equality. Even while promising a "different voice," women have found themselves quickly confronted with the practicalities of functioning within political institutions that may require behavior that is antithetical to their idea of "different." It will be important to watch this dynamic unfold as women's presence continues to grow in legislatures at the state and national levels. If women in government continue to be perceived as ineffective or no more effective than men in "standing for" the interests of women, then one of the primary arguments for women's election to positions of power will be undermined. The warnings of those wary of the "difference" argument's power to promote stereotypes and have unreasonable expectations of women will resonate. Columnist Ellen Goodman, writing after the 1992 elections, asked, "How long before we read the first story asking why six women in the Senate haven't changed the institution?"[64] If anything, as the number of women in Congress has increased, the rich diversity among women is more evident, which contributes to the mixed expectations for women's concerted behavior as a group. Working together across party and ideological lines, women have been able to add important issues to the public agenda. However, analysis presented in this chapter suggests that women's power beyond the agenda-setting stage of policy formation may still be limited by their lack of significant numbers and the influence that comes with leadership positions within institutions of government.

SEASONED OUTSIDERS: WOMEN AS POLITICAL ACTIVISTS AND AGITATORS

Many women and women's causes remain outside the realm of formal government. The second wave feminist slogan, "the personal is political" issued a direct challenge to mainstream politics to broaden its base to include the myriad of problems women face in everyday life. Issues that were previously removed from public discourse because they were defined as individual or private problems, such as abortion and reproductive rights, violence against women, pay equity, child care, sexual harassment, and housework, have been transformed into political issues by the women's movement. However, even as feminists directly challenged the definition of political as too exclusive, they were attacked for appearing to focus only on problems directly relevant to white, middle-class women.[65] Women of color and working-class women have participated in direct forms of political action for decades outside the confines of the organized women's movement, although their political activism is rarely included in discussions of women's political participation. Liberal feminists' willingness to engage the political system in seeking reform either from the inside or by using the system to produce changes in policy has been challenged by more radical feminists who argue that the location of women's oppression is more likely found in the family or the workplace.[66] A politics of engagement that seeks change outside the system by establishing autonomous programs or institutions but that enlists the system's aid (e.g., as a funding source) faces a variety of challenges. In the 1960s and 1970s, feminists created alternative institutions like battered-women's shelters, rape crisis centers, and health clinics. However, lack of funding for these institutions inevitably brought women back into contact with the state. By resolving the conflict of whether to remain an outsider or to work as an insider, feminists have broadened the possibilities for social change.[67]

This half of the chapter is devoted to examining post-suffrage political action strategies undertaken outside the traditional channels of government, such as through unions, community-based organizations, and other forms of grass-roots organizations. Nongovernmental organizations (NGOs) have been instrumental throughout the world in agitating for change in gender relations and in women's status. International conferences, treaties, and agreements have challenged the world's governments to take action in promoting women's equality. We will examine the role of the United Nations in promoting women's global equality through its many initiatives. The United Nations designated the year 2000 as "Women 2000" or "Beijing +5," a time for governments and NGOs around the world to take stock of progress in implementing the Platform for Action adopted in 1995 at the U.N. Fourth World Conference on Women held in Beijing. We will evaluate the U. S. government's standing on a number of global equality criteria. We will review the provisions contained in the Convention on the Elimination of all forms of Discrimination Against Women (CEDAW) and assess the rationale behind the opposition to CEDAW, particularly the opposition among women in the United States. Finally, the Senate has failed to ratify CEDAW in the twenty years since it was passed. We will examine the politics of relying on international treaties and conventions to pursue gender equality in the United States.

THE POLITICS OF DIRECT ACTION AND COMMUNITY ORGANIZING

Louise Tilly and Patricia Gurin describe the dimensions of women's politics as taking one of two forms: *politics* or *protopolitics*.[68] Politics is characterized by conventional action within institutions, organized interest groups and political parties, and through electoral politics. Protopolitics, by contrast, includes action by and within organizations that work outside the formal political arena. Protopolitical organizations are grounded in the collective identity formed through everyday life experiences. Women as a group have been marginalized in U.S. politics, but as we've seen repeatedly throughout history, within the group called *women*, some women are more "equal" than others. The mainstream women's movement has been criticized as being a white, middle-class, professional crusade that at best has ignored the plight of working-class, poor women, and women of color, and at worst, has sacrificed the interests of some women to expedite other women's entrance into the inner sanctum of political power. Neglected communities of women, defined by their color or class, have reacted by forming their own organizations and operating outside both the formal women's movement and the formal offices of government. On the other end of the spectrum, some women have organized with the conscious goal of maintaining and enhancing race, class, and gender divisions. Conservative, white, antifeminists have also organized as activists to maintain the status of their families by protecting their husband's place in the socioeconomic racial hierarchy.[69]

In all cases, women activists undergo an identity transformation as their individual identity becomes linked to a larger effort for social change. By forming or joining NGOs, women develop skills and attitudes that often propel them to action beyond their initial issues or interests. Activism also prompts women to reconsider the role gender plays in the structure of society and social problems. Women's daily lives provide the motivation to demand more in the way of rights, recognition, and agency. Although activism may develop around issues of community development and employment, the availability of low-income housing, public transportation, or environmental safety, the organizing principle centers on achieving justice. In describing her organization, one indigenous woman leader said, "This is a community political organization whose mission is to empower the disenfranchised, to achieve racial and gender equality, and social and economic justice. Our primary focus over the last few years has been doing work around environmental justice."[70] Indigenous women activists interviewed for a study of sixteen Native American and Latina associations shunned the label feminist even though they were actively working to transform patriarchal structures and relationships. They saw their political activism as indistinguishable from their cultural, ethnic, or racial identity. Central to their identity and notion of leadership is their relationship to their community and family. Themes of protection, justice, care, and equality run through their work.

Another useful way to conceptualize women's activism outside the formal channels of government is *two-tiered pluralism*.[71] In its ideal form, the pluralist theory of interest group participation presupposes that all interests have equal access to the policy process. Interests are served by forming groups that are dedicated to promoting those interests through the political process. The system is maintained because competing interests exist in a rough equilibrium with contrary interests balancing one another so that no one interest or set of interests dominates the political system or the policy outputs of the system. Two-tiered pluralism consciously recognizes the second-class status of minority groups and women relative to their ability to access the policy agenda. Political scientist Rodney Hero argues that "despite the equal legal and political status of minorities formally, distinct factors and processes have led to systematically lower political and social status."[72] The theory of two-tiered pluralism rejects the central patriarchal nature of a pluralism that ignores disenfranchised groups and instead recognizes their influence in enacting change. Rather than pursuing narrow policy directives, indigenous women activists are focused on "justice by increasing the participation and political effectiveness of their communities."[73] In the four examples that follow, women activists pursue interests that in many cases bring them into conflict with traditional political power structures.

Case 1: Increasing Funding for Public Education in Emerson, Massachusetts

In an interesting test of the insider-outsider strategies of political influence described here, Carolyn Howe investigated a community-based effort to fund public education in Emerson, Massachusetts.[74] In this case, two groups of citizens organized to urge voters to override Proposition 2½ (a Massachusetts law passed in 1980 that limited property tax increases to 2.5 percent per year). By referendum, citizens of Emerson, Massachusetts, could override the tax cap for one year so that they could raise $4.6 million for the Emerson Public Schools. The two groups differed both in demographic composition and their primary strategy. One group, comprised of local businessmen and politicians, pursued a traditional electoral strategy "aimed at (1) securing endorsements from key business, political, and religious organizations and (2) contacting voters likely to agree with the education override." The other group included primarily mothers of children who attended a local public elementary magnet school, as well as Anglo and Latino parents whose children attended other local schools. Their strategy was aimed at "educating and mobilizing networks of people at their children's schools."[75]

According to Howe, at their core, the two strategies could not have been more different. The Coalition for Emerson's Future, a registered political action group formed by the business and political leaders, hired two campaign professionals. The effort involved identifying precincts with high voter turnout in the last two citywide elections, targeting voters who were likely to support increased funding for education, and using phone banks to call supporters. Entire sections of the city dominated by white working-class, Latinos and African Americans were eliminated from this strategy based on low rates of voter turnout in previous elections. The goal of the Coalition for Emerson's Future was solely to pass the override referendum and raise immediate funds for the schools. They were not interested in developing coalitions across race, gender, and class lines to change the politics of Emerson. Meanwhile, the women associated with the magnet school were interested in more than simply passing the referendum. Recognizing that their voices were rarely heard within the elite power structures of state, city, and school governance, the women were most interested in developing a coalition of Anglo, Latino, and African American parents to become more active in school politics and in the related political power structures in the broader Emerson community. The Emerson Magnet School group organized parent phone trees to alert parents about meetings and the pending vote. Through chance, one of the group's members discovered the existence of the parallel effort by the coalition. Members of the magnet group were invited to attend a coalition meeting. The magnet group was quickly co-opted by the coalition and was used essentially as a volunteer base. The coalition minimized the momentum the magnet group had built early in their organizing efforts to reach out to disenfranchised communities. In the end, the referendum passed and voters approved the $4.6 million increase for the public schools, but nothing changed about the way politics was practiced as a result. In reflecting on the experience, Howe notes

> Rather than empowering people to take an active part in shaping the communities in which they live, the effort to save public school funding reinforced traditional ways of doing politics centered around an elite core of businessmen, politicians and party loyalists. What this story shows is the difficulty subordinate groups have in trying to politicize the struggles when they are in alliance with the very dominant groups they seek to challenge and whose interests are to prevent subordinate people from gaining power.[76]

This case illustrates the inherent contradictions in the two strategies' pursuit of change. On the one hand, the dominant group is most likely to pursue a strategy based on the rational interests of individuals. Collective power is an undesirable threat to the dominant group and is therefore avoided by depoliticizing the issue and constituencies. Alternatively, subordinate groups are most interested in gaining collective power to reshape the public agenda and include more interests relevant to class, gender, and race. This is accomplished by politicizing both the issue and the constituencies. The case of Emerson's public schools provides insights into the ways in which collective interests are often transformed and presented as individual interests in order to reduce the likelihood that the dominant power structure is challenged.

Case 2: MADRE: An International Human Rights Organization

In 1983, a group of women activists toured Nicaragua to assess the impact of the Contra war on women of the country. After seeing day-care centers, schools, and health clinics that had been bombed by the Contras, the women returned to the United States and founded MADRE. MADRE is an organization, founded and maintained in the United States, dedicated to building alternatives to war and violence, empowering women to address problems in their own communities, and shaping international human rights policy as it applies to women. It also mobilizes U.S. citizens to demand changes in government policy in support of the organization's goals. The group works in partnership with women's organizations in areas of conflict to provide direct relief in the form of food, shelter, and medical care. Through community development and training programs, women are encouraged to seek leadership roles in their communities that will enable them to shape government policy. MADRE has projects in Cuba, Guatemala, Haiti, Nicaragua, Palestine, Rwanda, and Chiapas, Mexico. In each case, MADRE establishes a partnership with local community-based women's organizations to develop programs that can meet local needs. Simultaneously, MADRE has also encouraged U.S. citizens to tour its projects through organized delegations and to then lobby the U.S. government to change policies that promote or facilitate conflict. MADRE has worked to change U.S. trade policies, end the embargo against Cuba, and end U.S. involvement in other countries' civil conflicts.

Case 3: New Right Women Fighting to Preserve Traditional Gender Roles

An interesting form of women's activism is exhibited by social conservative women of the *New Right*. These women present what can only be characterized as a paradox: They put traditional gender role protection at the heart of the movement, and yet political involvement brings New Right women directly into the very public sphere that they believe should be limited to men. Phyllis Schlafly links conservative women's public role to their obligation to a larger cause: "The Positive Woman accepts her responsibility to spin the fabric of civilization, to mend its tears, and to reinforce its seams. . . . God has a mission for every Positive Woman. It is up to her to find it and to meet the challenge."[77] Other female activists in the New Right have resolved their movement's cognitive dissonance by distinguishing between conventional and traditional values. Conventions do change with the times, and therefore changes in gender roles can be viewed as merely changing conventions without posing a threat to traditional values. Women in the paid labor force is a change in convention, but women rejecting male authority within the family is a threat to traditional values. Leaders of the women's arm of the New Right—Phyllis Schlafly and Beverly LaHaye, for example—have successfully mobilized women in the lower and middle classes on issues of equality characterized as men's liberation from responsibility for their families. Feminists are demonized as threats to a basic sense of fairness when they advocate a change to the traditional roles within families. The Equal Rights Amendment provided an incredible tool for mobilizing and organizing conservative women. Phyllis Schlafly warned women about the dangers the ERA posed to their security and that of their family:

Consider a wife in her 50s whose husband decides he wants to divorce her and trade her in on a younger model. This situation has become all too common, especially with no-fault divorce in many states. If the ERA is ratified, and thereby wipes out the state laws that require a husband to support his wife . . . the most tragic effect would fall on the woman who has been a good wife and homemaker for decades, and who can now be turned out to pasture with impunity because a new, militant breed of liberationist has come along.[78]

More recently Schlafly characterized affirmative action policies for women that are designed to break the glass ceiling as "unfair to the wives of the men who would be the losers in a system of Affirmative Action Quotas for executive women."[79]

Conservative women activists focus their attention on limiting government's expansion into the private sphere at the same time some feminists are claiming that women's lives and livelihoods depend on eliminating the barrier between the private and public sphere. Liberal feminists, in particular, argue that government is in the best position to end centuries of subordination within the private sphere. Once again, women find themselves divided and working at cross purposes.

Case 4: Women's EDGE: Trade Is a Woman's Issue

Trade and economic policies are rarely framed as gender issues. However, ample evidence suggests that trade and economic policies affect men and women differently. Likewise, policies have varying effects on developed and developing nations. Globalization of trade and trade policies have extended their impact on women. The Coalition for Women's Economic Development and Global Equality (Women's EDGE) works to put gender equality on the international trade agenda. Women's EDGE documents the impact of globalization and international trade policies on the lives of women and their families. When countries lower import tariffs to satisfy international trade rules, for example, women are affected more than men. Governments often cut spending on education or health, and public hospitals are privatized in an attempt to make up lost revenues. When fees are introduced into hospitals and schools, women and girls tend to make less use of them. Millions of women are employed by the textile and apparel industry. In recent years, the industry has become even more competitive, driving employers to move factories, drop wages, and increase working hours to remain solvent. Women employees are rarely in a position to prevent a company from moving or to bargain for safer working conditions. "Women make up 80 percent of developing country workers who manufacture products for export. They work up to 80 hours a week for as little as 18 cents an hour," says Elise Fiber Smith, who cofounded Women's EDGE in 1998.[80]

EDGE is particularly focused on watching the emergence of the World Trade Organization (WTO) and analyzing the impact that emerging global trade policies will have on women. The group is not antitrade, but rather it recognizes that world leaders see trade as an engine of economic development. The group's goal is to earn a seat at the table where trade decisions are being made. EDGE has been fairly successful in that effort over the past few years. In 1999, the U.S. Agency for International Development issued a paper that examined trade from a gender perspective for the first time and included policy recommendations. Gender specialists from NGOs like EDGE have also been included in the President's Advisory Committee on Trade Policy and Negotiations along with CEOs, heads of trade unions, and environmentalists. Working with other NGOs, EDGE formed the Gender and Trade Network, which comprises 1,200 economists, activists, and researchers from around the world. The network identifies gaps in research and has initiated a series of research projects on the effects of trade liberalization on women's lives. Both EDGE and the network have focused on developing a base of knowledge that enable them to participate fully in the development of trade policy in the next decade and beyond.

The four cases previously outlined represent only a small portion of the thousands of women who have been working in communities and across international borders to influence the development and implementation of policy in ways that support rather than disadvantage women. Women active in NGOs are no more likely to agree on a single strategy or area of greatest need than women serving inside government. The diversity of interests and organizational approaches advance women's interests despite obvious conflicts and contradictions. For example, MADRE focuses on direct intervention to address immediate relief needs while also mobilizing women and men in the United States to lobby their government against arming rebel causes and supporting violent regimes. EDGE, on the other hand, does not engage in direct service, but has instead adopted a broad research agenda that has enabled that group to provide government agencies and international organizations with information on trade policies that are fair to women.

INTERNATIONAL AGREEMENTS AND GENDER EQUALITY

The international women's rights agenda is in many ways facilitated and shaped by the United Nations. In 1975, the U.N. launched the decade for women with a world conference in Mexico City. In 1979, the U.N. General Assembly adopted the Convention on the Elimination of All Forms of Discrimination Against Women (CEDAW), an international bill of rights for women. Ratifying nations make a commitment to enact legislation and promote policies consistent with the treaty's conditions. As of 2001, the U.S. Senate has not ratified CEDAW. The decade for women concluded in Nairobi with the adoption of the

Forward Looking Strategies that specified the year 2000 for the achievement of specific goals related to women's equality, development, and peace.

The U.N. Fourth World Conference on Women, held in Beijing in September 1995, adopted a platform for action. The Beijing conference included a parallel meeting of activists and members of NGOs. More than 6,000 delegates participated in the Beijing Conference, and another 40,000 NGO representatives participated in the World Forum on Women. The Platform for Action, adopted by consensus of the 165 participating nations, focused on securing the following:

- *economic opportunity* for women, including the right to obtain a job, receive equal pay, and have access to credit and their own property, and that also encourages the world's governments to recognize, measure, and estimate the value of women's unpaid labor
- *education and health care* for women throughout their life cycles
- *personal safety* for women by adopting measures to eliminate violence against women in all its forms
- *a partnership with men* that will enable women to fully participate in the political and economic life of their countries
- *a balance between work and family responsibilities* by promoting shared family responsibilities and through government support for family-friendly workplace policies
- *reproductive rights* including the right of women to control their own fertility and equality in sexual relations
- *environmental justice* for women by promoting sustainable development and addressing the disproportionate impact of environmental problems on women and poor communities
- *respect and opportunity for girls* through education, eliminating prejudicial practices so that girls and boys can be valued equally in their families and in society
- *legal and human rights* by ensuring equality and nondiscrimination under the law, by knowing that human rights are women's rights and women's rights are human rights[81]

Prior to the 1995 Beijing Conference, President Clinton established the President's Interagency Council on Women (PICW). The PICW was charged with implementing the Platform for Action in the United States. In preparation for the Women 2000 Conference, the PICW published a comprehensive five-year progress report entitled *America's Commitment*.[82] The report details the programs in the United States designed to address concerns within each of the nine critical areas of concern set out in the Platform for Action. In many cases, programs existed long before the Beijing Conference. The PICW serves an important coordinating function in alerting women to programs supported by the federal government and directed at improving the status of women. While the report touts achievements in each area, it also lays out obstacles to further progress. In June 2000, delegates again convened in New York for a special session of the

United Nations, "Women 2000: Gender Equality, Development and Peace for the Twenty-First Century." This meeting, also known as "Beijing +5," served as an assessment of the world's progress on the Beijing Platform for Action.

Rating the United States on Progress Toward Gender Equality

Prior to the June 2000 meeting, women's organizations collaborated to produce a number of reports that assessed progress the United States has made in improving women's status in the nine critical areas of concern. The Women's Environment and Development Organization (WEDO) worked with seventeen other NGOs to produce a report entitled, *Women's Equality: An Unfinished Agenda*.[83] The report is described as a part of "a process by which U.S. women's organizations are holding their government accountable to the objectives of the Beijing Platform." The Beijing Platform for Action is a document of principles and recommended actions. It is not legally binding on any of the signatory nations. Because of the lack of enforcement mechanisms, NGOs have been very active around the world, developing ways to hold governments accountable for promises made in the platform. Equality Now, based in the United States, has initiated a project called, "Words and Deeds: Holding Governments Accountable." The project monitors countries around the world whose laws explicitly discriminate against women and violate the Platform for Action.[84] In addition to the *Women's Equality* report, WEDO and the Center for Women's Policy Studies have initiated a national campaign entitled, "Contract with Women of the USA." The contract's twelve principles are taken from the Beijing platform and have been an effective organizing tool for getting state and local governments to focus on the principles of equality.[85] More than 800 national and community-based organizations, members of Congress, state and city legislators, and thousands of individuals have signed the Contract with Women.

Before the June 2000 "Beijing +5" meeting in New York, US Women Connect issued a report card on the U.S. government's efforts to improve equality for women in America.[86] The *Report Card on US Government Action for Women's and Girl's Rights and Empowerment* graded the government's progress, using A (fulfillment of the Platform objectives), B (considerable action), C (some positive action; needs continued improvement), D (very limited action; needs great improvement), and F (total inaction or negative impact). The worst grade, F, was for the government's attempts to reduce poverty among women and girls. While the national poverty rate has decreased, the rate of women in poverty has increased during the period of review. The 1996 welfare reforms are blamed for reducing the average income of households headed by women by 35 percent and limiting poor women's access to education and training benefits, housing and food security, child care and child support. The best grade awarded was a B for increasing the number of women in power and in decision-making positions. The Clinton administration was applauded for appointing the highest number of women to positions of influence of any administration in history. Corresponding increases in women in the legislative branch, however, are lacking at every level of government. Despite its position as a global leader in democracy, the United States ranks only forty-second worldwide in terms of women in government. The United States also received a B for improving the institutional mechanisms for promoting women's equality. Citing President Clinton's creation of the PICW as a major step forward, the report cautions against too much optimism since there is no provision for the agency's continuation after 2000. In other areas, progress was noted in the government's effort to address violence against women through the passage of the Violence Against Women Act and the establishment of the Justice Department's Office on Violence Against Women. Major areas in need of attention are primarily related to soaring child poverty rates, erosion of affirmative action programs aimed at improving women's status in the labor market, gender inequities in pay and the Senate's refusal to ratify CEDAW, and the Convention on the Rights of the Child.

CEDAW: Establishing an International Standard for Women's Equality

The United Nations adopted the Convention on the Elimination of all forms of Discrimination Against Women on December 18, 1979. Prior to CEDAW, there was no convention that comprehensively addressed women's rights within political, cultural, economic, social, and family life. CEDAW provides a universal definition of discrimination against women:[87]

> Any distinction, exclusion or restriction made on the basis of sex which has the effect or purpose of impairing or nullifying the recognition, enjoyment or exercise by women, irrespective of their marital status, on a basis of equality of men and women, of human rights and fundamental freedoms in the political, economic, social, cultural, civil or any other field.

The construction of CEDAW is consistent with the legal equality doctrine of gender equality in that its articles require governments to take certain actions to guarantee women's rights. Article 4 permits affirmative action measures that accelerate equality and eliminate discrimination. In one of many controversial measures, Article 5 recognizes the role of culture and tradition, calling for the elimination of sex role stereotyping. Similarly, Article 10 makes equal access to all fields of education and the elimination of stereotyped concepts of men and women an obligation. Article 11 recognizes that the right to work is a human right and mandates the end of employment discrimination. Article 12 requires countries to take steps to eliminate discrimination in health care, including providing access to family planning. It further requires that steps be taken to ensure equality in marriage and in family relations. In short, CEDAW is similar to the failed Equal Rights Amendment in its attempt to redress discrimination

Encountering the Controversies of Equality

Women and World Politics

World politics has become increasingly feminized in the 20th century as women gained political power and exercised it. This evolution in the sexual basis of politics should be reflected in changes in international relations as the correlation between gender and antimilitarism decreases the use of force to solve international problems.

—Francis Fukuyama, 1998[1]

POLITICAL SCIENTIST Francis Fukuyama has posed a provocative proposition about biology, feminism, and international relations. Reviewing the literature on primate behavior, he noted three aspects that tie biology to social behavior: violence, the importance of coalitions, and that violence and coalition building are primarily the work of males. While female chimps could also be violent and also form coalitions, the most murderous violence was the province of males. ". . . female chimps have relationships; male chimps practice realpolitik." Fukuyama has traced the same violent and coalition-building tendencies to gain power through a number of primitive societies and concluded that there is "something to the contention of many feminists that phenomena like aggression, violence, war, and intense competition for dominance in a status hierarchy are more closely associated with men than women."

Feminists have characterized realist theories of international relations that view international politics as a struggle for power as a "gendered perspective," describing the behavior of states run by men rather than the behavior as states. Fukuyama said that the problem with the feminist view is that "it sees these attitudes toward violence, power, and status as wholly the products of patriarchal culture, whereas in fact it appears they are

by adopting laws that prohibit treating men and women differently on the basis of sex.

The United States was active in drafting CEDAW, and President Jimmy Carter signed it on July 17, 1980. It was passed out of the Senate Foreign Relations Committee in 1994, but the Senate has yet to ratify the treaty. As of June 2000, 165 countries have ratified CEDAW, the United States being the only developed nation that has not ratified the treaty. For CEDAW to be ratified, it needs two-thirds, or sixty-seven, affirmative votes in the Senate. The current Senate Foreign Relations Committee chair, Senator Jesse Helms, a Republican from North Carolina, has been a staunch opponent of CEDAW. Although the House has no formal constitutional role in ratifying treaties, Republican congressman Chris Smith, from New Jersey, has worked with Senator Helms to organize opposition to ratification. Helms and Smith have both objected to the emphasis on the legal equality standard that seeks to eliminate

rooted in biology." Lest the reader grow uncomfortable with a sense of "biological determinism," Fukuyama wrote, "biology is not destiny." However, there is sufficient evidence across a number of scientific domains to suggest that populations of men and women will act in certain predictable ways and that their behavior is not entirely shaped by culture and society. What will this mean for international relations in the future?

Fukuyama argued that as more women enter politics as voters and as political leaders, international relations between developed nations will become more "feminized." The violent and aggressive tendencies of men and of the states they lead will have to be constrained through a web of laws, agreements, and contracts rather than by external forms of aggression like war. As more women participate in politics, the positive effects of feminization will translate into less militarism. Citing the gender gap in foreign policy and national security issues, Fukuyama predicted that this will only occur in developed democracies, which are more likely to support the female franchise and women's participation in decision making than authoritarian states. This point leads to a caution: "If gender roles are not simply socially constructed but rooted in genetics, there will be limits to how much international politics can change. In anything but a totally feminized world, feminized politics could be a liability." The world will still have to deal with states that are run by young, unconstrained men.

What do you think?

How does the evolutionary biology argument differ from gender as an explanation for human behavior? What are the political implications for accepting the evolutionary biologist's claims? How might a *feminized* state's approach to conflict differ from that of a *nonfeminized* state? In what ways can this framework be used to analyze current conflicts in the world?

[1]Francis Fukuyama, "Women and the Evolution of World Politics," *Foreign Affairs* 77, no. 5 (September–October 1988): 24–41.

the differences between men and women. In a "sense of the Senate" resolution introduced by Helms on May 11, 2000, he urged rejection of CEDAW because it "demeans motherhood and undermines the traditional family."[88] In an earlier speech, Helms said "CEDAW ratification is about furthering an agenda which seeks to ensure abortion on demand, and which refuses to recognize any legitimate distinctions between men and women." Smith expressed the other major objection voiced primarily by ideological conservatives, "As a party to CEDAW, the U.S. would subject itself to the jurisdiction of a U.N. committee that was established to enforce compliance with CEDAW."[89] Opponents believe that the U.S. law would be superceded by the provisions of the treaty. However, an analysis by the State Department in the mid-1990s determined that U.S. law is consistent with the principles of CEDAW and that CEDAW is consistent with the Constitution.

Supporters have been frustrated by their inability to get a hearing before the

Senate Foreign Relations Committee. In October 1999, a delegation of ten congresswomen were ordered removed from a Senate Foreign Relations Committee hearing on China after they tried to present Senator Helms with a letter signed by 100 House members in support of CEDAW ratification.[90] On November 19, 1999, Senator Barbara Boxer, a Democrat from California, introduced a "sense of the Senate" resolution (cosponsored by seven other female Senators) to hold hearings and act on CEDAW. The resolution called for the Senate to act by March 8, 2000, International Woman's Day, and in honor of the twentieth anniversary of the treaty. No action was taken. Boxer re-introduced the resolution on April 12, 2000. State legislatures in California, Iowa, Massachusetts, New Hampshire, New York, North Carolina, South Dakota, and Vermont have endorsed U.S. ratification of CEDAW. In addition, some large city councils have taken similar action, and many professional organizations, such as the American Bar Association, have done the same.

Opposition to CEDAW is not limited to members of the Senate. Several women's organizations have taken a firm stand against the treaty. Women for Faith and Family, a U.S.-based organization of more than 50,000 Catholic women, strongly oppose ratification. In a statement issued in May 2000, the organization said, "The provisions of CEDAW seek to overcome injustices towards women by mandating sweeping social changes which embody the narrow ideological opinions and social analysis of militant feminism on a spectrum of issues concerning fundamental rights of women and of all human beings. . . . CEDAW is fundamentally flawed in its radical social analysis and totalitarian in its methods."[91] Likening it to an international version of the Equal Rights Amendment, they object primarily because the treaty attempts to eliminate the differences between men and women. Concerned Women for America calls CEDAW a "back-door ERA" and warns that feminists could use CEDAW to renew the drive for a federal ERA.[92] Conservative women's organizations also argue that CEDAW liberalizes abortion by requiring access to family planning for all women and that it destroys the traditional family structure since it urges a change in traditional roles that limit women's role in society. Others worry that provisions regarding education would amount to "gender re-education" since the treaty requires the elimination of stereotyped concepts of men and women in all forms of education.

Even without Senate action, the U.S. government has moved toward embracing CEDAW. The United States made ratification of CEDAW one of its public commitments in the 1995 U.N. Conference on Women in Beijing. Protests by NGOs at the time raised public awareness of the Senate's failure to hold hearings. On December 10, 1998, President Clinton issued Executive Order 13107, "Implementation of Human Rights Treaties" in which he established an interagency working group to implement America's obligations under U.N. treaties on human rights "to which the United States is now or may become a party in the future."[93] The arguments for and against the treaty strongly resemble the rhetoric of the ERA debate. The controversy also demonstrates the difficulty of creating an international agenda for women's equality that brings women together in pursuit of gender equality. There is no sex solidarity on the issue of gender equality among insiders or among outside activists.

CONCLUSION

Historically, women have been forced to act as *outsiders* in politics because of the legal and customary barriers to their direct participation as *insiders*. Contemporary female political actors, however, have a wide range of activities and strategies available in the pursuit of equality. Women elected to office who promise a different approach to governing do so in the hope of capitalizing on voters' positive gender stereotypes of women as moral, civic-minded, and dedicated to the interests of families, children, women, and those traditionally excluded from power. Outside the bounds of formal power, women continue to agitate for change here in the United States and globally. Women are more involved in politics, the political process, and in governing than at any other time in our history. However, women still encounter obstacles to their pursuit of equality. As a nation, the United States perceives itself as a leader in securing women's rights. The Senate's refusal to ratify CEDAW and its slow progress in addressing other areas of critical concern that were laid out in the Beijing platform suggest, however, that there is still work to be done. Analysis of international conferences suggests that the documents they produce effectively articulate women's rights, but "almost the entire value of the international document lies in their national implementation."[94] This suggests that there is a primary role for women, both inside and outside of formal political office, in continuing to shape policies that affect women and to pursue gender equality.

To this point, we have largely focused on how women have utilized politics to enter politics themselves, first as voters and later as public officials. The next three chapters of the book examine several broad policy areas to better understand how women shape and are shaped by public policies. The paradox of gender equality is integral to explaining both processes. Women shape public policy in a number of ways. In some cases, women's presence in legislative bodies makes it more likely that issues previously defined as *private* are transformed into *public* issues that can be addressed through the public policy process. Issues as diverse as domestic violence and quality child care have only recently been understood as problems that warrant attention in the public sphere. As activists and as officeholders, women can bring issues to the government's attention and influence the content of legislation. As administrators, they can influence how policy is implemented, enforced, and evaluated.

The policy process is normally conceived of in stages: problem identification and agenda setting, policy formation, policy adoption, policy implementation, and policy evaluation.[95] Policies regarding women have resulted from a multitude of converging forces that can't really be separated from historical circumstances. As we discussed in chapter 2, it is unlikely that women's suffrage would have been ratified without the inside lobbying strategy of Carrie Chapman Catt, the NAWSA, and the outside agitation by Alice Paul and the National Women's Party. By the time the legislation moved through Congress and was sent to the states for ratification, a majority of the public was convinced that allowing women to vote was the right and fair thing to do. It took more than seventy years for this to happen. Very few policymaking models adequately address the unique nature of policy affecting women. In most cases, patterns of slow, incremental change will only occasionally be broken with passage of landmark legislation or a single Supreme Court decision that immediately and significantly changes the status quo. Joyce Gelb and Marian Lief Palley utilize the convergence of interest group theory and social movement theory to examine the rise and fall of specific issues within the larger feminist movement. They find across a variety of policy areas that *role equity* issues usually produce successful change in women's status, while *role change* issues lead to intense and often unresolvable political conflict.[96] In this sense, role equity pursues equality as fairness while role change pursues equality as sameness. This conflict, as we've seen in previous chapters, is often most intensely felt and played out among women themselves. Organizations quickly form to advocate and oppose the new role status, extending the time it takes to form, adopt, and implement policy.

The paradox of gender equality can be found squarely at the center of most debates over policy affecting women. In chapter one, the paradox was framed in the form of a question: How can men and women be the same if they are different? The historic struggle to resolve the paradox has brought women into the public sphere and into politics primarily in search of individual agency. Yet women still occupy a primary role in the private sphere in relation to their families and particularly to their children. Separate spheres ideology presupposed that a division of labor is preordained by nature in which women were responsible for the home, the children, and the family, while men were economically and politically active in the public sphere. Public attitudes and public policy supported the gendered division of roles based on the strong belief that men and women were inherently different and therefore suited to play different roles. As public attitudes changed over time, policies changed as well. However, the division between the private and public spheres has not been entirely eliminated, and the underlying assumptions about men's and women's natural suitability for primary roles in the private and public spheres have not been entirely transformed. Contemporary policy debates therefore reflect all of the complexity, tension, and controversy created by the paradox of gender equality.

The next three chapters examine three broad policy areas that are at the heart of the paradox of gender equality: education, work, and family. Chapter 6 evaluates the role education has played in empowering women. Education sits at the intersection of the private and public spheres. Women were first permitted education to make them better mothers, wives, and homemakers. As more women were educated, the role of education changed and women demanded access to education at all levels and across all types of programs. It was not until Title IX was passed in 1972 that women were guaranteed universal access to equal education. The federal legislation could not, however, guarantee that men and women experienced education in the same way. Thus, while Title IX is consistent with the legal equality doctrine, ensuring equal access to education and all educational programs, there is some evidence consistent with the fairness doctrine that men and women learn differently and therefore should be educated differently. Chapter 6 examines the controversies associated with equality in education.

Chapter 7 looks at women's entrance into the labor force and the power of the paradox of gender equality in shaping their experience. Even more so than education, work exemplifies the contradictions that arise for women as a result of the paradox. Employment policy that is consistent with the legal equality doctrine is designed to treat men and women exactly the same. The Equal Pay Act of 1963, for example, mandates that men and women must be paid equally for doing the same job. However, the Equal Pay Act did not and cannot erase the centuries of influence of the separate spheres ideology that limited women's work to tasks consistent with their private sphere roles. Forty years after the Equal Pay Act, women still earn less than men. We will examine a variety of reasons for the wage gap, including women's concentration in low-paying jobs consistent with private sphere gender roles, discriminatory attitudes about why women work, and the periodic interruptions to women's labor force participation necessitated by childbirth. Although Title VII gave women a very powerful tool to combat overt discrimination in hiring and employment, it has done little to resolve the conflicts women face in balancing the responsibilities of home and work. The United States lags far behind other developed nations in enacting family support policies for this purpose.

Chapter 8 focuses on the family and the fertility and reproductive decisions women make in creating families. Many argue that women have been subject to the harshest forms of discrimination and oppression within the private sphere. Historically the family has been a private sphere matter and therefore not the subject of public policy initiatives. Once the absolute divide between the two spheres was broached and women became more active participants in the public sphere, family matters have received more public attention. While the legal equality doctrine appears to serve women's interests in the areas of education and work, it is not as effective in addressing the range of fertility and reproductive issues women face. Unlike the previous two policy areas where socially constructed gender differences are most at issue, reproductive and family issues also incorporate sex as well as gender differences between men and women. Women's claims to equality and autonomy are challenged by society's interest in promoting strong families and in reproducing and sustaining a robust population. Privacy has alternatively been used to promote and restrict women's rights. We will evaluate how effective public policy can be in addressing women's concerns in the private sphere and assess whether the private sphere remains a barrier to women's equality overall.

Notes

1. Harriet Woods, *Stepping up to Power: The Political Journey of American Women* (Boulder, Colo.: Westview Press, 2000), p. 163.
2. Hannah Fenichel Pitkin, *The Concept of Representation,* (Berkeley, Calif.: University of California Press, 1967).
3. Georgia Deurst-Lahti and Dayna Verstegen, "Making Something of Absence: The 'Year of the Woman' and Women's Political Representation," in *Gender Power, Leadership, and Governance,* eds. Georgia Deurst-Lahti and Rita Mae Kelly (Ann Arbor: University of Michigan Press, 1998), pp. 213–238.
4. Jane Mansbridge, "Should Blacks Represent Blacks, and Women Represent Women? A Contingent 'Yes,'" Politics Research Group, John F. Kennedy School of Government, Harvard University, 2000, accessed at *http://www.ksg.harvard.edu/prg/mansb/should.htm.*
5. Kim Fridkin Kahn, *The Political Consequences of Being a Woman* (New York: Columbia University Press, 1996), p. 137.
6. Jean Reith Schroedel and Nicola Nazumdar, "Into the Twenty-First Century: Will Women Break the Political Glass Ceiling?," in *Women and Elective Office,* eds. Sue Thomas and Clyde Wilcox (New York: Oxford University Press, 1998), pp. 203–219.
7. Mansbridge, "Should Blacks Represent Blacks."
8. Linda Witt, Karen M. Paget, and Glenna Matthews, *Running as a Woman: Gender and Power in American Politics* (New York: The Free Press, 1993), p. 268.
9. Ibid., p. 268.
10. Sue Thomas, "The Impact of Women on State Legislative Policies," *The Journal of Politics* 53, no. 4 (1991): 958–975.
11. Barbara Burrell, "The Political Leadership of Women and Public Policymaking," *Policy Studies Journal* 25, no. 4 (1997): 565–568.
12. Debra Dodson, ed., *Gender and Policymaking: Studies of Women in Office* (New Brunswick, N.J.: Center for American Women and Politics, Eagleton Institute of Politics, Rutgers University, 1991).
13. Freda Gehlen, "Women Members of Congress: A Distinctive Role," in *A Portrait of Marginality,* eds. Marianne Githens and Jewel Prestage (New York: David McKay, 1977).
14. Kathleen Frankovic, "Sex and Voting in the U.S. House of Representatives: 1961–1975," *American Politics Quarterly* 5 (July 1977): 515–530.
15. Susan Welch, "Are Women more Liberal than Men in the U.S. Congress?," *Legislative Studies Quarterly* 10 (February 1985): 125–134.
16. Barbara Burrell, *A Woman's Place is in the House: Campaigning for Congress in a Feminist Era* (Ann Arbor: University of Michigan Press, 1997). See, in particular, chapter 8.

17. Ibid., p. 158.

18. Sue Thomas, *How Women Legislate* (New York: Oxford University Press, 1994), p. 63.

19. Debra L. Dodson and Susan J. Carroll, *Reshaping the Agenda: Women in State Legislatures* (New Brunswick, N.J.: Center for American Women and Politics, Rutgers University, 1991).

20. John M. Carey, Richard G. Niemi, and Lynda W. Powell. "Are Women State Legislators Different?," in *Women in Elective Office: Past, Present, and Future,* eds. Sue Thomas and Clyde Wilcox (New York: Oxford University Press, 1998), pp. 87–102.

21. Ibid., p. 99.

22. Fact sheet compiled by the Center for American Women and Politics, Eagleton Institute of Politics (New Brunswick, N.J.: Rutgers University, 2001).

23. Sue Thomas, "Why Gender Matters: The Perceptions of Women Officeholders," *Women and Politics* 17, no. 1 (1997): 27–53.

24. Ibid., p. 29.

25. Carey, Niemi, and Powell, "Are Women State Legislators Different?," p. 91.

26. Marcia Lynn Whicker and Malcom Jewell,. "The Feminization of Leadership in State Legislatures," in *Women in Elective Office: Past, Present, and Future,* eds. Sue Thomas and Clyde Wilcox (New York: Oxford University Press, 1998), pp. 163–174.

27. Ibid., p. 174.

28. Cindy Simon Rosenthal, "Determinants of Collaborative Leadership: Civic Engagement, Gender, or Organizational Norms?," *Political Research Quarterly* 51, no. 4 (1998): 847–868.

29. Lyn Kathlene, "Power and Influence in State Legislative Policy Making: The Interaction of Gender and Position in Committee Hearing Debates," *American Political Science Review* 88 (1994): 560–575.

30. Lyn Kathlene, "In a Different Voice: Women and the Public Policy Process," in *Women in Elective Office: Past, Present, and Future,* eds. Sue Thomas and Clyde Wilcox (New York: Oxford University Press, 1998), p. 198.

31. Ibid., p. 199.

32. Janet Flammang, "Female Officials in the Feminist Capital: The Case of Santa Clara County," *Western Political Quarterly* 38 (1985): 94–118.

33. Cindy Simon Rosenthal, "Getting Things Done: Women Committee Chairpersons in State Legislatures," in *Women in Elective Office: Past, Present, and Future,* eds. Sue Thomas and Clyde Wilcox (New York: Oxford University Press, 1998), pp. 175–187.

34. For a discussion of the professionalization of women in the 1990s state legislatures, see Carey, Niemi, and Powell, "Are Women State Legislators Different?" For a discussion of the lingering gender differences in the compatibility of legislative service and private roles related to children and family, see also Debra Dodson, "Change and Continuity in the Relationship Between Private Responsibilities and Public Officeholding: The More Things Change, the More They Stay the Same," *Policy Studies Journal* 25, no. 4 (1997): 569–584.

35. Rosenthal, "Determinants of Collaborative Leadership," p. 184.

36. Kathlene, "In a Different Voice," p. 190.

37. Ibid., pp. 190–193.

38. Lyn Kathlene, "Alternative Views of Crime: Legislative Policy Making in Gendered Terms," *The Journal of Politics* 57 (1995): 696–723.

39. Kathlene, "In a Different Voice," p. 196.

40. Rosabeth Moss Kanter, "Some Effects of Proportion on Group Life: Skewed Sex Ratios and Response to Token Women," in *American Journal of Sociology* 82 (1977): 965–990.

41. Sue Thomas, "The Impact of Women on State Legislative Policies," *The Journal of Politics* 53, no. 4 (1991): 958–976.

42. Ibid., p. 967.

43. Angela High-Pippert and John Comer, "Female Empowerment: The Influence of Women Representing Women," *Women and Politics* 19, no. 4 (1998): 53–65.

44. Ibid., p. 62.

45. Lisa Jones Townsel, "Sisters in Congress prove they have what it takes to bring about change," *Ebony* 52, no. 5 (March 1997): 36–39.

46. Debra Dodson, "Representing Women's Interests in the U.S. House of Representatives," in *Women in Elective Office: Past, Present, and Future,* eds. Sue Thomas and Clyde Wilcox (New York: Oxford University Press, 1998), pp. 130–149.

47. Manon Tremblay, "Do Female MPs Substantively Represent Women? A Study of Legislative Behaviour in Canada's 35th Parliament," *Canadian Journal of Political Science* 31, no. 3 (September 1998): 435–465.

48. Ibid., p. 465.

49. Thomas, *How Women Legislate.*

50. Thomas, "The Impact of Women on State Legislative Policies," p. 973.

51. Lesley Primmer, "The Congressional Caucus for Women's Issues: Twenty Years of Bipartisan Advocacy for Women," in *The American Woman, 1999–2000,* eds. Cynthia B Costello, Sheri Miles, and Anne J. Stone (New York: Norton, 1998), pp. 365-375.

52. Irwin Gertzog, *Congressional Women: Their Recruitment, Integration, and Behavior,* 2d ed. (Westport, Conn.: Praeger, 1995), p. 188.

53. Ibid., p. 371.

54. Primmer, "The Congressional Caucus for Women's Issues," p. 367.

55. See WPI Web site: *http://www.womenspolicy.org.*

56. Dodson, "Representing Women's Interests in the U.S. House of Representatives," pp. 134–143.

57. Ibid., p. 134.

58. Ibid., p. 149.

59. Adrienne Elizabeth Christiansen, "Women and War: how 'power-over' politics silenced U.S. congresswomen in the Persian Gulf War," *The Humanist* 58, no. 1 (Jan.–Feb. 1998): 12–20.

60. For an interesting perspective on biological differences and aggression related to politics, see Francis Fukuyama, "Women and the Evolution of World Politics," *Foreign Affairs* 77, no. 5 (Sept.–Oct. 1998): 24–31.

61. Katha Pollitt, "Subject to Debate: Most Women in Congress Support Harsh Welfare Reform," *The Nation* 261, no. 19 (December 4, 1995): 697.

62. Ibid.

63. National Organization for Women, " 'Insider' Women Are Still Making a Difference," March, 1996, press release, accessed at *http://www.now.org/nnt/03-96/oped.html.*

64. Witt, Paget, and Matthews, *Running as a Woman,* p. 269.

65. Ann Bookman and Sandra Morgen, eds., *Women and the Politics of Empowerment* (Philadelphia: Temple University Press, 1988).

66. Claire Reinelt, "Moving onto the Terrain of the State: The Battered Women's Movement in the Politics of Engagement," in *Feminist Organizations: Harvest of the New Women's Movement,* eds. Myra Marx Ferree and Patricia Yancey Martin (Philadelphia: Temple University Press, 1995), pp. 84–104.

67. Ibid., p. 101.

68. Louise A. Tilly and Patricia Gurin, *Women, Politics and Change* (New York: Russell Sage Foundation, 1990), p. 7.

69. Kathleen M. Blee, introduction to *No Middle Ground: Women and Radical Protest,* ed. Kathleen M. Blee (New York: New York University Press, 1998), pp. 6–9.

70. Ibid., p. 52.

71. Rodney Hero, *Latinos and the U.S. Political System: Two-Tiered Pluralism* (Philadelphia: Temple University Press, 1992).

72. Diane-Michele Prindville and John G. Bretting, "Indigenous Women Activists and Political Participation: The Case of Environmental Justice," *Women and Politics* 19, no. 1 (1998): 41.

73. Ibid., p. 55.

74. Carolyn Howe, "Gender, Race, and Community Activism: Competing Strategies in the Struggle for Public Education," in *Community Activism and Feminist Politics,* ed. Nancy A. Naples (New York: Routledge, 1998), pp. 237–254.

75. Ibid., pp. 237–238.

76. Ibid., p. 251.

77. Rebecca Klatch, "The Two Worlds of Women of the New Right," in *Women, Politics and Change,* ed. Tilly and Gurin, p. 541.

78. Ibid., p. 539.

79. Susan Marshall, "Confrontation and Co-optation in Anti-feminist Organizations," in *Feminist Organizations: Harvest of the New Women's Movement,* ed. Myra Marx Ferree and Patricia Yancey Martin (Philadelphia: Temple University Press, 1995), p. 331.

80. Bharati Sadasivam, "For Women, A Place at the Trade Table," in *Women and Trade* Ford Report (New York: Ford Foundation, 2000), accessed at *http://www.womensedge.org/trade/fordfound.htm.*

81. "Recommended Actions from the Conference," accessed at *http://www.secretary. state.gov.*

82. Information can be accessed at *http://www.secretary.state.gov/www.picw/2000 Commitment/*

83. Available on-line at *http://www.wedo.org.*

84. Information can be accessed at *http://www.equalitynow.org.*

85. Information can be accessed at *http://www.wedo.org/news/june97/thousand.html.*

86. The *Report Card on US Government Action* can be accessed at *http://www. uswc.org/reportcards.html.*

87. For the full text of CEDAW, go to *http://www.un.org/womenwatch.*

88. Concerned Women for America, Laurel MacLeod and Catherina Hurlburt, "Exposing CEDAW," accessed at *http://www.cwfa.org/library,* September 5, 2000.

89. Women for Faith and Family, "WFF Statement on CEDAW," accessed at *http:// www.wff.org/CEDAW.html,* May 25, 2000.

90. Schmitt, Eric. "Helms Orders 10 Women from House Out of a Senate Hearing," *New York Times,* October 28, p. A-17.

91. Women for Faith and Family, p. 1.

92. Concerned Women for America, Laurel MacLeod and Catherina Hulbert, "Exposing CEDAW."

93. Concerned Women for America, Cliff Kincaid and Phyllis Schlafly, "Clinton's Power Grab Through Executive Orders," accessed at *http://www.cwfa.org/library,* January 20, 1999.

94. Hilary Charlesworth, "Women as Sherpas: Are Global Summits Useful for Women?" *Feminist Studies* 22, no. 3 (Fall 1996): 537–548.

95. James E. Anderson, *Public Policy-Making: An Introduction* (Boston: Houghton Mifflin, 1990).

96. Joyce Gelb and Marian Lief Palley, *Women and Public Policies: Reassessing Gender Politics,* 2d ed. (Charlottesville: University of Virginia Press, 1996), p. 9.

6

Education and the Pursuit of Equality

Education is a critical resource for human advancement at the individual and the societal levels. Education occupies a critical nexus for women between the private and public spheres. It isn't an accident that women won the right to be educated nearly 100 years before they embarked on the campaign for suffrage. Education empowers individuals to act on the basis of their self-interest, which is why it has been treated as a restricted commodity. Early nineteenth century Enlightenment theorists believed that education was crucial to developing the ability to reason and for attaining full citizenship. Therefore, only those who could become citizens needed to be educated, and that did not include women. Withholding education is a form of social control and a way of maintaining the status quo by ensuring that those at the bottom of the social hierarchy raise few objections.

We begin our discussion with the question, "Why educate women?" Although this may sound rhetorical today, in many countries and in some subcultures of the United States, education is still reserved almost exclusively for males or after a certain level is limited to males. Women's access to education in professional programs and in some institutions had been limited until Title IX, which was passed in 1972 as an amendment to the 1964 Civil Rights Act. Designed to address questions of gender equity in education by banning discrimination based on sex, Title IX receives the most public attention for what it has meant to girls' and women's athletics. In 1992, the American Association of University Women (AAUW) put the issue of gender equity in the classroom squarely before the public by issuing "How Schools Shortchange Girls," a major research study that documented how girls were being unfairly disadvantaged by common classroom practices that gave preference to boys and valued boys over girls. More recently, critics have charged that the situation is quite the opposite: Rather than schools' cheating girls, as the AAUW report charged, boys are now at a disadvantage and are suffering from discrimination in education.[1] We will evaluate both arguments. Finally, education is such a fundamental resource that its long-term influence is felt throughout a person's lifetime. We will examine the effect of education or the lack of education on women's status in the United States. The chapter concludes with an examination of issues in education facing future generations of citizens and policymakers.

A BRIEF HISTORY OF THE EDUCATION OF WOMEN

Education by its very nature empowers individuals, cultures, and nations to survive. From the beginning of human existence, informal education provided essential information about how to find and prepare food, build shelter, heal the sick, give birth to new life, and mourn the dead.[2] Access to formal education throughout time and regardless of place has been a restricted privilege. In Ancient Greece, for example, athletics, music, and reading were the formal educational requirements for young males destined for full membership in the citizen class. By the Middle Ages, daughters of royalty were sometimes tutored, but it was not until the nineteenth century that even a few men beyond royalty received a formal education. "Formal education was considered irrelevant for most free citizens, dangerous for men of lower status and for women, and even illegal for enslaved black people."[3] With very few exceptions, education for elite women was restricted to music, foreign language, and literature—all taught at home and for the express purpose of training women for their station in life.

The public debate over the character of women's education began in the seventeenth century in Europe and extended to the colonies. The dominant philosophy regarding women's education did not seek to enlighten and empower women, but rather to ensure that women remained confined to their "fortune and condition." Women's training focused on building moral character and developing the necessary submissive nature and skills to maintain a marriage, run a household, and supervise children. Women in the colonies taught religion, but only to other women. Women were permitted to preach only to other women and then only the words and thoughts derived from their husband's or minister's minds.[4] Women who demonstrated independence in thought or word were often declared insane and a threat to social order. The most famous example was the prosecution of Anne Hutchinson by the conservative religious authorities of the Massachusetts Bay Colony. Her banishment was a direct result of Hutchinson's overstepping the bounds of women's proper role.

Although Enlightenment theorists were a powerful influence on the expansion of education as a social good, women's education was still relegated to "patient submissiveness to male authority." Jean-Jacques Rousseau, who argued for the importance of education in reason to liberal theory's promise of human emancipation through government by consent, did not extend those same views to women's education. In *Emile* (1762), his treatise on the ideal education for a young man, Rousseau argued that the proper object of education for women was men. Anything beyond that was counterproductive since women's role and purpose was to marry and support their husbands, raise children, and manage the household. Educating women in reason and independence would not only be a waste, but it would also be a dangerous challenge to nature's designation of women as the object of men's pleasure.[5] Catherine MacCaulay and later Mary Wollstonecraft offered feminist critiques of Rousseau. In *Letters on Education*, published in 1790, MacCaulay asserted that men and women needed to understand each other better. Through coeducation, both men and women would develop the physical and intellectual powers required to accept the political responsibilities of the liberal state. If educated similarly, women could shoulder their share of these responsibilities. Likewise, Wollstonecraft, in *Thoughts on the Education of Daughters* and later *A Vindication of the Rights of Woman*, advocated coeducation, insisting that women also needed to develop independence, rationality, and competence. While she recognized that most women would become wives and mothers, she argued that women could best fulfill those roles if they first respected themselves as individuals.[6]

While Wollstonecraft herself was labeled a radical, her ideas nonetheless suffused the emerging philosophy of republican motherhood that had emerged in post-Revolutionary America. Women should be good "republican mothers" able to educate the sons of liberty, argued leading educational theorists of the time. Judith Sargent Murray, writing as "Constantina," provided the first American feminist voice regarding the education of women and was one of the first to challenge the prevailing notion that men and women were different by nature. Murray claimed that men and women were taught to be different:

> Will it be said that the judgement of a male of two years old is more sage than that of a female's of the same age? I believe the reverse is generally observed to be true. But from that period on what partiality! How is the one exalted and the other depressed, by the contrary modes of education which are adopted! The one is taught to aspire, the other is early confined and limited![7]

Access to education expanded in the United States throughout the 1800s. In the 1830s and 1840s, girls were admitted to free public elementary schools, particularly in the Northeast. Emma Willard opened the first "college" for women in 1821, the Troy Female Seminary. Prudence Crandall opened a similar academy for black women in 1833 only to be jailed and see her school burned to the ground.[8] Coeducational colleges developed in the 1830s, with Oberlin College in Ohio the first to admit both men and women, regardless of race. Women made up nearly one-third to one-half of the student body, and although allowed to mix freely with men in classrooms and during meals, were primarily admitted to the "Ladies' Department." The women's course of study omitted Latin, Greek, and higher mathematics. Women students were expected

Teachers and the Fight for Equal Pay, 1853

IN 1853, Susan B. Anthony, a teacher and prominent leader in the women's suffrage movement, attended an education conference in Rochester, New York. The discussion among the men present (the thousands of women in attendance were not permitted to participate in the proceedings) concerned the low regard in which teaching was held, compared with the professions of law, medicine, and the ministry. Anthony, after gaining permission to speak, identified patriarchy as the root of the wage and prestige gap:

> It seems to me, gentlemen, that none of you quite comprehend the cause of the disrespect of which you complain. Do you not see that so long as society says a woman is incompetent to be a lawyer, minister, or doctor, but has ample ability to be a teacher, that every man of you who chooses this profession tacitly acknowledges that he has no more brains than a woman? And this, too, is the reason that teaching is a less lucrative profession, as here men must compete with the cheap labor of women. Would you exalt your profession, exalt those who labor with you. Would you make it more lucrative, increase the salaries of the women engaged in the noble work of educating our future Presidents, Senators, and Congressmen.[1]

1. Gerda Lerner, *The Female Experience: An American Documentary* (Indianapolis: Bobbs-Merrill, 1977) pp. 234–236.

to wash and repair the clothing of the male students, as well as take charge of the dining hall tasks. When Lucy Stone, a future leader in the suffrage movement, was admitted to Oberlin, she was permitted to take the regular four-year collegiate course only after first completing the program of equal length in the Ladies' Department.[9]

Wheaton College was founded as the first real "women's college" in 1834, followed by Mount Holyoke in 1837. Iowa was the first state university to admit women, beginning in 1855. In 1904, Mary McCleod Bethune opened a small school for black women in Daytona Beach, Florida, which later became Bethune-Cookman College. By 1873, 60 percent of all American secondary schools had mixed-sex classes, and by the late 1880s, the majority of teachers were women.[10] As women joined the ranks of teachers in increasing numbers, the profession's prestige and salary began to fall. Kathryn Kish Sklar argues that the growth of mass education in the United States was accomplished cheaply as a result of low salaries for women. Low salaries were justified by three arguments: Women did not have to support families as men did. Women deserved less pay since they would quit their jobs when they married. Women's salaries were determined by the market, and since women had few options beyond teaching, they accepted whatever salary was offered, no matter how low.[11] Most schools *required* that women leave the teaching profession once they married, but women's entrance into paid teaching positions opened avenues to other "suitable" occupations over time and accorded some women new public stature within their communities. As more women were educated, the number of women's clubs and organizations dedicated to improving and expanding education increased dramatically throughout the 1870s.

In the twentieth century, the science of homemaking was introduced to the curriculum through courses in home economics, nutrition, psychology, sociology, and even in biology and chemistry. Educators reasoned that women also needed mathematics in addition to courses in the natural sciences to "help their children with their homework." The assumption that women's primary function was to marry and raise children remained dominant even as women entered higher education in greater numbers. Women's enrollment in college programs continued to ebb and flow throughout the century, dependent largely on the country's economic condition and men's needs. After World War II, for example, the percentage of women in higher education dropped substantially, reflecting the return of men to the classroom with federal assistance through the GI Bill. Women were encouraged to "return to normalcy," meaning that they were actively discouraged from seeking either education or employment beyond providing for the immediate needs of their family and home. By the early 1990s, women had surpassed men in enrollments in four-year colleges and universities in the United States.

LEGISLATING GENDER EQUITY IN EDUCATION: TITLE IX AND THE WEEA

The first major piece of legislation to address gender equality in education was not passed until 1972, the same year that the Equal Rights Amendment was sent to the states for ratification. Although discriminatory educational practices based on race had been addressed in Title VI of the 1964 Civil Rights Act, sex was not included anywhere in the Civil Rights Act except in Title VII, which dealt with employment. For many in the women's movement, issues of pay equity and employment discrimination were more overt and immediate barriers to women's equal status. While education plays an obvious and important role in preparing women for full employment, most schools were coeducational, thereby masking the many covert forms of educational discrimination against women. In 1970, President Nixon's Task Force on Women's Rights and Responsibilities called discrimination in education "one of the most damaging injustices women suffer."[12]

Title IX, also known as the Educational Amendments of 1972, banned sex discrimination in education at all levels of formal education. The language of this legislation mirrored other equal-protection legislation:

> No person in the United States shall, on the basis of sex, be excluded from participation in, be denied the benefits of, or be subjected to discrimination under any education program or activity receiving federal financial assistance.

Cosponsored by Congresswoman Edith Green and Senator Birch Bayh, the bill met little opposition from within Congress or from lobbyists when it was introduced. In fact, Green specifically asked women's organizations *not* to testify on behalf of the legislation fearing the publicity would attract opponents and endanger the legislation's chances for passage.[13] While the legislation was designed to eliminate the crippling barriers in all sorts of educational programs, institutions, and curriculum, the law is now almost exclusively described in relation to increasing women's access to sports programs—even in accounts of the women's movement or women's history.[14] The legislation specified that no federal funds could go to educational institutions that were already receiving federal dollars that practiced sex discrimination in any of its programs, including admissions, athletics, financial aid, counseling, facilities, and employment.

Provisions for enforcement of the legislation have been weak from the start. Women's rights organizations expended more energy protecting the legislation during its implementation than during its passage through Congress. The Department of Health, Education and Welfare (HEW) was charged with writing the specific implementation and administrative regulations. Enforcement rested with the Office of Civil Rights in the Department of Justice, where it remains today. Few objections have been raised over the provisions for equity in admissions policies or curriculum. Some conservative women's organizations have charged that efforts to promote gender equity in education, particularly through nonsexist curriculum and textbooks is detrimental to women's traditional role in society. As a result of Title IX regulations, schools dropped admissions quotas that limited the number of women enrolled in some professional programs (e.g., engineering, medicine, and law) and were required to evaluate men and women under the same set of admission standards. Congress did not, however, end single-sex education. Private, single-sex institutions were not required to change the character of their mission or their admissions process. The legislation merely prohibited public coeducational institutions from becoming single-sex in composition and required that once men and women were admitted, they had to be treated equally and have equal access to all aspects of the educational experience. This meant that girls could not be "advised" to pursue a traditional course of study, such as home economics, nor could boys be relegated to vocational courses like shop. Title IX, however, required gender-neutral counseling meaning that special efforts to redirect girls into nontraditional courses in higher mathematics, sciences, or vocational training were not permitted. Segregation by sex was still allowed in sex-education classes or in ability-grouped physical education classes, and school-affiliated organizations could maintain their traditional sex-segregation if they were purely social rather than academic or professional in character. This meant that social fraternities and sororities on college campuses could remain single sex.

Title IX and Equity in Athletics

The most immediate and vociferous opposition to Title IX came from college and high-school athletic directors and coaches. The National Collegiate Athletic Association (NCAA) initially tried to lobby HEW and Congress to exclude athletics from Title IX coverage. When total exclusion was unsuccessful, the NCAA argued, again unsuccessfully, that only the programs within an institution that actually received federal dollars should be subject to the equity provisions. Since few athletics programs at either the college or the high-school level are direct recipients of federal dollars, this interpretation would mean a de facto Title IX exemption for athletics. The Office of Civil Rights, the primary enforcement agency, refused the NCAA's efforts, maintaining that if any program took federal money, the entire institution was subject to Title IX compliance. In 1974, the NCAA supported the Tower Amendment, which would have exempted men's intercollegiate football and basketball (the revenue-generating sports). A House-Senate conference committee rejected the amendment, leaving the NCAA to challenge the constitutionality of the gender-equity provision in the courts. Although initially unsuccessful, a 1984 Supreme Court case, *Grove City College* v. *Bell*, temporarily gave Title IX opponents what they sought. The Court ruled that only those programs receiving federal funds must comply with the statute. Congress acted (over President Ronald Reagan's veto) in 1988 to reinstate the original intent of Title IX by passing the Civil Rights Restoration Act. Four years later, in *Cohen* v. *Brown University*, a federal court ruled that Brown University had violated Title IX's provisions when it cut two women's teams and two men's teams. Although the university cut the same number of varsity teams for men and women, several women on the gymnastics team filed suit claiming that the effect of Brown's action violated Title IX. Cutting the two women's programs had saved the university more than $62,000, while eliminating the two men's programs saved only $16,000. In other words, female athletes were disproportionately affected by the cuts.

The regulations under Title IX provide three ways an institution can show that it is providing equitable opportunities for women athletes. First, a school can show that the percentage of its female athletes is substantially proportionate to the percentage of women in its student body. Second, if there is not proportionality, schools are required to show that they are actively engaged in a meaningful process that will provide equity for women. And last, a school is in compliance if it is meeting the actual level of athletic interest among women. It is this third provision that has energized opponents to Title IX. In Brown University's case, the institution argued that while 51 percent of its student body was female, only 38 percent of its intercollegiate athletes were women suggesting that it was more than meeting the "interest test" required for compliance. It is difficult, however, to ignore the circuity of the interest argument. Girls and women are interested in sports when they have the opportunity to play sports.

Title IX's impact on women's interest and participation in sports was almost immediate and has been overwhelmingly successful. For example, in 1961, nine states actually prohibited interscholastic sports for females, presumably because of the stereotype that females were too delicate for physical activity and not suited for competitive sports. In 1971, only 7.5 percent of the nearly 4 million high-school athletes were female. By 1997, the twenty-fifth anniversary of Title IX, girls made up more than 40 percent of the 6 million-plus high-school athletes. Prior to Title IX, women made up 15 percent of college athletes, but received 2 percent of the total athletic budget. Between 1997 and 1998, women accounted for 40 percent of the student athletes at Division I institutions and received 40 percent of the athletic scholarships (up from 26 percent in 1996–97). While more than 51 percent of the undergraduates at Division I schools are female, women's programs accounted for only 36 percent of overall university athletic budgets, 32 percent of recruiting funds, and 28 percent of coaches' salaries.[15] On July 9, 1999, 90,185 people (including President Clinton) crowded into the Rose Bowl in Pasadena, California, to see the U.S. women's soccer team defeat China to win the World Cup. Not only was that the largest crowd ever, across all sports, to watch a women's sporting event, it was also the most-watched soccer event in U.S. history. An estimated 40 million viewers watched the game on television.[16]

Title IX has long been labeled "unfair" to males because, in the interest of equity, some institutions have chosen to cut male sports programs in order to move toward compliance. From the perspective of coaches and athletes whose budgets or prestige are likely to be reduced in the name of gender equity, Title IX promotes *discrimination*, a highly charged accusation. As John Weistart commented, "The particular rhetorical flourish that rallies these groups is the declaration that present policies under Title IX are 'affirmative action'—a not-so-subtle attempt to push the claims of women for recognition of their athletic aspirations into the swirl of anger that makes racial preferences such a political hot spot."[17] In 1995, J. Dennis Hastert, a former high-school wrestling coach and a Republican congressman from Illinois, attempted and failed on two successive occasions to cut funding for the enforcement of Title IX. In a 1998 speech he said, "The story is, the people who have gained are women's sports, and that is great. The sports that have lost are men's sports. . . . what we really want to do is treat kids fairly." Following Newt Gingrich's resignation as Speaker in 1998, Hastert became Speaker of the House, which puts him in a much better position to continue his fight against Title IX enforcement. In an ironic twist on the "fairness" claim, the U.S. Olympic Committee was concerned enough about the decline in U.S. medals in men's swimming and gymnastics to pledge $8 million from 1997 to the 2000 Olympic Games to help college conferences strengthen and restore their programs. Additionally, the Olympic Committee spent $4.4 million on men's gymnastics programs and built training centers in San Antonio, Minneapolis and Salt Lake City for the men's sports that some colleges no longer offer.[18]

Title IX opponents claim that "studies consistently find higher rates of in-

Title IX opened opportunities for girls and women of all ages to participate in athletics. In 1997, the twenty-fifth anniversary of Title IX, 40 percent of all high school athletes were female—over five times the number playing when Title IX was enacted in 1972. *David Young Wolff/PhotoEdit.*

terest in athletic participation among males, be they eighth-graders or college students."[19] As law professor Robert C. Farrell counters, "It is hard to have a high level of interest in a sports program that doesn't exist." The U.S. Court of Appeals agreed. In rejecting Brown University's "level of interest" argument, it stated, "To assert that Title IX permits institutions to provide fewer athletic participation opportunities for women than men, based upon the premise that women are less interested in sports than are men is among other things to ignore the fact that Title IX was created to remedy discrimination that results from stereotyped notions of women's interests and abilities."[20] In 1997, the Supreme Court refused to review the appeals court decision. The *Brown* decision should not be viewed too enthusiastically, however; after twenty-five years of Title IX enforcement, only 36 of the top 300 colleges and universities are in compliance.[21] In celebrating the twenty-fifth anniversary of Title IX, President Clinton extended the law's protections and announced more vigorous enforcement actions, prompting one administration official to say, "We are not stepping up our enforcement of Title IX, we are beginning it."[22]

The public is behind efforts to provide equity in sports. A 1999 CBS News poll found that more than 77 percent of adults supported gender parity in college sports, even if it meant cutting some men's teams.[23] Attendance at Women's World Cup Soccer matches, as well as enthusiastic crowds at Women's National

Basketball Association games, suggests that Title IX's impact on collegiate opportunities for women athletes extends beyond intercollegiate competition.

Title IX's Broad Impact on Access to Education

More women than ever before are enrolled in colleges and universities. The proportion of women enrolling in colleges and universities was at an all-time high in 2000 and 2001. In 1979, the number of women surpassed the number of men enrolled in college for the first time, and the upward trend has continued ever since. Most demographers expect that increase to continue, even as the proportion of male enrollees continues to decline. They also predict that between 1995 and 2007, the total number of both full- and part-time women students enrolled in college may increase by 19 percent to 9.2 million, compared with a 12 percent increase for men, to 6.9 million. Full-time enrollments show the largest gap, with the number of men expected to increase at less than half the rate of women. By 2007, 5.4 million women are expected to be enrolled full time, an increase of more than 30 percent since 1995. The 4.2 million men projected to be full-time students in 2007 represents only a 13 percent increase over the same time period.[24]

Although the trends are clear, the reason for the decline in male enrollments is not. Part of the change can be attributed to an increase in academic and professional opportunities for women that require a bachelor's degree. Some attribute the decline in male enrollments to a surging economy and more non-college-related options for men. "Men have more options than women when they graduate from high school. There's the military, trade unions, and jobs that require physical strength," said one director of admissions. "A young woman who wants to have a career may think she has to go to college, whereas men see other alternatives."[25] Colleges and universities must admit the best students in the applicant pool, regardless of gender, and the majority of those applicants are now female. Women tend to be better performers than men in high school and in college. Admissions officials at some institutions have started modifying their promotional material to appeal to male applicants in an attempt to attract more men to campus. The University of Dallas in Irving, Texas, brought back varsity baseball after a sixteen-year hiatus and added twenty-six additional men to the campus as a result. Other universities are using athletics, both varsity and intramural, to broaden the appeal of their campuses to male applicants. At the 2000 annual meeting of the National Association for College Admissions Counselors, two panel discussions addressed the absence of men in the college applicant pool.[26] During these panels, titled "Where Have all the Men Gone?" and "Are Our Boys at Risk?" participants confirmed the trend in declining male enrollments but offered few solutions beyond giving preferential treatment to men in the admissions process. The idea of preferential treatment for male applicants was met with interest, rather than scorn, by other admissions counselors in the audience.

TABLE 6.1 College Enrollment Rates of High School Graduates, by Sex: 1960–1998

Year	Total	Males	Females
1960	45.1%	54.0%	37.9%
1962	49.0%	55.0%	43.5%
1964	48.3%	57.2%	40.7%
1966	50.1%	58.7%	42.7%
1968	55.4%	63.2%	48.9%
1970	51.8%	55.2%	48.5%
1972	49.2%	52.7%	45.9%
1974	47.5%	49.4%	45.8%
1976	48.8%	47.2%	50.3%
1978	50.1%	51.0%	49.3%
1980	49.3%	46.7%	51.8%
1982	50.6%	49.0%	52.1%
1984	55.2%	56.0%	54.5%
1986	53.8%	55.9%	51.9%
1988	58.9%	57.0%	60.8%
1990	59.9%	57.8%	62.0%
1992	61.7%	59.6%	63.8%
1994	61.9%	60.6%	63.2%
1996	65.0%	60.1%	69.7%
1998	65.6%	62.4%	69.1%

Source: Bureau of the Census and Department of Labor, "College Enrollment of High School Graduates, Various Years," *Digest for Education Statistics, 1996,* Bureau of the Census (Washington, D.C.). Data can be found at *http://www. nces.ed.gov.*

Educational choices have economic consequences for both men and women. On average, male college graduates earn at least $23,000 a year more than men with only a high-school diploma, and the gap gets larger every year. And yet men account for 57 percent of the sixteen- to twenty-four-year-olds in the labor force who hold only a high-school diploma. With an edge in education, women could presumably quickly close the salary gap and move into positions of power as heads of corporations and political leaders. That is, if and only if, a college degree remains highly prized in the economic marketplace and, if and only if, the economic disadvantage that comes purely from being a female is somehow reduced. At a time when universities are competing with glitz and sports to attract male applicants and giving males a slight break on the admission standards, college-educated women in the full-time workforce still make only $4,708 more on average than high-school-educated men.[27] Why then are women choosing college and men choosing work? One reason may be that

TABLE 6.2 First Professional Degrees Awarded, by Sex and Race: 1996–1997

	Total*	Men	Women
Dentistry (DDS or DMD)	4.86%		
White		44.9%	21.0%
African American		1.9%	3.0%
Hispanic		2.5%	2.3%
Medicine (MD)	20.0%		
White		43.0%	27.9%
African American		2.7%	4.5%
Hispanic		2.5%	2.0%
Pharmacy (PharmD)	3.4%		
White		26.2%	41.3%
African American		2.4%	7.3%
Hispanic		.66%	1.5%
Veterinary Medicine (DVM)	2.81%		
White		31.0%	62.8%
African American		1.1%	1.5%
Hispanic		1.2%	2.1%
Law (LLB or JD)	51.5%		
White		46.0%	33.0%
African American		3.0%	4.4%
Hispanic		3.0%	2.5%

*The "Total" column represents the number of degrees in that field as a percentage of all professional degrees awarded.
Source: National Center for Education Statistics, "Completions" Survey, 1999, U.S. Department of Education (Washington, D.C.). This table can be accessed at http://www.nces.ed.gov (Table 279).

men have a clear edge in their interest in advanced technology and computer skills. Career Training Foundation, a nonprofit organization that supports U.S. trade and vocational schools, estimates that more than two-thirds of the people entering technology fields are male.[28] As the salaries for high-technology workers escalate and women lag behind men in choosing engineering, mathematics, and science as their major programs of study, the salary gap is ironically likely to increase even as women's edge in enrolling and earning bachelor's degrees continues to grow.

There is some evidence that women are making choices at the high-school level that will give them a wider variety of choices in college. In content-specific courses at the high-school level, girls continue to lag behind boys in entering science and higher mathematics courses in general. However, among college-bound males and females in the late 1990s, girls have caught up and in some cases exceed boys in years of study in science and math. The 1999 Profile of College-Bound Seniors shows that among those taking the SAT, 9 percent had more than four years of natural science courses. Within that 9 percent, 52 percent were female and 48 percent were male. Regardless of the science, a higher proportion of college-bound females completed natural science courses than college-bound males. The same trend was true for mathematics courses, including calculus. The only area in which the proportion of males was higher than that of girls was in computer math (59 percent male to 41 percent female).[29] At the college level, the number of women studying science and engineering increased from 16 percent in 1960 to more than 40 percent in 1990. The proportion of women earning doctoral degrees in science and engineering rose from 6.3 percent in 1960 to 27.7 percent in 1990. In both cases, however, growth has been more gradual than in all other disciplines.[30]

WEEA: Women's Educational Equity Act

Title IX requires gender-neutral treatment of men and women in education. The results have been more opportunities for women and fewer overt barriers to college admission and career choices. However, without proactive counseling and intervention strategies designed to increase the numbers of girls in nontraditional courses of study, the opportunities created by Title IX are likely to go unrealized. In 1974, Congress passed the Women's Educational Equity Act (WEEA), which authorized funds to promote bias-free textbooks and curriculum, support research on gender equity, and revamp teacher training programs. The effort was significantly underfunded by Congress and ignored by Republican administrations through Reagan and Bush. It was not until the American Association of University Women (AAUW) published its report, "How Schools Shortchange Girls" in 1992, that a credible effort to support WEEA materialized. Fiscal year 1996 had no appropriation for WEEA; however, between 1997 and 1999, funding remained constant at $3 million a year. As part of the original legislation, a national Equity Resource Center was established. It remains active as a clearing-house for teacher training, developing equity curriculum materials, and conducting research related to gender equity in education. The center's definition of gender equity in education addresses the chances for both females and males to learn in an environment free of limits:

> Gender equity is a set of actions, attitudes and assumptions that provide opportunities and create expectations about individuals, regardless of gender. Gender equity is a chance for females and males at learning regardless of the subject; preparing for future education, jobs, and careers; high expectations; developing, achieving and learning; equitable treatment and outcomes in school and beyond. Gender equity is linked to and supports race, ethnic, economic, disability, and other equity concerns.[31]

EQUITY IN ACTION: HOW GIRLS AND BOYS EXPERIENCE SCHOOL

The AAUW's 1992 report called immediate attention to a longstanding gender-equity problem. Although girls and boys attended the same classes within the same schools, their experience differed dramatically. "How Schools Short-change Girls" became a rallying cry for feminists to reexamine sexist attitudes in the classroom. As a result of the report, parents started paying more attention to their children's experiences in school.[32]

In 1982, the Project on the Status of Education of Women, a research effort commissioned by the Association of American Colleges (AAC), reported on the "chilly climate" for women in college classrooms. The research detailed the often subtle ways faculty treated male and female students differently. It found, for example, that female and male faculty alike were more likely to ask questions of male students, to focus more intently on the answers of male students, and to ask "higher order" critical questions of men, but not of women. In examples offered in class, males occupied the role of "professional," while women were more often the "client" or "patient," thereby making it difficult for women to view themselves in professional roles. Project researchers found more blatant examples of male faculty sexualizing female students and denigrating their future aspirations by treating them as less serious than those of male students. Similarly, they found the *attribution error* at work among faculty. A male's success was more often attributed to skill or ability, while a female's success was attributed to luck or a lack of difficulty with a task. The chilly climate has harmed both men and women. Women, over time, may grow to view their presence in a class or program of study as peripheral, having little expectation of participating in class discussions, and learn that their capacity for full intellectual development or career aspirations is limited. Male students are disadvantaged by not being challenged by all of their peers. Also, reinforcing any negative views of women may make their transition to the workplace more difficult and limit their ability to work with and view women as equals.[33]

Doonesbury   BY GARRY TRUDEAU

Two years later, in 1984, the same project released a study of the "chilly climate" facing women outside the classroom on college campuses. The study concluded that "even though men and women are presumably exposed to a common liberal arts curriculum and other educational programs during the undergraduate years, it would seem that these programs serve more to preserve, rather than to reduce, stereotypic differences between men and women in behavior, personality, aspirations and achievement."[34] The report went on to document experiences in support services, campus employment, admissions and financial-aid counseling, health care offered on campus, campus safety, and a lax attitude about harassment or degradation of women on campus that disadvantaged female students.

Both the AAC and AAUW reports peg the roots of the chilly climate to early educational disparities in elementary-school classrooms. In 1973, Myra Sadker published *Sexism in School and Society*. In many respects it was the first such book, written for teaches but released to a wider audience, that documented sex-segregated classes, gender bias in required textbooks, and sexist teaching and counseling practices. Myra Sadker, with her husband and intellectual partner, David, continued their research on bias in the classroom and in particular, on teachers' treatment of students. They published their results in *Failing at Fairness: How Our Schools Cheat Girls,* which was released in 1994. Coupled with the AAUW report, educators and parents could not ignore the findings on the treatment of girls in the primary-school classroom. The basic findings were these: Primary-school teachers tended to talk more to boys than to girls, teachers asked boys more "higher order" questions and worked with them to derive the answer rather than dismissing the first answer as wrong and moving on as they did with the girls. Teachers were also more likely to give boys specific instructions on how to complete an assignment but showed girls how to do it or did it for them. Additionally, teachers were more likely to praise boys for the content of their thinking as it was reflected in their work, whereas they praised girls for their neatness. The Sadkers' work was based on thousands of hours of classroom observations, many of which were videotaped. In the tapes, viewers could see teachers encouraging boys to work harder to answer to a question while silencing girls by quickly moving on after their answer was offered. The teachers were not acting maliciously, they were simply not aware of their actions nor of the detrimental consequences of their actions for girls.

The Backlash: How Schools Cheat Boys

Concurrent with the release of the previously mentioned studies on girls' educational experiences were several popular books on the psychological and intellectual development of girls in adolescence. Mary Pipher's *Reviving Ophelia* and Peggy Orenstein's *School Girls: Young Women, Self-Esteem, and the Confidence Gap* appeared in bookstores in 1994 and detailed the precipitous decline in intellectual confidence, voice, self-worth, and ambition in girls after about eleven years of age. Wildly popular with parents, educators, and women's groups, the books served to intensify the focus on girls. Congress responded by passing the Gender Equity in Education Act in 1994, which authorized additional research on girls' development, gender-equity issues in education, and strategies to counter bias where it exists.

Quietly at first, and then more stridently, boys' advocates began to object to all the attention showered on girls, presumably at the expense of boys. They cited U.S. Department of Education statistics showing that girls get better grades than boys, have higher educational aspirations, participate in advanced-placement classes at higher rates, and surpass boys in reading and writing skills. Studies of fourth, eighth, and twelfth graders show that girls are more "engaged" in school in almost all aspects. They are more likely to come to school prepared (with paper, pencils, books, and the like), and they are more likely to do assigned homework. By the time boys are seniors in high school, they were four times as likely as girls not to do their homework. Boys are more likely than girls to be suspended from school, be held back a grade, and to ultimately drop out of school altogether. Boys are three times as likely as girls to be diagnosed with some form of learning disorder and more likely to be involved with crime, alcohol, and drugs. Although girls attempt suicide more often than boys, boys are more often successful. [35]

In 1997, the Public Education Network (PEN), released a new teacher-student survey administered in grades seven through twelve, that seemed to directly contradict the findings of the AAUW-sponsored research: Contrary to girls' suffering neglect in the nation's classrooms, the PEN study found that boys consistently underperformed on a number of indicators. "Contrary to the commonly held view that boys are at an advantage over girls in school, girls appear to have an advantage over boys in terms of their future plans, teachers' expectations, everyday experiences at school and interactions in the classroom." [36] Most striking is the boys' perception, expressed by more than 31 percent of the boys in the study, that teachers do not listen to what they have to say. In contrast, only 19 percent of the girls shared this perception. Other studies released in the late 1990s offered similar findings relative to boys' current state of affairs. In almost all cases, girls outperformed boys, particularly on indicators related to school and aspirations for a college education.

The cover story of the May 2000 issue of *The Atlantic Monthly* was an article by Christine Hoff Sommers, titled "The War Against Boys." The article charged that the "crisis" in girls' education of the early 1990s was generated on false assumptions, based on "bad science," concocted by "girls partisans" for political purposes. In conclusion, Hoff Sommers writes,

> A boy today, through no fault of his own, finds himself implicated in the social crime of shortchanging girls. Yet the alleged silenced and neglected girl sitting next to him is likely to be the superior student. She is probably more articulate, more mature, more engaged, and more well-balanced. The boy may be aware that she is more likely to go on to college. He may believe that teachers prefer to be around girls and pay more attention to them. At the same time, he is uncomfortably aware that he is

considered to be a member of the favored and dominant gender. The widening gender gap in academic achievement is real. It threatens the future of millions of American boys. . . . In the climate of disapproval in which boys now exist, programs designed to aid them have a very low priority. This must change. We should call for balance, objective information, fair treatment, and a concerted national effort to get boys back on track. That means that we can no longer allow the partisans of girls to write the rules.[37]

The article prompted an outcry from many feminist quarters, particularly from those like Carol Gilligan and David Sadker, who were the objects of Hoff Sommers' critique. The response from readers was "swift and substantial."[38] Both the article and exchange of letters offer an extraordinary glimpse at the power of gender and the intensity with which gender operates in shaping our perceptions of important social questions, the facts gathered in order to answer those questions, and how the "facts" are interpreted in order to make public policy. There may well be another explanation for the mixed evidence on girls' and women's school experiences. Title IX was made into law in 1972, the AAUW report was based on schools in the mid to late 1980s, and the statistics offered to counter their findings are from the late 1990s. Rather than "bad science," perhaps the new statistics on women's performance in education reflect an outcome of gender-equity policy some thirty years later. Most scholars agree that gender equity in education is a pressing problem for both boys and girls. The odd mix of gender-neutral and gender-specific education policy currently on the books ensures that this debate will continue with each "side" armed with gendered facts to support its pursuit of equality in education.

EDUCATION'S LONG-TERM IMPACT ON WOMEN'S STATUS WORLDWIDE

In previous chapters we've addressed the question of women's agency, in other words, their ability to act by themselves and for themselves. Education serves as a vital resource in enabling women to exercise their agency as it relates to participation in politics, fertility issues, health decisions for themselves and their children, and the assurance of economic stability within their families. A tremendous body of research literature links women's education, employment, and empowerment.[39] In the United States, women's median income has increased both in real terms and relative to men's income largely as a function of the increase in women's level of education.[40] Studies document that increases in nutritional intake in households are a result of women's independent income. Research in India and elsewhere has shown a correlation between women's education, economic independence, and child survival rates.[41] Analysis by the U.N. Family Planning Agency has over the years illustrated that increases in educational attainment by women directly correlate with lower fertility rates, thereby easing the negative impact of population growth. Education also empowers women to use new communication technology to access information and to make their specific needs known to policymakers. As more women become policymakers themselves, there is evidence of a reciprocal impact on education for girls and women. In Bhopal, India, for example, the last four women rulers introduced compulsory education for girls that creates a standard for universal education for girls.

There remain challenges. Illiteracy among women remains an international problem, although in the last decade the gap between men and women has closed somewhat. UNESCO estimates that nearly two-thirds of the world's 876 million illiterates are women, and that number is expected to decline by only about 10 million by 2007.[42] Throughout the world, girls are more likely to leave school early because of family obligations. Boys too leave school early but more often because of economic reasons than to care for siblings or to perform unpaid household duties. Illiteracy rates among the young (ages fifteen through twenty-four) remain very high in countries where children are involved in economic activity. Census data collected in 2000 by the United Nations reported that more than one in four women between fifteen and twenty-four years old are illiterate.[43] Africa has one of the highest female illiteracy rates among young women (40 percent). In southern Asia, the UN estimates that 22 million girls and 13 million boys are not in school. The future impact on women, their families, and the world's economy will be severe.

EDUCATION ISSUES FACING FUTURE GENERATIONS IN THE UNITED STATES

Although women today enjoy unprecedented access to education and high achievement within educational programs, their success has not gone unnoticed and is not universally celebrated. When education is viewed as a zero-sum game, improvements in educational opportunities and performance for women are interpreted by some as discrimination against men. Title IX's requirement that institutions that receive federal dollars treat men and women equally in all aspects of educational programming, including athletics, does not specifically tell institutions how to accomplish gender equity. When universities choose to cut men's nonrevenue sports like wrestling, swimming, or gymnastics, in order to add women's programs in a move toward equity, it is an institutional decision, not one required by the policy. The perception is, however, that women's progress comes at men's expense. The controversy over how girls and boys are treated in the classroom has at its core the belief that when one sex is advantaged, the other must be disadvantaged.

The Unique Nature of Education as a Public Good

Education is unique in the sense that it is a commodity that has direct benefits for both society and the individual.[44] It is also a divisible or competitive good, meaning that it can be given to some and withheld from others. As we discussed earlier in this chapter, women and African Americans were barred from schools and even from privately acquiring the knowledge and skills an education provides. Laws now guarantee access to education for all. However, education is also a good that can be consumed differently by each individual even when everyone has access to the same presentation of the good. Sometimes this is an individual's choice, but in other cases, either through the socialization process or by subtle or not so subtle messages, individuals are directed to consume the good differently. Course-taking patterns suggest that men and women have consumed and may still consume education differently. The consequences of policy and individual choices are exhibited in the demographic characteristics of our population. Education plays a direct role in health, life expectancy, occupation and income, family size, and the quality of life citizens enjoy. Because of the importance of education, it remains a top policy priority in presidential campaigns and in successive sessions of Congress.

In the coming years, policymakers will be faced with making decisions about education policy that have direct gender implications even if not at first evident. For example, in the 2000 presidential campaign, both Al Gore, the Democratic candidate, and George W. Bush, the Republican candidate, talked about improving education. For George W. Bush, as well as many others, school vouchers offer one way to give parents more say in their children's edu-

TABLE 6.3 The Wage Gap by Education: 1999

	High School	Bachelor's	Master's
All Men	$32,098	$51,005	$61,776
White	$33,147	$51,606	$61,691
Black	$27,408	$40,805	$52,308
Hispanic	$25,291	$41,467	$50,410
All Women	$21,970	$36,340	$45,345
White	$22,247	$36,672	$45,772
Black	$20,609	$34,692	$41,780
Hispanic	$19,923	$31,936	$43,718

These figures represent the median earnings in 1999 for full-time, year-round workers, 25 years and older.
Source: The National Committee on Pay Equity, 2000.

cation. Vouchers would allow parents to enroll their children in the school of their choice, and the federal dollars dedicated to education would follow that child. In practice, this would mean that parents could choose to enroll their children in parochial schools with assistance from the government. It remains unclear how this might impact existing policy that requires gender equity in all aspects of an institution that receives federal funds. How might gender issues be treated in a Catholic school's curriculum or in a school that adheres to fundamentalist Christian tenets? If school vouchers are adopted, will there be Title IX issues? How strictly will the new administration enforce the provisions of Title IX when they conflict with other educational goals?

Single-Sex Schools

Another area facing policymakers in the future will be same-sex education. Title IX prohibits sex segregation in education only in vocational, professional, and graduate schools and in public undergraduate programs that have not limited admission to one sex from their founding. Unlike race equity and education, sex equity does not require integration in all schools and programs. In 1954, the Supreme Court reasoned in *Brown* v. *Board of Education* that separate can never be equal because of the perception of inferiority that race segregation entails. Neither the Supreme Court nor most feminists and policymakers, for that matter, have ever applied the same reasoning to sex-segregated schools. Because of the difference in how boys and girls experience education (which was described earlier in this chapter), many feminists actually advocate separate education for girls. Others argue that same-sex institutions are detrimental to females' development since they deny women the opportunity to compete with and interact with males as they will be required to do in the work force and in society. Largely because of this difference of opinion, the federal courts and policymakers have not adopted a view of educational equity that requires integrating males and females.

Although same-sex schools are not forbidden under Title IX or in most cases other federal laws, their popularity has waned throughout the 1970s and 1980s, leaving very few, mostly private, single-sex institutions in the 1990s. Legal challenges to single-sex institutions in the 1970s established that single-sex institutions were not inherently unconstitutional. The Supreme Court has allowed single-sex programs to remain if an individual denied admission cannot reasonably seek the same educational opportunity elsewhere or if the practice of limiting admission to one sex was arbitrary. For example, in the 1970 case of *Williams* v. *McNair*, men sought admission to then all-female Winthrop College in South Carolina. At the time, a U.S. District Court maintained Winthrop as a women's college, arguing that there were other coeducational colleges in South Carolina that offered similar liberal-arts programs to those offered at Winthrop. The plaintiffs in this case could not argue that the women-only admissions practice was arbitrary since South Carolina maintained separate state-supported institutions for men and for women (Winthrop for women, the Citadel for men). In that same year, however, a district court ruled that the University of Virginia[45] had to admit women because it offered a quality of education not available at other public institutions in the state. The first case the Supreme Court heard on this question came in 1982 in *Mississippi University for Women* v. *Hogan*. In this case, a male applicant to that school's nursing program was denied purely on the basis of his sex. The Supreme Court ruled that the gender discrimination was subject to scrutiny under the Equal Protection clause of the Fourteenth Amendment. This required the state of Mississippi to show that the admissions policy served an "important governmental objective" and that the single-sex admissions policy was "substantially related to the achievement of those objectives" (referred to as middle-level scrutiny). In this case, Mississippi failed to meet the test and males were admitted. The Court did not, however, directly address the constitutionality of state-supported, single-sex schools.

In 1996, the Court addressed this very question in *U.S.* v. *Virginia*. The case was brought by the U.S. government in an attempt to force the state of Virginia to admit women to the Virginia Military Institute (VMI). The case first entered the federal courts in 1992. At issue was the character of the program and whether a military-style program required VMI to retain its male-only admissions policy (the same set of questions applied to the Citadel in Charleston, South Carolina). The lower courts initially agreed that the single-gender character of VMI's adversative training program was essential, however, they ruled that Virginia had indeed violated the Constitution in denying women the opportunity for the same training. Virginia was given three options: admit women, establish a separate but equal program for women in the state, or convert VMI to a private institution. Virginia chose the second option and established the all-female Virginia Military Institute for Leadership (VMIL) at Mary Baldwin College. In 1996, the Supreme Court ruled that VMIL did not provide a substantially equal opportunity for women since VMI and VMIL were not of equal quality or stature in the state. Justice Ruth Bader Ginsberg issued the Court's majority opinion and came as close as the Court ever has to applying the same level of equal protection scrutiny to sex discrimination as it applies to race discrimination (called strict scrutiny). In a test now referred to as the "skeptical scrutiny" test, Ginsberg ruled that in discriminating on the basis of sex, the state must demonstrate an "exceedingly persuasive" justification for the action that bears a substantial relationship to important governmental objectives. The state also must describe "actual purposes" not rationalizations for differential treatment of the sexes. In other words, the state may not use stereotypic or traditional views of gender differences as its justification for different policies for men and women.[46] Immediately after the Supreme Court's decision, the Citadel announced that it too would admit women. VMI included women in its incoming class in 1997. In 2000, a woman was chosen as a battalion commander. Erin Nicole Claunch, with a 4.0 grade-point average, ranked 15th in her class of 298 and beat the average score for physical fitness among all

Encountering the Controversies of Equality

What About Men?

WOMEN'S STUDIES courses have proliferated on college and university campuses since they were first introduced in the 1960s. By some estimates, there are more than 700 organized programs in women's studies at all levels of education, from an undergraduate minor to a doctoral-degree program. Women's studies, by definition, focuses on transforming the "study of women," in which women are objects to "women's studies," in which women are subjects. But what about men?

Michael Kimmel is a professor of sociology who studies men and masculinity. He argues that understanding gender requires an examination of masculinity. "To fully integrate gender . . . we have to see both men and women as gendered . . . As gender inequality is reduced, the real differences among people—based on race, class, ethnicity, age, sexuality, as well as gender—will emerge in a context in which each of us can be appreciated for our uniqueness as well as our commonality."[1] Kimmel credits feminist

cadets. The appointment to battalion commander is based on academic performance, leadership ability and physical fitness and is one of the highest honors at VMI.[47]

Although largely settled in higher education, professional, and vocational programs, the issue of sex-segregated schools remains viable at the primary and secondary levels of public education. In 1996, the California legislature passed legislation authorizing $500,000 to districts that agreed to create all-boy or all-girl academies with equal facilities and agreed to evaluate the results of its pilot programs.[48] Several school districts have experimented with girls-only science and higher mathematics classes in an attempt to encourage more girls to continue with science and math. In 1998, Intel Corporation, as part of its "Women in Science" program, awarded several $75,000 grants to high schools and middle schools to mount a three-year pilot sex-segregated science class. Females make up about 29 percent of Intel's high-technology work force, and Intel designed the program to increase the number of women entering science.[49] In other areas, high schools have been experimenting with all-male English classes. In both cases the programs are designed to use a learning style that best suits the constituency and the subject matter in an area where students have traditionally shown weaknesses. There is little doubt that initiatives like these will continue—and continue to spark controversy since they introduce gender-specific educational practices in a field dominated by gender-neutral policies. There has not been a definitive legal ruling on whether separate-but-equal is acceptable for gender under these circumstances. The Of-scholars for focusing our attention on gender, but he challenges all scholars to examine the impact of gender on the experiences of both men and women and to make gender visible to men. Masculinity is a socially constructed manifestation of gender that warrants attention in classrooms and in scholarship. Just as there isn't only one female experience, there isn't only one male experience. ". . . [M]aking masculinity visible is the first step towards de-centering it as the unexamined norm."[2] Courses on men and masculinity first emerged in the 1980s, and now there are close to 100 such courses at colleges and universities.

What do you think?

In what ways is the study of gender enhanced by focusing on both women and men? In what ways might women's lives be improved by examining a masculine ideology? Are there reasons not to include men in the study of gender?

Are there any courses on men and masculinity at your institution? If not, should there be such a course?

1. Michael Kimmel, "Educating Men and Women Equally," *AAC&U on Campus with Women* 28, no. 3 (1999): 3.
2. Ibid., p. 15

fice of Civil Rights, however, has said that single-sex schools are an acceptable way to diversify educational choices as long as a district offers boys and girls the same classes and the same resources, as in the California example. When New York City established the Young Women's Leadership School in East Harlem, it prompted a warning from the Civil Rights Office. That warning cited a potential violation of Title IX unless New York developed an equal program and facility for boys. Many feminists remain wary of returning to the days of separate educations for boys and girls, even when they believe theoretically that girls may benefit from a single-sex education. Peggy Orenstein, author of *Schoolgirls: Young Women, Self-esteem and the Confidence Gap*, who has documented the problems of girls in schools, expressed concern for the Young Women's Leadership School in New York. "Beyond the legal issues, the creation of public girls' schools is risky," Orenstein said. "The United States has been down the separate-but-equal road before, and it was not a happy trip. Once institutionalized, who can guarantee that educational resources will be divided fairly?"[50]

CONCLUSION

Women were granted access to formal education nearly 100 years before they were granted access to the vote. Both of these rights have become powerful tools in the pursuit of equality. Because of the unique character of education as a "public good," one that benefits society and the individual, and because education is such a fundamental resource that is linked to myriad quality-of-life indicators, education policy is by its very nature contested ground. This chapter looked at the way public policy can lead society toward a more equitable distribution of educational access and content. Title IX has proven to be a powerful tool for changing the nature of education in the United States. Its detractors charge that gender-equity laws are unfair to males because they require that limited resources be redistributed among both males and females. This does, in many cases, require that exclusive privileges once granted to males alone be shared. Gender equity in education, at its most basic level, requires that boys and girls share equally in consuming the resources required to develop skills and acquire knowledge. It also requires careful attention to the process of education to ensure that boys and girls are learning in a bias-free atmosphere. Finally, gender equity in education requires that society presents both boys and girls with the full complement of life's opportunities beyond formal education. The next chapter examines how education is linked to work and wages. Education has permitted women to move from the private sphere to the public sphere, although as the next chapter shows, the move is far from complete.

Notes

1. See, for example, Christina Hoff Sommers, "The War Against Boys," *The Atlantic Monthly* (May 2000).

2. Hunter College Women's Studies Collective, *Women's Realities, Women's Choices*, 2d ed. (New York: Oxford University Press, 1995), chapter 11.

3. Virginia Sapiro, *Women in American Society: An Introduction to Women's Studies*, 4th ed. (Mountain View, Calif.: Mayfield Press, 1999), p. 146.

4. Ibid.

5. Nannerl O. Keohane, " 'But for Her Sex . . . ': The Domestication of Sophie," *University of Ottawa Quarterly* 49 (1980): 390–400.

6. Hunter College, *Women's Realities*, p. 374.

7. Judith Sargent Murray, "On the Equality of the Sexes," in *The Feminist Papers*, ed. Alice S. Rossi (Boston: Northeastern University Press, 1988), p. 18.

8. Sapiro, *Women in American Society*, p. 148.

9. Hunter College, *Women's Realities*, p. 382.

10. Kathryn Kish Sklar, "Catherine Beecher: Transforming the Teaching Profession," in *Women's America*. eds. Linda K. Kerber and Jane de Hart Mathews (New York: Oxford University Press, 1982), pp. 140–148.

11. Ibid.

12. President's Task Force on Women's Rights and Responsibilities, *Task Force Report: A Matter of Simple Justice* (Washington, D.C.: GPO, April 1970), p. 7.

13. Joyce Gelb and Marian Lief Palley, *Women and Public Policies: Reassessing Gender Politics* (Charlottesville: University of Virginia, 1996), p. 99.

14. See Ruth Rosen, *The World Split Open: How the Modern Women's Movement Changed America* (New York: Viking Press, 2000).

15. George J. Bryjak, "The Ongoing Controversy over Title IX," *USA Today Magazine* 129 (July 2000): 62.

16. Information can be accessed at *http://www.soccertimes.net/worldcup/1999/jul11.htm.*

17. John Weistart, "Equal Opportunity? Title IX and Intercollegiate Sports," *Brookings Review* 16, no. 4 (Fall 1998): 39–43.

18. Karen Goldberg Goff, "Does Athletic Equity Give Men a Sporting Chance?," *Insight on the News* 15, no. 2 (January 11, 1999): 38.

19. Bryjak, "Ongoing Controversy over Title IX."

20. *Cohen v. Brown University,* 991 F. 2nd 888. 1993; F. Supp. 185 (D.R.I. 1995).

21. Weistart, "Equal Opportunity?" p. 39.

22. Joe Leo, "Gender Police: 'Pull Over!,'" *US News and World Report,* 124, no. 11 (March 23, 1998): 11.

23. Bryjak, "Ongoing Controversy over Title IX."

24. Shannon Dortch, "Hey guys: Hit the Books," *American Demographics* 19, no. 9 (September 1997): 4–10.

25. Ibid., p. 6.

26. Notebook. *The Chronicle of Higher Education* (October 20, 2000): A29.

27. "Where the Boys Aren't," *US News and World Report* 126, no. 15 (February 8, 1999): 46.

28. Ibid.

29. Information can be accessed at *http://www.collegeboard.org/sat/cbsenior/yr1999/NAT/cbs1999.html.*

30. Leslie A. Barber, "U.S. Women in Science and Engineering, 1960-1990: Progress toward Equity?," *Journal of Higher Education* 66, no. 2 (March–April 1995): 213–235.

31. Information can be accessed at *http://www.edc.org/Women'sEquity.*

32. American Association of University Women, *How Schools Shortchange Girls: A Study of Major Findings on Girls and Education* (Wellesley, Mass.: Wellesley College Center for Research on Women, 1992).

33. Roberta M. Hall and Bernice R. Sandler, "The Classroom Climate: A Chilly One for Women," Project on the Status and Education of Women (Washington, D.C.: Association of American Colleges, 1982).

34. Roberta M. Hall and Bernice R. Sandler, "Outside the Classroom: A Chilly Campus Climate for Women?," *Project on the Status and Education of Women* (Washington, D.C.: Association of American Colleges, 1984).

35. Christine Hoff Sommers, "The War Against Boys."

36. Public Education Network, "The American Teacher 1997: Examining Gender Issues in Public Schools" (Rochester, N.Y.: Louis Harris and Associates, 1997).

37. Excerpt from "The War Against Boys" by Christine Hoff Sommers, from *The Atlantic Monthly*, May 2000. Copyright © 2000. Reprinted by permission of the author.

38. See both the article and the reader letters, accessed at *http://theatlantic.com/issues/2000/05/sommers.htm*.

39. United Nations Development Programme. 2000. *Women's Political Participation and Good Governance: 21st Century Challenges*. New York: United Nations Development Programme. Accessed at *http://magnet.undp.org*.

40. Cynthia Costello and Barbara Kivimae Krimgold, eds., *The American Woman 1996–1997: Women and Work* (New York: Norton, 1996), p. 23.

41. Amartya Sen, *Development as Freedom* (New York: Knopf, 1999).

42. United Nations, *The World's Women 2000: Trends and Statistics* (New York: United Nations, 2000), pp. 86–87.

43. Ibid., p. 88.

44. Margaret M. Conway, David W. Ahern, and Gertrude A. Steuernagel, *Women and Public Policy: A Revolution in Progress*, 2d ed. (Washington, D.C.: CQ Press, 1999), p. 19.

45. *Kirstein* v. *University of Virginia*, 309 F Supp 184 (1970).

46. *U.S.* v. *Virginia*, 976 F2d 890 (1992); 52 F3d 90 (1995); 116 Sct 2264 (1996).

47. American Association of University Women, "Breaking Barriers at VMI," *Outlook* 94, no. 2 (2000): 52.

48. Tamar Lewin, "Experimentation with Single-Sex Education is on the Rise," *New York Times*, 9 October 1997.

49. Information can be accessed at *http://www.mtdemocrat.com/news/intel60598.shtm*.

50. Peggy Orenstein, "All-Girl Schools Duck the Issue," *New York Times*, 1996 July 20, p. 19.

Women and Work: In Pursuit of Economic Equality

EVEN MORE than education, work exemplifies the contradictions of the paradox of gender equality. Although separate spheres ideology may have faded over time as *the* primary organizing principle of gender relations, its legacy is very much alive today in how women and men experience work. Title VII makes it illegal to restrict jobs to one sex or the other based purely on sex or stereotypical assumptions about gender-linked abilities, but gender segregation is pervasive throughout the labor force. Three-quarters of all women who work do so in just twenty occupations, each of which is nearly 80 percent female.[1] The economy is organized into "men's jobs" and "women's jobs," which is eerily consistent with the public-private sphere division of labor. For example, 1996 Bureau of Labor statistics reported that women made up 98 percent of the nation's preschool teachers, 84 percent of its elementary school teachers, 96 percent of its child-care workers, and 79 percent of its health-care workers. Alternatively, males made up 98 percent of the nation's firefighters, 74 percent of its physicians, 97 percent of its construction workers, and 99 percent of its auto mechanics.[2] If all occupations enjoyed the same level of prestige and pay, gender segregation in the labor force would not disadvantage women; however, that is not the case.

The median income for all full-time male workers in 1996 was $25,272 compared with $21,528 for all full-time female workers.[3] Moreover, even when men and women were similarly educated and working in the same profession, women were more likely to be at the bottom of the wage and prestige scales. For example, women constitute 26 percent of all lawyers in the United States, yet only 2 percent of the partners in major law firms. Women represent only 6 percent of the senior executives in *Fortune 500* companies and earn roughly two-thirds the salaries of their male counterparts. Women's concentration in low-paying, service-sector jobs also contributes to their high poverty rates. Are the disparities between men and women in employment a result of socialization and education, employment discrimination, negative public attitudes about women's work, or a result of women's choices?

This chapter examines women's entrance into the labor force and assesses the power of the paradox of gender equality in shaping their experiences. Employment policies consistent with the legal equality doctrine have been very effective in expanding occupational choices for women and in regulating the workplace to limit forms of discrimination such as sexual harassment. Gender-neutral policies in employment are designed to guarantee women equal pay for equal work, equal access to social security and other employment-related benefits, and equal access to opportunities for advancement within their careers. The Equal Pay Act of 1963 guarantees that men and women will be paid equally for doing the same job. Title VII of the 1964 Civil Rights Act prohibits discrimination on the basis of sex in hiring and employment. Affirmative-action policies in force until recently have ensured that women could not be ignored in hiring and promotions. The reality of women's experiences, however, suggests that gender-neutral policies do not aid in balancing the responsibilities of work and family nor do they credit women for the impact of their family responsibilities throughout their lifetimes, particularly in retirement.

Gender-neutral policies work best for women who most resemble the male model of employment, but since 63 percent of women with preschool age children are in the work force and nearly 90 percent of all women will bear a child in their lifetimes, few women fit that male model.[4] Gender-specific policies in employment that would grant women accommodations for childbirth, family obligations, and frequent interruptions in their participation in the labor force are nearly impossible to design without violating the prohibitions of sex discrimination so central to Title VII. As a result, policies such as the Family and Medical Leave Act (FMLA) were consciously designed to benefit both men and women in balancing family obligations with employment and do not specifically deal with women's experience. Likewise, although childcare is theoretically a family issue relevant for both male and female employees, the reality is that women are more often responsible for finding quality childcare and dealing with the daily logistics of children. The absence of federal childcare policy is felt more acutely by women than by men in the work force. When policies are gender neutral but affect men and women differently, women are almost always disadvantaged. Most often the root of the policy's disparate impact is in the persistence of separate spheres ideology and the attitudes that put women in the private sphere and men in the public sphere. When women are active in both spheres (home and work), they retain full responsibilities in both and face what sociologists have labeled the "double day." In this light, we will examine the impact of the wage gap, the status of childcare policy, social security, and the proposals to privatize social security. Ambivalent public attitudes about women's participation in the public sphere and paid labor force are apparent in the expectation that most women are supposed to handle their responsibilities at home as well as at work. Attitudes about women and work intersect with race and class bias in shaping economic policies aimed at poor women and their children. In this light, we will examine recent welfare reform legislation and evaluate its impact on women's poverty rates.

WOMEN ENTER THE WORK FORCE: A BRIEF HISTORY

Men and women have always worked. The industrial revolution moved the means of production from the homestead to the factory. As a result, the value of labor was assessed in the currency of money rather than the sustainability of one's family. In pre-industrial society, although men and women performed different tasks, both men's and women's work was necessary for survival.[5] There was little distinction between home and the workplace because they were often one and the same. In Colonial America, the home was the center of production, with men working in the fields and women tending to the home by cooking, cleaning, bearing and caring for the children, and manufacturing the goods the family needed to survive. Women did spinning and weaving, made soap, candles, and shoes, among other things. What their families did not consume, women offered for sale, which brought in additional income for the family.[6] However, industrialization changed the means of production and the division of labor between men and women. The value attached to gendered work became more starkly differentiated. So much so that participants in the Seneca Falls Convention in 1848 included among their demands issued in the Declaration of Sentiments women's ability to work and be fairly compensated.

Early in our nation's history, women entered the paid labor force in large numbers as teachers, seamstresses, domestics, or mill operators—occupations clearly consistent with their private sphere roles. In 1860, women comprised 10.2 percent of the free labor force. Almost one out of every ten free women over the age of ten were wage earners. That women *could* work in other, less-traditional venues was clearly demonstrated in the labor patterns of female slaves. Not only did African female slaves work side-by-side with men in the fields, they tended to domestic chores for the master as well as for their own family. Prior to the Civil War, the slave labor force included nearly 2 million women. Their entry into the paid labor force is reflected in the proportion of women working after the next census. In 1870, 13.7 percent of women worked for pay, making up 14.8 percent of the nation's total work force. By 1910, one out of every five workers was a woman, representing three times the number of female wage earners in 1870.[7] Since 1870, the proportionate increase in the number of employed women has exceeded the proportionate increase of employed men in every decade.[8]

Domestic work dominated women's choices for paid labor during the first

Women sorting peas in a Carter seed factory in 1918. Although one-fifth of all women worked for wages by this time, they were limited in the type of job they could hold. *Hulton Getty Picture Archive.*

phases of economic assimilation. In 1870, seven out of every ten women workers were servants. As new jobs opened in factories, retail stores, offices, and classrooms, the proportion of women working as domestic servants fell.[9] Employment patterns were still sex segregated. In industry, women were concentrated in those that manufactured cloth, clothing, or food or tobacco products. In the expanding white-collar sector, women were also relegated to a limited range of low-level jobs, such as teachers, nurses, office workers, salesclerks, and switchboard operators.[10] Women employed in these capacities were likely to be young, urban, unmarried, and the daughters of recent immigrants. The sole exception was the African American woman worker who might have been of any age and more likely to have been married while employed.

White women's youth was evidence of work's temporary nature for women of this period. The average white woman worker viewed employment as a temporary phase that would come to an end once she married. This attitude perpetuated from the start of women's wage-earning employment the expectation that women worked to contribute to the family but not to independently provide for their own support. Women's short time in the labor force limited her earning potential since, by definition, she was a perpetual newcomer to the work force, viewed as temporary and therefore not worth training for higher-paying skilled jobs. She was, therefore, relegated to the lowest-level jobs with little or no possibility of economic security or advancement.

Cultural pressure on women to adhere to the "domestic ideal" of hearth and home directly collided with increasing opportunities for women in the economy.[11] Even if employers were willing to accept women as full work-force participants, eligible for any job at any salary, the majority of the public was not. As Theodore Roosevelt wrote at the turn of the century, "If the women do not recognize that the greatest thing for any woman is to be a good wife and mother, why, that nation has cause to be alarmed about its future."[12] Thus the history of women and work is characterized by the often conflicting forces of economy and culture. In times of crisis, the nation accepts and in fact relies on women's labor. Although more often than not, once the crisis passes, women are expected to return to the domestic ideal. After recruiting women into the work force in unprecedented numbers during World War II, the government implemented a "return to normalcy" campaign to convince women to leave the work force to men and return to their responsibilities at home. By that time, however, most of the social prohibitions against married women working had fallen by the wayside, a direct result of women's wartime experiences. Women had learned to accommodate the dual burdens of work and family. Women's participation in the post–WW II labor force continued to increase, and by the late 1960s, nearly 40 percent of all women were employed outside the home.[13]

Women's labor history is also a history replete with contradictions about race and class. While middle- and upper-class white women aspired to and were in fact pressured to adhere to the domestic ideal, working-class, poor women, along with women of color and recent immigrants, were not included in the ideal. The economic realities of low salaries meant that most working-class men could not be their families' sole wage earner. That was particularly true for recently emancipated slaves. Survival often required that women and their children entered the paid labor force and accepted whatever low-paying, high-risk jobs that were available. As white women moved from domestic labor to clerical and sales positions, African American women took their place. The percentage of African American women domestic workers increased from 38.5 percent in 1910 to 59.9 percent in 1940. Over the next two decades, African American women diversified their labor participation to include manufacturing and clerical work. By the late 1960s, only 20 percent of working African American women were employed in private households.

Women's working conditions were also hampered by their exclusion from organized labor movements. During the first half of the nineteenth century, unions did not accept female members. By 1920, only 7 percent of women belonged to unions, compared with 25 percent of men.[14] Women in some industries attempted to form their own labor organizations (e.g., the Working Girl's Societies, the Women's Trade Union League). Women's unions tried unsuccessfully to alter the beliefs that women were temporary workers who were motivated only by the opportunity to earn "pocket money" to supplement their husband's income, or alternatively, that working women were selfishly pursuing a career at the expense of their family responsibilities at home. These attitudes about women's motivations for work persisted well into the twentieth century.[15]

By the mid-nineteenth century, approval of working women was conditional at best. Employment was only acceptable for women at opposite ends of the age spectrum, for those without children or whose children were grown, and for those who were willing to settle for part-time, low-wage positions. But by the 1960s, pressures of inflation collided with the rebirth of the feminist movement to produce an "awakening" among women as a group and within the larger public's consciousness. As a result, the proportion of all types of women in the work force rose. The job prestige gap between white and African American women continued to close. In 1996, two-thirds of African American women and three-fourths of white women held white collar jobs. Two-income families are now the norm across class and race, but the ambivalence over women's dual roles in the private and public spheres persists. In 1997, 61 percent of all families (both with children and childless) and 71 percent of families with children were characterized as "dual-worker families."[16]

Gender Socialization and Attitudes About Work

Gender specialization in work and the expectations for work relative to gender may develop in early childhood, built on a foundation of separate spheres ideology. Studies show that girls over five years old not only spend more time on household chores than boys do, they also begin doing chores at an earlier age.[17] Girls specialize in cooking and cleaning (jobs that are performed regularly), while boys were more likely to take out the garbage and help with yard work (jobs that are performed less frequently). Because parents view regularly performed chores, such as washing dishes, as contributing to the good of the family, they are usually done without pay (allowance), while such infrequent tasks as washing the car are likely to be compensated. Boys are more likely to find a neighborhood "market" for outdoor chores like shoveling snow or raking leaves, but girls are less likely to earn money cleaning a neighbor's house (although she may earn money by babysitting and is more likely to perform that task than her brother). Children have reason to conclude that the tasks males occasionally perform have monetary value, but the tasks females frequently perform do not. "Children have reason to think that boys labor for payment, while girls 'labor for love'. . . . The sexual division of children's play and labor induces both boys and girls to see housework and child care as women's responsibility, a responsibility that, ideally, is performed with love and pleasure. If housework, especially child care, is a woman's labor of love, equity does not come into the picture."[18]

In studies of the division of household labor between adults, women consistently perform more hours of labor in the home, regardless of race, class, education, and occupational status. The inequities are even greater among couples with children. Somewhat surprisingly, men and women accept inequities at home and see them as "fair." When married women who work outside the home are doing 66 percent of the housework, they judge the division fair. It is only when their portion of housework approachs 75 percent do they judge the distribution as unfair to themselves. Men, on the other hand, view their doing about equal hours of housework (48 percent) as unfair to themselves and see the division as fair when they perform about 36 percent of the labor.[19]

Why have women willingly accepted this "double burden" of carrying the majority of the housework and child care on top of a full-time job outside the home? Again the answer can be found in the separate spheres ideology. Virginia Valian, author of *Why So Slow? The Advancement of Women*, suggests three reasons. First, both men and women see equity as a relevant concept in the workplace, but neither sees home as the workplace. Because taking care of the family is a labor of love for women, demanding equity makes her appear heartless. "Women have learned to help others directly, by caring for them, even if that help comes at their own expense. Men, on the other hand, have learned to help others indirectly, by earning money to provide material well-being and educational opportunities."[20] Second, because of years of socialization in non-overlapping roles, men and women define certain jobs as feminine and others as masculine, making it particularly difficult for a man to retain his masculinity when performing "feminine" jobs in the home. Finally, men tend to compare themselves with other men and women compare themselves with other women. Particularly if men and women compare their own division of labor within their marriage with that of their parents, both husband and wife view themselves as "better off" than either of their parents. Both men and women believe (correctly in most cases) that contemporary men are doing substantially more than their fathers ever did, particularly in the area of child care. This relieves men of the responsibility for equal housework and denies women grounds (or so she perceives) for demanding a more equitable division of labor in the home.[21] This leaves women to figure out ways to combine a professional career or full-time job with the demands of the home and children and defines resolving work and family pressures as a female problem rather than a human one. Thus, the need for higher-quality, more-affordable child care, family-leave policies, and more flexible work hours are all defined within the policy process as "women's issues." The burden of finding solutions in the absence of government action is squarely placed on women in most cases. Placing these issues on the public policy agenda is crucial for women's continued advancement within the economy.

LEGAL PATHS TO EQUALITY: EQUAL PAY, TITLE VII, AND AFFIRMATIVE ACTION

Women's work, as we saw earlier, is largely a function of the interplay of the economy and cultural sex-role expectations. As the need for more workers put more women in the work force, women themselves sought opportunities beyond those prescribed by traditional gender roles. In this sense, they were aided by government. As the need for skilled workers surpassed the available male labor pool, the National Manpower Council, the Department of Labor, and the Women's Bureau joined forces to explore ways to develop women's labor potential. In 1957, these organizations issued a report affirming that the principles of equality of opportunity and pay should apply to women as well as men.[22] The women's movement, largely dormant at this point anyway, did not immediately seize on this report as an opening because it was experiencing internal divisions over the pursuit of equal opportunities at the expense of protections for women workers. In this sense, the first equal-employment laws were not a direct result of actions by the women's movement, but rather they happened despite inaction and division within the movement.

The two paths to equality that stemmed from the paradox of gender equality were both evident as the government struggled with how to extend women equal-employment rights. On the one hand, a strictly gender-neutral approach guaranteed legal equality for men and women in the workplace, assuming that men and women experienced the workplace in similar ways. In passing the Equal Pay Act of 1963, Congress guaranteed women equal pay for work equal to that of male employees. Title VII of the 1964 Civil Rights Act prohibits discrimination of both men and women in employment on the basis of sex. Alternatively, gender-specific policies recognize differences between men and women. In enacting protective legislation, popular with progressives and social-reform feminists in the early twentieth century, the government attempted to protect women from long hours or dangerous working conditions and to accommodate their "special burden" related to bearing (and raising) children. Liberal feminists argue that protective legislation, regardless of its intent to favor women, will in the end disadvantage and stigmatize women. The passage of Title VII essentially ended the debate over which path the government would pursue. In addition, women have directly benefited from affirmative-action policies that were set in motion by executive orders 11246 and 11375. While affirmative action initially appears to contradict the equality doctrine and the ideology of individualism, women nonetheless advocated the inclusion of sex in affirmative-action policy. With the exception of affirmative action, the history of gender antidiscrimination employment law in the United States is one that has been based on the legal equality doctrine. While this approach appears to promise women equal employment conditions through strictly gender-neutral policy, the results have been mixed.

The Equal Pay Act of 1963

The Equal Pay Act of 1963 was not the government's first foray into regulating pay equity. Largely as a way to prevent employers from dampening wages by hiring women, the government required that women and men be paid equally at several points prior to 1963. The Fair Labor Standards Act of 1938 prohibited classifying jobs and wages according to age or sex and provided a minimum wage for some job classifications and required fair treatment for wage and hourly workers. When women flooded the work force during both world wars, government took action to alleviate the fear that women in men's jobs would depress wages. Policy dictated that women holding "men's jobs" be paid "men's wages." Hardly a statement on gender equality, the policy was designed to protect men's jobs and wage rates. Since attitudes about women working were still largely ambivalent, policy directed at equalizing wages based on a doctrine of equality did not surface until the Kennedy administration sent an equal-pay bill to Congress. The Women's Bureau, led by Esther Peterson, argued that "fairness" dictated equal pay for men and women. Initially, the Women's Bureau pursued "equal pay for comparable work" but relented under pressure from employers who argued that defining comparable work would invite excessive government intrusion. Given the persistence of the "dual labor force," both Congress and the law's detractors in industry were confident that an equal-pay law within the context of a sex-segregated workplace would not jeopardize men's jobs or wages. By the time Congress took action, twenty-three states already had equal-pay laws on the books.

The federal law requires that when men and women perform the same (or substantially same) job in the same place and under the same conditions, they must receive equal pay.[23] However, seniority, merit, and measures related to the quantity and quality of the work provide a legal basis for pay differentials as do "any other factor other than sex." Initially the law, which was an amendment to the Fair Labor Standards Act, covered only wage and hourly employees and exempted employers with fewer than twenty-five employees. In 1972, the law's protections were extended to workers in small firms not covered by

Encountering the Controversies of Equality

Equal Protection Versus Protectionism

IN PREVIOUS chapters we have discussed the debate among feminists in the women's movement about protectionist legislation designed to insulate women from dangers in the workplace. Those who favor equality characterized by the legal equality doctrine view protectionist legislation as detrimental to women's cause since it limits a woman's ability to independently set the terms for her labor and to choose where, when, and for how long she works. Alternatively, those who favor equality characterized by fairness argue that a woman's reproductive role requires that she be accommodated in the workplace. Both sides agree that protectionist legislation is theoretically designed to favor women, however, the two sides differ on whether the implementation of protectionist policies work to the advantage or disadvantage of women. The debate effectively ended with the adoption of Title VII of the Civil Rights Act of 1964. Title VII required equal treatment of men and women and prohibited employment discrimination on the basis of sex. The exceptions are noted in chapter seven.

Recently, the protectionist debate has been renewed over the issue of fetal protection policies adopted by many private-sector employers in the 1980s and 1990s. Once again the question is raised about gender equality and occupational health and safety. Fetal protection policies restrict women from certain jobs deemed by employers to be potentially hazardous to women and fetuses. As many as 20 million women may have already been excluded from certain jobs, usually the highest paying jobs, as a result of exclusionary policies. In *United Auto Workers* v. *Johnson Controls, Inc.* (1991),[1] the United States Supreme Court held that fetal protection policies violated Title VII because the

minimum-wage laws, professionals including teachers, and to state and local government employees. Enforcement moved from the Department of Labor exclusively to the Equal Employment Opportunity Commission (EEOC) in 1978, but that move did not result in more stringent application of the law. Primarily, enforcement is the result of an individual or group of workers filing a claim with the EEOC. The prevailing 25 percent wage gap in 2000, some thirty-seven years after the law was passed, suggests that both the law and its enforcement have not rectified the problem of wage discrimination.

Title VII of the 1964 Civil Rights Act

Now singularly powerful in combating gender discrimination in employment, Title VII of the 1964 Civil Rights Act resulted from an amendment offered by Congressman Howard Smith, a conservative southern Democrat from Vir-

policy constituted disparate treatment on the basis of sex since employees were classified by gender and reproductive capacity rather than by individual circumstances. In addition, the Court found that the policy was not justified under the bona fide occupational qualification (BFOQ) defense to sex discrimination. Johnson Controls argued that it was permitted to bar fertile women to protect their potential offspring and that a BFOQ of "sterility" was justified. The company further claimed that the BFOQ was closely related to job skills and aptitudes because it was necessary to ensure the safe and efficient production of batteries. The Court disagreed, saying in essence that an employer was not permitted to discriminate against women based on their potential for pregnancy unless it prevented them from doing their jobs. Treating all female employees as potentially pregnant constitutes discrimination on the basis of sex. The Court did not directly address questions of an employer's responsibility to provide a safe workplace for all employees regardless of sex, the argument about potential tort liability and business solvency, or the existence of fetal rights.

What do you think?

Who are fetal protection policies designed to protect?

Consider the practical result of the Supreme Court's decision. Under this reasoning are all fetal protection policies illegal forms of sex discrimination? Under what circumstances might the Court permit an employer to maintain a fetal protection policy?

Protective laws make women's reproductive function paramount, however, equal employment laws ignore women's reproductive function. Men are rarely included in fetal protection policies and yet they too play an important role in reproduction. Is there an alternative approach to solving this problem for both men and women?

1. *U.A.W. v. Johnson Controls, Inc.* 499 US 187 (1991).

ginia. Smith was determined to undermine the prohibitions against race discrimination at the core of the Act by suggesting that men and women should be treated equally in the workplace. He was sure that the inclusion of sex along with race, color, religion, or national origin would derail the bill, if not in the House, in the Senate. Without the amendment, many argued that white women would have been the only workers unprotected from employment discrimination under federal law. While accounts of his precise motivations vary, the Smith amendment did, in fact, survive to become one of the most powerful federal antidiscrimination employment laws. The inclusion of sex along with the other protected categories was opposed by several prominent women's organizations, including the President's Commission on the Status of Women, the Women's Bureau, and the American Association of University Women. Their opposition arose mainly in response to the issue of "protective" legislation for women and the recognition that special accommodations for women would no longer be permitted under Title VII.[24] The law has since been amended three

TABLE 7.1 World's Women Earn Less: Women's (nonagricultural) wages as a percentage of men's

Percent	Country
92%	Tanzania
92%	Vietnam
91%	Australia
89%	Sweden
86%	Colombia
85%	Kenya
84%	Jordan
83%	Denmark
81%	France
81%	New Zealand
80%	Egypt
80%	Italy
77%	Finland
77%	the Netherlands
76%	Brazil
76%	Germany
75%	Belgium
75%	Israel
75%	Mexico
75%	United States
71%	Singapore
69%	Ireland
68%	Thailand
63%	Canada
61%	the Philippines
61%	Chile
60%	Syria
59%	China
54%	South Korea
51%	Japan
42%	Bangladesh
40%	Russia

Source: Naomi Neft and Ann D. Levine, *Where Women Stand, 1997–1998* (New York: Random House, 1997), p. 71.

times. The first change extended the authority of the EEOC and expanded coverage to include public employers and educational institutions. The second amendment, known as the Pregnancy Discrimination Act (1978), declared that classifications based on pregnancy and pregnancy-related disabilities fall within the meaning of "sex" under Title VII. Third, The Civil Rights Act

(1991) amended Title VII to reverse the effects of several Supreme Court rulings in the late 1980s that made job discrimination suits harder to win.

The EEOC, now responsible for administering all of the nation's equal protection provisions, was created under this Act and charged from the start with developing guidelines for Title VII's implementation. It was clear that the EEOC was not going to be very ambitious in writing guidelines on sex discrimination, and women's organizations like the newly formed National Organization for Women (NOW) rallied to pressure the agency to act more diligently. The specific provisions in Title VII most relevant to sex discrimination are found in section 703(a):

> It shall be an unlawful employment practice for an employer (1) to fail or refuse to hire or to discharge any individual, or otherwise to discriminate against any individual with respect to his compensation, terms, conditions, or privileges of employment, because of such individual's race, color, religion, sex, or national origin; or (2) to limit, segregate, or classify his employees or applicants for employment in any way which would deprive or tend to deprive any individual of employment opportunities or otherwise adversely affect his status as an employee, because of such individual's race, color, religion, sex, or national origin.[25]

An important exception to Title VII's coverage arises from what is called a Bona Fide Occupational Qualification (BFOQ):

> Notwithstanding any other provision of this subchapter (1) it shall not be an unlawful employment practice for an employer to hire and employ employees . . . on the basis of his religion, sex, or national origin in those certain instances where religion, sex, or national origin is a bona fide occupational qualification reasonably necessary to the normal operation of that particular business enterprise. . . .[26]

Like many policies passed by Congress, the basic provisions and language of Title VII have been subject to interpretation by the Supreme Court. Two of the statute's critical phrases have provided the basis for such cases. Title VII prohibits discrimination practices "because of sex." Congress did not specify exactly what it intended in choosing this particular language, so the courts decided what each means through a succession of cases. In 1912, Justice Holmes best articulated for the Court the basic principle of the equal-protection clause that allows some sex-based laws to stand, even today in the face of Title VII's prohibition of sex discrimination: "The Fourteenth Amendment does not interfere [with state legislation] by erecting fictitious equality where there is real difference."[27] Unlike race, which the Court views as an immutable characteristic that bears no relationship to job performance, sex is assumed to create real and meaningful differences in a man's or a woman's ability to get and hold some jobs. However, the determination of the relevance of sex differences to employment cannot, the Court ruled, be based on assumptions of women as a group or any stereotypical characteristics as a group and must be based in fact.

One of the first Title VII cases brought on the basis of sex, *Phillips* v. *Martin Marietta*, was decided in 1971. In this case, Ida Phillips challenged the

Martin Marietta Corporation's policy against hiring women with preschool children, although it had no such policy against hiring men with preschool children. Two lower courts ruled that the employment policy did not violate Title VII since it did not rely solely on sex, but also relied on a criterion "other than sex" (preschool children). The Supreme Court rejected the "sex plus" criterion as a violation of Title VII's intent.

Several cases have been brought before the courts on the basis of the BFOQ exception to Title VII. One of the earliest, *Weeks v. Southern Bell Telephone and Telegraph* (1969), challenged a rule that prevented women, but not men, from holding positions that required lifting more than thirty pounds. Lower courts ruled that the company had based its decision to limit women's employment on stereotypes rather than on real abilities of its employees or applicants. Similarly, in *Rosenfeld v. Southern Pacific Company* (1971), the Ninth Circuit Court of Appeals ruled against Southern Pacific's policy of excluding women from certain jobs that were deemed "unsuitable" for women because (1) they involved irregular hours and lifting weights of up to twenty-five pounds; and (2) state laws limited working conditions for women under a variety of protective statutes. The court ruled that neither reason constituted a BFOQ exception to Title VII because both relied on stereotypes of women's abilities rather than on a finding of fact.[28]

BFOQ defenses constitute a large number of employment discrimination cases. Some of the most important rulings defining permissible BFOQ defenses have involved a male plaintiff bringing suit to open occupations previously limited to women. In *Diaz v. Pan American World Airways, Inc.* (1971), Celio Diaz applied for a job as a flight attendant, but was refused employment because of his sex. Pan Am's policy of hiring only women as cabin attendants raised the question of whether an employee's sex in situations where the public expected to find one sex or the other (customer preferences) constituted a legitimate BFOQ. The Supreme Court reversed a lower court's support for the policy ruling that Title VII only permits sex to operate as a BFOQ when it is reasonably necessary to the operation of a business. The Court left open the possibility that there might be some instances when "the essence of the business operation would be undermined by not hiring members of one sex exclusively," but that Pan American had not argued that female flight attendants were essential to their business success.

Ten years after the Pan Am ruling, another case involving an airline's hiring policy refined the Court's test for business necessity. In *Wilson v. Southwest Airlines Company* (1981), Southwest Airlines argued that female flight attendants were necessary to the financial success of its business in the highly competitive aviation industry. Southwest Airlines had adopted a public relations campaign based on an image of female sexuality that catered to the almost exclusively male business travelers. Using the slogan, "We're Spreading Love All Over Texas," Southwest gained on its competitors throughout the 1970s. When sued for its refusal to hire male flight attendants, Southwest Airlines argued that in this case, sex operated as a BFOQ since their financial success depended on the appeal of their female flight attendants. In its decision, the Supreme Court created a two-pronged test based on two questions: (1) does the job under consideration require that the worker be of one sex only? *and* if so, (2) is that requirement reasonably necessary to the essence of the employer's business? In requiring affirmative answers to both questions, the Court sought to retain Title VII's intent. Since Southwest Airline's primary business was providing safe air transportation, requiring flight attendants to be female was not reasonably necessary to the essence of safe travel. The Court concluded, "Sex does not become a BFOQ merely because an employer chooses to exploit female sexuality as a marketing tool or to better insure profitability."[29]

Under some conditions, however, sex does serve as a legitimate BFOQ, but they are few. For example, conditions of privacy warrant one sex exclusively (restroom attendant or undergarment fitter) as do jobs that require authenticity, such as an actor or actress playing a particular role in a movie or play. A 1977 Supreme Court ruling in *Dothard* v. *Rawlinson*, however, disappointed most feminists. In rejecting a woman's bid to become a prison guard in an Alabama state penitentiary, the Court allowed Alabama to discriminate against qualified women applicants because of the dangerous conditions in Alabama's prison system. While allowing that unconstitutional overcrowding creates a danger to men as well as women, the Court nonetheless held that "a woman's ability to maintain order . . . could be directly reduced by her womanhood. . . . There would also be a real risk that other inmates deprived of a normal heterosexual environment would assault women guards because they were women."[30] This ruling was very narrowly written and did not even extend to most other state prisons that attempted to prohibit female guards. However, as Justice Thurgood Marshall pointed out in his dissenting opinion, the majority opinion "regrettably perpetuates one of the most insidious of the old myths about women—that women, wittingly or not, are seductive sexual objects." Most jobs now have been ruled open to both sexes. Proving gender discrimination at all stages of employment, however, is difficult.

In most cases, enforcement of Title VII occurs in reaction to a complaint filed by an individual or group with the EEOC. There are primarily three types of proof of discrimination. The first is proof of *prior intent to discriminate* requiring written or sworn oral testimony that there was intent on the employer's part to discriminate against one sex in hiring, promoting, paying, or providing benefits. While there were blatant cases of intent throughout the 1970s, more recent cases have not presented such clear proof and have mostly fallen under either *disparate treatment* or *disparate impact*.

Disparate treatment refers to an employer deliberately favoring or disadvantaging one group protected under Title VII over another. In these cases, the burden of proof falls on the plaintiff, who must demonstrate that the disparate treatment is due to sex rather than some legitimate reason unrelated to sex. In short, the person making the charge is required to counter the employer's defense with hard evidence to the contrary. When a group files suit, evidence may take the form of statistics showing a pattern of discrimination in hiring over time or that women are underrepresented in the company's employee or applicant pool relative to those qualified to hold the position in the population at large. Alternatively, if an individual files suit, evidence is often difficult to obtain. Disparate impact cases arise where an employer's policies appear to be gender neutral, but have the effect of treating men and women differently. For example, minimum-height requirements or the ability to lift a certain weight or the need to travel for extended periods of time. A defense in this case requires the employer to prove that the requirements are related to the job and that they constitute a business necessity. In other words, if the qualifications for a position list the ability to lift more than 75 pounds, but in performing the job, the employee is never asked to lift heavy loads, the business-necessity defense is not legitimate and instead the qualifications constitute Title VII discrimination. The burden of proof in demonstrating a "business necessity" in these cases lies with the defendant (the employer), and the plaintiff is not required to prove that the company intended to discriminate through its hiring practices.[31] As a result of the Civil Rights Act of 1991, the courts are now bound by legislation to hold employers responsible for demonstrating that their employment practices, which may result in a disparate effect, are related to a legitimate business necessity.

Affirmative Action Policies: Executive Orders 11246 and 11375

In 1965, President Lyndon Johnson signed executive order 11246, which required companies that do business with the federal government to take "affirmative action to ensure that applicants are employed, and that employees are treated during employment without regard to their race, color, religion or national origin."[32] The Office of Federal Contract Compliance was established within the Department of Labor to enforce the order. Unlike Title VII, sex was not included in the original affirmative-action order. However, pressure from women's organizations and others convinced the Johnson administration to sign executive order 11375 (1967), which included sex among the protected categories in affirmative-action policies. Unlike Title VII or the Equal Pay Act, both of which require employers to treat similarly situated men and women in a similar manner, affirmative action has gone a large step further. Recognizing that today's inequalities are rooted in past discrimination, affirmative action requires that employers consciously monitor their employment practices and take action if women are underrepresented or have been underrepresented in the past. Affirmative action takes the form of a proactive remedy to past discrimination. As such, critics of the policy have long referred to affirmative action as "reverse discrimination." The Supreme Court, however, has made it very clear that a lawful affirmative-action program "must apply only to qualified candidates, have a strong reason for being developed, and be narrowly crafted to minimize negative effects."[33] This means that a program cannot legally promote unqualified candidates at the expense of qualified individuals, nor can an affirmative-action program use quotas, contrary to popular anti-affirmative-action political rhetoric.

Studies consistently document the persistence of discriminatory treatment based on race and gender. Tests conducted by the Fair Employment Council of Greater Washington continue to find that white applicants are favored over minority applicants who have identical credentials. The Fair Employment Council sends paired "testers," one white and one black, to apply for the same job. Although each person has identical work experiences, backgrounds, demeanor, interviewing skills, and physical builds, a 1992 study found that almost half of the white testers received job offers, compared with only 11 percent of the African American applicants.[34]

Although many of the most vehement attacks on affirmative-action policies have come at the expense of racial minorities, women of all races stand to lose a considerable tool in the pursuit of equality if the principles of affirmative action are undermined or ruled unconstitutional. Studies show that African American women, long relegated to the bottom of the ladder in hiring, salary, and promotion, have gained both in employment opportunities and wages as a result of affirmative action laws.[35] All women seem to have gained as a result of an increase in the public's consciousness of equal opportunity and diversity in the workplace and in admissions to professional schools. The rise in the number of women entering law and medical programs, while not directly due to affirmative-action policies per se, can be positively linked to greater awareness of gender balance in admissions.

During the 1980s and the Reagan administration, a conservative Supreme Court did significant damage in both practice and concept to affirmative-action principles. While the Civil Rights Restoration Act of 1988 and the Civil Rights Act of 1991 reversed many of the Court's more damaging rulings on federal equal employment opportunity law, it would, nevertheless, be fair to say that the climate in the United States toward affirmative action has remained hostile throughout the 1990s. In November 1996, 54 percent of California's electorate voted for Proposition 209, labeled the California Civil Rights Initiative by its proponents. The proposition prohibited the implementation of race and gender affirmative-action programs and has resulted in dramatic changes in admission practices in the state's extensive college and university system. While the country remains divided over the politics of affirmative-action policy, the principle of distributing opportunities evenly across the sexes and across racial lines retains support.

THE IMPACT OF FEDERAL POLICIES ON WOMEN'S WORK EXPERIENCES

There is ample evidence that the three major federal policies previously described have not entirely eliminated discrimination in employment for women, nor have they fundamentally altered the ways in which men and women experience the workplace. The "dual labor force" is still intact even in the face of advances that women have made in the professions. Women are still more heavily concentrated in "women's jobs" at the low end of the pay and prestige scales and less likely to carry the benefits that provide health care for themselves and their families. The wage gap remains real, even accounting for occupational differences and education. Over the course of her lifetime, the AFL-CIO estimates that a 29-year-old college-educated woman in 1998 will lose $990,000 because of the wage gap.[36] Workplace climate issues were raised in a very public way in both Clarence Thomas's Senate confirmation hearings and in President Clinton's impeachment hearings in the House of Representatives and trial in the Senate. Sexual harassment remains a very real threat to many women's security and advancement, even though stricter laws have been established to punish offenders. In this section, we will examine how contemporary women enter and experience the workplace three decades after the major federal equal employment laws were passed.

Women in the Professions

The combination of Title IX (discussed in the previous chapter) and federal affirmative-action goals have motivated professional programs to examine their admissions policies and the gender balance in their classrooms. Title IX eliminated quotas for women in specific programs, allowing women to compete for admission on their merits. The result was a steady increase in the number of women enrolled in law, medicine, engineering, science, and dentistry postgraduate programs. Between 1974 and 1994, overall job growth was the fastest for managers and other professionals; in 1994, 7 million women held managerial and professional positions, almost double the number in 1974.[37]

Using both aggregate data (all men and women) to examine trends and cohort data (men and women born in the same year) to compare men and women with identical education and backgrounds, Virginia Valian examined men's and women's advancement in the professions. She made sure to note similarities in "human capital," a variable that represents education, experience, and other qualifications and is often used to dismiss the size of the wage gap. Valian nevertheless found that men in business, medicine, government, and the law advanced more easily than women in the same professions.[38] In 1978, two women were heads of *Fortune* 1,000 companies in the United States; in 1994 that number remained unchanged. In 1996, four women headed up *Fortune*

FIGURE 7.1 Pay Ratios of Women to Men by Level of Education

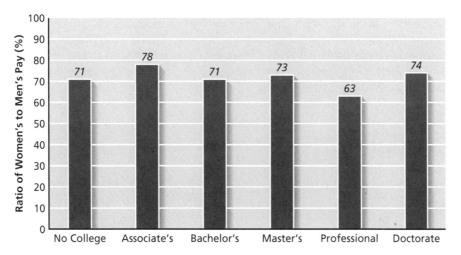

Source: U.S. Bureau of the Census, 1996. Data is for full-time workers age 25 and older.

1,000 companies. In 1990, women made up less than one half of 1 percent of the most highly paid officers and directors of 799 major companies. A 1996 review of the 1,000 largest firms in the United States found that women held only 1 percent of the top five jobs in those corporations. As Valian points out, these figures relied on aggregate data and therefore did not take into account years of experience, age, and other factors directly related to achieving the highest positions in business. However, when she examined the relative progress made by men and women in the same cohort and with college degrees and MBAs, she found that men were promoted more quickly and advanced to higher salary grades more quickly than women did. The situation was similar for engineers. Women were overrepresented in lower-prestige ranks, and men were overrepresented in higher-prestige ranks, even though both the men and the women had identical training, education, and experience. She concluded, "In engineering, as elsewhere, men accumulate advantage more easily than women do."[39]

In 1996, an American Bar Association panel revealed that although women constituted 23 percent of the law profession, bias against women still pervades the profession.[40] The problem is as much a sticky floor as it is a glass ceiling. The income gap between male and female lawyers begins during the first year of practice and widens from there. During the early 1990s, women suffered disproportionately from the glut of lawyers, and their rates of promotion to partner fell more steeply than men's. Although nearly 50 percent of law-school students are women, they're taught by an almost exclusively male faculty. In medicine, women fared better salarywise when pay was based on hourly wages, with female doctors earning nearly 87 percent of male doctors' earnings.

However, 55 percent of women, compared with 42 percent of men practiced in the three lowest-paying specialties—pediatrics, general practice, and general internal medicine. Conversely, only 14 percent of women worked in the four highest-paying fields (radiology, general surgery, anesthesiology, and subspeciality surgery), compared with 27 percent of men.[41] Valian found that men and women choose specialties that are congruent with gender expectations and that senior medical staff encouraged young medical students to choose specialties that conformed to gender roles.

Sexual Harassment

Sexual harassment is a form of gender discrimination in employment and educational institutions that is covered under Title VII and Title IX, respectively. In 1980, the EEOC defined sexual harassment as a form of discrimination:

> Unwelcome sexual advances, requests for sexual favors, and other verbal or physical conduct of a sexual nature constitute sexual harassment when (1) submission to such conduct is made either explicitly or implicitly a term or condition of an individual's employment; (2) submission to or rejection of such conduct by an individual is used as a basis for employment decisions affecting such individual; or (3) such conduct has the purpose or effect of unreasonably interfering with an individual's work performance or creating an intimidating, hostile, or offensive working environment.[42]

The EEOC's regulation encompasses the two most common types of harassment: quid pro quo (an exchange of favors) and creating a hostile environment. The standards for applying Title VII to allegations of sexual harassment in the workplace were developed by a series of federal circuit court decisions and the EEOC before a case ever reached the Supreme Court. In 1986, ruling in *Meritor Savings Bank* v. *Vinson,* the Court outlined a pattern of proof of hostile environment cases in which the plaintiff must show that

> (1) she was subjected to unwelcome sexual conduct; (2) these were based on her sex; (3) they were sufficiently pervasive or severe to create an abusive or hostile work environment; and (4) the employer knew or should have known of the harassment and failed to take prompt and appropriate remedial action.[43]

The Court specifically took note of the EEOC guidelines in deciding the Meritor case, which prompted the lower courts to do the same. In determining the character of "unwelcome" sexual advances and the severity of an abusive or hostile work environment, the courts have tended to use a "reasonableness standard." This means that, under similar circumstances, would a "reasonable person" in the harasser's position have known the behavior was unwelcome? Feminists objected to this standard, arguing that harassers are usually men and that men do not have a good track record on understanding the seriousness of sexual harassment or the difference between "teasing" and "harassment." The Court later adopted a "reasonableness" standard related to the victim's perspective, noting that the previous standard ran the risk of reinforcing the prevailing level of discrimination. In *Ellison* v. *Brady*, the Ninth Circuit Court of Appeals adopted the perspective of a "reasonable woman." In ruling, the court was careful not to establish a higher level of protection for women (a fear expressed by some liberal feminists), noting, "a gender-conscious examination of sexual harassment enables women to participate in the workplace on an equal footing with men. By acknowledging and not trivializing the effects of sexual harassment on reasonable women, courts can work toward ensuring that neither men nor women will have to 'run a gauntlet of sexual abuse in return for the privilege of being allowed to work and make a living.'" Thus, when a male plaintiff alleges a hostile environment, the standard would be that of a "reasonable man."

The courts' willingness to hold an employer accountable for the behavior of its managerial and supervisory employees has prompted most businesses and schools to develop policies on sexual harassment. These policies include guidelines on how to report incidents of harassment and procedures for an internal resolution of the complaint. A victim of sexual harassment may always file a sex-discrimination claim with the EEOC. In the wake of the Anita Hill-Clarence Thomas hearings in 1991, the EEOC reported a 60 percent increase in the number of complaints in the nine months following the televised hearings. Included in the Civil Rights Act of 1991 are provisions allowing victims of sexual harassment to sue for monetary damages (up to $300,000). In 1993, the Supreme Court ruled in the case of *Harris* v. *Forklift Systems* that the victim of sexual harassment need only demonstrate impairment of work or education to prove that an environment is hostile. Lower courts had been heading toward requiring evidence of severe psychological harm.

The Pay Gap

Ironically, while Title IX and Title VII opened doors to education and employment in well-paying professions previously limited to men, the Equal Pay Act, the first among the major federal equality initiatives, has not effectively guaranteed women equal pay for equal work. Regardless of occupation, level of experience, skills, or education, the pay gap remains. Women lawyers make on average $300 a week less than their male colleagues, women secretaries earn about $100 a week less than male clerical workers, female physicians' median weekly income is nearly $500 a week less than that of their male colleagues. Male college faculty earn nearly $170 a week more than women in the same rank, and male elementary school teachers take home about $70 more a week than female teachers.[44] On average, women earn 74 cents for every dollar a man earns. That means that if you are "an average woman accountant in the United States, you work Monday through Friday to earn what the man at the next desk has earned by noon on Wednesday."[45] The gap is much larger for women of color. African American women earn 67 cents and Latinas 58 cents

TABLE 7.2 Women's Earnings as a Percent of Men's Earnings, 1979–1999

	Annual	Weekly	Hourly
1979	59.7%	62.5%	64.1%
1981	59.2%	64.6%	65.1%
1983	63.6%	66.7%	69.4%
1985	64.6%	68.2%	70.0%
1987	65.2%	70.0%	72.1%
1989	68.7%	70.1%	75.4%
1991	69.9%	74.2%	78.6%
1993	71.5%	77.1%	80.4%
1995	71.4%	75.5%	80.8%
1997	74.2%	74.4%	80.8%
1999	72.2%	76.5%	83.8%

Source: Department of Labor, Women's Bureau, February 2000, accessed at *http://www.dol.gov.wb*.

for every dollar a man earns. Only Asian Pacific American women (80 cents) and white women (75 cents) do better than the average. As a result of the wage gap, 16 percent of all African American and Latina working women and their families live below the poverty line—more than double the rate for all women workers (7.7 percent in 1996).[46]

Early in 1997, the AFL-CIO Working Woman's Department conducted a national study of the issues facing working women. The "Ask a Working Woman" survey reported that equal pay is the top concern among 94 percent of full-time working women, while only 62 percent reported that they currently earn equal pay. Two-thirds of the working women said they contributed at least half of their household's income. More than half (52 percent) of the married women contributed half or more of their household income. Second on the list of top concerns among 87 percent of the women was affordable health insurance. Ranking third among women (79 percent) were pension and retirement benefits. Of those surveyed, 30 percent lacked health insurance, and 33 percent lacked pension benefits. Later that same year, the AFL-CIO and the Institute for Women's Policy Research conducted a follow-up study on the pay gap itself. That study's results are presented in "Equal Pay for Working Families" and the analysis is based on state-by-state breakouts of pay data collected by the Census Bureau and the Bureau of Labor Statistics.[47] The study reports that the wage gap varies by state. Women who work full-time in Indiana, Louisiana, Michigan, Montana, North Dakota, Wisconsin, and Wyoming receive, on average, 70 percent of men's wages. Women fare best (on average 80 percent of men's wages) in Arizona, California, Florida, Hawaii, Massachusetts, New York, and Rhode Island. However, the study found that in the District of Columbia, the lowest overall gap (97 percent) is largely a result of the very low wages of minority men. Men working in predominantly female occupations across all states lost an average of $6,259 a year as a result of depressed wages in those occupations.[48] The report emphasizes that since most families with children are supported by two-wage earners (71 percent), equal pay is essential to family support. In 1977, 54 percent of married women were wage earners, compared with 66 percent twenty years later.[49]

In marking the thirty-fifth anniversary of the Equal Pay Act, the Clinton administration in 1998 called on Congress to strengthen the enforcement of the law in recognition of the wage gap. In 1999, Clinton included a call for tougher enforcement of the EPA in his State of the Union Address.[50] In his fiscal-year 2000 budget, President Clinton included more than $14 million dollars designated to close the wage gap, largely through tougher enforcement provisions and federal legislation that would allow unlimited compensatory and punitive damages to be awarded in cases of wage discrimination. The Department of Labor and the Equal Employment Opportunity Commission (EEOC), both charged with enforcing provisions in the law, have stepped up their efforts accordingly. In January 1999, Texaco agreed to pay a record $3.1 million to female employees who had consistently been paid less than male employees. The settlement included more than $900,000 in salary increases and more than $2.2 million in back pay.[51]

Equal Pay Day, celebrated each year in early April, marks the day on which women "catch up" to men in terms of wages. It also sparks a barrage of criticism about the focus on the wage gap by many who say that the gap is an artifact of women's choices and not a result of gender discrimination in hiring, promotions, or pay. Labeling the wage gap a product of the popular media culture's "women as victims" theory, Diana Furchtgott-Roth and Christine Solba of the ideologically conservative American Enterprise Institute and the Independent Women's Forum, argue that self-selected statistics and anecdotal evidence have led women and policymakers to believe a myth.[52] The myth of the pay gap stems, they argue, from faulty methodology and an unwillingness to admit that women have made progress in the last three decades. They also argue that the "glass ceiling," for example, reflects the lack of qualified women in the pipeline for top corporate positions and not systematic discrimination as reported by the Glass Ceiling Commission (created as a result of the Civil Rights Act of 1991). The Glass Ceiling Commission reported that women held only 5 percent of the top management posts in *Fortune* 1,000 industrial and in *Fortune* 500 service companies. Furchtgott-Roth and Solba argue that since women were not well represented in professional schools in the 1950s and 1960s, few would have the requisite qualifications (an MBA and twenty-five years of experience) to hold industry's top positions and therefore would not be among those at the top of their professions today.[53] This is true since many professional programs did not admit women until required to do so by Title IX, passed in 1972. While Furchtgott-Roth and Solba may label the delay in women's "earning" the experience necessary to be CEO of *Fortune* 500 companies a "pipeline" problem, it also represents the effects of systematic discrimination.

With regard to the pay gap, Furchtgott-Roth and Solba focus on the "choices" women make. For women and men with similar education, continuous years in the work force, age, and occupation, the "adjusted wage gap" is much smaller (though it still exists). The difference appears to stem from women's "choice" to have children. Citing a study of women who received their college degrees around 1972, Furchtgott-Roth and Solba note that "among those who have had a successful career, as indicated by income level, nearly 50 percent were childless."[54] Comparing men and women with the same experience and education in 1991, women without children averaged 95 percent of men's wages while women with children made just 75 percent of men's wages. The presence of children accounted for women's, but not men's lower wages, according to two other studies they cited. This, they argued, is due to a woman's choice to spend time with her children, accept more flexible, lower-paying jobs to do so, or to aspire to less demanding occupations in anticipation of having children. In this sense, the "pink ghetto" of lower paying jobs represents an "oasis" to women who plan to have children.

Copley News Service.

[T]he choices women make *outside* the workplace have significant consequences for their achievement *within* the workplace and that women, like men, can make it to the top—but not without sacrifice. What appears to be happening (and what those who cite discrimination ignore) is that women in many professions are making decisions to balance work and family priorities and that those decisions can result in fewer women reaching the top of their fields. Those who measure success solely by women's performance in the professional world rarely recognize that trend. Many mothers with small children give high priority to spending time with them and are willing to risk higher rates of absenteeism and thus fewer opportunities for promotions. It may be unfair that the bulk of child-raising responsibilities continues to fall to mothers rather than fathers, but it is not clear that most women see motherhood as a burden. . . . A preference for more time at home with less pay and less job advancement over more time at work with more pay and advancement is a legitimate choice for women.[55]

Of course, what this argument fails to address is the persistent dominance of the separate spheres ideology that places almost exclusive responsibility on women for both bearing and raising children. Presumably, having children is a choice made jointly and shared by a man and woman; however, the cost in this case for an "individual choice" falls solely on women in the form of lower wages, forgone promotions, and lost economic opportunities.

LIMITS OF THE LEGAL EQUALITY DOCTRINE IN PROMOTING ECONOMIC EQUALITY

Policies designed on the legal equality doctrine are gender neutral in their intent yet not always in their impact. Title VII and the Equal Pay Act have neither substantially changed the demographics of the labor force by ending sex segregation and eliminating the pay gap nor made it legally possible for women to ascend to the highest positions in proportion to their presence in the work force. The limits to women's promotions once they've been hired by a company have been labeled the *glass ceiling*. Further, some issues go unaddressed by gender-neutral policies. The character of the workplace has not changed significantly in response to the likelihood that both a husband and a wife will be full-time wage earners for the length of their working lives. This leaves issues of child care and family responsibilities to individuals to handle as best they can, and since women still carry the primary responsibility for home and children even when working full-time, these *private* decisions have fallen to women more often than not. As a result, women's work lives are interrupted to bear and care for children in ways that men's are not. In addition to contributing to the pay differential, women are also disadvantaged in retirement. Social security benefits are calculated based on lifetime earnings, and women consistently draw lower benefits than men. These issues are discussed below.

The Glass Ceiling

The barrier that prevents otherwise qualified women from attaining the highest positions, along with their corresponding prestige and pay, has been labeled the *glass ceiling*.[56] Titles IX and VII allowed women to make tremendous gains in education and in the workplace. There are few overt barriers to jobs for women today. However, in 1999, there were only two women CEOs of *Fortune* 500 companies. Although women made up 49 percent of managerial and professional specialty positions in 1999, they constituted only 3.3 percent of the top earners. Overall 11.9 percent of corporate officers and 11.2 percent of board directors were women. While white women face a glass ceiling, women of color have characterized it as a "concrete ceiling." In 1999, women of color made up just 1.3 percent of corporate officers in *Fortune* 500 companies and 1.9 percent of board directors in *Fortune* 1,000 companies.[57] Surveys of women of color in management reveal that a lack of networking opportunities is perceived as the number one barrier to advancement. A vast research literature documents the power of the "old-boys' network" in excluding women's participation in the types of informal informational exchanges that result in client referrals and overall advancement in an organization.[58]

Rather than having employment policies that are obviously discriminatory, organizational culture and practices have created the glass ceiling. Ingrained in

"Aha! Just as I suspected!"

these cultures are traditional assumptions about gender stereotypes that can influence women's ability to reach the highest levels in a profession. Research suggests that both men and women perceive successful managers as those with more male characteristics than female characteristics. Women managers are perceived as less aggressive and independent than their male colleagues, although women are thought to have better interpersonal skills.[59] The characteristics that are valued and encouraged in an organization can often be gleaned from its mission statement and official publications. Companies that use motivational metaphors that draw on male-associated sports or military references and that make little positive mention of women in presentations of their corporate image are unlikely to have many women in top positions.[60]

Comparable Worth

The Equal Pay Act of 1963 was written to enforce equal pay for the same work but has done little to address the effects of employment patterns that show many women doing "women's work" and therefore receiving "women's wages." Advocates of the original EPA gave up the words "equal pay" for "comparable work" in order to get the bill passed. In recent years, however, the concept of comparable worth has returned as a public-policy issue. Comparable worth legislation would ensure that women who work as *prison matrons*, for example, would be paid the same as men who work as *prison guards*. Similarly, 911 dispatchers would receive the same pay as emergency operators at the Fire Department, a social worker's wages would equal those of a probation officer, and a nursery worker who tends children would not be paid less than a nursery worker who tends plants.[61] In an attempt to garner public support, advocates of comparable worth have adopted the rhetoric of "paycheck fairness." As we have seen repeatedly, a change in the status or conditions women face is much more likely to be accomplished in the name of "fairness" than in the pursuit of "sameness." Some opponents of comparable worth still worry that men's wages will be depressed under comparable worth. Others recognize the large redistribution of income that would be required to eliminate the dual labor market.

Tom Harkin, a Democratic senator from Iowa, and Eleanor Holmes Norton, the Democratic delegate from the District of Columbia, have sponsored the Fair Pay Act. This bill would prohibit wage discrimination on the basis of sex, race, and national origin, by "requiring employers to provide equal pay for work of equal value, whether the jobs are the same or not." The bill would also ban retaliation against workers who challenge pay practices or seek to disclose wage information, and would require employers to file wage information annually with the EEOC. The AFL-CIO, as well as other unions and many women's organizations have supported this route to reducing the pay gap. Businesses and manufactures are strongly opposed, because of the inherent costs in equalizing wages and the disclosure requirements. In a separate effort to strengthen and enforce the Equal Pay Act, Tom Daschle, Democratic senator from South Dakota, and Rosa DeLauro, Democratic congresswoman from New York, have proposed the Paycheck Fairness Act. This bill would strengthen the penalties that courts may impose for equal pay violations and provide compensatory as well as punitive damages, in addition to back pay, to individuals denied equal pay for equal work. In addition, this bill would authorize class-action lawsuits and would direct the Department of Labor to provide public information about strategies for eliminating wage discrimination and to issue guidelines for evaluating jobs.

Child Care

The issue of child care was politicized seemingly overnight as two women were forced to withdraw their nominations for attorney general of the United States under the newly elected Clinton administration in 1993. Zoe Baird, the first female nominee for attorney general, was forced to withdraw her nomination because of allegations related to employment and payroll taxes for her nanny. Kimba Wood, President Clinton's second choice for the post, was also forced to step down over similar issues related to her child-care arrangements. Clinton's third choice, also a woman, was not subject to this line of inquiry since Janet Reno was unmarried and without children. No previous nominee had ever been questioned about his child-care arrangements during Senate confirmation hearings. Then, on February 4, 1997, the country and the world learned of the death of eight-month-old Matthew Eappen, allegedly at the hands of his 18-year-old British au pair, Louise Woodward. In all three of these cases, public reaction centered on choices that women with full-time jobs made about child care. Deborah Eappen, Matthew's mother, was publicly vilified for leaving her son with an au pair when she returned to work part-time as an ophthalmologist. Baird and Wood were painted as "yuppie moms," abusing the tax code by paying for child care under the table instead of paying payroll taxes as required by law. The fact is that child care is largely an underground industry in the United States, only loosely regulated, largely unsupported by federal or state dollars, and subject to market forces that make child-care workers some of the lowest paid members of the work force.

The demographics of the full-time work force have changed dramatically over the last thirty years, but the social support structures to help families care for children, the elderly, or the ill have not changed substantially. For families with children between the ages of three and five, child care is the third greatest expense after housing and food.[62] Finding adequate child care is a widespread problem that cuts across all demographic boundaries. Sixty-three percent of women with children under age six work, and 78 percent of women with children between the ages of six and seventeen have jobs. One quarter of all households with children under the age of eighteen are headed by a single female.

Policy solutions to families' changing needs have been slow to materialize.

Unlike equalizing pay or opening educational programs to women, a single policy or government program on child care is not likely to fit every family's needs. Even more central to the problem is the public's ambivalence over women's dual role as both a mother and a full-time employee. This is not a new problem and individuals left on their own to find solutions to the dilemma of raising children and working full-time are also not a new phenomenon. In 1993, President Clinton signed the Family and Medical Leave Act (FMLA), allowing individuals to take up to twelve weeks of unpaid leave to care for a newborn, a sick child or family member, or to deal with their own illness. However, FMLA covers only a small percentage of the work force, and two-thirds of employees who needed and were eligible for FMLA did not take it because they could not forgo the income.[63] Infants and toddlers demand time and constant attention, while older elementary-school children demand less time, but their parents need more flexible schedules to meet with teachers and attend school-related events during traditional work hours. The parents of teenagers report that they need the ability to leave work on a moment's notice to deal with emergencies. Thus, families with children of various ages continue to seek solutions that best accommodate the stresses of combining work and raising children. Often one parent (most often the mother) will drop out of the work force to care for very young children until they enter kindergarten at the age of five. In doing so, those parents severely limit their long-term wage-earning capacity, risk the erosion of job-related skills and knowledge, and reduce the size or security of their pension. Alternatives to parent-centered child care come in many forms, ranging from part-time or full-time in-home care to group daycare outside the home. There are advocates for each form of care, but government subsidies are only available to poor families with children in group daycare programs. Tax credits and deductions for childcare expenses benefit mainly the middle and upper classes, but do nothing to address the accessibility and quality of child care.

Even as we begin a new century, women's full-time employment is not an assumption but rather is still treated as an anomaly or a "social problem." Although the United States professes to care deeply about its children, the culture of limited government, individualism, and familial autonomy and privacy conspire to worsen an old problem: Who will care for the children? As we said earlier, the assumption that women will not only bear children but also take primary responsibility for their care stems from the separate spheres ideology and therefore eliminates men from the very definition of the problem. The question of "who will care for the children" does not include fathers in its implicit or explicit assumptions. *Working father* is not a part of our modern lexicon—in fact, it seems redundant in ways that *working mother* does not. This dichotomy negatively affects both men and women, but for women the consequences are likely to be economic. Why isn't child care viewed like education, as a "public good" (see previous chapter)? In the same way that education benefits both the individual and larger society, doesn't society have an interest in ensuring that generations of children become competent adults? If there is a social contract to educate all citizens, why isn't there one to care for the nation's infants? The answer is in the pervasive influence of gender-specific expectations that stem from the separate spheres ideology. Furthermore, the question of child care, like that of education, cannot be understood without recognizing the power of class in defining the problem. While middle-class women are being pressured to stay home with their children, *in the interests of their children,* poor women are being told to join the work force, *in the interests of their children.* In other words, for professional women, no child care is good enough to justify leaving their children to go off to work, but for poor women, no child care is bad enough to justify providing public support for them to stay home with their children.[64]

Government initiatives on child care have been spotty at best. In times of national crisis (an economic depression or a war), when women were *needed* to work, the government has taken a more active role in providing assistance with child care. However, once the crisis passed, government's involvement virtually vanished. Between the mid-1950s and 1970s, as women's full-time participation in the work force became more the norm than the exception, government tax deductions or tax credits encouraged private solutions to a very public problem. Public child care was provided in the 1960s concurrent with the growth in public housing to combat poverty. Thus the link between public child care and public assistance for the poor precluded a national discussion about the public's responsibility for universal child care that other developed, primarily European nations provide.[65] Congress attempted to address the need for universal child care in 1971 in the Child Development Act, which would have created a network of childcare facilities with fees based on a family's income. The public's negative reaction to out-of-home care as the standard prompted a presidential veto and shelved the discussion for nearly twenty years. In the 1990s, when it was evident that women's participation in the full-time work force not only included the majority of women and women with small children, but that women would work throughout the course of their lifetime rather than for a short time before marriage and children, government began to re-examine the issue. In 1990, Congress passed the Child Care and Development Act. Consistent with other "new federalism" programs of the decade, Congress authorized funding in the form of block grants to states, which allowed each state to decide how the money will best serve its needs. On the one hand, this allowed a state to experiment with childcare strategies that were tailored to its unique constituencies and needs. Alternatively, by not providing uniform standards for quality, training, and services, the Child Care and Development Act did not do anything to standardize the accessibility or quality of child care nationally. Further, 75 percent of the block-grant funding was targeted for low-income families, which perpetuated the myth that child care was a class issue. In the fall of 1997, the Clinton administration convened a White House Conference on Child Care. The result was a proposal to increase tax credits for child care and improve the quality and accessibility of childcare centers.

The organized women's movement has largely stayed away from the childcare issue, fearing that linking child care to women's rights would merely reinforce the perception that women are solely responsible for children and their care. The character of the definition of child care might have been very different if feminists had worked to define the issue as public, rather than private, in nature. If that were the case, rather than women's rights and children's interests opposing each other, child care might have been perceived as a family rights issue.[66] In the 1980s and into the 1990s, child care became yet another weapon the far right used to suggest that feminists were out of step with mainstream American "family values." Women in the workforce were demonized as selfish by those who cared for their children full-time. Women in the full-time work force felt guilty (a feeling that is fueled by the popular culture), anxious about their childcare arrangements, and exhausted from juggling both work and family. Women who stay at home with their children are subject to derision and often made to feel backward or unambitious by their peers. Whether they work part-time, work from home, or work as full-time caregivers, women who stay at home are anxious and exhausted from the nonstop demands of child care. Neither the public nor women themselves have fully supported either choice. As with other political and economic rights, the question, "who will care for the children" divides women rather than unites them around a common interest. Without a consensus that child care is a public good that should be subject to shared costs and responsibilities across all citizens, the government, employers, and parents will continue to wrestle with the vagaries of the private market in finding suitable childcare arrangements. Employers, while excused from any government-mandated responsibility for providing child care as an employment benefit, are left to deal with the consequences of the incompatibility of family and work responsibilities of both male and female employees.[67] Men, although not usually the primary caregiver in the family, are increasingly partnered with women who work full-time, which leaves men without anyone at home to organize the affairs of the family. Sociologist Arlie Hochschild contends that men and women have actually increased their time at work, contrary to their claims of wanting to spend more time with their children and families. The reason, she explains, is that the work environment is less stressful, more orderly, and one in which they feel more competent.[68]

Attempts to create family-responsive workplaces have been met with mixed success. Companies that invest in child care, family benefit packages that include flextime, or other work arrangements have benefited by increased profits, less turnover, and lower rates of absenteeism among employees.[69] However, policies vary considerably, and the policies on paper may not reflect the reality of the practice. Most human-resource scholars admit that the financial incentive is probably not large enough to get companies to invest heavily in family benefits. In fact, employers might have more of an incentive to steer clear of employees who plan to have or already have children (most of whom are young women).[70] This leaves government to take a larger role in providing a policy that supports families. Optimally, the solution would allow parents to make choices about the form and duration of the care their children receive from others. While disincentives for parents who choose to stay at home with their children should be minimized, the assumption that only women can care for children should be actively challenged by policy alternatives that grant men and women equal opportunities to care for their families.

Strengthening Family and Medical Leave

The Family and Medical Leave Act was passed by Congress several times and vetoed several times before it was finally signed into law as the first act of a new Clinton administration in 1993. FMLA provides up to twelve weeks of unpaid job-protected leave to care for a newborn child or a sick family member, or to deal with one's own illness. Although it is a step in the right direction, FMLA only covers employers with fifty or more employees. Recent proposals introduced in the 106th Congress attempted to extend FMLA coverage to employers with twenty-five or more employees, to eliminate the hours-of-service requirement (currently an employee has to have worked for 1,250 hours in the last year to qualify for coverage), to allow employees to take FMLA leave to address domestic-violence situations, and to extend FMLA to allow parents to attend and participate in school events, teacher-parent conferences, and field trips.[71] The Clinton administration also instructed the Department of Labor to investigate the feasibility of using unemployment insurance funds for FMLA leave. Results of the National Study of the Changing Workforce suggest that women's choice to work part-time to care for children or family limits their ability to access FMLA leave. Although 86 percent of fathers covered under FMLA had worked the required 1,250 hours, only 73 percent of mothers met that requirement. As a result, the study estimated that only 41 percent of employed women were covered by FMLA, compared to 49 percent of men.[72] Even when employees are covered by FMLA, the likelihood is that their leave must be unpaid. Two-thirds of workers who are eligible for leave opt not to take it because of financial reasons, and one in eleven who used FMLA was actually forced onto public assistance to make ends meet. Of 158 countries around the world, 130 have leave policies for parents, and 98 percent of those offer paid leave. Three countries included in the survey provided unpaid leave—the United States, Ethiopia, and Australia.[73]

Americans strongly support providing paid family leave. In a Center for Policy Alternatives survey, 68 percent of women and 56 percent of men would be more likely to vote for a candidate who favors expanding the FMLA. One option for paid family leave, called Baby UI, is under consideration in thirteen states. This option would apply unemployment insurance benefits to leave taken for caring for a new baby or a newly adopted child.[74] The National Partnership for Women and Families (NPWF) strongly supports legislation to allow states to use unemployment insurance and temporary disability insurance to fund paid parental leave. In a survey, sponsored by Zero to Three, Civitas, and the Brio Corporation, released in October 2000, 80 percent of adults and

88 percent of parents with children six or younger support "paid parental leave that allows working parents of very young babies to stay home from work for their children."[75] The same survey found that 85 percent of adults support expanding "disability or unemployment insurance to help families afford to take time off from work to care for a newborn, a newly adopted child, or a seriously ill family member." Fourteen percent of those surveyed said that they opposed such measures. Both business and government get mediocre marks from survey participants on their efforts to make changes in the workplace that would help workers meet the needs of their young children. Fifty-nine percent of those surveyed said that employers are doing a fair or poor job, whereas 63 percent said that government is doing a fair or poor job in assisting workers.

Opponents of the regulations to allow states to use unemployment insurance funds to pay for family leave argue that the practice will be too expensive and will bankrupt states' unemployment insurance funds, particularly in times of economic recession when unemployment rates are high.[76] The Employment Policy Foundation (EPF) characterizes the policy change as "pitting the 'haves' (those with jobs) versus the 'have-nots' (the unemployed)."[77] EPF cautions that notification and reporting requirements can limit personal freedom and privacy rights. In response to unfavorable comparisons of the current FMLA with more generous European family leave policies, the EPF argues that the U.S. economy benefits from a free-market approach that allows workers to negotiate benefits privately with their employers. Many businesses objected to the Family and Medical Leave Act when it was first introduced, arguing that mandated employee benefits would bankrupt many companies.

Women in Retirement: Social Security and Private Pensions

The current social security system was established under the Social Security Act in 1935. Numerous changes have been made since its inception, but the basic philosophy has remained intact. The social security system is an example of a gender-neutral law because it does not treat men and women differently in the law itself, though men and women experience the system quite differently as a result of differences in employment and wage patterns. Social security is particularly important for women because women are less likely than men to have a private pension. They also live an average of seven years longer than men, and because of pay inequities and time spent away from work to raise children, women have lower lifetime earnings than men. In 2000, women made up 60 percent of social security beneficiaries. Half of the women age 65 and older would be poor if not for social security benefits, and for 25 percent of elderly women who live alone, social security is their only source of income. Without social security, the poverty rate for women over 65 would have been 52.9 percent in 1995.[78] Although some adjustments to the laws have been

Is Social Security Reform Good for Women?

IN ASSESSING the various reform proposals, the National Council of Women's Organizations has developed a "Women's Checklist to Strengthening Social Security."[1] Use this checklist to evaluate reform proposals currently under consideration. In each case, does the proposal:

- *Continue to help those with lower lifetime earnings, who are disproportionately women?* The current benefits formula compensates women and other low-wage earners for lower lifetime earnings. Any reform proposal should adopt a similar progressive benefit formula that replaces a larger share of low-income workers' past earnings as a protection against poverty.
- *Maintain full cost-of-living adjustments?* The current social security system protects against inflation, a crucial protection against the erosion of benefits. This feature is particularly important to women because they live, on average, seven years longer than men. Women also rely more on social security for their total retirement income since they often lack private savings or pension funds.
- *Protect and strengthen benefits for wives, widows, and divorced women?* Social security's family protection provisions help women the most by providing guaranteed, inflation-protected, lifetime benefits for widows, divorced women, and the wives of retired workers. While theoretically, spousal benefits accrue to both men and women, figures show that 63 percent of female beneficiaries age 65 and older receive benefits based on their husbands' earning records, while only 1.2 percent of males receive benefits based on their wives' earning records. These benefits go some way toward offsetting the wage disparity between men and women.
- *Preserve disability and survivor benefits?* Social Security now provides benefits to 3 million children and the remaining parent in the event of a premature death or disability of a working parent. Two out of five of today's twenty-year-olds will face premature death or disability before reaching retirement age. Spouses of disabled workers or widows and widowers of workers who die prematurely receive guaranteed lifetime benefits.

made to recognize women's increased participation in the labor force, the social security system is premised on the 1930s traditional gender roles in families, which characterizes a tiny fraction of modern families. Social security was intended to be a supplement to private pension plans and savings accumulated over the course of a lifetime, but only about half of men and a quarter of retired women earn additional income from private pensions.

Social security is a pay-as-you-go system, meaning that current payroll taxes are used to pay benefits to current retirees. In 1983, Congress increased the payroll tax rate to ensure that social security took in more than it paid out in anticipation of a bulge in retirees when the baby boomers started to retire. As a result, there is a surplus of funds, but still nearly 90 percent of that money is required to cover the costs of current retirees. Without changes to the system,

- *Ensure that women's guaranteed benefits are not subject to the uncertainties of the stock market?* Current proposals to divert payments from the social security system into individually held private stock accounts, whose returns would be dependent on volatile investment markets, would not be guaranteed to keep pace with inflation nor provide spousal benefits and could reduce the retirement income of many women. Without the guarantees of a shared insurance pool, cost-of-living increases, and spousal and lifetime benefits, many women could outlive their assets.
- *Address the caregiving and labor force experience of women?* The current system is based on marriage and work patterns that have changed dramatically. The benefit formula, which generally helps those with low lifetime earnings, also favors those with thirty-five years of work force participation. Many women fall short of this mark because they drop out of the labor market to care for children or the elderly. The effects of sex-based wage discrimination during their working years are not fully offset by more generous benefits to low earners. Therefore, at the same time the fiscal integrity of the system itself is under consideration, issues such as divorce, absence from the work force for caregiving responsibilities, and the difference in current benefits between one- and two-income families needs to be considered as well.
- *Further reduce the number of elderly women living in poverty?* Social security has helped to reduce the poverty rate among women older than sixty-five from 35 percent in 1959 to less than 11 percent in 1996. Without social security, the poverty rate among elderly women would be greater than 50 percent. Yet, unmarried women still suffer disproportionately: Single, divorced, and widowed women over sixty-five have a poverty rate of 22 percent, compared to 15 percent for unmarried men and 5 percent for married couples.

1. National Council of Women's Organizations, "Women and Social Security Project," accessed at *http://www.women4socialsecurity.org.*

social security will remain solvent and able to pay 100 percent of promised benefits until 2037. Social security benefits are protected from erosion by inflation because the annual cost of living adjustment is indexed to inflation.

Under the current social security system, workers are eligible to retire with full benefits at age sixty-five and to receive partial benefits at age sixty-two. However, for workers born after 1937, eligibility for retirement with full benefits is age sixty-seven. Social security benefits are based on the thirty-five years of highest taxable earnings of at least $520 each quarter of the year. The benefit formula is a progressive calculation, and the five lowest earning years (including years with zero earnings) in an individual's working life are dropped. A married person is eligible for the larger of either 100 percent of his or her own retired-worker benefit or 50 percent of his or her spouse's retired-worker benefit. A woman whose benefit, based on her own work record, is less than or equal to the spousal benefit she could claim is said to be "dually entitled" and does not gain additional benefit from having worked. A man is similarly entitled to benefits from his wife's accounts, but in reality nearly all who use the spouse's benefit are women. This may change if more men opt to help raise children by either reducing the number of hours they work or by leaving the paid labor force entirely for a period of time.

Widows and widowers are entitled to 100 percent of the deceased spouse's retired worker benefit, if it is larger than his or her own benefit. A divorced person who was married for at least ten years, who is not married at age sixty, and whose former spouse is still living is entitled to spousal benefits equal to 50 percent of the former spouse's benefit (if greater than 100 percent of his or her own benefit). Divorced persons married at least ten years are also eligible for survivor benefits when the former spouse dies, at the 100 percent rate that applies to widowed spouses. Social security also includes disability insurance.[79]

Several reform proposals are being actively considered in Congress. The most common type of reform includes some aspect of privatization of the current system by diverting some or all of the current payroll tax dollars to an individually held, private investment account. The plans differ in how much would be diverted (all or only a percentage) and in what type of private account the money would be invested. Some people would like to see individual reform initiatives that will invest primarily or solely in equities (stocks), whereas others would prefer a more conservative investment strategy in bonds or in some split between the two that could change over the course of one's lifetime, becoming more conservative as retirement nears. Some plans call for collective investment of the trust fund assets or the collective investment of only some of the assets to try to increase the size of the trust fund itself. The Task Force on Women and Social Security, a joint project of the National Council of Women's Organizations and the Institute for Women's Policy Research, has made several proposals that would strengthen social security for women.[80] Among its many recommendations is the provision of a "family service credit," which could include an earnings credit and a provision for a number of "drop out years" in calculating benefits.

THE CONSEQUENCES OF A GENDERED ECONOMY: THE DEMOGRAPHICS OF POVERTY

The single best predictor of poverty in America is gender. Add to that the presence of children and the absence of marriage, and you have the "feminization of poverty" in the United States. The phrase "feminization of poverty" was coined to characterize the growing numbers over the last three or more decades of single, female-headed households living in poverty.[81] The reasons for single-parent households headed by women vary. Fewer women are getting and staying married. As of 1995, close to 45 percent of women were unmarried. About two-thirds of all first marriages end in separation or divorce. Additionally, half of all females over sixteen years old have custody of a minor child, and of these women, one out of every three is not married. This means that one woman out of every six is a single mother.[82] Two out of every three mothers have a job outside the home, although because women work on average fewer hours per week than men and earn less than men, women's average annual earnings stand at about half those of men. Because of the changes in the marketplace, there are fewer high paying, low-skill jobs available for men and women. The "deindustrialization" of America has reduced the number of manufacturing jobs to one-sixth of all jobs available.[83] Conversely, service and retail jobs now make up more than half of the jobs available, and that proportion is expected to increase in the coming years. Wages paid in manufacturing jobs outpaced those paid in the service sector by nearly 85 percent in 1995. In this sense, both men's and women's earning power has declined, so even among married couples, both husband and wife are likely to work full-time to support the family.

In sum, there are a variety of contradictory trends that contribute to the disproportionate number of women who live below the poverty line. Fewer women are married, although nearly half of all women have children and nearly 90 percent of women in the United States will have children at some point in their lives. A single head of household with minor children, regardless of sex, is at a severe disadvantage since he or she will be required to do both the unpaid labor of the household as well as to work for a living outside the home. When a woman is the single head of a household, this problem is made worse because women's wages are lower than men's. Households with children must either contract for child care or work only part-time and provide some measure of care themselves. With either option, the household income is diminished. Add to this, the contradictory messages men and women receive about the importance of "family." We value children in theory, but we do not value the care of children enough to pay professional childcare workers adequately or to set up social support systems (e.g., social security) based on life choices to care for children. Individuals are largely on their own to figure out how to care for their children and work full-time to support their families. Communal support structures are largely absent, even though there's much talk about communal responsibility. Additionally, we lack consensus on the very definition of a family (see more on this topic in the next chapter). Finally, although we believe that having a job is crucial to supporting one's family and serving as a contributing member of the community, there is a deficit in the proportion of jobs available and those that provide a "living wage." The growth in low-wage, service-sector jobs and the decline of high-wage manufacturing jobs have resulted in a situation where in 1995, 12 percent of adults under age sixty-five were living below the poverty line yet holding a full-time, year-round job.[84] Changes in the economy and cultural contradictions have resulted in increasingly shrill rhetoric about poor people and their "responsibility" for their circumstances. Within this context, Congress and the Clinton administration negotiated major changes to the welfare system in the United States in 1996.

The Gender Implications of Welfare Policy and Welfare Reform

Welfare policy in the United States began more than eighty-five years ago with state-level mothers' pension policies, which were designed to reduce poverty of mothers without husbands. The New Deal nationalized mothers' pensions with the Aid to Dependent Children (ADC) program. The ADC program was based on a number of assumptions about gender, poverty, and the need to lift single women "toward the norms of Anglo-American, middle-class culture," argues historian Gwendolyn Mink.

> From these premises followed prescription for the supervision of 'welfare mothers' to ensure their assimilation of proper family values. The welfare policies that surrounded these innovations radiated stigma, judgment, and anxiety over deviations from those values. Yet they simultaneously acknowledged the economic needs of poor, single mothers as legitimate and asserted confidence that diversely situated mothers could be led to a universal cultural and family ideal.[85]

Mink states that aid to single mothers went from a program in the 1930s, which was designed to supervise and educate women to enable them to make choices that more closely approximated the dominant cultural norm, to one in the 1960s, which focused on the choices and behaviors of welfare mothers and disputed women's entitlement to support. ADC was modified to include a grant to mothers as well as children in 1950, and then it became Aid to Families with Dependent Children (AFDC) in 1962. During that time, the program's goals and focus shifted from ensuring that children did not grow up in poverty for lack of a male breadwinner to those that enforced gender ideology and racial and cultural control.[86] As barriers to eligibility and moral supervision were lowered, more women of color joined the program and the public's perception that women on welfare "don't deserve it" increased.

Pressure throughout the 1980s and 1990s to "end welfare as we know it" was rooted in a variety of myths about welfare recipients and cultural stereotypes about women in general—specifically African American women. Prior to national work requirements and time limits imposed by the 1996 legislation, 43 percent of AFDC recipients either combined work with welfare or cycled between the two, and 56 percent of AFDC recipients were continuously enrolled on welfare for fewer than two years.[87] Furthermore, welfare payments alone never enabled a woman and her children to escape poverty. In 1996, the maximum AFDC benefit for a family of three in New York, the most generous state, was $703 a month, while the maximum payment in Mississippi, the least generous state, was $120 a month. In 1996, a family of three was below the poverty line when its annual income was $12,980 ($1,082 a month) or less. Even with food stamps, the combined benefit in the most generous state was only $935 a month—well below the poverty standard. The median combined payment per month was only 65 percent of the poverty line.[88] AFDC families were allowed to own a car as long as its value did not exceed $1,500. They were allowed to have no more than $1,000 in cash, checking, savings, or other assets, and once on welfare, families could keep only $50 of any child-support payments, with the balance going back to the state. Welfare, although designated as an antipoverty program, did not "pay" women enough to escape poverty, nor did it provide incentives to get the education and training that would allow women to seek jobs above poverty-level wages, nor did it address that fact that a single woman did not have a "wife" at home to care for her children when she did enter the work force to support her children.

The Heritage Foundation, a conservative think tank, promoted another dominant myth—that welfare was "breaking the national bank." In a 1994 report, it stated, "In 1992, federal, state, and local governments spent $305 billion on means-tested welfare programs for low-income Americans. Welfare now absorbs 5 percent of the GNP, up from 1.5 percent in 1965 when the War on Poverty began."[89] In fact, spending on both welfare and Medicaid declined between 1980 and 1993 when the two programs combined to make up 0.7 percent of the gross domestic product and 2.4 percent of the federal budget. Contrary to Heritage's assertion that welfare cost the nation $305 billion, total government spending (state and federal) on women and their children in 1992 (for AFDC, food stamps, and Medicaid for AFDC families) was $70.5 billion. By comparison, the value of the tax exemption for employer-sponsored health insurance in the same year was $47 billion, and the mortgage deduction from income taxes was $49 billion. Relative to other government "welfare" programs, AFDC and its companion support programs were not disproportionately high.[90]

Political scientist Jyl Josephson argues that the negative public focus on welfare mothers is a result of both the social construction of their gender, race, and class-based roles and the labeling of their behavior as *deviant*. Members of Congress "argued that women who were single parents should be in the work force, and that they were using their children as an excuse not to work."[91] Utilizing a framework first developed by Schneider and Ingram, she says that AFDC and other forms of public assistance were fairly easy targets for elimination by policymakers. Politicians could appear tough without appearing mean and fiscally responsible without appearing punitive. And since the focus was on the mother's deviancy, the effect on millions of children could be safely ignored.

The reform package passed by Congress and signed by President Clinton in 1996, called the Personal Responsibility and Work Opportunity Reconciliation Act (PRWORA), has as its centerpiece a replacement for AFDC, known as Temporary Assistance to Needy Families (TANF). The basic goal of the new program is to replace government assistance with earnings. In addition, funding is accomplished through block grants to the states, which are given the authority to design and administer welfare programs within their boundaries. The entitlement to public assistance was ended with the 1996 legislation. States have designed programs around work requirements, allowing recipients to keep a larger percentage of the wages they earn and to still be eligible for assistance, education, and training programs to develop job skills. These programs offer support that is limited to two to five years (over a person's lifetime in most cases), have increased efforts to collect child support from biological fathers, and have given more attention to childcare demands. Since TANF was passed, the number of families receiving public assistance in most states has decreased, but the reasons for the decline are not clear. Community-based non-profit service providers report that more families are seeking assistance in soup kitchens and shelters. Beyond the effects within individual communities, researchers at the Economic Policy Institute estimate that an influx of low-skilled workers into the work force will increase the competition for already underpaid occupations and will most likely drive down wages. They concluded that the work requirements under the 1996 reforms would drive down the average hourly wage for the bottom third of the work force by 12 percent—from $5.47 an hour to $4.82 an hour. Even working forty-hour weeks, a single, hourly wage-earner cannot support a family.

Other reforms to the welfare programs now designed and administered by the states include behavior modification tactics. For example, Learnfare suspends payment if a child misses a certain number of days of school or gets a failing grade; The Family Cap freezes benefits at their current level when another child is born to a poor mother receiving cash assistance; Bridefare gives small monetary benefits for marrying the father of a child; and Shotfare denies a family benefits if immunization records are incomplete for any child.[92] Other states have offered incentives for implanting the contraceptive Norplant (the next chapter examines coerced contraception). While behavior modification reflects the legislation's focus on individual responsibility, it also operates on often faulty assumptions about poor mothers' motives. Children of welfare families miss school more often than other children because their transportation is more tenuous, their housing is more subject to instability that can often lead to periods of homelessness, and the vagaries of the low-wage job market may necessitate moving several times throughout the school year to follow available jobs. Domestic violence may prevent a woman from marrying the biological father of her child, although monetary incentives to the contrary may lure women into dangerous relationships.

The implications of the 1996 welfare reforms are only now becoming evident. States will no doubt make changes as programmatic evaluations are completed. However, the character of the reforms adopted in 1996 are so dramatically different from any of the other federal benefit programs, one wonders whether single mothers will remain the country's best scapegoat. Positive incentives are few and far between in the current policy, and the expectation that single mothers will be able to move off of public assistance on the basis of an hourly wage job that does not provide health, pension, or childcare benefits is unrealistic at best. TANF eliminated a welfare mother's ability to choose education over an hourly wage job in order for her to continue to receive benefits, thereby further limiting her long-term earning power.

CONCLUSION

In this chapter we have covered a lot of topics related to work, the economy, wages, and the different ways men and women experience the labor market over the course of their lifetimes. It is clear that society has not resolved its ambivalence over women in the full-time work force, even though the majority of women and the majority of women with small children are full-time participants in the economy. Antiquated notions of why women work reinforce "pink ghettos" of low-wage occupations primarily held by women and also depress women's wages overall. The wage gap not only deprives women and their families of income now, but it also reduces retirement benefits. While Title VII and Title IX have opened doors to women's employment and educational opportunities, the Equal Pay Act has been largely ineffective in equalizing wage rates for men and women. Women and their partners are left alone to negotiate child care and other caregiving arrangements when both are working full-time. If one partner stops working for any length of time to care for children or an ailing family member, he or she risks erosion of employment skills, a reduction in overall earnings, as well as a loss in pension and other retirement benefits. The United States has yet to develop a universal system of child care that is integrated with the educational system to provide a single stream of child development assistance. Given the current conservative social forces stressing the autonomous family unit, free from government intrusion, it is unlikely that the Congress and administration will be very aggressive in exploring more comprehensive solutions to the childcare problem. The next generation of men and women entering the work force will face wage inequities and the struggle to reconcile work with family issues.

Is a gender-neutral approach to employment policy effective for women or does gender neutrality merely increase the burden on women to work full-time in both the paid and unpaid labor sectors? Our analysis in this chapter suggests that the policies adopted in the 1960s and still subject to interpretation by the courts today have not been sufficient to change the character and existence of the dual labor market, the wage gap, or the "glass ceiling" and "sticky floor" problems. A majority of women entering the work force today will hold a wage-earning job until retirement. Some women may still opt to drop out of the work force entirely to bear and raise children, but most will either stay in the work force or return once their children have started school. Some women will work because they find it fulfilling. Most women, however, will work for their lifetime out of economic necessity. As we have noted in previous chapters, until public attitudes catch up with the realities of women in the work force, public policy is unlikely to address the most pervasive problems women face.

Notes

1. Sharlene Hesse-Biber and Gregg Lee Carter, *Working Women in America: Split Dreams* (New York: Oxford University Press, 2000), p. 54.

2. Bureau of Labor Statistics, 1996. *Employment and Earnings,* January 1997, Tables 11 and 18.

3. Ibid.

4. Hesse-Biber and Carter, *Working Women in America,* pp. 167–168.

5. Eleanor Flexnor and Ellen Fitzpatrick, *Century of Struggle: The Women's Rights Movement in the United States* (Cambridge: Harvard University Press, 1996).

6. Hesse-Biber and Carter, *Working Women in America,* p. 18.

7. Nancy Woloch, *Women and the American Experience* (New York: Alfred A. Knopf, 1984), p. 220.

8. Julie A. Matthaei, *An Economic History of Women in America: Women's Work, the Sexual Division of Labor, and the Development of Capitalism* (New York: Schocken Books, 1982).

9. Woloch, *Women and the American Experience,* p. 221.

10. Ibid., p. 220.

11. Ibid., p. 221.

12. Maxine L. Margolis, *Mothers and Such: Views of American Women and Why They Changed* (Berkeley: University of California Press, 1984), p. 195.

13. Hesse-Biber and Carter, *Working Women in America,* p. 37.

14. Rosalyn Baxandall, Linda Gordon, and Susan Reverby, *America's Working Women: A Documentary History—1600 to the Present* (New York: Vintage Books, 1976), pp. 255–256.

15. Ann Gordon, Mari-Jo Buhle, and Nancy Schrom, "Women in American Society: An Historical Contribution," *Radical America* 5, no. 4 (1971): 3–66.

16. "Equal Pay Helps Men Too," AFL-CIO fact sheet, accessed at *http://www.aflcio.org/women/.*

17. J. J. Goodnow, "Children's Household Work: Its nature and functions," *Psychological Bulletin* 103 (1988): 5–26.

18. Virginia Valian, *Why So Slow? The Advancement of Women* (Cambridge, Mass.: MIT Press, 1998), p. 33.

19. Ibid., p. 40.

20. Ibid., p. 44.

21. Ibid.

22. National Manpower Council, *Womanpower* (New York: Columbia University Press, 1957).

23. *Equal Pay Act of 1963.* 77 Stat. 56 (1963).

24. J. Ralph Lindgren and Nadine Taub, *The Law of Sex Discrimination*, 2d ed. (Minneapolis, Minn.: West Publishing, 1993), pp. 145–146.

25. Ibid., pp. 146–147.

26. Ibid., p. 174.

27. *Quong Wing v. Kirkendall*, 233 US 59, 63 (1912).

28. Lindgren and Taub, *Law of Sex Discrimination*, p. 177.

29. *Wilson v. Southwest Airlines.*

30. *Dothard v. Rawlinson*, 433 US 321 (1977).

31. *Griggs v. Duke Power Company*, 401 US 424 (1971).

32. *Executive Order 11246.* 30 F.R. 12319, 1965.

33. Jocelyn C. Frye, "Affirmative Action: Understanding the Past and Present," in *The American Woman 1996–1997: Women and Work*, eds. Cynthia Costello and Barbara Kivimae Krimgold (New York: Norton, 1996), p. 35.

34. Ibid., pp. 37–38.

35. Roberta Ann Johnson, "Affirmative Action and Women," in *Women in Politics: Outsiders or Insiders?*, ed. Lois Duke Whitaker, 3d ed. (Upper Saddle River, N.J.: Prentice Hall, 1999), pp. 334–352.

36. For the full report, go to *http://aflcio.org/publ/press98/pr0901.htm.* To calculate the impact of the wage gap on your own lifetime earnings, go to the AFL-CIO's Equal Pay Web site at *http://www.aflcio.org/women/equalpay.htm.*

37. Cynthia B. Costello, Shari Miles, and Anne J. Stone, *The American Woman 1999–2000* (New York: Norton, 1998).

38. Valian, *Why So Slow?*, pp. 190–191.

39. Ibid., p. 198.

40. Nina Bernstein, "Report Shows Setbacks for Women Lawyers," *New York Times*, 14 January 1999, section 4, p. 5.

41. Valian, *Why So Slow?*, p. 208.

42. Dorothy McBride Stetson, *Women's Rights in the USA: Policy Debates and Gender Roles*, 2d ed. (New York: Garland Publishing, 1997), p. 317.

43. Lindgren and Taub, *Law of Sex Discrimination*, p. 217.

44. National Committee on Pay Equity, "Equal Pay by Occupation," analysis of 1997 Household Data Annual Averages (Washington, D.C.: Bureau of Labor Statistics, 1999).

45. Linda Tarr-Whelan, "Women: Essential for the Success of the New Economy" (speech delivered at the Trans-Atlantic Women in the New Economy Summit, 11 Downing Street, London, England, 2000), accessed at *http://www.stateaction.org.*

46. "It's High Time—Past Time—for Women of Color to Earn Equal Pay," AFL-CIO fact sheet, accessed at *http://aflcio.org/women/f_color.htm.* (2000).

47. Heidi Hartman, Katherine Allen, and Christine Owens, "Equal Pay for Working Families: National and State Data on the Pay Gap and its Costs," A Joint Research Project of the AFL-CIO and the Institute for Women's Policy Research, 1998, accessed at *http://www.iwpr.org* and on *http://aflcio.org/women.*

48. Ibid., pp. 1–3.

49. Information can be accessed at *http://aflcio.org/women/eqp_men.htm.*

50. Transcript can be accessed at *http://cnn.com/ALLPOLITICS/stories/1999/01/19/sotu.transcript.*

51. Timothy S. Bland, "Equal Pay Enforcement Heats Up," *HRMagazine* 44, no. 7 (1999): 138–143.

52. Diana Furchtgott-Roth and Christine Solba, *Women's Figures: An Illustrated Guide to the Economic Progress of Women in America* (Washington, D.C.: AEI Press and the Independent Women's Forum, 1999).

53. Ibid., pp. 18–19.

54. Ibid., p. xx.

55. Ibid., p. 19.

56. Federal Glass Ceiling Commission, *Good for Business: Making Full Use of the Nation's Human Capital* (Washington, D.C.: Government Printing Office, 1995).

57. Catalyst, "The Glass Ceiling in 2000: Where are Women Now? Labor Day," fact sheet, accessed at *http://www.catalystwomen.org.*

58. See Hesse-Biber and Carter, *Working Women in America,* pp. 163–173.

59. Gregory Northcraft and Barbara A. Gutek, "Point-Counterpoint: Discrimination Against Women in Management—Going, Going, Gone or Going but not Gone?," in *Women in Management: Trends, Issues, and Challenges in Managerial Diversity,* ed. Ellen A Fagenson (Newbury Park, Calif.: Sage, 1993), pp. 219–245.

60. Albert J. Mills, "Organizational Culture," in *Women and Work: A Handbook,* eds. Paula J. Dubeck and Kathryn Berman (New York: Garland Press, 1996), pp. 321–322.

61. Ellen Goodman, "Equal Pay Struggle Continues," *Times-Picayune,* 16 March 1999, p. 5B.

62. U.S. Bureau of the Census, *Statistical Abstracts: 1997* (Washington, D.C.: Bureau of the Census, 1997), table 711.

63. Center for Policy Alternatives, 2000. "Women's Voices 2000: Women and Time," accessed at *http://www.stateaction.org/programs/women/voices/time.cfm.*

64. Ellen Goodman, "Who Gets Blamed for Matthew's Death? The Working Mother, of Course," *Boston Globe,* 26 October 1997, p. E7.

65. See Janet C. Gornick, Marcia K. Myers, and Katerin E. Ross, "Supporting Employment of Mothers: Policy Variations Across Fourteen Welfare States," *Journal of European Social Policy* 7 (1997): 45–70.

66. Sonya Michel, *Children's Interests/Mother's Rights: The Shaping of America's Child Care Policy* (New Haven, Conn.: Yale University Press, 1999).

67. Jennifer L. Glass, and Sarah Beth Estes, "The Family Responsive Workplace," *Annual Review of Sociology* 23 (1997): 289–314.

68. Arlie Russell Hochschild, *The Time Bind: How Work Becomes Home and Home Becomes Work* (New York: Holt, 1997).

69. Glass and Estes, "The Family Responsive Workplace," p. 312.

70. P. Kingston, "Illusions and Ignorance about the Family Responsive Workplace," *Journal of Family Issues* 11 (1990): 438–454.

71. Information can be accessed at *http://www.lpa.org/lpapublic/policy/status/fmla. htm.*

72. Costello and Krimgold, *Women and Work*, p. 85.

73. "Family Leave Benefits," accessed at *http://www.stateaction.org/issues/workfamily/ famleave/index.cfm.*

74. Ibid.

75. National Partnership for Women and Families, "Public Support for Family Leave Benefits Growing," news release, October 4, 2000, accessed at *http://www.national partnership.org.*

76. See information from the Employment Policy Foundation, accessed at *http://www. epf.org.*

77. Ibid.

78. Information can be accessed at *http://www.women4socialsecurity.org.*

79. This summary is based on information from the Institute for Women's Policy Research, 2000. "Research-in-Brief," IWPR publication no. D437RB.

80. Heidi Hartman, Catherine Hill, and Lisa Witter, "Strengthening Social Security for Women: A Report from the Working Conference on Women and Social Security," Warrenton, Va., July 19–22, 1999, accessed at *http://www.irp.org.*

81. Mwangi S. Kimenyi and John Mukum Mbaku, "Female Headship, Feminization of Poverty and Welfare," *Southern Economic Journal* 62, no. 1 (July 1995): 44–53.

82. Randy Albelda and Chris Tilly, *Glass Ceilings and Bottomless Pits: Women's Work, Women's Poverty* (Boston: South End Press, 1997), p. 3.

83. Ibid., p. 6.

84. Ibid., p. 9.

85. Gwendolyn Mink, "Welfare Reform in Historical Perspective," *Social Justice* 21, no. 1 (Spring 1994): 114–132.

86. Ibid., p. 117.

87. Heidi Hartmann and Roberta Spalter-Roth, "The Real Employment Opportunities of Women Participating in AFDC: What the Market Can Provide," *Social Justice* 21, no. 1 (1994).

88. Albelda and Tilly, *Glass Ceilings and Bottomless Pits*, p. 13.

89. Ibid., p. 100.

90. Ibid., pp. 102–103.

91. Jyl Josephson, "Gender and Social Policy," in *Gender and American Politics: Women, Men, and the Political Process*, eds. Sue Tolleson-Rinehart and Jyl J. Josephson (Armonk, N.Y.: M. E. Sharpe, 2000), p. 151.

92. Albelda and Tilly, *Glass Ceilings and Bottomless Pits*, p. 116.

The Politics of Family and Fertility: The Last Battleground in the Pursuit of Equality?

THE PREVIOUS chapter examined the effectiveness of gender-neutral laws in ending employment discrimination and analyzed the limits of the legal equality approach to reconciling women's dual roles in the private and public spheres. Family policy and issues of reproduction and fertility pose the greatest challenges to feminists when choosing a path toward equality. Gender-neutral laws are nearly impossible to construct, considering the central role biological differences play in this area. Gender neutrality in family law or policies related to pregnancy often obscure the ways in which women are disadvantaged. For example, a law that prevents firefighters from breast feeding their babies between calls only affects women, although it presumably applies to all firefighters regardless of gender. In *General Electric* v. *Gilbert* (1976), the Supreme Court ruled that a policy that distinguishes between pregnant and nonpregnant persons does not constitute sex discrimination against women.[1] A legal equality doctrine is much more difficult to adopt in family and fertility policies because in many cases women's biological differences are paramount and are magnified by the socially constructed gender roles. Yet, gender-specific laws that apply to women only and that are based on their biological functions are often discriminatory in their application. The debate over which path to equality is most advantageous for women is vividly displayed with regard to family and fertility issues.

This chapter surveys the laws that apply to the formation, maintenance, and dissolution of families constructed through marriage. Although nearly half of all marriages end in divorce, marriage remains the primary mechanism by which families are defined and recognized under the law. The increase of female, single-parent households challenges society to examine government programs that support children and women who must work outside the home. The presence of children in a woman's life directly challenges her autonomy. This chapter also examines reproductive policy. By regulating access to contraception and reproductive services, a state can regulate women's sexuality and reproductive choices. We will evaluate under what circumstances the state has a legitimate interest in regulating reproduction and how such regulations affect women's claims to autonomy. Should women be able to contract freely for their reproductive labor, just as men are constitutionally free to contract for their productive labor? Surrogacy, contract pregnancy, and *in vitro* fertilization present society with an entirely new set of issues. While sex is conceptually different from gender, emerging fertility technology may further blur or entirely erase the lines between sex and gender. Will fertility technologies liberate women from their biological role in reproduction in ways that promote equality or will the science of fertility and reproduction serve as another form of patriarchal control? What impact will changes in reproductive technology have on defining and forming families in the United States? These broad questions form the basis of our examination of women's attempts to reconcile their role within families with their expanding role in the public sphere. As we'll see, public policy in this area both assists and hinders women's pursuit of equality.

THE DEMOGRAPHICS OF MODERN FAMILIES

American families are quite diverse in their forms. The traditional patriarchal family model of two parents—a male breadwinner and a stay-at-home mother—with two or more children characterizes less than a quarter (about 22 million) of all U.S. households. The 1996 census counted 100 million households in the United States, 30 million of which comprised single men or women, making single-individual households more prevalent than the "traditional family" model. The most common type of household is the two-wage-earning married couple with or without dependents. These households account for about 34 percent of the total. Female-headed households constitute about 13 percent, with single males heading up about 3 percent of households overall. Gay and lesbian couples account for about 5 percent of all households, although census statistics catagorize them as single, or as a male- or female-headed household.[2]

American men and women are marrying later in life. In 1995, the average age at first marriage was 24.5 years for women and 26.9 years for men—the highest average age recorded in the twentieth century. In 1996, almost 19 percent of women and 28 percent of men in their early thirties had never been married. About half of all marriages end in divorce and almost 80 percent of divorced people remarry, creating "blended families." The divorce rate slowed considerably in the early part of the 1990s, perhaps because men and women are marrying later.[3]

The definition of "family" now encompasses a variety of forms, including same-sex couples with children. *Mark Richards/PhotoEdit.*

While all ethnic and racial groups have experienced changes in marriage and divorce patterns, the change has been particularly pronounced for African American women. In 1970, 62 percent of black women over the age of eighteen were married, 5 percent divorced, 16 percent widowed, and 17 percent never married. In 1995, 40 percent of African American women over eighteen were married, 13 percent divorced, 11 percent widowed, and 36 percent never married. The differences in 1970 among whites, African Americans, and Hispanics were relatively minor, yet the marital status of black women today contrasts sharply with both white and Hispanic women.[4]

CREATING FAMILIES THROUGH MARRIAGE

In 1976, the California Supreme Court ruled that actor Lee Marvin had to honor a prior agreement with Michelle Triola, who had been his nonmarital partner for seven years, that provided her with support and a share of their property should their relationship end. In issuing its ruling, the court took the opportunity to express society's view of marriage:

> We take this occasion to point out that the structure of society itself largely depends on the institution of marriage; and nothing we have said in this opinion should be taken to derogate that institution. The joining of man and woman in marriage is at once the most socially productive and individually fulfilling relationship one can enjoy in the course of a lifetime.[5]

Marriage is both an individual choice and a social expectation. For women, the institution of marriage has historically been the most oppressive force in denying women the rights, privileges, and obligations of full citizenship. Chapter one reviewed John Stuart Mill's characterization of marriage as a form of slavery. Under coverture marriage, a husband's identity entirely subsumed his wife. As a result, a woman was wholly subject to her husband's will and dependent on his willingness to provide support for her and their children. In entering coverture marriage, women relinquished control of all property and assets that she might have inherited from her family. Any assets that the couple might have accumulated during their marriage were considered the husband's property exclusively, including the household goods, the wife's clothing, and even the children. Coverture entitled the husband to expect obedience, maintenance of the household, supervision of the children, and unlimited access to the marital bed. Coverture obligated a man to provide the necessities, but nothing more. Should a wife rebel, common law provided for "mild correction." Throughout most of the nineteenth century, women's invisibility under coverture denied them political, social, and economic rights in the public realm. Although there were exceptions, such as prenuptial or postnuptial agreements that granted women control of their property, most laws that addressed women's property rights were not established until the late 1840s. Since property formed the basis of most economic and political rights in the United States, without property rights married women remained civilly dead.

Although coverture has largely faded as the standard for modern marriage, its vestiges remain in the patriarchal traditions and laws associated with forming a family through marriage. Family policy is not covered under the Constitution and has largely been left to the states to manage. Most of the laws or court interpretations of statutes have evolved over time and do not express a coherent view of "family life" in the United States. Laws regarding marriage usually have to do with establishing a minimum age for males and females to marry, specifying property rights, providing for custody and care of children produced within a marriage, and setting the conditions under which a couple may divorce. In each of these areas, marriage policy is intended to promote social order and protect property interests. Therefore it can be difficult to talk about women's rights within a marriage or how marriage policy might either advance or hinder women's pursuit of equality. For the most part, the character of family life once the family unit is formed is considered a private matter and not subject to the intrusions of public policy in the same ways that education and employment were in the last two chapters. For women, the private nature of the family has left them largely unprotected from the power of patriarchy. Is it possible to talk about women's rights or women's equality within a family or are all individual rights subsumed by the interests of the family unit as a whole?

Men and women who come together in marriage, or even those who choose to live together without being married, can more or less negotiate their own set of gender roles with minimal interference from the state for as long as the union holds. However, they cannot escape the gender roles built into the U.S. tax code, the consequences of a largely absent family support system even in the face of women's increased participation in the labor force, insurance regulations, or divorce, child custody and support laws. Furthermore, marriage is legal only for a woman and a man. Legal marriage carries with it access to a variety of benefits: the right to share medical benefits, inherit a pension, or access spousal social security benefits. Other family constellations, while increasingly prevalent in the United States, have not been recognized by law or supported by public policy. Some large employers have granted access to employment benefits, such as health insurance, to "domestic partners" even in the absence of state laws.

Vermont was the first state to pass a law that allowed full and equal civil legal status to gay and lesbian couples, although not the right to legally marry. Hawaii attempted to recognize same-sex unions and give them the same legal privileges as heterosexual marriages. In response, Congress passed the Defense of Marriage Act (1996), which exempted other states from having to legally recognize such unions within their own state boundaries. If the right to marry is understood as a fundamental right flowing from the right to privacy, the question of same-sex marriages is far from settled. In *Loving* v. *Virginia* (1967), the Supreme Court struck down Virginia's antimiscegenation statute prohibiting interracial marriage, citing both the Equal Protection clause of the Fourteenth Amendment and the fundamental right to marriage derived from the constitutional right to privacy. Furthermore, the Court did not say that the Lovings had a constitutional claim to a mixed-race marriage, but rather a fundamental right to marry. Although several states had antimiscegenation statutes and marriage between blacks and whites was culturally vilified, this did not dissuade the Court from supporting the right to marry.[6] This would suggest that it is only a matter of time before the constitutionality of same-sex marriages or state-enacted bans on same-sex marriages reach the Supreme Court.

THE DEVELOPMENT OF CONTEMPORARY MARRIAGE

Political scientist Dorothy McBride Stetson characterizes the development of modern marriage as the result of three theories: unity, separate but equal, and shared partnership.[7] Unity, defined by coverture to render husband and wife one legal entity, characterized marriage through the early 1900s and was slowly replaced by a theory of separate spheres that lasted throughout the 1960s. Within the "separate, but equal" theory of marriage, each individual made a separate but equally important contribution to the union. This period was defined by traditional sex roles in which the male was the family breadwinner and the female was in charge of the home and children. Women in this capacity were glorified by the "cult of domesticity" and were urged to invest themselves in homemaking with the same fervor that a male invested in his paid employment. An explosion of consumer goods and new household appliances relieved women of much of the drudgery of housework and reinforced the primacy of the woman's role as household manager. While a woman was not considered a legal dependent of her husband within a marriage, she was severely disadvantaged by this theory should her marriage dissolve. Women who "stayed at home," as the theory prescribed, found themselves without adequate education or training, without an employment history or job skills necessary to support themselves and their children, and without a credit history necessary to qualify for a mortgage or even to rent housing if the marriage ended in divorce. The courts most often required a husband to support his ex-wife with alimony and child-support payments, but her standard of living declined substantially, even with such court-ordered monetary support. Furthermore, most states granted a divorce only if one party was determined to have been at fault as a result of serious abuse, neglect, abandonment, or adultery. No-fault divorce, permitting a couple to part without publicly establishing blame, was first established in California in 1969. As more women entered the labor force and increased their overall participation in the public sphere, the theory of marriage characterized as a shared, equal partnership became the norm. The equal partnership theory was defined in 1970 by a National Organization for Women task force as "an equal partnership with shared economic and household responsibility and shared care of the children."

The transition from "separate, but equal roles" to "shared, but equal roles" is hardly complete as the previous chapter revealed, and most marital relationships remain asymmetrical. While the majority of state laws now recognize men and women as equal partners in a marriage, reality has not yet caught up with the law. Men and women both struggle to balance the need for two incomes with the problems created by the absence of a full-time family caretaker and household manager. Public policy has not kept pace by providing family support structures, even though the laws regarding marriage, divorce, child custody, and support have become, for the most part, gender neutral. In this

Encountering the Controversies of Equality

Domestic Violence Then and Now

DOMESTIC VIOLENCE is an issue that sits at the intersection of the private and public spheres. The context in which domestic violence is defined affects the remedy available. Under coverture laws of marriage, men were allowed to administer "corrections" to their wives since they were legally responsible for their wives' debts and conduct.[1] Just as parents were entrusted to discipline their children, a husband as the patriarchal head of a family was entrusted to discipline his wife. The phrase "rule of thumb" is said to have arisen in this context. A husband's legitimate authority to use force against his wife or children was limited to the use of a stick no larger in diameter than his thumb. One of the causes the temperance movement took up was to stop women from being physically abused by their husbands. Drunken husbands not only spent the family's wages but also often returned from a night of drinking to physically assault their wives and children. Activists urged reform of divorce laws to permit women to escape domestic violence.

In the 1970s, the battered women's movement reflected the divide among feminists. Some argued that the best way to help women end the violence in their lives was to provide them with services (e.g., shelter, police protection, legal aid, and counseling) within the conventional social service sector. Other more radical feminists believed that domestic violence stemmed from economic dependency and would not cease until the

case, gender-neutral policy does not disadvantage women's rights specifically but rather disadvantages women *and* men within the family unit.

Although the notion of a marriage contract is largely outdated, the concept of rights and obligations in a legal marriage retains some viability in the law. Originally, marriage contracts detailed the duties and obligations of both parties in a marriage. The husband was responsible for support, and in return, the wife owed her husband household, domestic, and companionship services.[8] As we saw in chapter 2, anti-ERA forces objected to a blanket legal equality for women under the Equal Rights Amendment, fearing that husbands would no longer be obligated to provide financial support for their wives and families. Traditionalists then did not care that the presumption of marital support arose from coverture or that husbands and wives were already both liable in most states for joint debt—the war of public opinion is waged on rhetoric and image, not merely on fact. Today most courts obligate spouses to support one another according to circumstances rather than generalized gender roles. Although most marital obligations were unenforceable in court, there were and still are consequences for women stemming from this contractual conception of marriage and the theory of unity.

basic structural gender arrangements in society changed. They favored creating autonomous alternatives to the patriarchal family and economic structures.[2]

Addressing domestic violence must begin by moving the definition of the problem from the private sphere to the public sphere. When women's battery is defined as a family problem, public institutions are unlikely to interfere. Thus, police departments have been slow to intervene in domestic disputes until recently. A national coalition of feminist organizations successfully lobbied Congress to pass federal legislation on domestic abuse. The Violence Against Women Act of 1994 (VAWA) charges the Justice Department with collecting data on domestic abuse, provides money to state and local governments to fund efforts to provide services to victims and abusers, and identifies domestic abuse as a gender-based crime, which has allowed victims to sue their batterers in federal court.

What do you think?

What are the causes of domestic violence? Are they different today than they were in the 1800s?

In 1992, females made up 70 percent of all murder victims who were killed by intimate acquaintances. In what ways does this statistic reflect the power of gender in society?

How can the problem of domestic violence best be addressed today? Is this a public policy issue?

1. William Blackstone, *Commentaries on the Laws of England* (London: Strahan, 1803).
2. Gretchen Arnold, "Dilemmas of Feminist Coalitions: Collective Identity and Strategic Effectiveness in the Battered Women's Movement" in *Feminist Organizations: Harvest of the New Women's Movement*, eds. Myra Marx Feree and Patricia Yancey Martin (Philadelphia: Temple University Press, 1995) pp. 276–290.

Until the Equal Credit Opportunity Act was passed in 1974 (and since amended in 1977 and 1988), women were routinely denied credit because lenders assumed that married or unmarried, women were not economically responsible individuals. When a woman married, many credit-card lenders automatically canceled cards that were in her birth name and reissued joint accounts in her husband's surname. If the marriage dissolved, through divorce or death, women did not qualify for credit since their credit history was based on their husband's. Women were often required to have a male (husband, father, brother) cosign loan agreements. When applying for a mortgage or joint credit with her husband, a wife was required to provide information about her birth-control practices and her intentions to bear children. Only half the wife's salary was included in calculating assets to determine the size of a mortgage a couple could afford, based on the assumption by leaders that women were not autonomous economic entities. The Equal Credit Opportunity Act, as amended, required lenders to base their credit decisions solely on an individual's ability to repay the debt, rather than on sex, race, national origin, or age. Further amendments in 1988 opened the door to commercial lines of credit for women entrepreneurs.

Coverture and the theory of unity rendered the husband and wife one person in the eyes of the law. As such, husbands and wives could not sue each other in civil court nor be compelled to testify against each other in criminal court. Over time, the private nature of family and marriage reinforced interspousal immunity, even though other legal changes granted women independent public standing, including the ability to make contracts. Courts did not want to settle disagreements between a husband and wife. In this sense, interspousal immunity has complicated a battered woman's ability to bring civil suits against her husband. Domestic violence has been ignored until recently because of the private nature of marriage. Because of the concept of "conjugal rights" inherent in the marriage contract, a wife could not charge her husband with rape. The "marital exemption" to state rape laws has only been addressed within the last decade, and as of 1996, three states still retained a full marital exemption. Two of those states have since adopted laws that more directly address domestic violence.

Violence within a marriage raises questions of justice. Philosopher Susan Moller Okin argues that marriage and the family as currently practiced in the United States are unjust institutions.[9] While she acknowledges that talking about "justice" is difficult in such an intimate and private setting, justice nonetheless should govern marital unions and the families that result. Okin believes that the roots of injustice can be found in the vulnerabilities created by traditional expectations of women, both in paid labor and in the family. She argues that the "division of labor within marriage (except in rare cases) makes wives far more likely than husbands to be exploited both with the marital relationship and in the world of work outside the home." Traditional gender role expectations developed in childhood have led both men and women to anticipate a certain division of labor within a family, based on the "husband as provider, wife as full-time care giver" model, which in most cases does not mirror reality. Since the majority of women (including mothers of small children) are in the paid work force, they end up doing a disproportionate share of the labor at home and outside the home (since they work longer hours for less pay). They are disadvantaged in the workplace because the professions or occupations that provide the flexibility needed to raise children are often in traditionally female occupations, which pay less. Even if that isn't the case, women find themselves in professional settings that assume a full-time "wife" at home and do not support combining work and family in any sort of equitable manner. At home, they must deal with the unequal distribution of labor within the family. Even as wage earners, women do the majority of child care and household chores—the unpaid work of a family.

> One cannot even begin to address the issue of why so many women and children live in poverty in our society, or why women are inadequately represented in the higher echelons of our political and economic institutions, without confronting the division of labor between the sexes within the family. . . . Thus it is not only itself an issue of justice but it is also at the very root of other significant concerns of justice, including equality of opportunity for children of both sexes, but especially for girls, and political justice in the broadest sense.[10]

In most cases, Okin argues that this imbalance of power, based on the traditions of gender, are *nondecisions*—assumed rather than decided. The lack of a consensus on the norms and expectations of marriage makes avoiding vulnerabilities more difficult. Reality no longer reflects our expectations that are born of traditional gender roles. Since what a family should be differs from what many families experience, we should strive to create diverse expectations that allow all types of families to flourish and do not make one sex vulnerable to power differentials that result from an asymmetrical division of labor.

THE LEGACY OF PATRIARCHY

American culture is devoid of public rites that symbolize the passage from childhood to adulthood, except for marriage. It is no surprise then that a lot is invested in the marriage ritual and ceremony. Young girls are socialized early to anticipate and plan for their wedding, a cost traditionally the responsibility of the father of the bride. The ceremony itself is a mix of civil and religious symbolism. White, the traditional color of a woman's gown, symbolizes purity, and the veil worn by many brides is a holdover from the days when the wedding was the first time a bride and groom met. The ring exchange originally symbolized the exchange of property that was negotiated in a marriage contract. Weddings are usually public celebrations where friends and relatives join in recognizing the new union by contributing money and gifts for the couple's joint household. Although weddings now come in all varieties—from very traditional to religious, to purely civil ceremonies—the symbolism is an important aspect of joining a man and woman in legal marriage. The symbols also reproduce the patriarchal culture that has oppressed women within marriage for centuries, although most brides and grooms would not recognize them as such today.

Names

Most people incorrectly assume that women are legally required to take their husband's surname. This habit, however, is a result of common law or tradition rather than a requirement by statute. A holdover from the days of unity in marriage, a woman's adoption of her husband's name signals a new identity in marriage for women, but not for men. It also adds a "social marker" to women's identities that men do not share. Women are known as Miss, Ms., or Mrs. Each carries social information about marital status or, with "Ms.," a refusal to be traditionally labeled. Men, regardless of age or marital status, are simply addressed as "Mr." Customarily (and in a few states, legally), children produced in a marriage are registered with the state under the husband's last name. The use of patronymics (father's names) was important in establishing the continuity of lineage and property rights. Some states, notably Kentucky and Alabama, have required that married women use their husband's name on such state documents as a driver's license and taxes. This sex-based requirement, which is for women only, was upheld by the U.S. Supreme Court in 1971.[11] Only about 5 percent of high-school educated women, 15 percent of women with college degrees, and about 20 percent of women with postgraduate degrees use a surname other than their husband's.[12] The public is not entirely comfortable with women who use their birth names, even when it is used in conjunction with their husband's surname. A 1993 *Wall Street Journal*–NBC poll found that while 74 percent viewed first lady Hillary Rodham Clinton as a positive role model, only 6 percent favored her using "Rodham" in her name, and 62 percent were opposed to it. Another study conducted that same year found that 25 percent of southerners and 20 percent of people not from the South believed that the growing trend of women using their birth names "was a change for the worse."[13]

Domicile Laws

Domicile laws establish an individual's rights within a defined territory (most often a state) for the purposes of benefits and obligations. Since most laws regarding the family are state-based, establishing permanent residency is significant. In a holdover from the days of unity in marriage, many states follow the common law that assumes that a husband's residence constitutes the primary residence of a family. In the days when men provided sole financial support for the family, giving them precedence in the choice of domicile may have made sense. As women entered the work force on a more equal basis, where a family sets up residence is now subject to negotiation. A majority of the public, however, still believes a husband and wife should occupy one residence, and many state laws still assume that a wife has abandoned her husband if she refuses to move with him to another city. A 1985 survey showed that 72 percent of women and 62 percent of men believed that a woman *should* quit her job and move to another city if her husband got a job there, even if she had a good job in the city where they were currently living. Only 10 percent of women and 19 percent of men said that the husband should turn down the job.[14] The rise of commuter marriages, most often necessitated by two professional careers, has caused domicile laws to begin to change, but that's often on a case-by-case basis. Some women have found it easiest to get a court order recognizing their unique residence for the purposes of university tuition, taxation, voting, licensing, and jury duty, among others.

Property Rights

As we said earlier, coverture invested property rights entirely in the husband. The Married Women's Property Acts of the late 1800s permitted women to acquire and control property. In response, unity gave way to "separate property" rights for men and women. In reality, however, because women were still relegated to the home and unpaid labor in the home by separate spheres ideology and tradition, laws that allowed them to acquire property, enter into contracts, or engage in business were initially limited. Even as women entered the paid labor force, their wages usually contributed substantially less to their family's income than their husband's did. By 1993, forty-one states had laws in which "property follows title." In common-law property states, husbands and wives are entitled individually to control property—that is, whoever holds the title, owns the property. In many cases, however, because full-time homemakers had no visible source of income, the courts ruled that jointly acquired property or assets (including a joint bank account) were the husband's property. In common-law property states, the courts also paid close attention to who paid the bills in two-income families. Women sometimes found themselves without assets if they assumed responsibility for such consumables as food and the husband paid the mortgage and purchased durable goods, such as the family automobile. In community property states, both the husband and wife equally control assets acquired in marriage. Nine states—Arizona, California, Idaho, Louisiana, Nevada, New Mexico, Texas, Washington State, and Wisconsin—have some form of community property laws. Although exceptions have been made for individual inheritance or assets accumulated prior to the marriage, the courts in community property states view a couple as one economic unit. In many cases, courts used to give husbands control over the ongoing management of community property. This has now changed to reflect the theory of marriage as an equal partnership.[15]

DIVORCE

Divorce contributes significantly to poverty rates among women; this stems from the interplay of private and public patriarchy. Within a marriage, women contribute their unpaid labor, and if they work outside the home, their earnings provide less than one-third of the family income in most households. When a marriage ends in divorce, a woman's standard of living falls because her single wage must provide for herself and her children. A ten-year study in California estimated that after divorce, women's standard of living declined by 73 percent while men's rose on average by 42 percent.[16] Men are also more likely to remarry and to do so more quickly than women. One study estimated that the total family income of a divorced woman and her children was less than 50 percent of the family income prior to divorce, but as the custodial parent she needed approximately 80 percent of the total family income before the divorce to maintain the family's standard of living.[17]

Since marriage is a state-sanctioned, legal union, only the state can legally dissolve a marriage. Eighteenth-century feminists sought reforms to divorce law as a way of escaping abusive and dangerous marriages at a time when civil law did not recognize divorce. The state exercised its prerogative to encourage marriage even at the expense of women's physical safety and happiness. Prior to 1969 and California's adoption of "no-fault" divorce laws, most states required the party seeking a divorce to prove legitimate grounds for a separation. These most often included battering, abuse, abandonment, and (except for South Carolina) adultery. Evidence of fault was required even when both parties agreed to divorce. Reforms to state divorce laws began in the late 1960s and generally followed California's lead in adopting no-fault divorce laws. No-fault divorce is now available in all fifty states, although the application and disposition are very different. Irreconcilable differences or separation most often provide the grounds for contemporary divorce. States that recognize separation as grounds may require a couple to live in separate residences for a time (usually six months to two years) before granting a divorce.

In recent years, states have become alarmed at the rising divorce rates. In response, states have taken a renewed interest in legislating policy on marriage and divorce. For the most part, states have not returned to fault-based divorce, although some states have extended the waiting period for divorce or have required couples to get counseling when children are involved. Most states, however, have concentrated on encouraging couples to be more careful before entering into marriage in the first place. Some states now require couples to get "couples counseling" before issuing a marriage license. In 1997, Louisiana went a step farther and created voluntary "covenant marriages." Couples who choose a "covenant marriage" agree to seek counseling if problems develop in their marriage and will only be allowed to seek a divorce under certain severe circumstances (sexual abuse, adultery, abandonment) or after a two-year separation, very similar to the grounds of fault-based divorce. Arizona has since adopted similar legislation, and several other state legislatures have policies under consideration. Couples with a "regular marriage" may retroactively petition the state for a covenant marriage by declaring in a written affidavit to the court that "marriage is for life" and by agreeing to abide by the guidelines of a covenant marriage.

Property, Benefits and Support After Divorce

While real property assets are fairly easy to divide and most states require an equitable division of real property, benefits awarded by a third party (health insurance, pension rights, stock options) or an increase in earning capacity derived from a professional degree are more difficult to divide. Since community property laws dominate most states, any assets or property acquired while married is subject to equitable division by the court. More than half the states consider pensions marital property and subject to division. Federal law covers access to social security or military pension benefits after divorce as long as the couple has been married for ten years or more (see chapter 7). An employer is required to continue health insurance coverage for a period of one year. The most difficult concept for the states to grasp, however, involves "human capital." In the 1970s and 1980s, the popular press was full of stories about professionally successful husbands who were divorcing their wives after several decades of marriage in favor of a younger woman even though the first wife had often supported the family financially during her husband's years in law school or medical school. In almost all cases, the courts determined that earning capacity and educational degrees cannot be divided. However, several courts have used a man's earning capacity and a woman's contribution to developing his earning capacity to determine the amount of alimony payments. Others have required a husband to reimburse his wife for the cost of his education.

Alimony is yet another holdover from the theory of unity. A husband's obligation for financial support extended past the marriage if the husband sought the divorce or was determined to be at fault. During the marriage reforms of the 1970s, alimony laws were rendered "gender neutral" allowing the courts to require support payments to either husband or wife. In *Orr v. Orr* (1979), the U.S. Supreme Court ruled that sex-based alimony laws violated the equal-protection clause of the Fourteenth Amendment. The end to fault-based divorce also diminished the presumption that alimony is compensation for harm. It is rare that either spouse is now ordered to make support payments indefinitely. Short-term payments may be ordered to ease the transition from marriage to a single-wage status. Alimony may also be awarded to allow a spouse to receive job training or earn a college degree or as a one-time financial award. In many cases, the trend toward gender-neutral, no-fault divorce laws have not benefited women, particularly those who pursued a traditional gender role within their marriage. These women suffer a dramatic loss of income and social status when their marriage ends.

Child support is different from alimony. Both parents may be ordered to provide support for their children, regardless of the custody arrangements. Noncustodial parents are much less likely to actually pay court-ordered support (and are more likely to be fathers). Congress has reacted by strengthening enforcement of child-support provisions. In 1975 Congress created the Child Support Enforcement program that was designed to collect unpaid child support from noncustodial parents. While billions of dollars have been collected and redistributed, that amount represents a very small proportion of what is actually owed. In 1996, as a part of the welfare reform bill known as the Personal Responsibility and Work Opportunity Reconciliation Act, Congress again strengthened collection provisions by creating state and federal databases to help locate noncustodial parents. Using motor-vehicle, tax, and public-utilities records has allowed authorities to track noncustodial parents across state lines. New penalty provisions have revoked motor vehicles, as well as professional and recreational licenses issued by the government, for nonpayment. It is too soon to evaluate whether the new law will help children receive support payments they are owed.

TOWARD A GENUINE FAMILY POLICY IN THE UNITED STATES: WHAT WOULD IT TAKE?

Family policy, largely related to marriage and divorce laws, is administered almost exclusively by the states. This has resulted in an uncoordinated patchwork of laws and policies that are targeted at specific issues or problems. When federal legislation is layered on top of state statutes, the result is often more confusion than support for families. Determining what families need from government is made all the more difficult because of our inability to clearly define "family." Public and private employer policies aimed at parents and children necessarily exclude couples who choose not to have children. Does this unlawfully deny child-free couples a social or employment benefit? The debate over "family values" waged in a political context is laden with values regarding which type of family constellation should be rewarded or discouraged. Conservative Christians have entered politics in large numbers during the last decade to influence policy in favor of the "traditional family"—though the definition of the "traditional family," even according to this group, now includes two wage earners. The rhetoric of "family values" is designed to exclude single heads of households (whether by circumstance or choice), and same-sex households. Given this political context, what type of family policy might we expect in the coming years?

Regardless of which political party controls the federal government, families of all types have put pressure on those in office for more help in accommodating the stresses associated with juggling work and family. The Family and Medical Leave Act (1993), discussed in the previous chapter, was the first parental-leave policy enacted in the United States. Most now believe it does not go far enough and should be strengthened. Although the right of the mother to leave employment after pregnancy was affirmed internationally in the United Nations' International Labour Office Maternity Protection Convention, adopted in 1952, the United States lagged far behind other nations in even meeting the bare minimum requirement of twelve weeks of maternity leave. Of the 138 U.N. member nations, the United States was the only country that made this leave optional. In other countries, a mandatory minimum is enforced, and in several, the minimum leave is compulsory.[18] Parental leave, entitling both mother and father to spend time with their children, is offered in 36 of 138 member nations. In 25 nations, including 9 of the 14 European Union members, parental leave is paid. The most generous parental- or maternity-leave policies offer high levels of compensation to offset a loss of earnings overall. In all cases, job guarantees are built into the policy so that parents are not penalized for taking time off.

Internationally, support for families takes a variety of forms. Whether any one country has adopted a policy relating to family support depends on a number of factors, including structural economic factors (capitalist versus socialist economy), need created by changing social and economic factors, and the activity of family advocacy groups, employers and business owners, women's

TABLE 8.1 International Maternity Leave Benefits, 1998 Selected Countries from each Region of the World

Country	Length of Leave	Portion of Wages Paid	Provider of Coverage
Congo	15 weeks	100%	50% employer; 50% social security
Kenya	2 months	100%	employer
Morocco	12 weeks	100%	social security
Nigeria	12 weeks	50%	employer
Somalia	14 weeks	50%	employer
South Africa	12 weeks	45%	unemployment insurance
Argentina	90 days	100%	social security
Bahamas	8 weeks	100%	40% employer; 60% social security
Brazil	120 days	100%	social security
Chile	18 weeks	100%	social security
Cuba	18 weeks	100%	social security
Haiti	12 weeks	100% for 6 weeks	employer
Honduras	10 weeks	100% for 84 days	33% employer; 67% social security
Mexico	12 weeks	100%	social security
Venezuela	18 weeks	100%	social security
Bangladesh	12 weeks	100%	employer
Cambodia	90 days	50%	employer
China	90 days	100%	social security
India	12 weeks	100%	employer; social security
Iran	90 days	66.7% for 16 weeks	social security
Iraq	62 days	100%	social security
Israel	12 weeks	75% up to a ceiling	social security
Saudi Arabia	10 weeks	50% or 100%	employer
Australia	1 year	0	————
Austria	16 weeks	100%	social security
Canada	17–18 weeks	55% for 15 weeks	unemployment insurance
Denmark	18 weeks	100% up to a ceiling	social security
France	16–26 weeks	100%	social security
Germany	14 weeks	100%	social security to a ceiling; employer
Italy	5 months	80%	social security
Japan	14 weeks	60%	social security; health insurance
Portugal	98 days	100%	social security
Spain	16 weeks	100%	social security
United Kingdom	14–18 weeks	90% for 6 weeks, flat rate thereafter	social security
United States	12 weeks	0	————

Source: United Nations, Table 5.C in *The World's Women 2000: Trends and Statistics* (New York: United Nations, 2001), p. 140.

organizations, and religious groups. These "policy inputs" influence the "policy output" in each country and help explain why there are differences across national boundaries.[19] Family policy may take the form of cash benefits or assistance (health insurance, education, social security, or employment) to boost the family's standard of living; indirect cash transfers in the form of tax credits or deductions for dependent children, family allowances, means-tested family benefits; employment benefits granted to workers with family responsibilities (maternity and parental leave, childcare leave); direct services to families (on-site child care, after-school programs); housing subsidies for families with children; or legislation that is consistent with the state's population policies (access to contraception, abortion services, infertility treatments, or adoption). The United States has a large number of policies at the state and federal levels that affect families, but the dominance of attitudes that support family autonomy and limited government involvement, as well as the reinforcement of gender ideologies, have limited the coherence and reach of family policy. The next section of this chapter explores the link between population and family policy: the issue of fertility. Fertility and issues of population growth or limits even more directly target women and are rarely gender neutral. When policy is crafted to be gender neutral, it rarely benefits women in their pursuit of equality. The physical aspects of pregnancy, childbirth, and lactation render gender-neutral strategies largely useless because they focus first on sex and second on gender. Unlike education, employment, or family support where socially constructed gender ideologies are most profoundly related to women's disadvantages, fertility issues focus first on sex and secondarily on gender.

CONTROLLING REPRODUCTION

A woman's individual interest in regulating fertility and reproduction is directly connected to issues of private and public subordination. Yet since human reproduction is also social and cultural reproduction, controlling the quality and quantity of reproduction has long interested the state. It is the social aspect of reproduction that gives women these socially constructed gender expectations that are not only related to childbearing but also have to do with child rearing and motherhood. A state's survival depends on successive generations of children who have been properly guided to mature citizenship. A state's interest in regulating fertility and reproduction therefore is also directly related to women's subordination. In the United States, reproductive policy is not as explicitly stated as it is in other nations, yet it is present nonetheless. Such policies are complicated by the dominance of individualism and a liberal approach to policy creation. In most areas of U.S. constitutional law, the interests of the individual outweigh the interests of the state, unless the state can prove a "compelling state interest" that would warrant intruding on individual rights. In the area of reproduction, however, it is less clear whether individual rights reign supreme, most particularly women's individual rights.

The U.S. Supreme Court has extended the individual's right to privacy to some reproductive decisions (birth control, access to abortion in the first trimester), but has not required the states to support these "rights" if an individual cannot afford to purchase them on the private market. Some areas of reproductive policy and decision making do not conform well to a rights-based interpretation. Some people argue that the right *not* to reproduce is every bit as fundamental as the right to reproduction. Christine Overall contends that a woman has no moral obligation to have a child against her will. "Women who do not have access to contraceptive devices and abortion services are, as a result of 'biological destiny,' victims 'of a sort of reproductive slavery.'"[20] Alternatively, Sara Ann Ketcham argues that there is an inherent asymmetry between the right not to reproduce and the right to reproduce that stems from reproduction's inclusion of other people. Therefore the rights and interests of others (father, child, society) must also be taken into account in protecting an individual's right to reproduce.[21] The first perspective is most directly relevant to contraception and abortion rights. The latter directly concerns the movement to endow the fetus with rights that are equal to those of the woman.

Individual Access to Contraception

The history of reliable contraception in the United States is a relatively short one. It has only been within the last forty years that women have been able to access to methods of contraception that are safe, reliable, and entirely within their control. The Food and Drug Administration (FDA) approved an oral contraceptive for women ("the pill") in 1960. While condoms and diaphragms were revolutionized in the nineteenth century as a result of changes in rubber manufacturing techniques, the pill represented the first new technology in contraception. The pill was followed by FDA approval of the sponge in 1983 (though no longer available in the United States). Then came the cervical cap in 1988, and in 1990, a long-acting reversible contraceptive implant (known popularly as Norplant and effective for up to five years). Depo-Povera, an injectable contraceptive that is effective for up to three months, had been widely used in other countries prior to its approval for use in the United States. Additionally, the FDA approved the sale of female condoms in the 1990s. Sterilization, however, remains the most widely chosen form of contraception for women.

Development and dissemination of contraceptives depends in large part on the public's attitude toward sexuality, current birth rates, and the positive or negative consequences of population growth. Prior to the Civil War, many states permitted abortion until "quickening," but soon after the Civil War's conclusion, most states banned abortions. Succumbing to the pressure to reproduce and new restrictive attitudes toward sexuality that were promoted by organized religion, Congress passed the Comstock laws in 1873. These laws were ostensibly designed to control pornography but defined pornography as any information or product distributed for the prevention of conception or for causing unlawful abortion. The statute, in effect, likened contraception to obscenity and made it illegal to distribute information on contraception or contraceptive devices. Various social sectors supported restricting contraceptives, and doctors were among them. In their eyes, contraception violated nature, bred immorality, damaged health, and violated the sanctity of motherhood.[22] Many women, particularly those in the middle and upper classes, viewed contraception as a direct challenge to marital fidelity and their corresponding sphere of authority. Poor and uneducated women were most disadvantaged by unintended pregnancies and were especially vulnerable to public campaigns devoted to suppressing information or medical services. Middle- and upper-class women participated in an informal but extensive network of information, access to birth control devices illegally imported from Europe, and access to relatively safe, but still illegal, abortions.

Birth-control advocates like Margaret Sanger and Emma Goldman worked most directly with poor, working-class women, many of whom were recent immigrants. In addition to stressing that giving birth to too many children or not adequately spacing pregnancies was harmful to women's health, Emma Goldman, a socialist active in the labor movement, was also interested in limiting the influx of child labor, which drove down wages for everyone.[23] Immigrants were the targets of a robust eugenics (selective breeding) movement that thrived by promoting fears of "race suicide" if white, middle-class birthrates declined and poor immigrant populations increased unchecked. These seemingly contradictory interests forged a nascent birth-control movement that directly violated the Comstock laws. By 1914, Margaret Sanger, who had been radicalized by her experiences with the left and a year in France, began to publish a monthly called *Woman Rebel* in which she eventually promoted contraception as a woman's right:

> A woman's body belongs to herself alone. It does not belong to the United States of America or any other government on the face of the earth. Enforced motherhood is the most complete denial of a woman's right to life and liberty. Women cannot be on an equal footing with men until they have full and complete control over their reproductive function.[24]

Many issues of the *Woman Rebel* were confiscated by the post office under the Comstock laws. While the newsletter did not include information on contraceptive techniques, it did publish letters from desperate readers begging for information. In response, Sanger published a brochure entitled *Family Limitation: A Nurse's Advice to Women*. Between 1914 and 1917, more than 160,000 copies were distributed, although Sanger fled to England during some of that time to avoid further prosecution under the obscenity laws. In 1916, Sanger opened the first birth-control clinic in the United States in Brooklyn, New York.

A court decision in 1918 allowed physicians to disseminate "advice to a married person to cure or prevent disease"—a clear reference to venereal disease and a cover for distributing contraception to married women. Medicalizing the birth-control issue allowed Sanger to solicit support and cooperation from physicians, and in 1921 she formed the American Birth Control League (ABCL). By the 1940s, the ABCL gave way to the Planned Parenthood Federation of America in recognition of contraception's transformation into a "family planning" tool. Sanger's legacy extended into the 1960s when Planned Parenthood challenged a Connecticut law that prohibited the sale, advertisement, or manufacture of birth-control devices. The Connecticut law also prohibited married couples from using contraception. In 1965, the U.S. Supreme Court delivered its decision in *Griswold* v. *Connecticut,* declaring that Connecticut's law was an unconstitutional violation of the right to privacy of married persons. The Court extended the fundamental right of procreative choice and privacy to unmarried persons with the ruling in *Eisenstadt* v. *Baird* (1972). The fundamental right to privacy established in the *Griswold* and *Eisenstadt* rulings was extended to cover a woman's right to abortion services in 1973.

Individual Access to Abortion Services

The issue of abortion, much more so than contraception, has divided families, political parties, and the nation. Abortion "rights" were most clearly established in the Supreme Court ruling in *Roe* v. *Wade* (1973), although by the time Roe was decided, more than thirteen states had reformed and liberalized their abortion laws. More than likely state-level reforms would have continued had the Court not acted, but slowly and in a patchwork fashion. Almost everyone agreed that abortion reforms were necessary to protect women from physical injury and death at the hands of illegal abortionists. Just because abortion was illegal did not prevent it from occurring, and the dire consequences of botched abortions cut across all races and socioeconomic groups.

Justice Harry Blackmun, writing for the seven-vote majority in *Roe* v. *Wade,* used the trimesters of pregnancy as benchmarks to balance a woman's privacy interests with the state's increasingly legitimate interests in protecting a fetus as it approached viability outside the womb. In the first trimester, a woman's right to make private choices is protected from state interference (although later decisions have allowed the state to regulate the conditions under which a woman exercises her "right"). During the second (fourth through sixth month) and third (seventh month through birth) trimesters, the state gains grounds to regulate abortions "in ways that are reasonably related to maternal health" or to restrict its use entirely by the third trimester, except when necessary to protect the life or health of the mother. While the decision nationalized women's rights to a legal abortion within the first three months of a pregnancy, it also muddied other issues surrounding reproductive rights by rooting the decision in privacy doctrine. In *Harris* v. *McRae* (1980), the Court held that the right to privacy does not compel states to pay for poor women's abortions. The separation of public and private, enunciated in *Roe* and *Harris,* was used in 1989 (*Webster* v. *Reproductive Health Services*) to allow states to prohibit abortions from being performed in public facilities or by public employees. The public-private distinction was used again in 1996 to uphold the ban on furnishing abortion information and counseling to poor women by federally funded family-planning agencies (*Rust* v. *Sullivan*).

In other cases, the Court has allowed states greater leeway in establishing limits on a woman's right to abortion services as long as the regulations do not create an "undue burden" on the woman seeking an abortion. A state regulation is defined as an undue burden "if its purpose or effect is to place a substantial obstacle in the path of a woman seeking an abortion before the fetus attains viability."[25] In 1992, *Planned Parenthood of Southeastern Pennsylvania* v. *Casey* upheld most of Pennsylvania's regulations, including an "informed consent" provision, a twenty-four-hour waiting period, and parental consent for women who were minors. The only provision the Court declared an "undue burden" was the requirement that women notify their husbands prior to having an abortion. Thirty-one states enforce parental consent or notification laws for minors seeking an abortion. Forty-five percent of minors who have had abortions told their parents, and 61 percent underwent the procedure with at least one parent's knowledge.[26]

Two decisions delivered at the conclusion of the 1999–2000 term reversed the Court's trend in recognizing more active regulatory action by the states. In *Hill* v. *Colorado* the Court was asked to consider the constitutionality of a statutory buffer zone (in this case eight feet) around abortion clinics and around individuals who were entering the clinics. Antiabortion protesters set up human barricades around abortion clinics and harassed women on their way in and out of the clinics, urging them not to "kill their baby." In this case, the free speech interests of the protesters were weighed against the woman's right to abortion services. The six-to-three majority in *Hill* upheld Colorado's "zone of separation" statute, arguing that the law was a reasonable restriction on the First Amendment right of so-called sidewalk counselors to protest, educate, or counsel outside a health-care facility. While the Court recognized that the right to free speech includes the right to try to persuade others to change their views, "The First Amendment does not demand that patients at a medical facility undertake Herculean efforts to escape the cacophony of political protests."[27] A second case, *Stenberg* v. *Carhart*, dealt with the issue of late-term abortions and a state's ability to prohibit all late-term abortions (known as "partial birth" abortions by opponents). This case was more closely decided by the Court in a five-to-four decision and turned on the question of a woman's health. Justice Stephen Bryer, writing for the majority, said "a risk to a woman's health is the same whether it happens to arise from regulating a particular method of abortion, or from barring abortion entirely." This decision supports a doctor's determination of what is in the best interests of the woman's health over the state's outright ban of certain abortion procedures. However, this decision also demonstrates how vulnerable *Roe* v. *Wade* may be in the future. Justice Clarence Thomas wrote a dissenting opinion in which he detailed his fervent opposition to *Roe* v. *Wade*. During Thomas's confirmation hearings he claimed that he had no opinion on abortion or the *Roe* v. *Wade* decision. Clearly he has, as the youngest member of the Court, at fifty-two years old, found his voice and seems poised to exert influence on this issue in the future.

RU-486 Gains Approval

On September 28, 2000, the FDA approved Mifepristone, also known as RU-486, to terminate early pregnancies (defined as forty-nine days or less). RU-486 was developed in 1980 and has been in use in Europe and China by more than 620,000 women since it came on the market in 1988. The drug is administered in pill form in doses spaced two days apart. Women are required to return to their doctor fourteen days later to make sure that the pregnancy has been terminated. Mifepristone causes an abortion by blocking the action of progesterone, a hormone essential for sustaining pregnancy. The drug prevents an embryo from attaching to the uterine wall during the earliest stages of gestation. At this point in a pregnancy, an embryo is no larger than a grain of rice. This treatment regimen is effective in about 95 percent of all cases. Under the terms of FDA approval, Mifepristone can be distributed by physicians who must also be able to provide surgical intervention in cases of incomplete abortion or severe bleeding (or they must have made plans in advance to have others provide such care). Side effects from RU-486 include cramping (sometimes severe) and bleeding over a period of nine to sixteen days. The advantages to Mifepristone are that surgical complications are avoided and that it can be administered much earlier in a pregnancy than a surgical abortion, which is generally not performed until the sixth or seventh week of pregnancy. One disadvantage is that the process may take several days rather than one visit to a clinic or hospital.

Opponents of RU-486 in the United States have cited the dangers to women in using the drug. As Republican Congressman J. C. Watts remarked, "Do-it-yourself abortion has no place in civilized society." Columnist Anna Quindlen observed that RU-486 is an exercise in self-determination for the woman who chooses to use it. "She is in charge of the decision, the mechanism and the process, not a dupe and not a victim; the choice is quite literally in her hands."[28] After twenty years, women in the United States now have access to a nonsurgical abortion alternative. It remains to be seen how many doctors will prescribe Mifepristone under the FDA's guidelines. Considering the diminishing access to surgical abortions in the United States (86 percent of U.S. counties do not have abortion providers), this drug marks a major advance in a woman's right to choose.

The Demographics of Abortion

Today, as in earlier eras, whether legal or illegal, abortion in practice is not limited to a particular type of woman. An estimated 43 percent of women will have at least one abortion by the time they reach forty-five years of age. Each year, two out of every ten women from fifteen to forty-four years old have an abortion; 47 percent of them have had at least one previous abortion, and 55 percent have had a previous birth. Fifty-eight percent of women who had abortions in 1995 were using contraception during the month they got pregnant. Nine in ten women at risk of an unintended pregnancy are using a contraceptive method. Women who seek abortions are likely to be younger than twenty-five (52 percent); women twenty to twenty-four obtained 32 percent of all abortions; and 20 percent of abortions performed in 1995 were performed on teenagers. While white women obtained 60 percent of all abortions, their abortion rate is considerably lower than that of minority women. African American women are more than three times as likely as white women to have an abortion, and Hispanic women are more than twice as likely. Catholic women are 29 percent more likely than Protestant women to seek an abortion, although their overall rates of abortion are comparable to the national abortion rate. Two-thirds of all abortions are performed on never-married women. About 14,000 abortions are performed every year following rape or incest. Of the 50 million abortions performed each year worldwide, more than 40 percent are obtained illegally.[29]

Compared to the abortion rates of other nations, the United States is relatively high among developed nations at a rate of 23 per 1,000 women of childbearing age. While some opponents of abortion lay the blame on what they view as extremely "permissive" abortion policy, research conducted by the Alan Guttmacher Institute (AGI) released in the report *Sharing Responsibility: Women, Society and Abortion Worldwide*, attributes the high U.S. abortion rate to a high unintended pregnancy rate. Citing developed countries in Western Europe with substantially lower abortion rates and more permissive policies (including full funding of the procedure under national health programs in many cases), AGI concludes that contraceptive availability and use accounts for much of the difference.[30] The Netherlands is consistently classified among countries with the least restrictive abortion policies and ranks among the lowest abortion rates per 1,000 women in the world.

In any given year, 85 of 100 sexually active women who do not use contraception will become pregnant, while only one in eight women who use an oral contraceptive (the most commonly used reversible method) will become pregnant. One of the major barriers to contraceptive use in the United States is cost. Cost for supplies alone can be approximately $360 a year for oral contraceptives, $180 a year for injectable Depo-Povera, $450 or more for Norplant implants, and $240 for an IUD insertion.[31] Most women rely on employer-based private health insurance to pay for their health care, although most private plans do not cover the entire cost of contraception and many do not cover any of the cost. This more than likely accounts for women paying 68 percent more in out-of-pocket health expenses than men do. Public funding is restricted to those who qualify for Medicaid or Title X coverage for care in publicly funded clinics. The result is that most women face financial as well as logistical barriers to receiving reliable contraception. AGI estimates that providing full coverage of contraceptive care for women under employment-based plans would cost only $21.40 per employee per year. A nationwide poll found that 78 percent of privately insured adults would support contraceptive coverage, even if it increased their costs by $5 a month (fourteen times the amount estimated for the additional coverage).[32]

On December 13, 2000, the Equal Employment Opportunity Commission (EEOC) ruled that employers discriminate against women when they offer insurance coverage for preventative health care, such as drugs to lower blood pressure, but exclude prescription contraceptives.[33] Although the ruling only applies to the two women whose complaints prompted the EEOC's ruling, the decision provides guidance to employers and the courts on interpretation of the Pregnancy Discrimination Act, which forbids workplace discrimination against women because of pregnancy, childbirth, or related conditions. "Contraception is a means to prevent, and control the timing of, the medical condition of pregnancy," the decision read. "In evaluating whether respondents have provided equal insurance coverage for prescription contraceptives, therefore, the Commission looks to respondents' coverage of other prescription drugs and devices, or other types of services, that are used to prevent the occurrence of other types of medical conditions."[34] The Equity in Prescription Insurance and Contraceptive Coverage Act has been stalled in Congress since 1997, although thirteen states have passed laws requiring most insurance plans that pay for prescription drugs to include contraceptive coverage.

Public Opinion on Abortion

Overall, U.S. public opinion favors maintaining a woman's right to choose abortion, although support for abortion rights appears conditional. A 1998 survey by the *New York Times* found that 61 percent supported abortion during the first trimester, but only 15 percent supported it in the second trimester. Further, as social commentator Wendy Kaminer reports, "People seem inclined to prohibit abortions when women have them for the 'wrong reasons.'"[35] The public is most disapproving of women who have abortions because they want to finish school or pursue a career; 70 percent said that they did not believe that abortions should be available to women who want to terminate their pregnancy for career-related reasons. Less than half of those surveyed (42 percent) supported abortion for teenage girls who wanted to finish school or continue their education. Only 43 percent said that abortion should be available to low-income women who could not afford another child. The strongest support was for women who terminated their pregnancies for health reasons or because there was a strong suspicion of fetal deformity.[36]

The public attitudes expressed in the *Times* survey appear to run contrary to recent state welfare reforms that withhold additional public support on the birth of an another child. These attitudes also seem to contradict economic rationality since women without an education cannot earn a sufficient wage to support a child and will be dependent on public assistance, private agencies, or family for support. Do romanticized attitudes toward motherhood account for these findings? Wendy Kaminer attributes the rather harsh attitude toward

Encountering the Controversies of Equality

Can a Feminist Be Against Abortion?

THIS CHAPTER discussed abortion as one of many reproductive issues facing women. The ability of women to control their fertility and reproduction and the belief that women must be able to act autonomously are central tenets of feminism. Reproduction has been so central to women's subordination within the family and in perpetuating traditional sex roles that have relegated women exclusively to the private sphere. In response, feminists have focused a great deal of energy obtaining and sustaining broad reproductive rights that allow women to make choices about whether or not they bear children, as well as how many children they will have and when they will have them. While abortion has become the public focus in this effort, access to safe, effective, and affordable contraception is at the heart of reproductive rights. The Supreme Court's ruling in *Roe v. Wade* (1973) has become a focal point for both those who support a woman's right to terminate an unintended pregnancy and those who believe that abortion is morally wrong. These two positions were quickly labeled as *pro-choice* and *pro-life*—labels that presumably characterize the first principles on which each position operates. Framing reproductive rights in a way that centered on abortion and polarized these two dichotomous positions once again divided women in seemingly unproductive ways. As a result, the label pro-life feminist seems like an oxymoron. Is it possible to be fundamentally opposed to abortion and be a feminist?

Feminists for Life (FFL) was organized in 1972 and heads what has become known as the "Pro-Woman, Pro-Life" movement.[1] Citing the pro-life positions of early suffragists, such as Mary Wollstonecraft, Susan B. Anthony, and Elizabeth Cady Stanton, FFL argues that abortion is a symptom of much deeper social problems affecting women's

women who say they are not ready for the changes a child would require in her life to an unwillingness to grant women autonomy:

> The abortion debate is not simply about the nature of a human fetus; it is, in large part, about the nature of a woman. Is it natural for her to put motherhood second—or to choose not to become a mother at all? Is it natural for her to demand the same right to self-determination that fully democratic societies have always granted men?[37]

WOMEN'S RIGHTS VERSUS FETAL RIGHTS

Liberal theories grounded on individual rights provide one philosophical basis for feminists to make equality claims in a number of areas, as we've seen in previous chapters. Liberal feminists have been both lauded and derided for their emphasis on gaining equal status with men *within* the current political, social, and economic system. Critics of liberal feminism often point to the lim-

lives. "When a man steals to satisfy hunger we may safely assume that there is something wrong in society—so when a woman destroys the life of her unborn child, it is an evidence that either by education or by circumstances she has been greatly wronged."[2] They also argue that abortion simply frees men from yet another responsibility, and they define abortion as the "ultimate act of violence against women and children." By profiling accomplished women who oppose abortion, FFL attempts to highlight women's unique life-giving capacity as a source of strength in the pursuit of equality and a larger public role. The group's rhetoric also equates the life of the woman and the fetus, "We believe in a woman's right to control her body and she deserves this right no matter where she lives; even if she is still living inside her mother's womb." For those active in FFL, abortion relieves society of the duty to address structural barriers to women's full equality. In their view, abortion is yet another tool to control women and sustain patriarchal domination. As member Juli Wiley says, "We seek the ultimate justice: A society that bends to women's biological identity, rather than insisting that women change their biological identity through abortion."

What Do You Think?

In what ways is this position consistent with feminism? In what ways are there contradictions?

How does equating the rights of a woman and a fetus square with feminist ideology?

How might FFL respond to the claim that they are calling for a feminist utopia that does not address the immediate needs of women in this world?

Construct a short dialogue of exchange between a Pro-Life Feminist and a Pro-Choice Feminist—where are the points of agreement and disagreement?

Can a woman be a feminist and against abortion?

1. Accessed at *http://www.feministsforlife.org.*
2. Mattie Brinkerhoff, 1869. Quoted in "Are all feminists pro-abortion?" accessed at *http:www.lifesa.asn.au.*

its of using a male standard of equality to judge women's status. Successful claims advanced on the basis of the legal equality doctrine are most often made under the banner of *fairness*—that is, if men retain certain rights, privileges, or obligations that further their status purely on the basis of gender, fairness dictates that women be treated equally by erasing gender/sex from the statute or policy in question. Alternatively, the other approach in pursuit of equality argues that fairness requires the law to treat men and women differently. How do these two paths to gender equality apply to pregnancy, reproduction, and regulating emerging fertility technologies?

The rulings in *Griswold* and *Roe* ground women's reproductive liberty in the constitutional right to privacy. Privacy in this sense is understood as a limit on government's intervention in personal decisions or conduct. Individuals have a fundamental "right to be let alone," according to the decision in *Griswold*. However, the Court's ruling in *Harris* raises questions about whether a negative view of privacy is sufficient to guarantee women the fundamental right to "personhood" (autonomy) in reproductive decision making. A right to obtain an abortion that cannot be exercised solely because of one's inability to pay rings hollow for many feminists. Does government have an affirmative obligation related to the exercise of privacy rights?

Feminist legal scholar Catherine MacKinnon has argued that locating women's reproductive rights in the privacy doctrine merely serves to reinforce the subordination women experience as a result of the public/private dichotomy. The assumption that women can exercise autonomy within the private sphere is faulty, she argues, and cites as evidence the lack of support for a woman's right to refuse sex. If unintended pregnancy is a result of unintended sex (she argues here that men control sexuality entirely), then privacy understood as a negative right rather than a positive duty on government to provide termination of the unintended pregnancy merely reinforces women's subordination as a group to men as a group.[38] In this sense, " . . . *Roe* v. *Wade* presumes that government nonintervention into the private sphere promotes a woman's freedom of choice. . . . But, the *Harris* result sustains the ultimate meaning of privacy in *Roe*: Women are guaranteed by the public no more than what we can get in private—that is, what we can extract through our intimate associations with men. Women with privileges get rights. . . . So women got abortion as a private privilege, not as a public right. . . . Abortion was not decriminalized, it was legalized."[39] MacKinnon charges that in the case of abortion specifically and reproductive rights more generally, "privacy" shields and protects the very source of women's subordination—the private sphere. Within the private sphere, women are left to negotiate their rights as individuals who are segregated from the interests of women as a group. This, she argues, is why women cannot be effectively organized around the issue of abortion. "This is an instance of liberalism called feminism, liberalism applied to women as if we *are* persons, gender neutral. It reinforces the division between public and private that is *not* gender neutral. It is at once an ideological division that lies about women's shared experience and that mystifies the unity among the spheres of women's violation."[40]

Whether or not you accept MacKinnon's line of reasoning, there is an interesting dilemma posed by *Harris* in which the Court ruled that the government does not have to fund poor women's abortions through Medicaid. Privacy only guaranteed the *decision* whether or not to terminate her pregnancy, not the ability to carry out the decision. The government in this case supports only one decision—the decision to continue the pregnancy. But, how does this square with welfare reform provisions for a "family cap" or a limit to public assistance when an additional child is born? It would seem that government now supports neither decision—or rather the law may support both decisions, but for poor women, reality permits neither.

When Rights Are in Conflict: State Intervention

In recent years there has been a growing trend toward greater state intervention in the lives of pregnant women in the name of fetal protection. This intervention includes state-compelled medical treatment, arrest and incarceration of drug-addicted pregnant women under child-endangerment laws or drug-distribution penalties, and workplace restrictions that apply to both pregnant and potentially pregnant women. Central to each of these areas is the competition of rights between the woman and the fetus. Some scholars have argued that the extension of "rights" to a fetus is possible due to advances in technology that have allowed the public to see the fetus as it develops recognizably human features long before viability.[41] *Roe* tips the balance from the interests of the individual (the woman) to the state at the point of fetal viability. As technology has gradually moved the point of viability earlier in the pregnancy, in both reality and public perception, the state has taken a more aggressive role on behalf of the fetus, often at the expense of a woman's autonomy. More often than not, the public as been supportive of increased state intervention, especially when it comes at the expense of personal autonomy for poor women and women of color.

Compelling pregnant women to undergo medical treatment can be seen as enforcing the woman's duty to care for the fetus.[42] In the case of *In Re A.C.*, the court of appeals held that a trial judge's actions that compelled a woman who was twenty-six-and-a-half-weeks pregnant and dying of cancer to have a caesarean section violated a long tradition of an individual's right to accept or reject medical treatment and to maintain bodily integrity. At twenty-six weeks, the woman entered the hospital knowing that her illness was terminal and agreed to palliative care to extend her life until her pregnancy reached the twenty-eighth week (of forty weeks in a normal full-term pregnancy). Her condition worsened quickly and within four days she was intubated and unable to communicate further. The hospital immediately sought a declarative judgment from the court to intervene for the fetus as *parens patriae*. Doctors for the hospital testified that a fetus delivered at twenty-six weeks was viable (defined as "capable of sustained life outside of the mother, given artificial aid") and stood about a 50 percent chance of survival. There was no evidence offered that the woman consented to a caesarean delivery at twenty-six weeks, and her mother testified that she opposed intervention since she believed her daughter wanted to live to see the baby if delivered and that she would not have chosen to deliver a child with a substantial degree of impairment (fairly likely given the premature birth and the mother's medical condition). The trial court ordered the caesarean section, arguing that because the fetus was viable, "the state has an important and legitimate interest in protecting the potentiality of human life;" and further, that although there had been some testimony that the surgery would most likely hasten the woman's death, there had also been testimony that a delay would greatly increase the risk to the fetus.[43] The child died within two-and-one-half hours of the surgery, and the woman died two days later.

The appeals court based its reversal on several legal precedents, including an individual's right to make informed choices about treatment that includes the right to forgo treatment altogether and the court's inability to compel a person to permit significant intrusion on his or her bodily integrity even if the life of another person is at stake (e.g., compulsory bone marrow transplants for relatives). The court wrote, "It has been suggested that fetal cases are different because a woman who 'has chosen to lend her body to bring a child into the world' has an enhanced duty to assure the welfare of the fetus, sufficient even to require her to undergo caesarean surgery. Surely, however, a fetus cannot have rights in this respect superior to those of a person who has already been born. . . ."[44] Regardless of the appellate court's holding, forced caesarean surgeries continue.

A second area of states' attempts to regulate pregnant women's conduct is in regard to drug and alcohol use. Most often drug- or alcohol-addicted women are identified for state intervention and punitive action after they have given birth to a child that tests positive for drugs or exhibits symptoms of fetal alcohol syndrome. Some states have required medical personnel in public hospitals to report such findings to law enforcement officials. These laws have a disproportionate impact on poor women and women of color because they are more likely to seek prenatal care and deliver infants at public hospitals. Dorothy Roberts argues that hospitals that serve poor, minority communities have implemented infant toxicology tests almost exclusively. One trigger to testing is the mother's failure to obtain prenatal care, a factor highly related to race and income. In many cases, hospitals do not have formal screening criteria, but rely on hospital staff to identify women likely to be substance abusers and initiate testing on their infants. Racial stereotypes result in tests being performed almost exclusively on African American women and their babies.[45]

In Charleston, South Carolina, a "Search and Arrest" policy was instituted in 1989 at the Medical University of South Carolina (MUSC). Pregnant women who sought prenatal or medical care at the public hospital were targeted without a warrant or their consent for urine testing that looked for cocaine use. Positive test results were reported to local police who arrested more than thirty women in the five-year period the policy was in effect. Some women were arrested and jailed while they were still pregnant. Others were handcuffed and arrested immediately after giving birth or while still in their hospital beds. A subsequent change to the policy provided women with the option of undergoing treatment in lieu of arrest, but treatment options were limited and no provisions were made to allow women to set their affairs in order or arrange for care of their other children before entering residential treatment programs. Women who refused immediate admission to residential treatment programs were arrested and jailed. Ten women (all indigent and nine of whom are African American) filed suit, charging that the MUSC policy violated their constitutional right to medical care, violated their Fourth Amendment rights against unreasonable searches and seizures, undermined the doctor-patient relationship, and ultimately endangered the health of women and their babies.[46] On March 21, 2001, in the case of *Ferguson* v. *City of Charleston*, the Supreme Court ruled the South Carolina policy an unconstitutional form of search and seizure.

In another South Carolina case, *Whitner v. South Carolina*, the South Carolina Supreme Court upheld the use of the state's child-abuse and endangerment statute to prosecute cocaine-addicted pregnant women for child abuse. Although the word "child" in the statute is defined as a "person under the age of eighteen," the court held that a viable fetus met the definition and therefore warranted protection by the state. Generally these policies are promoted as deterrents to adverse behavior among other pregnant women, however, there is little evidence that arrest and prosecution deters drug or alcohol addiction in any form. More likely, these policies discourage other pregnant women from seeking prenatal care out of fear of criminal prosecution.[47]

Finally, increased regulation of pregnant or impregnable women takes the form of workplace exclusions in occupations deemed hazardous to fetal development. Under the guise of protecting women's health, fetal protection policies have proliferated within the past two decades. The underlying philosophy of fetal protection policies is similar to that expressed in *Muller v. Oregon* (1908), a case in which the U.S. Supreme Court upheld a limited workday for women only. Limiting working conditions (hours, minimum wage, and the like) for men was considered an arbitrary infringement on the right and liberty of the individual to contract in relation to his labor. The Court's reasoning was based on what was termed "general knowledge" about women's physical structure, the injurious effects on the female body of long hours on her feet, and maternal functions: ". . . as healthy mothers are essential to vigorous offspring, the physical well-being of women becomes an object of public interest and care in order to preserve the strength and vigor of the race."[48] Contemporary fetal-protection policies also speak to the question of maternal duty and responsibility (as well as liability issues for the employer involved). Although in this case, justification for maternal monitoring was grounded in the "rights" and interests of the fetus rather than in broad social reproductive policy goals. Individual women are viewed only within the context of reproduction in exclusionary workplace policies that bar women from certain positions designated as "hazardous." Ironically, fetal-protection policies are more likely to be in place in industries where women are not overrepresented, while the risks are greatest in industries where women constitute 75 to 80 percent of the work force (e.g., semiconductors, textiles, and hospitals). Fetal-protection policies that exclude women from the highest paying jobs are most often found in industries where women make up a small proportion of the total work force. The scientific evidence on which exclusionary policies are based is subject to debate and rarely considers paternal risk factors, either genetically at the point of conception or the risk of a male exposing a pregnant woman to toxins that are on his skin or clothing. Critics of exclusionary policies directed solely at women charge that blanket policies that treat women as a class fail to recognize women as individuals capable of making autonomous decisions and evaluating risks in employment. This "romantic paternalism" is strikingly similar to protectionist policies of the progressive era that were declared unconstitutional under Title VII.[49]

In each of these examples of increased government intervention in women's reproductive decisions and pregnancies, the intersection of race, class, and gender is unmistakable. Women of color and poor women are significantly more likely than middle- and upper-class white women to be prosecuted for drug addiction and child endangerment. The behavior and choices of all pregnant women are subject to intense scrutiny as fetal rights become more a prominent part of our public discourse. Women who do not fit the ideal of "motherhood"—those who receive public assistance, those who choose not to disrupt their careers with a pregnancy and opt for adoption or surrogacy, those who serve as surrogates or egg donors, and those who are battling addiction to drugs or alcohol—are all subject to public sanction at the hands of law enforcement, public opinion, and employers. In each case, pregnant women are hurled back in time to the days before women had access to the public sphere as fully responsible autonomous adults. Erosion of these rights and support for women's autonomy pose significant threats to women's equality.

TECHNOLOGY, REPRODUCTION, AND GENDER IDEOLOGIES

Scientific advances in the technology of reproduction have increased the demand for applying such technology to infertility. Estimates ten years ago showed that nearly 15 percent of all married couples have fertility problems.[50] It is estimated that the male sperm count has fallen by more than 30 percent in the last half century so that nearly a quarter of men now have sperm counts that are low enough to be considered functionally sterile. Similarly, the number of women experiencing fertility problems has also grown. Of those who are currently sterile, 40 percent attribute sterility to scarred fallopian tubes from pelvic inflammatory disease and other low-level gynecological infections. In addition to the physical aspects of consumer demand for fertility technology, changing social patterns have contributed to the trends as well. The wider acceptance of contraceptive use, abortion, and a growing trend among single women to bear and raise a child have all helped to decrease dramatically the number of infants available for adoption. The availability of fertility technology has increased the number of couples interested in producing "their own" child rather than having to navigate the complicated procedures involved with domestic and foreign adoptions. Finally, infertility increases with age in both men and women. People who have postponed marriage and parenting until after earning a degree and establishing their careers have, in turn, delayed childbearing until later in life.[51]

Consumer-driven demand for fertility technology, while presumably grounded in the most intimate desire for a child, has been criticized for "commercializing reproduction" and creating a market in women's reproductive labor. Treating women's reproductive labor as a commodity, similar to any other form of labor, presents society with a wide array of conundrums that are only now beginning to surface in the form of public policy. One of the first public exposures to contract pregnancy was the Baby M case in which the Sterns contracted with Mary Beth Whitehead to have her artificially inseminated with Richard Stern's sperm. On delivering the baby, Ms. Whitehead was promised $10,000. The specific terms of the contract were drawn up to avoid "baby selling" under New Jersey law. Although the baby was initially turned over to the Sterns, Ms. Whitehead subsequently changed her mind and sought custody of the child known in court documents as "Baby M." Whitehead argued that the bond between mother and child was more powerful than any contract. In 1983, the court sided with Ms. Whitehead and invalidated the surrogacy contract on the grounds that money exchanged for the purpose of adopting a child was illegal under New Jersey law and therefore the contract was unenforceable. The outcome of this highly publicized case once again focused public attention on women's reproductive roles that conflict with social expectations. Those sympathetic to Whitehead's claims pointed to the Sterns' wealth, two-career status, and impatience with the adoption process as evidence that they were unfit as parents, compared with Ms. Whitehead who already had children of her own, a stable marriage, and was motivated out of a desire to help infertile couples realize their dream. Ms. Stern, diagnosed with multiple sclerosis, was criticized for putting her own health interests ahead of having "their own" children.

Another surrogacy case was argued in California in 1993. In this case, the surrogate, Anna Johnson, was implanted with an embryo created by the Calverts (*Johnson v. Calvert*). When she gave birth to the child, Ms. Johnson informed the Calverts that she did not intend to relinquish her parental rights. The court in this case assumed that both Anna Johnson and Crispina Calvert had claims to maternity and that the outcome would therefore turn on the parties' intentions in entering the surrogacy agreement. The court ruled in favor of Ms. Calvert by reasoning that she alone intended to be a parent to the child from the outset. Ms. Johnson had entered the agreement as a result of other motivations. The "natural mother" was identified as "she who intended to procreate the child—that is, she who intended to bring about the birth of a child that she intended to raise as her own."[52] Note that the court intentionally (although seemingly obliviously) links the physical ability to bear a child with the social responsibility of raising a child in a seamless definition of *natural* motherhood, defined most prominently by the intention of raising the child.

The policy status of surrogacy, contract pregnancy, and *in vitro fertilization* techniques that result in embryos being created outside the womb is unclear. Sex and gender are interwoven, but rarely consciously disentangled in the public dialogue on the social desirability of de-coupling traditional heterosexual intercourse from reproduction. Regulations are substantially behind medical technology and are largely driven by a reaction to events already unfolding (e.g., cloning). The question of whether reproductive technologies liberate women or serve as yet another tool of patriarchal control dominates feminist literature on the subject. While technology seems to have helped infertile women, single women, and women without heterosexual partners bear children, it directly challenges our definition of family, our understanding of the link between sex and gender, and women's biological and sociological role in reproduction. Is surrogacy exploitation akin to prostitution? Should women be able to contract for their reproductive labor as freely as they do for other types of labor? Do reproductive technologies devalue women's reproductive role or liberate women from the subordination inherent in biological reproduction? These questions and more will face future generations of men and women as well as policymakers and politicians.

CONCLUSION

A variety of issues related to the family will face future generations of citizens and policymakers. The very definition of what constitutes a family is being contested today. Vermont was the first state, but probably not the last, to recognize civil unions and give them something approaching the status of marriage so that same-sex couples could access state and employer benefits. New reproductive technologies have allowed same-sex couples, whether male or female, to genetically contribute to the conception of a "child of their own." Women's biological and sociological roles in relation to reproduction are less clear than they have ever been. How will these issues be resolved?

The policy process is not particularly well-equipped to deal with such intimate and complex issues. The same claim to privacy that gives women choices in reproductive decisions also surrounds and isolates them as individuals subordinated within families in the private sphere. Domestic violence, marital rape, and poverty conditions have all been beyond the scope of politics and government action relatively recently in our history. More so than in other issues we've discussed in this volume, family and fertility decisions present women with direct challenges to their autonomy. When women were defined solely within the private sphere, they were virtually invisible. As women have become more active in politics and the public sphere, they have transformed previously private issues significant to their lives and livelihoods into issues legitimate for public policy. However, as government has become more involved in these issues, women's interests as autonomous individuals run the risk of being subsumed by larger social interests. Particularly in the area of reproduction and fertility concerns, women as individuals risk becoming an invisible interest in public policy debates. As we saw in chapter 5, electing more women to public office does not in itself guarantee that women's interests will be promoted.

How will women and men resolve these tensions created by the paradox of equality? There is no clear path to women's equality in the family and in reproductive choices. The legal equality doctrine's gender-neutral approach does not seem appropriate when the issues are tied directly to women's biological sex as well as socially constructed gender roles. The persistence of patriarchal culture, however, makes it difficult to determine what is fair treatment for women under the fairness doctrine. Betty Friedan has argued that the only way to resolve these seemingly intractable issues is to redefine the context of the problem from judging *equality* within a legal framework to judging it in the context of the substantive *quality* of men's and women's lives. This, she argues, calls for a reconceptualization of how to balance work (public sphere) and family (private sphere).[53] This new equality is not equality between men and women but in the substantive areas in which their lives converge. This is the challenge for the coming century as men and women continue their pursuit of equality.

Notes

1. *General Electric* v. *Gilbert,* 429 US 125 (1976).
2. Rosemary Radford Ruether, "Diverse Forms of Family Life Merit Recognition," *National Catholic Reporter* 36, no. 32 (June 16, 2000): 19.
3. Cynthia B. Costello, Shari Miles and Anne J. Stone, *The American Woman 1999–2000: A Century of Change* (New York: Norton, 1999), p. 190.
4. Ibid., pp. 191–192.
5. Virginia Sapiro, *Women in American Society: An Introduction to Women's Studies,* 4th ed. (Mountain View, Calif.: Mayfield 1999), p. 398.
6. William M. Hohengarten, "Same-sex marriage and the Right of Privacy," *Yale Law Journal* 104, no. 6 (April 1994): 1495–1531.
7. Dorothy McBride Stetson, *Women's Rights in the USA: Policy Debates and Gender Roles* (New York: Garland Press, 1997), pp. 178–183.
8. Sapiro, *Women in American Society,* pp. 392–393.
9. Susan Moller Okin, *Justice, Gender, and the Family* (New York: Basic Books, 1989).
10. Ibid.
11. *Forbush* v. *Wallace,* 341 F. Supp. 241 (1971).
12. Sapiro, *Women in American Society,* p. 392.
13. Nancy McGlen and Karen O'Connor, *Women, Politics and American Society,* 2d ed. (Upper River Saddle, N.J.: Prentice Hall, 1998), pp. 214–215.
14. Sapiro, *Women in American Society,* p. 392.
15. Stetson, *Women's Rights in the USA,* p. 192.
16. Lenore J. Weitzman, *The Divorce Revolution: The Unexpected Social and Economic Consequences for Women and Children in America* (New York: Free Press, 1985).
17. Hunter College Women's Studies Collective, *Women's Realities Women's Choices: An Introduction to Women's Studies* (New York: Oxford University Press, 1995), p. 249.

18. United Nations, *The World's Women 2000: Trends and Statistics* (New York: United Nations Publications, 2000), p. 133.

19. Anne H. Gauthier, *The State and the Family: A Comparative Analysis of Family Policies in Industrialized Countries* (New York: Oxford University Press, 1996), pp. 3–4.

20. Robert Blank and Janna C. Merrick, *Human Reproduction, Emerging Technologies, and Conflicting Rights* (Washington, D.C.: Congressional Quarterly Press, 1995), p. 4.

21. Sara Ann Ketchum, "Selling of Babies, Selling of Bodies," in *Feminist Perspectives in Medical Ethics*, eds. Helen B. Holmes and Laura M. Purdy (Bloomington: Indiana University Press, 1992), pp. 284–294.

22. Nancy Woloch, *Women and the American Experience* (New York: Alfred A. Knopf, 1984) p. 365.

23. Ibid., p. 367.

24. Quoted in Woloch, 1984, p. 369.

25. *Planned Parenthood of Southeastern Pennsylvania* v. *Casey,* 112 S Ct 2791 (1992).

26. Alan Guttmacher Institute, "Induced Abortion," *Facts in Brief,* 2000, accessed at *http://www.agi-usa.org/fb_induced_abortion.html.*

27. California Abortion and Reproductive Rights Action League, *"Hill* v. *Colorado:* Summary of the Court's June 28, 2000 Decision," accessed at *http://www.choice.org/court2000/hillsummary.html.*

28. Anna Quindlen, "RU-486 and the Right to Choose: Cheering, wailing, hailing, damning—the abortion pill is important but no panacea," *Newsweek* (October 9, 2000), p. 86.

29. Ibid.

30. Alan Guttmacher Institute, *Sharing Responsibility: Women, Society and Abortion Worldwide* (New York: AGI, 1999).

31. Alan Guttmacher Institute, "U.S. Policy Can Reduce Cost Barriers to Contraception" in *Issues in Brief* (New York: AGI, July 1999), accessed at *http://www.agi-usa.org/pubs/ib_0799.html.*

32. Ibid.

33. Tamar Lewin, "Agency Finds Many Health Plans Should Cover Contraceptive Costs," *New York Times,* 15 December 2000, p. A1.

34. Ibid.

35. Wendy Kaminer, "Abortion and Autonomy," *The American Prospect* 11, no. 14 (June 5, 2000), accessed at *http://www.prospect.org/archives/v11-14.*

36. Ibid.

37. Ibid.

38. Catherine A. MacKinnon, "Privacy v. Equality: Beyond *Roe* v. *Wade,*" in *Mary Jo Frug's Women and the Law,* eds. Judith G. Greenberg, Martha L. Minow, and Dorothy E. Roberts, 2d ed. (New York: Foundation Press, 1998), pp. 737–742.

39. Ibid., p. 741.

40. Ibid., p. 742.

41. Robert H. Blank, "Reproductive Technology: Pregnant Women, the Fetus, and the Courts," in *The Politics of Pregnancy,* eds. Janna C. Merrick and Robert H. Blank (New York: Haworth Press, 1996), pp. 1–18.

42. Greenberg, Minow, and Roberts, *Mary Jo Frug's Women,* p. 772.

43. In *Re A.C.,* Court of Appeals of the District of Columbia, En Banc, 573 A2d 1235 (1990).

44. Greenberg, Minow, and Roberts, *Mary Jo Frug's Women,* p. 754.

45. Dorothy E. Roberts, "Punishing Drug Addicts who have Babies: Women of Color, Equality, and the Right of Privacy," in *Mary Jo Frug's Women,* p. 772.

46. Center for Reproductive Law and Policy, "U.S. Supreme Court Hears Arguments in *Ferguson* v. *City of Charleston*" (2000), accessed at *http://www.crlp.org/100400 ferguson.html.*

47. Robert H. Blank, *Fetal Protection in the Workplace* (New York: Columbia University Press, 1993), p. 14.

48. J. Ralph Lindgren and Nadine Taub, *The Law of Sex Discrimination,* 2d ed. (Minneapolis, Minn.: West Publishing Co., 1993), p. 39.

49. Blank, *Fetal Protection,* p. 99.

50. Robert H. Blank, *Regulating Reproduction* (New York: Columbia University Press, 1990), p. 13.

51. Ibid., p. 15.

52. Greenberg, Minow, and Roberts, *Mary Jo Frug's Women,* pp. 796–798.

53. Betty Friedan, *The Second Stage* (New York: Summit Press, 1986).

9

Conclusion: New Challenges in the Pursuit of Equality

OUR EXAMINATION of women's pursuit of equality has focused on the complexities, tensions, and controversies created by the paradox of gender equality—that is, how to reconcile demands for gender equality with sex differences between men and women. Two major paths have been forged in attempting to resolve the paradox and improve the status of women. The difference between the two approaches lies in how the implications of sex differences are understood. Advocates of the *legal equality doctrine* believe that women can never achieve equality as long as they are treated differently from men. "Difference" in this context always means inferior. By removing sex as a method of categorizing individuals, women will be free of the discriminatory institutional, legal, and political barriers erected purely on the basis of sex that have historically prevented them from full participation in society. Using the legal equality doctrine, women and men are made the same in the eyes of the law, and therefore cannot be treated differently (with a few remaining exceptions). Critics of this approach argue that since men and women are in fact biologically different, erasing their legal differences but not their real differences will merely burden women further. Advocates of the *fairness doctrine* believe that sex differences have significant consequences for how men and women live in the world. Women are disadvantaged, and equality is not meaningful when their unique biological role is ignored as it would be under the legal equality doctrine. Using the fairness doctrine, laws that recognize and accommodate women's physical differences will thereby promote women's equality in reality.

As we have seen throughout this text, women do not agree among themselves on the meaning or even on the desirability of equality as defined by these two paths. Sex alone does not create a binding political identity among women, nor does it foster a group consciousness that mobilizes women around the issues of gender equality. Feminism, one manifestation of women's political consciousness, has not always provided an effective political mobilizing ideology because it too encompasses the paradox of gender equality. Feminism encourages unity among women even while recognizing women's diversity. The same sorts of socioeconomic and political cleavages that divide men from one another also divide women and have proven difficult to overcome in adopting a single approach to resolving the gender paradox. Yet all women share one condition purely on the basis of their sex—a subordinate position within the gender hierarchy of *patriarchy*. Patriarchy privileges men over women, regardless of class, race or ethnicity, sexuality, or political ideology. The pernicious influence of the separate spheres ideology has combined with patriarchy's male privilege to render women's pursuit of equality an enduring political challenge. Private patriarchy (families) combined with public patriarchy (economy, politics and public policy) creates a system that has historically submerged women in the private sphere, rendering them nearly invisible in the public sphere until the mid-1800s. The quest for women's rights can thus be characterized as a movement to gain women's autonomy and full citizenship in the public sphere.

This book has traced women's historical progress in their fight for autonomy and equality. Early women activists had obvious hurdles to overcome, starting with the debilitating fact that women were not permitted to speak aloud in a public forum. Without a public voice, women could neither articulate their own interests nor expect their interests to be represented in politics or policy. The first manifesto of women's rights, the Declaration of Sentiments, adopted in 1848 at the Seneca Falls convention, included the demand for women's voices to be heard within their marriages, families, communities, and the larger political system. Today the Declaration of Sentiments provides a good framework for evaluating women's progress toward equality. Participants at the Seneca Falls meeting thought their demand for the vote was the most radical of the Declaration's eleven resolutions that participants adopted. It was, as you recall from chapter 2, the only resolution that was not adopted unanimously. In retrospect, the third resolution called for an even more fundamental transformation. It read, "Resolved, That woman is man's equal—was intended to be so by the Creator, and the highest good of the race demands that she should be recognized as such." It is a simple declaration of equality between men and women that is missing from the nation's founding documents. It took suffragists seventy-two years to win the elective franchise, but such a clear declaration of equality between men and women has yet to be embraced as fundamental U.S. law. The Equal Rights Amendment was never ratified as an amendment to the Constitution. Moreover, its international equivalent, the Convention on the Elimination of all forms of Discrimination Against Women, has yet to be ratified by the Senate in the twenty years since its adoption. Does that matter? Perhaps not if women have achieved equality without having the words codified into law. Where do women stand today?

In many ways, this question returns us to where we began. To evaluate women's status relative to equality, we have to have some established standard

Encountering the Controversies of Equality

Will You Have to Move in Pursuit of Equality?

THE INSTITUTE for Women's Policy Research (IWPR) regularly conducts research on the status of women's rights in the United States in all fifty states. Because we are governed by a federal system, there is substantial variation between states on policies that promote women's rights and opportunities. In its most recent report, issued in November 2000, the IWPR found substantial variation in women's political participation, employment and earnings, economic autonomy, reproductive rights, and health and well-being.[1] Their most disturbing finding, however, was that women have yet to achieve equality with men in any state, even in those with better policies for women. Within each of the five domains of women's rights, IWPR has created a composite index to represent women's achievement, which then allows the organization to rank the states overall and within each domain. Overall, Connecticut and Vermont received the highest rankings, appearing in the top ten states on four of the five composite indices and in the top third on all of the composite indices. Conversely, Mississippi ranked the

of judgment that we presently do not have. We do not have a consensus on the meaning of gender equality in theory or in practice. Women among themselves do not even have a consensus on the desirability of equality as a shared goal. That said, women's movements have unquestionably influenced women's private and public status in the United States through their pursuit of equality along a number of paths. This final chapter examines three areas in which women have demanded an expansion of rights, beginning with resolutions adopted at the Seneca Falls meeting. Each of the following sections briefly summarizes women's advances and identifies areas in which women are still struggling to define and achieve equality. In setting a future agenda for women's equality, we will evaluate the challenges that lie ahead in resolving the paradox of gender equality in the twenty-first century.

ELECTIVE FRANCHISE AND POLITICAL REPRESENTATION

Although all women were enfranchised in 1920 with the ratification of the Nineteenth Amendment, it took more than seventy years and countless campaigns led by three generations of suffragists to win the vote. Women were

lowest of the fifty states, joined by Alabama, Tennessee, Arkansas, Kentucky, and South Carolina. In examining the results of this report (which can be found on *http:// www.iwpr.org*), consider the implications of federalism for women's rights and the pursuit of equality.

What do you think?

As you prepare to graduate and establish residence in a state, will you take into consideration the policies and opportunities each state affords women? Which of the five indicators will be most important to your decision?

Where does the state where you currently reside rank?

In what ways are women disadvantaged by the power of the states in the U.S. system of government? Are there any advantages to federalism relative to women's rights?

How does the variation in women's rights and status square with the Constitution's guarantee of equal protection?

How might the status of women look different if the Equal Rights Amendment had been ratified? Would there still be variation across the states?

1. Institute for Women's Policy Research, "Overview of the Status of Women in the States," 2000, can be accessed at *http://www.iwpr.org*.

slow to use their vote, and it took several more decades for the number of women voters to approximate the number of women who were eligible to vote. Women now regularly vote at higher rates than men do in most national elections, but with what results? Having the vote is not synonymous with using the vote to promote women candidates or a women's political agenda. Attracting the "women's vote" could potentially mean the difference between victory and defeat for a party or candidate, and so the gender gap and courting women's votes remain salient features of contemporary political campaigns. Although men and women voted differently in the 2000 presidential contest, women voters did not determine the outcome. A majority of women (54 percent) voted for Democrat Al Gore, while a majority of men (53 percent) voted for Republican George W. Bush. There was an 11 percentage point gender gap between women who preferred Gore and men supporting Bush. In several Senate races, however, the gender gap and women's clear preference for the Democratic candidate did provide the margin of victory.[1] As a result of the 2000 elections, a record number of sixty-one women were voted into the House of Representatives and a record thirteen women will serve in the Senate. Whether "women's interests" will be more effectively advanced remains to be seen.

In chapter 5, we saw that political representation can take on a variety of forms. Descriptively, women are better represented in the 107th Congress than ever before by virtue of the increase in numbers of women elected. But women will be equitably represented only when they hold roughly half the seats in the legislature. As more women get elected to public office at all levels and become political role models, more women may view public service as a viable option and the pace of women's election to office may quicken. Former Governor Christine Todd Whitman, of New Jersey, said recently, "Parents come up to me and say, you know, you're really a role model for my daughter, who now believes she can be anything that she wants to be."[2] However, unless women in office also provide substantive representation by *acting for* women's interests, the status of women overall is unlikely to change. This is more difficult to accomplish because women do not agree on a single set of "women's interests." The research on women's behavior in office defines women's interests as those "where policy consequences are likely to have a more immediate and direct impact on significantly larger numbers of women than men."[3] Using this measure, women's interests are closely linked to social policies, which are not necessarily the same as feminist issues. Women's issues therefore have included both feminist (such as pay equity, violence against women, reproductive choice) and traditional interests (family and children, education, health and welfare).[4] The dichotomy is another indication of the division among women along basic ideological lines as well as by political party. Research on women's voting records and impact on shaping the legislative agenda within institutions suggests that the election of feminists constitutes the best guarantee of connecting descriptive with substantive representation. Feminists are more likely to speak and act in favor of women's interests.[5] Will we see women run as self-identified feminist candidates? That seems unlikely, given the ambivalence the public, and particularly women, express about feminism as an ideological marker. Research on women's effectiveness in office also shows that until women occupy leadership positions within the institution, they are less likely to shape the overall agenda to include women's issues.

These findings leave future activists with two primary tasks: Elect more gender-conscious women to office and work to reelect those who have already been elected so that they will be eligible to assume positions of leadership. Both of these goals require a mobilized electorate of men and women who value equality and believe that the aims of gender equality can be promoted within the political system. Meeting these goals also requires more women who are willing to run for public office. The research in chapter 3 clearly shows that when women run for office, particularly in open-seat contests, they have an equal or a better chance of winning than men. A number of initiatives are underway to recruit and support women candidates, particularly young women. The age gap between men and women first elected to office remains an impediment to women seeking progressively higher office and in winning leadership posts within their current chamber. Term limits have some positive influence on legislatures where few women are already serving, but there is also evidence that term limits negatively affect women's representation in states where they have already been successful in raising their numbers. A number of countries have implemented quotas for electing women to party slates or to seats within parliament, and in doing so have successfully increased the number of women in office.[6] The United States is unlikely to adopt such an approach. However, the Women's Environment and Development Organization in conjunction with Beijing+5 recently launched initiatives like "50-50 in 2005: Get the Balance Right!" These and similar candidate-recruitment efforts described in chapter 4 will ultimately be successful in identifying, recruiting, and supporting women candidates for public office. As the number of women in office grows, the diversity of political agendas will likely increase as well, meaning that women as a group may be better represented. But women's interests in terms of gender equality may not be better represented unless women themselves come to share a single view of equality as a goal.

MARRIAGE AND FAMILY RIGHTS

The Declaration of Sentiments was primarily concerned with changing the common law practices associated with coverture. In coverture marriage, a woman as an individual was "covered" by her husband's identity and was no longer able to exercise independent control over anything in her life, including her property, wages, household goods, and her children. Marriage reforms consistent with the legal equality doctrine now view men and women as equal partners in a marriage. Whether this arrangement results in real equality for women often depends on a family's socioeconomic status. For a woman with children, divorce means a substantial reduction in her standard of living even as her ex-husband's standard of living rises. A woman's ability to survive as her household's only wage earner without relying on public assistance is directly related to her position in the work force and her ability to stay employed if she has children.

Reliable, high-quality childcare is an issue for all working parents, but particularly for single parents. Although public support for federally sponsored child care solutions remains well above 80 percent, Congress has yet to act. This may have less to do with the estimated price tag than with persistent public attitudes that support women's traditional role. Eighty-two percent of the adults (87 percent of the men and 78.1 percent of the women) in the 1996 General Social Survey agreed that women are biologically better suited to care for children. This does not directly translate into equally robust support for a return to the separate spheres of labor. Only 14.9 percent of all adults in 1996 (down from more than 35 percent in 1976) agreed that "women should take care of running their homes and leave running the country up to men."[7] However, respondents still expressed ambivalence about women's full participation in the labor force when she has children. When asked if everyone benefits if women take the main responsibility for care of the home and children, while men take the main responsibility for supporting the family financially, well over half of the adult population is in agreement (67.8 percent in 1996).

Resolving the division of family and work-force labor will be a primary issue facing men and women in the future. Policies consistent with the legal equality doctrine are more problematic in this area than in any other because of the weight that biological differences have when assigning reproductive responsibilities. Beyond the physical implications of pregnancy, attitudes about women's sociological responsibilities for children and home also complicate developing gender-neutral family policies. Gender-specific policies carry the danger of reinforcing attitudes about women's natural fit in the private sphere at the risk of further exclusion from the public sphere. In the meantime, women are significantly disadvantaged in the work force because of the expectation that they continue to maintain the primary responsibility for the children and home. A substantial portion of the pay gap is attributed to differences in men's and women's length of employment experience. When children come into a family, their presence is associated with lower wages for women, but not for men.[8] Women suffer more interruptions to their participation in the labor force due to childbearing. These realities have implications not only for women's current paychecks, but also for retirement income from social security and private pensions, which are based on an individual's time in the paid workforce and rate of pay. Current proposals for social security reform that emphasize privatizing the system may have negative implications for women if such changes do not also account for the differences in men's and women's employment patterns.

It may be that many of these issues cannot be resolved by public policy. As attitudes about what constitutes a family change to permit more variations on the traditional heterosexual, middle-class model, women and men alike will need to reevaluate and perhaps rearrange their priorities to more equitably balance work and family life. New reproductive technologies will only complicate our national attempts to define "the family." Women are divided on issues of surrogacy or egg donation that turn what was traditionally viewed as unpaid reproductive labor into paid productive labor for some women. Is this liberation from the confines of sex-linked reproductive responsibilities or sexual exploitation of women?

The political culture in the United States has not supported government's intervention into the private domain of family and children until relatively recently. Even now, government's participation is limited to protecting the health and safety of individuals within families and not in providing financial and programmatic aid to families struggling to balance work and family responsibilities. The Family and Medical Leave Act of 1993 is a pale comparison to family-support programs provided in many other nations (see chapter 7). Efforts to strengthen the legislation to provide paid leave funded by state unemployment insurance funds have been met with strong opposition. There is little evidence that a national childcare policy is at the top of any legislative agenda. Until women and men reach the point where both are faced with the same challenges, it seems unlikely that a government policy will be the mechanism that produces real change. As we discussed at the end of chapter 5, policies that are designed to promote role equity (equality defined as fairness) have been more successful than policies designed to promote role change (equality defined as sameness). Balancing family with other public responsibilities presents a complicated case for this framework. Because men and women continue to hold fairly traditional attitudes about the division of labor within the family and private household (see chapter 7 on gender socialization and work), even women see their additional family responsibilities as "fair" up to a point. Until these attitudes change, it is unlikely that the public will pressure policymakers to produce solutions.

EDUCATION, EMPLOYMENT, AND ECONOMIC OPPORTUNITIES

Because women were legally excluded from all colleges and universities, as well as from most occupations, the Declaration of Sentiments demanded women have access to education and employment opportunities. Today, Title IX (discussed in chapter 6) and Title VII (discussed in chapter 7) guarantee that access to educational institutions and most occupations cannot be denied on the basis of sex. These two pieces of legislation have been powerful tools for women in developing the "human capital" necessary to broaden economic opportunities. Human capital, which includes education and experience in the labor market, is often viewed as the most important determinant of wages.[9] Wages, of course, are an important determinant of security, health, and quality of life. As we have seen in the previous three chapters, gender-neutral access to education or employment does not necessarily ensure that the experience itself is comparable for men and women. In an effort to improve the quality of education, several current reform proposals call for vouchers that would permit parents to use federal education dollars to send their children to any school (public or private) that the parents choose. It is unclear whether federal gender-equity legislation would apply in private school settings under these circumstances, even when public money is paying for a student's tuition. Unless gender equity remains a priority in the changes that are being made to the way children are educated, gains in this area for women will be vulnerable.

Most of the world's poor are women (an estimated 70 percent).[10] The poverty rates for women in the United States, particularly among women with children and the elderly, remain startlingly high in 2001. Even as the nation prospered, the proportion of women living below the poverty line has increased. There are a number of explanations for women's overrepresentation among the poor (see chapter 7). The 1996 changes to the nation's welfare policy are likely to impact women's poverty rate. Across the nation, fewer women have applied for welfare benefits, but it is not clear whether the decline is because they are gainfully employed and earning wages sufficient to support their families. At the same time that welfare rolls are shrinking, private charities report serving more families than in years prior to the reforms. Addressing women's poverty will require attention to the impact of sex segregation in the work force, disparate classroom experiences and counseling in grade and high schools, the limits imposed by the glass ceiling and the sticky floor, and particularly the pay gap.

The pay gap, although a strikingly consistent 25 percent across hourly and salaried occupations, remains the subject of debate. Some attribute the pay differential between men and women to "choices" each makes regarding employment, education, and family. The portion of the pay gap that remains unexplained by differences in education, occupation, union membership, and labor market experience, however, is estimated at roughly 12 percent.[11] This is the portion of the pay gap that is attributed to gender discrimination. A study using 1990 Census data on workers from all sectors of the economy found that a substantial portion of the pay gap (one quarter) is a result of differences in pay between men and women working in similar jobs and establishments.[12] Even when there are differences in workplace productivity, the pay differential is significantly lower than the productivity differential. A recent study found that "at the margin" women were 85 to 96 percent as productive as men but were paid only 66 to 68 percent as much as men.[13] These disparities, due purely to sex, are precisely the type of discrimination the Equal Pay Act of 1963 was designed to eliminate. However, nearly forty years after the policy was enacted, women still earn less than men even when performing the same job in the same sector of the economy. The pay gap has indeed declined over the past three decades, but it has not disappeared. Women with college degrees will still earn less on average than men with college degrees ($14,665) and only slightly more ($3,193 a year) than white men with high-school diplomas (see Table 6.3).

The reasons for the pay gap are varied and complex, but it is real. The burdens and costs incurred by women in bearing children are not distributed equally across the population, even though the benefits to reproducing the population are clearly shared. Until this facet of gender inequality is addressed, the pay gap, sex segregated occupations, and poverty will remain pervasive problems that are nearly immune to solutions in the legal equality tradition. In this case, policies requiring gender equality have made some inroads into changing attitudes about women's roles, but they have not entirely erased the effects of centuries of influence of the separate spheres ideology. Since the separate spheres ideology locates women firmly in the private sphere, gender-specific policies run the risk of reinforcing attitudes that limit women's ability to participate fully in the public sphere. For example, in 1989, Felice Schwartz, president of Catalyst, an organization dedicated to improving women's access to top-level jobs,[14] proposed that employers distinguish employees as either "career primary" or "career and family."[15] Under this design, women who did not plan to interrupt their employment to have children could operate on the "sprint" career model as their male peers do, while women who are "career and family" designated could work more flexible schedules with slower promotion expectations. The second track was immediately dubbed the "mommy track." Although theoretically this looks like a good solution to the dual pressures women in particular face in juggling work and family, there are significant problems associated with the policy. First, women's pay and prestige in the workplace are reduced by her obligations to family. If this is the result of a real choice, perhaps that is an option some women would gladly take. However, there might also be instances where women are "tracked" by employers in ways that do not reflect the individual's choice, thereby further legitimating sex discrimination. Further, the "mommy track" reinforces the idea that family is women's work and perpetuates the sex-linked division of labor in both the private and public spheres. In this area, as in others, we are left with a complex dilemma. Gender neutral policies do not appear to go far enough in recognizing the different challenges women face either as a result of biological reproduction or sociological expectations. However, gender-specific policies, even when theoretically designed to help women can often carry the very real danger of reinforcing discriminatory practices and attitudes that disadvantage women.

WHERE DO WE GO FROM HERE?

As we reach the end of this volume and our analysis of the gender paradox, where do men and women stand after more than 150 years of effort toward a resolution to the paradox? We must conclude that men and women are more equal today than at any other time in U.S. history, but the paradox has not been entirely resolved. In a variety of contexts, men and women lead very different lives and in some cases, women are decidedly disadvantaged because of their gender. Public attitudes about gender roles in society have changed to support women as participants in the public sphere, although as we've seen, there are limits to the autonomy women are extended. Feminism remains the ideological challenge to gender hierarchy that limits women's full participation and autonomy, but feminism faces a direct challenge to its own legitimacy as an organizing philosophy for women. While public opinion polls show women increasingly support efforts to change their status (78 percent of women favored such efforts in 1994 compared to 57 percent in 1974),[16] women's ambivalence over feminism and the organized women's movement as appropriate tools continues. In 1991, Susan Faludi published *Backlash: The Undeclared War Against Women,* in which she documented the negative responses to women's gains. One aspect of the backlash she describes is that a growing number of women (primarily white, middle-class, college-educated, and professionally successful) call themselves feminists, but are publicly hostile to current feminist arguments and organizations.[17] She attributes this to an antifeminist strategy to oppose women's gains, not only in the name of women as the antisuffrage and anti-ERA forces did but also in the name of feminism itself.[18] Other fissures within feminism look like a generation gap. Young women in their twenties have attracted publicity in recent years with books that appear to take the second-wave feminists (in many cases, their own mothers) to task in ways very similar to the generational divide among feminists in the 1920s. "Older feminists" are criticized for concentrating on legal solutions to discrimination rather than focusing on developing their own potential as women. Many of these tracts encourage women to express their sexuality as a sign of power.[19]

There are signs of a "third wave" of feminism: In 1992, in the wake of the William Kennedy Smith rape trial and the Clarence Thomas–Anita Hill hearings, more than 100 young feminists gathered in New York City and organized a network they called "The Third Wave." The vision, articulated by organizers, was "to become the national network for young feminists, to politicize and organize young women from diverse cultural and economic backgrounds, to strengthen the relationships between young women and older feminists, and to consolidate a strong base of membership that can mobilize for specific issues, political candidates, and events."[20] Even among women who are not associated with an organization, the tendency of third-wave feminists is to focus more broadly and integrate women's concerns with larger issues related to justice, including racism, poverty, and environmental issues. Betty Friedan, a founder of the second wave of feminism, said of the third wavers, "Young women are the true daughters of feminism; they take nothing for granted and are advancing the cause with marvelous verve. If they keep doing what they are doing, thirty years from today we may not need a feminist movement. We may have achieved real equality."[21] The challenge of gender equality is now in your hands.

Notes

1. "Gender Gap in the 2000 Elections," fact sheet compiled by the Center for American Women and Politics, Eagleton Institute of Politics (New Brunswick, N.J.: Rutgers University, 2001), accessed at *http://www.cawp.rutgers.edu.*

2. Quoted at *http://www.befearless.oxygen.com.*

3. Susan J. Carroll, *Women as Candidates in American Politics,* 2d ed. (Bloomington: University of Indiana Press, 1994), p. 15.

4. Manon Tremblay, "Do Female MPs Substantively Represent Women? A Study of Legislative Behaviour in Canada's 35th Parliament," *Canadian Journal of Political Science* 31, no. 3 (1998): 440.

5. Ibid., p. 465.

6. R. Darcy, Susan Welch, and Janet Clark, *Women, Elections and Representation,* 2d ed. (Lincoln: University of Nebraska Press, 1994), chapter seven.

7. NORC, 1996. General Social Survey Cumulative Data File.

8. "Explaining the Trends in the Gender Wage Gap," The Council of Economic Advisers, 1998, accessed at *http://www2.whitehouse.gov/WH/EOP/CEA/html/gendergap.html.*

9. Ibid., p. 6.

10. Ruth Leger Sivard, *Women: A World Survey* (Washington, D.C.: World Priorities), 1995.

11. Ibid., p. 9.

12. Bureau of the Census, "New Evidence on Sex Segregation and Sex Differences in Wages from Matched Employee-Employer Data," prepared by Kimberly Bayard, Judith Hellerstein, David Neumark, and Kenneth Troske for the International Symposium on Linked Employer-Employee Data, Bureau of the Census (Washington, D.C., April 1998).

13. Judith Hellerstein, David Neumark, and Kenneth Troske, "Wages, Productivity and Worker Characteristics," working paper 5626, National Bureau of Economic Research, June 1996.

14. See the Catalyst Web site, accessed at *http://www.catalyst.org.*

15. Felice N. Schwartz, "Management, Women and the New Facts of Life," *Harvard Business Review* 67 (January–February 1989): 65–76.

16. Roper Center for Public Opinion Research, "Virginia Slims Polls," Storrs, Conn. (n.d.). Survey question: "There has been much talk recently about changing women's status in society today. On the whole, do you favor or oppose most of the efforts to strengthen and change women's status in society today?"

17. See Susan Faludi, "I'm Not a Feminist, But I Play One on TV," *MS.* 5, no. 5 (April 1995).

18. See, for example, Elizabeth Fox-Genovese, *Feminism is Not the Story of my Life: How Today's Feminist Elite Has Lost Touch with the Real Concerns of Women* (New York: Nan A. Talese, 1996); Camille Paglia, *Vamps and Tramps* (New York: Vintage, 1994); or Christine Hoff Sommers, *Who Stole Feminism? How Women have Betrayed Women* (New York: Simon & Schuster, 1994).

19. See Katie Roiphe, *The Morning After: Sex, Fear, and Feminism* (Boston: Little, Brown, 1993); Rebecca Walker, ed., *To be Real: Telling the Truth and Changing the Face of Feminism* (New York: Anchor Books, 1995); or Naomi Wolf, *Fire with Fire: The New Female Power and How to Use it* (New York: Fawcett Combine, 1993).

20. Beth Dulin, "Founding Project Challenges Young Feminists," *New Directions for Women* 21, no. 1 (1993): 33.

21. Joannie M. Schrof, "Feminism's Daughters," *U.S. News and World Report* (September 27, 1993).

Suggested Readings and Web Resources

Chapter One

Sandra Lipsitz Bem, *The Lenses of Gender: Transforming the Debate on Sexual Inequality* (New Haven, Conn.: Yale University Press, 1993).

Nancy Cott, *The Grounding of Modern Feminism* (New Haven, Conn.: Yale University Press, 1987).

Jean Beth Elshtain, *Public Man, Private Woman: Women in Social and Political Thought*, 2d ed. (Princeton, N.J.: Princeton University Press, 1981).

Sherrye Henry, *The Deep Divide: Why American Women Resist Equality* (New York: Macmillan, 1994).

Mark E. Kahn, *The Gendering of American Politics: Founding Mothers, Founding Fathers, and Political Patriarchy* (Westport, Conn.: Praeger, 1999).

John Stuart Mill, "The Subjection of Women" in *The Feminist Papers*, edited by Alice S. Rossi (Boston: Northeastern University Press, 1972).

Carole Pateman, *The Sexual Contract* (Stanford, Calif.: Stanford University Press, 1998).

Carole Pateman, *The Disorder of Women: Democracy, Feminism and Political Theory* (Stanford, Calif.: Stanford University Press, 1989).

Virginia Sapiro, *A Vindication of Political Virtue: The Political Theory of Mary Wollstonecraft* (Chicago: The University of Chicago Press, 1992).

Chapter Two

Susan D. Becker, *The Origins of the Equal Rights Amendment: American Feminism Between the Wars* (Westport, Conn.: Greenwood Press, 1981).

Carol Ellen Dubois, *Feminism and Suffrage: The Emergence of an Independent Women's Movement in America 1848–1869* (Ithaca, N.Y.: Cornell University Press, 1978).

Eleanor Flexnor and Ellen Fitzpatrick, *Century of Struggle: The Woman's Rights Movement in the United States*, enlarged edition (Cambridge, Mass.: Harvard University Press, 1996).

Aileen Kraditor, *The Ideas of the Woman Suffrage Movement: 1890–1920* (New York: Norton, 1981).

Jane Mansbridge, *Why We Lost the ERA* (Chicago: University of Chicago Press, 1986).

Susan Marshall, *Splintered Sisterhood: Gender and Class in the Campaign against Woman Suffrage* (Madison: University of Wisconsin Press, 1997).

Nell Irvin Painter, *Sojourner Truth: A Life, A Symbol* (New York: Norton, 1996).

Gilbert Y. Steiner, *Constitutional Inequality: The Political Fortunes of the Equal Rights Amendment* (Washington, D.C.: Brookings Institution, 1985).

Doris Stevens, *Jailed for Freedom: American Women Win the Vote*, edited by Carol O'Hare (1920; reprint, Troutdale, Ore.: New Sage Press, 1995).

Rosalyn Terborg-Penn, *African American Women in the Struggle for the Vote, 1850–1920* (Bloomington: Indiana University Press, 1998).

National Women's History Project: *http://www.nwhp.org*.

Places Where Women Made History: *http://www.cr.nps.gov/nr/travel/pwwmh/*.

Women's Rights National Historical Park: *http://www.nps.gov/wori/wrnhp.htm*.

The National Women's Hall of Fame: *http://www.greatwomen.org*.

Chapter Three

Jo Freeman, *A Room at a Time: How Women Entered Party Politics* (Lanham, Md.: Rowman & Littlefield, 2000).

Kathleen Hall Jamieson, Richard Johnston, and Michael Hagen, "The Primary Campaign: What did the Candidates Say, What did the Public Learn, and What did it Matter?" (Philadelphia: Annenberg Policy Center, University of Pennsylvania, March 27, 2000): *http://www.appcpenn.org*.

Wendy Kaminer, "Crashing the Locker Room," *The Atlantic* 270, no.1 (July 1992): 58–70.

Karen M. Kauffman and John R. Petrocik, "The Changing Politics of Men: Understanding the Sources of the Gender Gap," *American Journal of Political Science* 43, no. 3 (July 1999): 864–887.

Richard Seltzer, Jody Newman, and Melissa Vorhees Leighton, *Sex as a Political Variable: Women as Candidates and Voters in U.S. Elections* (Boulder, Colo.: Lynne Rienner Publishers, 1997).

Virginia Sapiro, *The Political Integration of Women* (Urbana: University of Illinois Press, 1983).

Sidney Verba, Kay Lehman Schlozman, and Henry E. Brady, *Voice and Equality: Civic Voluntarism in American Politics* (Cambridge, Mass.: Harvard University Press, 1995).

Center for American Women and Politics, Eagleton Institute of Politics, Rutgers University: *http://www.rci.rutgers.edu/~cawp*.

Feminist Majority: *http://www.feminist.org.*

National Women's Political Caucus: *http://www.nwpc.org.*

Women's Policy, Inc.: *http://www.womenspolicy.org.*

Women Leaders Online: *http://www.wlo.org.*

Chapter Four

Maria Braden, *Women Politicians and the Media* (Lexington: University of Kentucky Press, 1996).

Barbara Burrell, *A Woman's Place is in the House: Campaigning for Congress in the Feminist Era* (Ann Arbor: University of Michigan Press, 1994).

Kathleen Dolan, "Gender Differences in Support for Women Candidates: Is there a Glass Ceiling in American Politics?" *Women and Politics* 17, no.2 (1997): 27–41.

Irwin L. Gertzog, *Congressional Women: Their Recruitment, Integration and Behavior*, 2nd edition (Westport, Conn.: Praeger, 1995).

Amy Handlin, *Whatever Happened to the Year of the Woman: Why Women Still Aren't Making it to the Top in Politics* (Denver, Colo.: Arden Press, 1998).

Kathleen Hall Jamieson, *The Double Bind: Women and Leadership* (New York: Oxford University Press, 1995).

Kim Fridkin Kahn, *The Political Consequences of Being a Woman* (New York: Columbia University Press, 1996).

Tanya Melich, *The Republican War Against Women: An Insider's Report from Behind the Scenes* (New York: Bantam Books, 1996).

Linda Witt, Karen M. Paget, and Glenna Matthews, *Running as a Woman: Gender and Power in American Politics* (New York: Free Press, 1993).

Harriet Woods, *Stepping Up to Power: The Political Journey of American Women* (Boulder, Colo.: Westview Press, 2000).

"Pipeline to the Future: You Women and Political Leadership," Lake Snell Perry and Associates for the White House Education Project Fund, April 12, 2000: *http://www.womensleadershipfund.org/*

EMILY's List: *http://www.emilyslist.org.*

The Wish List: *http://www.thewishlist.org.*

Gender Gap: *http://www.gendergap.com.*

The White House Project: *http://www.thewhitehouseproject.org.*

Women Count: *http://www.womencount.org.*

The Women's Campaign School: *http://www.wcsyale.org/contents.html.*

Women Under Forty PAC: *http://wufpac.org.*

National Organization for Women: *http://www.now.org.*

National Political Congress of Black Women: *http://www.npcbw.org.*

League of Women Voters: *http://www.lwv.org.*

National Federation of Republican Women: *http://www.nfrw.org.*

Women's National Democratic Club: *http://www.democraticwoman.org.*

Chapter Five

Mary Anne Borrelli and Janet M. Martin, editors, *The Other Elites: Women, Politics, Power in the Executive Branch* (Boulder, Colo.: Lynne Rienner Publishers, 1997).

Myra Marx Ferree and Patricia Yancey Martin, editors, *Feminist Organizations: Harvest of the New Women's Movement* (Philadelphia: Temple University Press, 1995).

Karen Foerstel and Herbert N. Foerstel, *Climbing the Hill: Gender Conflict in Congress* (Westport, Conn.: Praeger, 1996).

Temma Kaplan, *Crazy for Democracy: Women in Grassroots Movements* (New York: Routledge, 1997).

Georgia Duerst-Lahti and Rita Mae Kelly, editors, *Gender Power, Leadership, and Governance* (Ann Arbor: University of Michigan Press, 1995).

Jane Mansbridge, "Should Blacks Represent Blacks, and Women Represent Women? A Contingent 'Yes'," Politics Research Group (John F. Kennedy School of Government, Harvard University, 2000): *http://www.ksg.harvard.edu/prg/mansb/should.htm*.

Nancy C. Naples, editor, *Community Activism and Feminist Politics: Organizing Across Race, Class and Gender* (New York: Routledge, 1998).

Diane-Michele Prindville and John G. Bretting, "Indigenous Women Activists and Political Participation: The Case of Environmental Justice," *Women and Politics* 19, no.1 (1998).

Cindy Simon Rosenthal, *When Women Lead: Integrative Leadership in State Legislatures* (New York: Oxford University Press, 1998).

Sue Thomas, *How Women Legislate* (New York: Oxford University Press, 1994).

Women 2000/Beijing +5: *http://www.un.org/womenwatch/confer/beijing5/*

Text of CEDAW: *http://www.un.org/womenwatch/daw/cedaw/*

Report Card on US Government Action: *http://www.uswc.org/reportcards.html*.

UN Division for the Advancement of Women: *http://www.un.org/womenwatch/daw*.

Womankind Worldwide: *http://www.womankind.org.uk*.

Global Fund for Women: *http://www.globalfundforwomen.org*.

National Foundation for Women Legislators: *http://www.womenlegislators.org*.

.Institute for Women's Policy Research: *http://www.iwpr.org*.

Women's International Network New: *http://www.feminist.com/win.htm*.

Chapter Six

American Association of University Women, *How Schools Shortchange Girls: A Study of Major Findings on Girls and Education* (Wellesley, Mass.: Wellesley College Center for Research on Women, 1992).

Roberta M. Hall and Bernice R. Sandler, "The Classroom Climate: A Chilly One for Women," Project on the Status and Education of Women (Washington, D.C.: Association of American Colleges, 1982).

Roberta M. Hall and Bernice R. Sandler, "Outside the Classroom: A Chilly Campus Climate for Women?," Project on the Status and Education of Women (Washington, D.C.: Association of American Colleges, 1984).

Christine Hoff Sommers, "The War Against Boys," *The Atlantic* (May 2000).

John Weistart, "Equal Opportunity? Title IX and Intercollegiate Sports," *Brookings Review* 16, no. 4 (Fall 1998): 39–43.

The Women's Educational Equity Act Equity Resource Center: *http://www.edc.org/ womensequity.*

International Federation of University Women: *http://www.ifuw.org.*

American Association of University Women: *http://www.aauw.org.*

National Women's Studies Association: *http://www.nwsa.org.*

Women's College Coalition: *http://www.academic.org.*

Working Groups on Girls: *http://www.girlsrights.org.*

Girls, Inc.: *http://www.girlsinc.com.*

Chapter Seven

Randy Albelda and Chris Tilly, *Glass Ceilings and Bottomless Pits: Women's Work, Women's Poverty* (Boston: South End Press, 1997).

Sharlene Hesse-Biber and Gregg Lee Carter, *Working Women in America: Split Dreams* (New York: Oxford University Press, 2000).

Sara M. Evans and Barbara J. Nelson, *Wage Justice: Comparable Worth and the Paradox of Technocratic Reform* (Chicago: University of Chicago Press, 1989).

Claudia Goldin, *Understanding the Gender Gap: An Economic History of American Women* (New York: Oxford University Press, 1990).

Janet C. Gornick, Marcia K. Myers, and Katerin E. Ross, "Supporting Employment of Mothers: Policy Variations Across Fourteen Welfare States," *Journal of European Social Policy* 7 (1997): 45–70.

Arlie Russell Hochschild, *The Time Bind: How Work Becomes Home and Home Becomes Work* (New York: Holt, 1997).

Julie A. Matthaei, *An Economic History of Women in America: Women's Work, the Sexual Division of Labor, and the Development of Capitalism* (New York: Schocken Books, 1982).

Sonya Michel, *Children's Interests/Mother's Rights: The Shaping of America's Child Care Policy* (New Haven, Conn.: Yale University Press, 1999).

Diana Furchtgott-Roth and Christine Solba, *Women's Figures: An Illustrated Guide to the Ecnomic Progress of Women in America* (Washington, D.C.: AEI Press and the Independent Women's Forum, 1999).

Virginia Valian, *Why So Slow? The Advancement of Women* (Cambridge, Mass.: MIT Press, 1998).

AFL-CIO: *http://www.aflcio.org/women.*

The Glass Ceiling: *http://www.theglassceiling.com.*

National Partnership for Women and Families: *http://www.nationalpartnership.org.*

Employment Policy Foundation: *http://www.epf.org.*

Catalyst: *http://www.catalystwomen.org.*

U.S. Equal Employment Opportunity Commission: *http://www.eeoc.gov/*

National Committee on Pay Equity: *http://www.feminist.com/fairpay/*

Families and Work Institute: *http://www.familiesandwork.org/*

Chapter Eight

Robert H. Blank, *Fetal Protection in the Workplace* (New York: Columbia University Press, 1993).

Robert H. Blank, *Regulating Reproduction* (New York: Columbia University Press, 1990).

Robert Blank and Janna C. Merrick, *Human Reproduction, Emerging Technologies, and Conflicting Rights* (Washington, D.C.: Congressional Quarterly Press, 1995).

Susan Chira, *A Mother's Place: Taking the Debate about Working Mothers beyond Guilt and Blame* (New York: HarperCollins, 1998).

Cynthia B. Costello, Shari Miles and Anne J. Stone, *The American Woman 1999–2000: A Century of Change* (New York: Norton, 1999).

Anne H. Gauthier, *The State and the Family: A Comparative Analysis of Family Policies in Industrialized Countries* (New York: Oxford University Press, 1996).

Betsy Hartmann, *Reproductive Rights and Wrongs: The Global Politics of Population Control* (Boston: South End Press, 1995).

Alison M. Jaggar, editor, *Living with Contradictions: Controversies in Feminist Social Ethics* (Boulder, Colo.: Westview Press, 1995).

Eileen L. McDonagh, *Breaking the Abortion Deadlock: From Choice to Consent* (New York: Oxford University Press, 1996).

Ellen H. Moskowitz and Bruce Jennings, editors, *Coerced Contraception? Moral and Policy Challenges of Long-acting Birth Control* (Washington, D.C.: Georgetown University Press, 1996).

Susan Moller Okin, *Justice, Gender, and the Family* (New York: Basic Books, 1989).

Peggy Orenstein, *Flux: Women on Sex, Work, Love, and Life in a Half-Changed World* (New York: Doubleday, 2000).

Laura M. Purdy, *Reproducing Persons: Issues in Feminist Bioethics* (Ithaca: New York University Press, 1996).

Kate Conway-Turner and Suzanne Cherrin, *Women, Families, and Feminist Politics: A Global Exploration* (New York: Harrington Park Press, 1999).

Andrea Tone, editor, *Controlling Reproduction: An American History* (Wilmington, Del.: Scholarly Resources Books, 1997).

ACLU Reproductive Rights: *http://www.aclu.org/issues/reproduct/hmrr.html.*

Reproductive Health and Rights Center: *http://www.choice.org.*

Alan Guttmacher Institute: *http://www.agi-usa.org.*

International Planned Parenthood Federation: *http://www.ippf.org/*

Center for Law and Reproductive Policy: *http://www.crlp.org/*

Feminists for Life: *http://www.feministsforlife.org/*

Susan B. Anthony List: *http://www.sba-list.org/index.cfm.*

Index

Abolition movement, link with suffrage movement, 35–38, 40–42, 43
Abortion
    approval of RU-486, 265
    demographics of, 265–267
    and ERA opponents, 60
    feminists opposed to, 268–269
    and electoral gender gap, 77–78
    impact on political participation, 82
    individual access to, 263–264
    legislative voting records on, 138
    and opposition to CEDAW, 163, 164
    pre-Civil War, 261
    public opinion on, 267–268
    women's caucus position on, 146–147
    women's positions on, 87
    See also Reproductive policy
Adams, Abigail, 7
Affirmative action, 157, 161, 200, 207, 214–215
AFL-CIO, 216, 220, 225
African Americans
    and abolition movement, 40–42, 43
    and affirmative action policies, 215
    candidates, stereotyping of, 115
    gender gap in voter turnout, 73

participation in suffrage movement, 39–42, 43, 44, 45
African American women
    cultural barriers to political activity, 89
    feminism of, 25–26
    impact of affirmative action on, 215
    marital status of, 246
    officeholders, political behavior of, 143–144
    position on reproductive rights, 146–147
    presidential appointments of, 126
    and wage gap, 219–220
    and welfare system, 236
    women's rights organizations for, 44
    in work force, 60, 201, 203–204
Age
    and marriage, 245
    and voter turnout, 73, 74–75
    of women candidates, 108, 109, 123–124, 284
Agency for International Development, U.S., 158
Aid to Dependent Children (ADC), 236
Aid to Families with Dependent Children (AFDC), 149, 236–237

Work force, women in (*cont.*)
  and comparable worth policies,
    225–226
  equal-employment laws for, 206–215
  and equality-difference paradox,
    200–201
  and Equal Pay Act, 207–208
  as ERA debate issue, 59
  Family and Medical Leave Act,
    230–231
  and fetal protection policies, 12–13,
    208–209, 273
  and gender segregation, 199–200
  and gender socialization, 204–206
  and glass ceiling, 223, 224–225
  impact of deindustrialization on, 235
  impact of educational equity on,
    183–184, 189
  limits of legal equality for, 223
  Marxist-social feminism's focus on, 24
  and sexual harassment, 218–219
  as single parents, 234–235
  social security and private pensions,
    231–234
  Supreme Court discrimination rulings,
    211–214
  and Title VII of Civil Rights Act,
    208–214
  and wage gap, 219–223, 288–289
  women in the professions, 216–218
  See also Employment discrimination;
    Wage and prestige gap
World Anti-Slavery Convention, 38
World Forum on Women, 159
World Trade Organization (WTO),
  157
World War II, and women in work force,
  203

"Year of the Woman," 96, 105
Young Women's Leadership Institute,
  124
Young Women's Leadership School, 195
Young Women Vote '98, 123–124